Polish Cinema Today

Polish Cinema Today

A Bold New Era in Film

Helena Goscilo and Beth Holmgren

LEXINGTON BOOKS
Lanham • Boulder • New York • London

Published by Lexington Books
An imprint of The Rowman & Littlefield Publishing Group, Inc.
4501 Forbes Boulevard, Suite 200, Lanham, Maryland 20706
www.rowman.com

6 Tinworth Street, London SE11 5AL, United Kingdom

British Library Cataloguing in Publication Information Available

Library of Congress Cataloging-in-Publication Data

Library of Congress Control Number: 2021933357

ISBN 978-1-7936-4165-6 (cloth)
ISBN 978-1-7936-4167-0 (pbk)
ISBN 978-1-7936-4166-3 (electronic)

To Wiesiek and Elżbieta Oleksy, whose friendship over the years transformed Łódź into a "pleasure dome" and second home
HG
To Mark Sidell, whose wizardry enables my adventures in cinema, and my students, whose discussions of Polish film continually inspire and surprise me
BH

Contents

Acknowledgments

First and foremost, our most profound gratitude goes to the formidably talented, committed members of the Polish film industry—directors, scriptwriters, camera crews, actresses and actors, composers, and others—who in "the worst of times" (the 1990s) and "the best of times" (2005–now) have continued to produce original, challenging, and thought-provoking screen experiences for viewers at home and abroad. Second, we owe thanks to Marek Haltof, Ewa Mazierska, Andrzej Werner, and Mateusz Werner for their surveys of Polish film; Marcin Adamczak for his foundational work in film distribution studies; and Elżbieta Ostrowska for the inspiring sophistication of her scholarship on a wide array of filmic topics. And we would be remiss if we did not express our appreciation for the persistence of Eric Kuntzman and the professionalism of Kasey Beduhn, both at Lexington Books, who responded so enthusiastically to our undertaking and shepherded the project through the pandemic to its completion. To Tatiana Melnikova, we render homage for the bold creative image that appears on our book's cover. Finally, I (HG) am pleased to acknowledge that to be collaborating again with my cowriter (and coeditor on three previous projects) qualifies as that rare phenomenon—an intellectual sizzle, partially sparked by decades of affection and the happy appearance of Georgie offscreen. And I (BH) have been thrilled to perform a true coauthoring duet with my favorite collaborator on our most exciting book to date, with my pleasure in analyzing great film more than matched by my pleasure in reading my partner's incisive scholarship.

Introduction

Why Polish Cinema Today?

In 2013, acclaimed American director Martin Scorsese launched an ambitious festival showcasing "The Masterpieces of Polish Cinema" in screenings throughout the United States, Canada, and the United Kingdom.[1] This project took shape after Scorsese accepted Polish filmmaker Andrzej Wajda's 2011 invitation to receive an honorary doctorate at the prestigious Łódź Film School, an institution that furnished the blueprint for Scorsese's alma mater, what is now the Maurice Kanbar Institute of Film and Television at New York University. In his acceptance speech, the American filmmaker attested to the powerful influence that Polish cinema had exerted on him since his student days: "The school nurtured in me an unshakeable belief in artistic expression grounded in Italian neo-realism, French New Wave, and Polish cinema—the great sweeping, humanistic, intimate, and profound films that were an integral part of what, looking back, seems more and more like the golden age of international cinema."[2] Scorsese's substantial tribute to this "golden age" entailed curating, with consultation, twenty-one Polish films that he had digitally restored by a team of experts; screening these films on tour over a two-year period; and packaging the restored DVDs for purchase in three boxed sets. All of the selected films, ranging chronologically from Andrzej Munk's *Eroica* (1957) to Krzysztof Kieślowski's *A Short Film about Killing* (1987)—and including only one film by a female director, Agnieszka Holland—were made during the People's Republic of Poland (commonly referred to as the PRL or *Polska Rzeczpospolita Ludowa*, from 1945 to 1989)—that is, before the end of the Cold War and Poland's independence from the Soviet bloc.

There is never a bad time for high-profile international publicity, especially for a relatively small national film industry avid for a global market. Covering Scorsese's "Polish Masterpieces" 2015 tour in the United Kingdom, British journalist Geoffrey Macnab implies that contemporary Polish cinema has not tinkered with its Cold War-era winning formula: "It surely isn't a coincidence that [Paweł] Pawlikowski's Oscar-winning *Ida* is set in the early Sixties, shot in black-and-white, and self-consciously evokes the golden era in Polish film-making."[3] Yet Scorsese's canonization of a "golden age" inclusive of PRL-era Polish cinema in the 2010s proved unintentionally ironic, given the bold innovations by Polish filmmakers and the film industry from the early 2000s up to the present day. Scorsese's reverential "look backward" for the classics obscures a phenomenal new age in twenty-first-century Polish cinema that is at once accretive and audacious, encompassing well-made genre films and quite astonishing arthouse productions, and evincing greater thematic and stylistic diversity than ever before. After roughly a decade of economic set-backs, slowly evolving systems of distribution and marketing, and young film professionals' highly limited access to education, on-the-job experience, and feature debuts, the Polish film industry at last has emerged as a strong con-tender in the European and even global markets. Post-communist Polish film is no longer an example of a Hollywood-derivative capitalist dismantling of a paradoxically socialist golden age. Over the last two decades, Polish film has been flourishing as vibrant, sophisticated art and entertainment eagerly con-sumed domestically and increasingly well-received and distributed abroad. Our coauthored volume, *Polish Cinema Today*, which draws on current scholarship in Polish film production and distribution studies, as well as film criticism, reviews, and interviews with directors and actors, seeks to expand the present cinema's currency, showcasing its key films by theme and close analysis for film scholars, students, and cinephiles the world over.

THE TRANSFORMATION OF THE
POLISH FILM INDUSTRY

The transition of the Polish film industry from a socialist state enterprise into a system equipped to manage a Hollywood-dominated capitalist market was predictably rugged, but also surprisingly liberatory, for it eventually entailed breaking free from the elitist professional restrictions of Poland's "golden age." Film scholar Marek Haltof recapitulates the familiar transition story very well—the "1989 Freedom Shock" that initially excited filmmakers with the abolition of political censorship, even as it toppled them from their ped-estal as prophets and teachers, overwhelmed them with imported Hollywood blockbusters that lured away domestic viewers, and left them scrambling for funding no longer provided by the state.[4] The economic blow to the Polish film industry was exacerbated by new consumer options that gutted cinema attendance: the circulation of pirated VHS tapes as well as access to satellite and cable TV. Between 1990 and 1992, cinema ticket sales plummeted from 38 million to 10.5 million annually.[5] Nor was the film industry prepared at this point to lure potential moviegoers into theaters. "Distribution" under socialism was confined to reproducing and shipping film copies, with nary a thought about marketing.[6]

At the same time, this crisis encouraged the improvisation and emergence of new professionals in the industry, according to Marcin Adamczak, a leading scholar in the fledgling field of Polish film distribution studies.[7] In counterpoint to the narrative about film production's post-1989 free fall, Adamczak elaborates on a three-stage development of the film distribution market from the late 1980s up to the present day, beginning with the appearance of "an interesting generation of cultural entrepreneurs"—figures such as Sławomir Salamon and Roman Gutek, who initially served as professional intermediaries between film producers and cinema owners.[8] These intermediaries had been shaped by their experience in the amateur Film Discussion Clubs that thrived in late socialist Poland—all of them drawn to good film, attentive to audience interests, proficient in organizing film programs, and, post-1989, well-known film festivals.[9] For example, Salamon, a mathematician by training, stumbled into his future as a powerful distributor at the suggestion of Agnieszka Holland in the late 1980s. The director had returned to Poland with her new film, *Zabić księdza* (To Kill a Priest):

> At that time I was already involved in organizing film screenings, and I toured with her around Poland with one copy of the film. One day, on our way to Gorzów, we had a conversation about what I could do in the film industry, since I did not have the temperament of a director and I could not be an actor either; Agnieszka said: "Maybe you could work in distribution? It is all about numbers and so boring."[10]

Roman Gutek blazed a more specialized trail in distribution, promoting "*auteur* and experimental cinema in the late 1990s" and building Gutek Film in the 2000s, which now "includes a distribution company, three film festivals (including New Horizons, one of the biggest arthouse film festivals in Europe), a system of indirect or direct control over the repertoire of at least several cinemas, and a strong educational division that organizes screenings for schools."[11]

The second stage in Adamczak's history of the post-1989 distribution market is marked by the widespread establishment of multiplex cinemas in Poland in the late 1990s. As in the United States and Western Europe, the multiplexes, strategically situated in shopping malls, reshaped "the whole social phenomenon of movie-going," "reinforcing the concept of cinema as a realm of pleasure, relaxation, and casual entertainment."[12] As multiplexes garnered the dominant position in the Polish film market, they stopped the economic free fall of film consumption, ensuring strong ticket sales and ensconcing the leading distribution companies still operative in Poland today. They also began to condition audience expectations for the different kinds of cinematic entertainment on offer. Though Hollywood blockbusters continued to attract the greatest box office, moviegoers could choose among a slowly increasing assortment of films produced during the first decade of the twenty-first century.

Adamczak dates the start of the third, ongoing stage in market development to 2010–2011, but it bears noting that the phenomenon powering it had transformed film *production* a decade prior.[13] The digitalization of cinemas, Adamczak points out, resulted in a whopping increase of films—from 224 produced in 2005 to 335 in 2017—and a concomitant 57 percent increase in cinema screens on which to show them. Putting the horse back in front of the cart, other film scholars argue that the digital revolution put high definition, cheap digital cameras and digital editing into the hands of many semi-established and nascent filmmakers and allowed them to experiment with feature film production at last. Mateusz Werner credits the digital revolution in large part with "the eruption of independence in the film industry in the late 1990s," "a reaction of young artists to having no chance in the mainstream."[14] Joanna Rożen-Wojciechowska underscores how the digital revolution and a burgeoning audience fascinated by new independent films liberated Polish filmmaking from a production system made cumbersome by the need for huge financial investment and star directors with well-established filmographies and Łódź School degrees: "Independent, low-budget films were . . . the only way into the film industry for young filmmakers anxious to make their first film after graduating from film school. The movie business stagnation of that period left the new crop of filmmakers with no outlet for their creative energies. The indie scene, with its cheap, digital format, allowed them to begin immediately, rather than wait for the situation to improve."[15] Nor did an aspiring filmmaker need any formal film school training. Werner names several successful directors who leapt into film as amateurs—Jacek Borcuch, Przemysław Wojcieszek, Piotr Matwiejczyk, and Bodo Kox.[16]

Both Werner and Rożen-Wojciechowska remark on the award-winning breakthrough in 2003 for Polish directors embracing digital technology. At the major national film festival in Gdynia that year, Dariusz Gajewski's first feature film, *Warszawa* (Warsaw), won the Golden Lions Award, its top honor, while the more experimental feature, *Dotknij mnie* (Touch Me), an exposé of the world of homeless Poles, filmed by handheld camera and written and directed by Anna Jadowska and Ewa Stankiewicz, nabbed first prize in the category of "independent film" for its "cinematic truth, formal invention, innovative storytelling, and ruthless exposure of Polish reality."[17]

As Werner argues more generally, the works of these and other Polish directors successfully debuting in the twenty-first-century project "authentic communication" with viewers in lieu of formulaic strategies derived from genre films to thrill or please.[18] Their films showcase directors confidently mapping their own worlds and telling stylistically diverse stories that speak to an ever-maturing domestic audience.

Nevertheless, the digital revolution alone could not address the challenges that a turbulent market economy posed to underwriting Polish film production. State support was desperately needed by the mid-2000s, according to Jerzy Płażewski: "not only were the new grants getting smaller and smaller, but the amounts which had already been allocated suffered from delays, which hindered the release of even the all-but-completed movies. The situation got so bad that by 2005, the government owed [film] producers PLN 35 million [35 million zlotys] (with the production cost of an average movie amounting to 1–3 million)."[19] It was at this crisis point that the Polish Parliament, pressed by the Ministry of Culture and the extraordinary efforts of deputy Agnieszka Odorowicz, passed the June 7, 2005, "Act on Cinema" and established the Polish Film Institute (Polski Instytut Sztuki Filmowej or PISF) "modeled on those of other European nations."[20] Weighing in on Polish film production in 2012, Adamczak pronounces the PISF "something of a production hegemon . . . provid[ing] up to 50% of a film's production costs, although this limit could be increased to 90% for films that are deemed to exhibit particularly strong artistic promise, but little commercial potential."[21] Six years later, Adamczak and his coauthor, Agnieszka Orankiewicz, applaud PISF for its much broader portfolio of "subsidies, loans, and sureties to producers," for such investment supports both arthouse film and "popular genre cinema," and "thus builds a basis for a well-functioning film industry."[22]

RECURRING THEMES IN POLISH CINEMA TODAY

Compared with the "golden age" of socialist-era cinema, twenty-first-century Polish films are no longer wholly preoccupied with a black-and-white struggle between an oppressive, dysfunctional state and alienated Polish workers, farmers, and professional intelligentsia. Instead, the establishment of democracy and its disappointments, the onslaught of a global market and its inequities, the emergence of a more diverse society insistent on equal rights for all in partial emulation of the EU template for Europe, and the public and scholarly license to investigate long silenced crimes committed during the Holocaust and Cold War—all of these phenomena have attracted the critical and creative attention of Polish filmmakers and screenwriters in the last two decades. For example, screen images of the Catholic Church have undergone a revolution as younger Poles increasingly criticize and move away from religious dogma. During the Cold War, the church and its clergy had functioned admirably as a buttress for political resistance to the state, yet, in post-communist Poland, this institution now wields tremendous and largely unchecked conservative power. While several films bordering on hagiographies pay homage to officially canonized priests and nuns, other features treat the lamentable dilemma of children's and adolescents' sexual abuse by members of the Catholic clergy. These "exposés" include recent documentaries that have shaken the Polish population and have joined international voices protesting the secretive, ineffectual habits of Catholicism's upper echelon. For decades, the latter's paramount goal of protecting the reputation of the church has prompted them to ignore or camouflage local priests' malfeasance by merely relocating them from one parish to another, hence permitting them to continue their abusive practices elsewhere.

In conjunction with their challenge to Catholic religious conservatism, which prescribes premarital chastity, women's subservience as wives and mothers, and postmarital monogamy, twenty-first-century Polish films have focused on the warts and wounds of family relations, women's negotiation of profound social changes under the new regime and the concomitant market economy, and, perhaps most strikingly, the sexual behavior of Polish women belonging to various generations. No longer constrained by censorship, contemporary cinematic images of gender have toppled decades of mythic male heroism by spotlighting male weakness and female strength as well as women's desperate escape from control. Previously exalted as the bedrock of society and the stronghold of psychological sustenance for the individual, family in recent screen offerings emerges as a source of strife and trauma. Within that context, the apotheosized mother of numerous verbal and visual texts has yielded to darker, often destructive concepts of maternity even as her role of unappreciated family safekeeper continues to be acknowledged, if only because paternity appears as inadequate. Such revisionist scenarios often spring from the rejection of puritanism in screen portrayals of female sexuality, which reflect the postfeminist stance of directors and the enlightened world at large, which does not equate enjoying sex with sluttishness.

In like vein, the contentious issue of homosexuality and lesbianism has fueled several fine films in tune with the universal acceptance of what are inaccurately labeled "alternate sexualities," but at odds with the current right-wing populist Law and Justice government's ideology of childbearing heteronormativity. While the Ordo Iuris (Legal Order) organization—one of Poland's most influential pressure groups, with its founder, Aleksander Stepkowski, a spokesman of the Supreme Court—anathematize LGBTQ rights as the onset of Armageddon[23] and the recently reelected president, Andrzej Duda, has declared the LGBTQ movement as "worse than Nazism," a significant portion of Poland's educated, urban population and filmmakers such as Olga Chajdas, for example, view the struggle for same-sex rights as liberating, which her well-received film *Nina* (2018) makes clear. While Jan Komasa's *Suicide Room* (Sala samobójców 2011), which drew large audiences, offers a sympathetic portrayal of its young protagonist's fluid sexual identity, the world-renowned Krzysztof Warlikowski—the openly gay founder and artistic director of Warsaw's New Theater, hailed as a member of "the reforming vanguard of theatrical language in Europe"[24]—as well as Rafał Trzaskowski, the capital's broadly admired, energetic, LBGTQ-supportive mayor, subvert the PRL-era's reactionary conceptions of sexuality.

Polish misadventures with global capitalism, including the competitive market for creating blockbuster movies, have yielded two types of films in this "new era"—stories about migrant laborers and their families, and genre films (detective stories, thrillers) about nonpolitical crime. The first type tends to be artistically ambitious, focusing on the experiences of those who emigrate for work overseas or those left behind, dependent on their emigrant partner's success to provide a decent life for their families. Tales of Polish migrants "in search of bread" date back over a century, though the old stories primarily feature poor peasants coming to America. In the twenty-first century, the migrants on the screen are highly educated and skilled, but nonetheless unable to achieve middle-class status at home. To a great degree, these films reflect Poles' abiding perception of themselves as a nation abandoned by the West after World War II and therefore unfairly disadvantaged vis-à-vis historically fortunate Western nations in Europe and North America. At the same time, such films offer well-informed and empathetic glimpses into Polish provincial life in small towns and villages—its lack of amenities and employment opportunities, alternately stressed and supportive family life, and the natural beauty in what has become known as "Poland B."

Kindred shifts have occurred in films dramatizing crime, which during PRL repeatedly (and justifiably) identified the state as corrupt and morally unsound on multiple fronts. As amply demonstrated by American film from its very birth, capitalism and crime go hand in hand, and post-1989 Polish features have experimented with gusto in the previously sidelined popular genre of individual and mob crime. They have had to compete with foreign film industries far more practiced and successful in the production of genre film. If their foray into narratives about serial killers has fallen short of their sophisticated handling of other criminal scenarios, Polish series recently streamed on Netflix suggest that directors increasingly bring originality and conviction to that subgenre.

In their coverage of Poland's twentieth-century past, twenty-first-century films benefit from the abolition of political censorship, though this advantage does not automatically guarantee their high quality. As satisfying as it is to denounce the Soviet Union as Poland's actual Cold War enemy in lieu of the United States, the consequent binary usually results in too schematic or melodramatic a plot. Some films revisiting the Cold War have attracted enthusiastic audiences by focusing on historical sidebars that could not be screened before 1989, such as the intimate role of secret police informants in the lives of famous dissidents or the whip hand that the secret police exercised over regular cops. The most artistically successful films on this period experiment with outsized characters and dark humor, switching the roles of victimized dissidents and villainous informants to render dissidents eccentrically criminal or informants heroic in their unabashed sacrifice of their bodies and normal lives.

The most nationally provocative historical films in this new era, however, investigate how Polish Catholics were active perpetrators of the Holocaust—as informers, blackmailers, thieves, and murderers of Polish Jews. One could argue that such productions are designed to bait the right-wing Law and Justice Party. But these films' accusations are aimed at a deeper target. As at least two generations of Holocaust scholars in Poland have discovered through their research, these feature films, like the documentaries that preceded them, strike at the heart of postwar Poles' national identity as the martyrs of World War II. As in other interwar European countries, so in Poland, the National Democrats, a violently anti-Semitic party, molded the mindset and behavior of many Polish Catholics, particularly in the provinces, and the Catholic Church, in contrast to its dissident role during the Cold War, largely supported the National Democrats' agenda. It is likely that more films representing the very disturbing "local Holocaust" in Poland will be ventured by filmmakers, and it is certain that Polish scholars specializing in Jewish Studies will respond to these efforts with historically grounded praise or criticism.

THE STRUCTURE OF *POLISH CINEMA TODAY*

Since we conceived of *Polish Cinema Today* with multiple diverse readers in mind, we organized our selective coverage and analyses of Polish films into thematic chapters to help teachers and students develop their research and curriculum on global cinema. Each thematic turn locates new Polish films in specific transnational historical and theoretical contexts. Here film scholars and students will find fascinating Polish examples as they explore worldwide screen representations of such topics as religion in society, the experience of migration, nationalist identity vis-à-vis ethnic minorities, changing gender constructs and roles, discrimination against/tolerance of LGBTQ citizens, and new developments of popular film genres ranging from police procedurals to thrillers.

We also designed the volume as a guide for the general cinephile, for those who love good movies or perhaps those who have watched the Polish masterpieces recommended by Scorsese and are eager to sample what Polish directors are producing today. In order to satisfy all three intended audiences—teachers, students, and movie lovers—we have eschewed survey-style coverage to focus on specific films that we recommend and, in many cases, films that have elicited strong responses and lively discussions in the courses we have taught. Our framing of these films thus includes their national sociopolitical context as well as transnational theme. Our analyses provide pertinent information about the directors, actors, and other talents as needed, and highlight the films' formal features, such as mise-en-scène, camerawork, editing, and sound, as well as their modification of genre conventions. In a few instances, we examine a single film from two different thematic angles, for we deemed that "double take" imperative.

Chapter Synopses

Chapter 1: Saints and Sinners: The Polish Catholic Church in Close-up

The formidable importance of the Catholic Church in Polish culture throughout the centuries has resulted in numerous films' engagement with a broad range of religious topics. Whereas earlier significant cinematic offerings explored demonic possession or sin in the midst of the sacred (*Sister Joanna of the Angels*, *The Devil*), more recent fare has focused primarily on two polar extremes: the deeds of saintly figures within the church (*Faustyna*, *Popieluszko*, *Jasminum*), on the one hand, and corruption and sexual crimes committed by its representatives, on the other (*Kler*). The latter orientation has coincided with documentaries (*Only Don't Tell Anyone*) and publications (*In the Closet of the Vatican*) exposing both real and perceived misdeeds throughout all levels of the Catholic Church hierarchy, as well as the concerted efforts of its upper echelons to cover up the behavior of those entrusted with hearing confessions and leading exemplary lives "in the service of God." Paweł Pawlikowski's Oscar-winning *Ida* stands apart from these two categories, intent instead on examining what becoming a nun means to a novice unaware of her Jewish background and her family's fate during the Nazis' invasion in World War II.

Chapter 2: Wandering Poles: Lost or Left in Migration

Poland's 2004 acceptance into the European Union initially signaled an important step toward greater economic parity between a highly developed Western Europe and a much less developed Eastern Europe stymied by its decades within the military-industrial complex of the Soviet bloc. Nevertheless, EU membership has exacerbated rather than altered Poles' perception of themselves as a nation of workers to be outsourced. Recent Polish cinema reflects solely on the experiences of Polish immigrants and migrant laborers abroad and the families they leave behind. Films focusing on Poles attempting to relocate to more prosperous parts of Europe either chronicle their eventual rebellion against the rigid, punitive laws of a "nanny state" (*Strange Heaven*) or reveal the elusiveness, moral compromise, and psychological toll of complete assimilation (*Beyond Words*). Those films trained on the relations between migrant providers and their families from the vantage point of a provincial Poland empathetically depict parental self-sacrifice and the painful consequences of family separation (*Silent Night*, *Wild Roses*). In contrast to the films about immigrant relocation, they also question the worth of "moving West" in their portraits of ambitious migrant providers who either dismiss or presume to control the modest dreams and desires of their families at home.

Chapter 3: All in the Family: The Ties That Bind and Blight

Recent Polish film challenges the country's hardy tradition of championing the family as a stronghold of intimacy, dependability, and social cohesion. Directors examine painful fissures within the family structure (*Silent Night*), alienation between generations and individuals (*The Last Family*), and the failure of parents to provide a safe harbor for their offspring. More particularly, exploration of the maternal role, immemorially based on the paradigm of the Catholic Madonna, exposes women's indifference to that function at best (*Mother to Her Own Mother*) and their readiness to murder their offspring at worst (*Son of the Snow Queen*). At the same time, several films demonstrate how the death of the strong, loving mother who constitutes the backbone of the family leads to the latter's disintegration and a loss of identity in one of her daughters (*33 Scenes from Life*), and in another case, a son's finally successful attempt at suicide (*The Last Family*). Films devoted to family issues present a dispiriting landscape, and many bleak examinations of motherhood show fathers as weak, self-preoccupied, or completely absent. Little better—or even worse—as husbands, men are insensitive, unfaithful, and immature, especially at times of crisis (*Love*, *Fugue*). Ultimately, the family emerges as a source of uncertainty and psychological ordeal.

Chapter 4: Rescreening Christian-Jewish Relations in Interwar, Wartime, and Postwar Poland

Jews made up the largest, most influential ethnic minority in Poland's various political incarnations for 1,000 years before the Holocaust. But the massacre of 90 percent of their population during the Holocaust and the deportation of 13,000 more in the government-directed purge of 1968 left a tremendous absence in what was once Poland's primarily bicultural society. The post-1989 Jewish revival in Poland has strived to commemorate the lost, diverse world of the Polish Jews by restoring Jewish heritage sites, hosting at least forty annual Jewish cultural festivals, establishing Jewish Studies programs in universities, and creating major institutional resources such as museums and community centers. In the spirit of the revival, the documentary *Po-Lin: Scraps of Memory* offers a well-intentioned cinematic primer on interwar Jewish life, piecing together a mosaic of home movies made by visiting relatives to Jewish shtetls. *Po-Lin* fails, however, to remind viewers that its footage was not designed to package the Jewish world for postwar Polish approval. Feature films still concentrate on the Holocaust, but directors are taking greater risks in challenging a Polish national martyrology. *In Darkness*, based on a true story of Jews surviving the Holocaust in the sewers of Lwów, veers from the convenient binary of gentile rescuer/Jewish victim by rendering its Christian "helper" a boor rather than a saint and its Jewish protagonists proactive and psychologically complex. In *Ida*, a novice about to take her vows suddenly learns of her Jewish heritage and her church's silence about its activities during the war, and must help reinter family members killed by the Christian family trusted to hide them. In *Aftermath*, two brothers unearth the fact that their father and one-time neighbors massacred local Jews on their family farm and stole their property.

Chapter 5: Crime à la Carte: Death and Double-Dealing

Unlike in the United States, crime as a cinematic genre never took firm root in socialist Poland. Once the country freed itself from Soviet shackles, however, crime suddenly flourished on the Polish screen in multiple forms, ranging from political betrayals (*Blindness*) and desperate citizens' violent elimination of threatening mobsters (*The Debt*) to influential functionaries' financial scams (*Closed Circuit*) and serial murders (*The Red Spider* and *Sleep, My Darling*). Directors based most of these offerings on actual events and cast some of Poland's best actors in the major roles, with outstanding results in the case of *The Debt* and *Closed Circuit*. Yet, despite comparably fine performances in films about serial killers, lack of experience in this profoundly American and Scandinavian genre betrays weaknesses in script, plot development, pacing, and mise-en-scène—the last resulting also from financial constraints. Their flaws notwithstanding, *I'm a Murderer* and kindred fare shine in their astute psychological insights into the sui generis byways of criminal minds.

Chapter 6: Cold War Retakes in the Twenty-first Century

Whereas American and British films tend to represent the Cold War as a deadly game of espionage, involving the superman feats of a Bond or the spycraft of covert government agencies, twenty-first-century Polish cinema on the Cold War focuses on the antagonistic, toxic relationship festering between Poland and its influential superpower, the Soviet Union. This chapter examines in depth two films that bookend this relationship—*Katyń* (2007) and *The Dark House* (2009). Marking the Soviet atrocity that catalyzed the Cold War between the USSR and Poland, *Katyń* contextualizes and then represents the covert massacre of 22,000 Polish officers by the Soviet secret police in 1940. *The Dark House*, in turn, depicts the events leading to a triple homicide in southeastern Poland in the late 1970s and a reopened investigation into that crime conducted during martial law in the early 1980s. It thus gauges the demoralizing effects of the Soviet system on the Poles, demonstrating how the local secret police incessantly interfere with regular police business to political ends. Twenty-first-century Polish film also explores how the new class order imposed by Soviet dominance resulted in new sorts of romantic mésalliances. In the "love stories" of *Little Rose* and *The Reverse*, affairs between the secret police/police informants and members of the intelligentsia reveal very different responses to "sleeping with the enemy." In *Cold War*, however, the working-class informant pays dearly to protect her intellectual lover and manages to salvage their "great love," if not their lives.

Chapter 7: Female Sexuality with and without Apologies

For decades, under the influence of the Polish Catholic Church, the long-standing identification of womanhood with the Virgin Mary and the kenotic mother constrained the concept of women's sexuality. Recent directors of such films as *Little Rose*, however, rescue sexual desire as a healthy, natural drive from the exclusive province of men, equating female lust with boundless energy and the life force. Indeed, prostitution (*Elles*), casual sexual encounters according to the woman's terms (*The Lure*), and incestuous sexual congress (*Shameless*) complement the conventional notion of intercourse as a part of heterosexual love, legitimated by marriage and the desire to procreate. By doing so they join the rest of Europe in recognizing the diversity of individual sexual orientations and their praxis. Moreover, the life and works of Poland's renowned but long-unacknowledged female sexologist, Michalina Wisłocka, finally has been transferred to the screen (*The Art of Loving*) in all her extravagant, unorthodox boldness. In their nonjudgmental portrayals of womanhood and female bodies, such films have reconfigured the terms of cinematic gender acceptability in Poland.

Chapter 8: Male Gays under a Female Gaze

Homosexuality rarely surfaced on the Polish screen under socialism, which either ignored or marginalized it through simplistic or opprobrious portrayals. After 1989, directors turned to the topic, which increasingly complicated issues of sexual identity throughout the world have rendered crucial. Three female directors belonging to different generations tackle homosexuality with nuance and sympathy in *The Lovers from Marona, Torpor,* and *In the Name of . . .*—the last conveying the torments of an empathetic, committed priest who struggles against his proscribed desire, but finally succumbs to the overtures of a youth who admires and pursues him. These thoughtful investigations contrast dramatically with the conventional—indeed, hackneyed—approach to homosexuality by the young male director Tomasz Wasilewski in *Floating Skyscrapers.* Though the film's camerawork deservedly received plaudits, Wasilewski's depiction of gay men's existence in contemporary society and especially the latter's homophobic brutality is an alienating throwback to films about same-sex love of the 1970s, such as *The Boys in the Band* and similar Anglophone fare, which cannot help but strike the viewer as musty and reductive in today's world.

We undertook the writing of *Polish Cinema Today* partially out of shared enthusiasm for an extraordinary new body of work in global film and in part because we have delighted in and benefited from collaborating on important projects for over thirty years. Our coauthorship reflects two different voices, but represents hundreds of hours of reading, revising, and learning from each other's scholarship in our quest to give nonspecialists the best English-language critical introduction to Polish film in the twenty-first century.

HG and BH

NOTES

1. Marta Jazowska, "Martin Scorsese Presents 21 Masterpieces," October 14, 2013, *culture.pl.* https://culture.pl/en/article/martin-scorsese-presents-21-masterpieces. Accessed December 27, 2020.

2. "Martin Scorsese Explains His Fascination with Polish Cinema," January 30, 2014, *culture.pl.* https://culture.pl/en/article/martin-scorsese-explains-his-fascination-with-polish-cinema. Accessed December 27, 2020.

3. Geoffrey Macnab, "Martin Scorsese Celebrates Masterpieces of Polish Cinema from *Ashes and Diamonds* to *Black Cross*," *The Independent*, April 17, 2015, https://www.independent.co.uk/arts-entertainment/films/features/martin-scorsese

-celebrates-masterpieces-polish-cinema-ashes-and-diamonds-black-cross-10182411 .html. Accessed December 27, 2020.

4. Marek Haltof, "A Fistful of Dollars: Polish Cinema after the 1989 Freedom Shock," *Film Quarterly* 48, 3 (Spring 1995): 23.

5. Marcin Adamczak, "Zderzenie z globalizacją," *Kino*, 6, 2019: 24.

6. Marcin Adamczak, "Hard Power and Film Distribution: Transformation of Distribution Practices in Poland in the Era of Digital Revolution," *Studies in Eastern European Cinema* 11, no. 3 (2020): 246.

7. Adamczak credits Edward Zajiček as the initiator of this field, a film scholar who was "also an active member of the community." "His research focused on problems of profitability in film business, work conditions in the industry, historical research on the interwar period market, and the production history of Polish cinema." "Hard Power and Film Distribution" (2020): 244.

8. Adamczak, "Zderzenie z globalizacją," 25; Adamczak, "Hard Power and Film Distribution," 246.

9. Adamczak, "Hard Power and Film Distribution," 247.

10. Marcin Adamczak and Agnieszka Orankiewicz, "Film and Finance. An Attempt at a Statistical Comparison of the Attendance Results and Ratings of Polish Films in the Years 2012–2015," *Images. The International Journal of European Film, Performing Arts and Audiovisual Communication* 32 (2018): 198.

11. Adamczak, "Hard Power and Film Distribution," 247.

12. Adamczak, "Hard Power and Film Distribution," 248.

13. Adamczak, "Hard Power and Film Distribution," 249.

14. Mateusz Werner, "Whatever Happened to Polish Cinema after 1989?" *Polish Cinema Now! Focus on Contemporary Polish Cinema*, ed. Mateusz Werner (London, Warsaw: Adam Mickiewicz Institute, John Libbey Publishing Ltd., 2010), 17.

15. Joanna Rożen-Wojciechowska, "The Phenomenon of Polish Independent Cinema in 1989–2009," *Polish Cinema Now!* . . . (2010), 141.

16. Mateusz Werner, "Whatever Happened to Polish Cinema after 1989?" *Polish Cinema Now!*, 17.

17. Joanna Rożen-Wojciechowska, "The Phenomenon of Polish Independent Cinema in 1989-2009," *Polish Cinema Now!* . . . (2010), 144.

18. Mateusz Werner, "Whatever Happened to Polish Cinema after 1989?" *Polish Cinema Now!*, 20.

19. Jerzy Płażewski, "Polish Cinema—A Return to Market Economy," *Polish Cinema Now!* 155–156.

20. Jerzy Płażewski, "Polish Cinema—A Return to Market Economy," *Polish Cinema Now!* 156–157; Marcin Adamczak, "Polish Cinema after 1989: A Quest for Visibility and a Voice in the Market," *Illuminae* 24, no. 4 (88) (2012): 50 (45–58). See also the volume that Adamczak coedited with Marcin Malatyński and Piotr Marecki—*Restart zespołów filmowych* (Kraków-Łódź, 2012) and Ewa Mazierska's *Polish Postcommunist Cinema: From the Pavement Level* (Bern: Peter Lang Publishing, 2007).

21. Adamczak, 2012, 51.

22. Marcin Adamczak and Agnieszka Orankiewicz, "Film and Finance," (2018): 205, 207.

23. See Josephine Huetlin, "Here's Who Drives the Anti-LGBTQ Agenda in Poland Elections," *The Daily Beast*, July 13, 2020, at https://www.thedailybeast .com/in-polands-elections-heres-who-drives-the-anti-lgbtq agenda?fbclid=IwAR2tM HbERvTdH7izDbBPxM3wiK0ByV9L2sIzI4s6lxga7LPCig_woEhBsQ0. Accessed December 19, 2020.

24. See "Krzysztof Warlikowski Director 20/21 Artist" at https://www.operade-paris.fr/en/artists/krzysztof-warlikowski. Accessed December 19, 2020.

Chapter 1

Saints and Sinners

The Polish Catholic Church in Close-up

THE CITADEL OF POLISH TRADITIONS

The Polish Catholic Church occupies a unique place among religious institutions worldwide owing to the vagaries of the country's disastrous history. A stronghold of conservative values as regards its representatives' ecumenical mandatory celibacy and prohibition of its believers' use of contraception, as well as their access to abortion and divorce, the Catholic Church proved a vital sanctuary for Polish culture when the three partitions of 1772, 1793, and 1795 divided Poland among Russia, Prussia, and Austria, respectively. After the last partition erased the *Respublica* (Polish state) from the map of Europe, faute de mieux the church assumed the role of quasi-archivist and champion of national mores until 1918, when Poland regained its status as an independent entity. Similarly, during the Soviet era, the church symbolized political resistance to the Soviet Union, solidifying the imbrication of religion and politics that most recently has taken an unexpected turn—one of reactionary complicity. Given the historic role of the church as the repository of centuries-old Polish culture, today even atheists are reluctant to criticize Poland's Catholic Church, for doing so implies a lack of appreciation or ignorance of its admirable role in preserving the country's rich cultural heritage for more than a century.[1]

It bears remembering that Poland during the so-called Golden Age of the Polish-Lithuanian Commonwealth (late fifteenth to mid-seventeenth century) was internationally renowned as a powerful multiethnic country with a thriving intellectual atmosphere hospitable to diverse nationalities and religions.[2] The partitions and, subsequently, World War II and the aftermath of the Soviet takeover dramatically altered the nature of Polish politics, social hierarchies, and its everyday life.[3] The election of Karol Wojtyla (1920–2005) as Pope John Paul II in 1978 (until 2005) brought positive international attention to

Poland inasmuch as the well-traveled, second-longest-serving Pope worked to improve the relations of the Catholic Church with Islam, Judaism, and the Eastern Orthodox Church. Widely admired despite his doctrinaire views, he inspired the 2005 TV miniseries by Giacomo Battiato, *Karol: A Man Who Became Pope* (Polish: *Karol—Człowiek, który został Papieżem*; Italian: *Karol, un uomo diventato Papa*), also released in movie theaters. Its unexpected success prompted the creation of a sequel titled *Karol: The Pope, the Man* (2006), tracking his life from his papal inauguration to his death. And Krzysztof Zanussi, whose films variously engage Catholicism, released a biopic titled *Z dalekiego kraju* (From a Distant Country: Pope John Paul II 1981) as well as a screen adaptation of Karol Wojtyla's play *Brat naszego Boga* (Our God's Brother 1997), written before he became Pope. Few developments in twenty-first-century Polish history boosted the reputation of its Catholic Church, as did Wojtyla's papacy and the films about his life. In the last year revelations about his knowledge of sexual abuse within that church and silence about it, however, have somewhat diminished his image.

Though Poland remains a profoundly devoted Catholic country, recent tendencies show a decline in both membership and observance of Mass and official church holidays.[4] Especially the younger generations of Poles recently have balked at the reactionary attitudes of their country's church toward contraception, abortion, and various forms of sexual identity and intimacy, as evidenced in the repeated mass demonstrations of women against proposed abortion bans[5] as well as the protests by proponents of sexual liberalism against violations of LGBTQ rights, in which government and church speak with one voice.[6] And recent events and publications have tarnished the reputation of the Catholic Church, both in the West and in Poland,[7] where exposés of priests' sexual misconduct have resulted not only in their removal from office amid scandals but also in documentation of the church's long-standing habit of ignoring reports of such malfeasance or simply transferring "lapsed" priests to another parish. A March 2019 study commissioned by the Episcopal Conference of Poland that coordinated data from over 10,000 local parishes revealed that from 1990 to mid-2018 "church official received abuse reports concerning 382 priests." Seemingly, 625 children, most aged fifteen or younger, "were sexually abused by members of the Catholic clergy"—a figure that many believed underestimated the real extent of the problem.[8] For many years, the role of the Polish Catholic Church in both culture and politics has shielded it from critical scrutiny, but that situation seems to be changing today. Indeed, with World War II and the Soviet period receding into the increasingly distant past, Polish millennials may be unaware of or indifferent to the historical significance of Poland's Catholic Church, particularly in light of globalization and the minimalization of national differences within popular culture. Among the younger generations throughout Europe, technology rather than religion tends to provide answers to the questions preoccupying them. Today in Poland the image of the Catholic Church is undergoing revision in both everyday life and on screen, as I argue below.

THE CHURCH IN WESTERN AND POLISH CINEMA

More than a half-century ago an opinionated, polemical review essay by the immensely influential French Catholic critic André Bazin divided films about the church (or what he called "religious films") into three categories: "Stations-of-the-Cross" narratives (e.g., *Quo Vadis?*), hagiographies, and stories about priests and nuns.[9] Strikingly, Bazin remains a critic routinely cited nowadays, either in an adoptive or disputative mode, for his impact on film theory and criticism would be difficult to overestimate. Largely though not entirely leaving aside his first two categories, which others have discussed,[10] I focus on the last group, especially screen offerings since the late 1980s.

Whereas Anglophone cinema has produced approximately one hundred films about Catholic priests and roughly forty movies about nuns during the last sixty-plus years, Polish screen features of its Catholicism total under twenty narratives, half of them biopics.[11] Such a discrepancy may be accounted for, at least partially, by various factors: the greater number of films released in the West, particularly Hollywood; the lofty status and perceived stability of the Polish Catholic Church, which Poles may have deemed above analysis and criticism; and the preponderance of "faithful" Catholics among the Polish population, including those employed in cinema, vis-à-vis the multireligious Anglophone West, which harbors skepticism about sundry aspects of Catholicism while also addressing them. Anglophone films on the subject of priests' religious conflicts include lighthearted comedies (e.g., *Keeping the Faith* 2000), intense psychological explorations, such as Alfred Hitchcock's *I Confess* (1953) and Ulu Grosbard's *True Confessions* (1981), melodramatic examinations of gay priests (e.g., Antonia Bird's *Priest* (1994) and John Patrick Shanley's *Doubt* (2008)), and a diverse array of cinematic investigations into religious orders that continue to challenge individual choices in light of church dogma during increasingly secular approaches to everyday modern life.

Nuns' battle with their psychology and sexual impulses have yielded more modest cinematic fare, but several memorable instances include Henry Koster's *Come to the Stable* (1949), John Huston's *Heaven Knows, Mr. Allison* (1957), Fred Zinnemann's *The Nun's Story* (1959), Norman Jewison's *Agnes of God* (1985), Peter Mullan's *The Magdalene Sisters* (2002), and Maggie Betts's *Novitiate* (2017). Moreover, a recent French-Polish award-winning film titled *Les Innocentes* (The Innocents 2016), based on historical events and directed by Anne Fontaine, tackles the harrowing subject of Soviet soldiers' rape of

Benedictine nuns in a Warsaw convent in 1945 and their resultant pregnancies. As an astute reviewer noted, the film "is most interested in exploring how the atrocities test the sisters' religious faith."[12] *The Innocents* is akin to a recent series of Polish films that examine the brutality of World War II and its aftermath to reappraise a given country's "crimes against humanity" that have been denied or simply buried along with the victims of those atrocities: most notably Andrzej Wajda's *Katyń* (2007; discussed in chapter 6), Wojciech Smarzowski's *Róża* (Rose 2011) and *Wołyń* (Volhynia 2016), Władysław Pasikowski's *Pokłosie* (Aftermath 2012; analyzed in chapter 4), Paweł Pawlikowski's *Ida* (2013), and Ryszard Bugajski's *Zaćma* (Blindness 2016). While movies spotlighting Poles' barbarous actions, such as *Aftermath*, have elicited indignant denial and opprobrium in Poland, films focused on Polish victimhood, such as *Katyń*, predictably have found favor on home terrain, though these have largely avoided the issue of individuals victimized by Catholic clergy.

A striking recent development in Poland's Catholic Church that begs for interpretation has been an increase, noted in 2014, in the number of diocesan and religious priests, with ordinations outpacing deaths. Consequently, Poland "has the 2nd-highest number of diocesan priests in Europe (after Italy) and the 3rd-highest number of religious priests (after Italy and Spain)." At the same time, the period has witnessed a decrease in female religious communities,[13] with women who entered religious orders numbering 566 in 2000, but only 177 in 2017.[14] Without jumping to conclusions, one may consider the possibility that Polish priests' molestation, not only of children, which has attracted considerable media attention in recent months, but also of nuns may be at least partially responsible for this trend. Ursuline Sister Jolanta Olech, secretary general of the Warsaw-based Conference of Higher Superiors of Female Religious Orders, told Poland's Catholic Information Agency, KAI that "sexual abuse of nuns by clergy has long been a problem in Poland—and it's a very painful matter." Noting that during the twelve years she has occupied her position, "very painful" cases have come to her attention, which is why she "welcomed Pope Francis' Feb. 5 [2019] call for action against offending clergy." One young nun, apparently, "had been forced to leave her order after becoming pregnant, while the priest who fathered her child had remained in his post without 'any serious consequences for his behavior.' "[15] Yet, Polish cinema has not hesitated to pay homage to those whose religious commitment and fervor seem beyond reproach.

APOTHEOSIS AND SAINTHOOD

The Mystery of Mysticism: Faustyna *(Faustina 1995),* Jerzy Łukaszewicz

Łukaszewicz's brief biopic of the nun Maria Faustyna Kowalska (1905–1938) tackles the complicated task of portraying a mystic. Beatified by Paul

John II in 1993 and canonized in 2000, the young Maria Faustyna had visions of Jesus Christ that earned her the title of Apostle of Divine Mercy. Given her biography, Łukaszewicz's film faced the fraught challenge of conveying the transcendent convincingly. One specialist in film commenting on Polish religious biopics stated, *"Faustyna* is for me the only film in this group that succeeds in conveying spiritual experience, which, one expects, should be the main effect of a biopic of a religious figure."[16] Yet Faustyna's mysticism presents enormous difficulties for a director intent on capturing the extraordinary experiences that testify to her saintliness. "It may be," speculated James B. Anderson, "that the most intriguing facet of mystical writing, poetry or prose, is that the element of obscurity and mystery never diminishes."[17] The same obtains in film, though the viewer has the opportunity to share the mystic's visions owing to the visual nature of cinema. As Anderson rightly contends, the general characteristics of mysticism include the following:

(1) the mystical acts are interior, secret and intimate;
(2) they are intuitive rather than ratiocinative;
(3) they are built upon discipline and negation of the senses,
(4) which results in a state of darkness;
(5) the acts are motivated by love for and desire for union with the Divine Being, which is its ultimate consummation.[18]

One of the reasons that *Faustyna* seems so persuasive is the ability of Łukasiewicz, in the span of 75 minutes, to implement all these principles.[19]

From our first glimpse of Faustynka as a seven-year-old (Zosia Kondraciuk) dressed in white, with a flower garland on her head, running through the fields to join rural dancers to the adult Faustyna's (Dorota Segda)[20] last words on her deathbed about mercy as the cardinal divine attribute, Łukasiewicz highlights her passionate devotion to only two phenomena: Jesus Christ and hard work. Her visions of Christ, rooted in her childhood, breed skepticism of all around her, including her mentor and confessor, Father Sopoćko (Krzysztof Wakuliński), her envious fellow nun, Feliksa (Agnieszka Czekańska), who in her old age (Danuta Szaflarska) narrates Faustyna's biography and her own regret for her past behavior, and those in whose midst Faustyna stands out by virtue of her exclusive, steadfast dedication to God. Most of Faustyna's "dialogue" is with Christ, albeit we hear only her side of it ("You can do everything"; "Jesus, I have faith in you"; "Jesus, take me"/"Ty wszystko możesz," "Jezu, ufam Tobie," "Jezu, zabierz mnie"). Her interaction with everyone else consists largely of references to her visions or statements about Christ's glory and compassion. The film preempts inaccessibility to her manifestly rich inner world on the viewer's part by the iterated incomprehension of all the religious people with whom she lives and works on a daily basis. As the convent's Mother Superior acknowledges at Faustyna's bedside, she understands nothing and feels like a child beside the young nun. The mystery of mysticism, in other words, remains precisely that, emphasized by Faustyna's explicitly articulated happy bewilderment at having been chosen for such ecstasy-inspiring visitations when all she possesses of value is her heart. And the music of composer Wojciech Kilar (1932–2013), known for his contribution to Wajda's films and numerous Hollywood offerings, harmonizes beautifully with the aura of transcendence that envelops *Faustyna*.

Łukasiewicz uses conventional religious symbolism such as the radiance of the sun and its rays, and especially in the second part of the film frames Faustyna in nature, where she toils even after being diagnosed with tuberculosis. Assigned the bakery as her workplace, she kisses the bread that is "the staff of life" and treats her older companion there with kind consideration, also bolstering her spirits and making light, literally and metaphorically, of their frequently demanding work. Apart from divine visitations, however, there is nothing extraordinary about Faustyna's life, the importance of which is entirely internal, for the mystery of her visions is a mystery impenetrable to others, including viewers. Her biography, in other words, comprises her intimate relationship to Christ, and the political engagement central, for example, to the priest Popiełuszko (in life and in the film about it) never even remotely impinges on her consciousness. The film's hazardous principle of selectivity succeeds in transposing temporality from the horizontal to the vertical axis. Not breadth but depth defines her being, and her spirituality and profound tranquility are abetted by Kilar's affective, delicate score. Her death of tuberculosis at the age of thirty-three inevitably conjures up Christ's age at his crucifixion, but the film makes no effort to draw that all too obvious analogy. Segda's skillful acting, which earned her an award in 1996 as best Polish actress of the year,[21] makes for a wholly convincing mystic, while the "mystical aesthetic" of the film, in Anderson's felicitous phrasing, "is more mystical than aesthetic."[22]

The Politicized Saint: Popiełuszko: Wolność jest w nas *(Popiełuszko: Freedom Is within Us 2009), Rafał Wieczyński*

Unlike Łukasiewicz's exalted depiction of a live icon, Wieczyński's approach to Popiełuszko is decidedly low-key and down to earth, treating him as a balanced, determined man inspired by inner strength to perform risk-laden but largely unexceptional deeds. Renowned throughout Poland for his courageous opposition to communism and his unflagging support of Solidarność, Jerzy Popiełuszko (1947–1984) was killed by agents of Służba Bezpieczeństwa (Security Service of the Ministry of Internal Affairs), who subsequently were convicted of the murder. Beatified by Pope Benedict XVI in 2010 as a martyr for his continuation of a hardy tradition within the Polish

Catholic Church—political resistance through sermons that inspired congregations during a yet again troubled period of Poland's history—he inspired two feature films that border on hagiographies: Agnieszka Holland's *Zabić księdza* ("To Kill a Priest" 1988) and Wieczyński's *Popiełuszko: Freedom Is within Us.*[23]

Holland has discussed the copious difficulties in making "To Kill a Priest"—one of her earliest films, before she established herself internationally. Coping with a dialogue in English and shooting in France, not Poland, according to her, were most problematic.[24] With the French Christopher Lambert in a remarkably diffident performance as Popiełuszko and most of the cast Americans (notably, Ed Harris as the secret agent responsible for the murder), the film does not fully belong to Polish cinema. It received largely poor reviews, though film scholar Paul Coates, while acknowledging the film as "ideologically flawed," found it sufficiently complex to warrant analysis.[25] And some critics, such as Roger Ebert, struggled to find positive aspects in an "ineptly made" film that, he contended, "might have seemed more convincing if it had been made in Polish and subtitled in English."[26] Indeed. Wieczyński's *Popiełuszko*, by contrast, not only is profoundly Polish but also benefited from the intervening years, which witnessed the move to beatify Popiełuszko (2010), providing the kind of apotheosis intrinsic to hagiography.

Wieczyński made a number of wise choices, above all in casting Adam Woronowicz (b. 1973) in the titular role, for his understated demeanor nicely conveys the quiet conviction and serenity that the film emphasizes while avoiding "larger than life" heroics. Secondly, considerable screen time is devoted to Solidarność (1980–), the period of Martial Law (December 1981–July 1983), and the protests of the era that had the priest's unwavering support. The many newsreel shots lend authenticity to the depiction of the sociopolitical context that made a genuine hero of the charismatic young priest, whose sermons were broadcast through Radio Free Europe, thereby increasing his mass popularity. Thirdly, the film starts with Popiełuszko's boyhood in 1953 and his bond with a father who despises Soviet power, then moves to his stint in the army, where his religious convictions land him in trouble, which leaves him unmoved, for by then he has become convinced that "freedom is within one." As a priest he serves the population on a day-to-day basis with mundane acts, taking a pregnant woman to doctors, giving money to those in straitened circumstances, hearing confessions in the midst of mayhem, and comforting anyone in need of a reassuring word. Rather than elevating him to superhuman status, Wieczyński shows him as likable, simple in his dealings with others, and able to forge human relations with people: tellingly, much of the time he appears in standard secular clothes, not a cassock.

The film also forgoes sensationalism and bathos in the portrayal of his murder. Shot in darkness, which makes it difficult to see exactly what transpires, the sequence merely has viewers hear his quickened breath and murmur of "Jezu" (Jesus) as the attackers beat him to death and throw him into the Wisła/Vistula River. Even the shots of traumatized public reaction are brief and circumspect. Though both Popiełuszko and other representatives of the Catholic Church appear in a wholly positive light, the film shows remarkable restraint in portraying the life of a modest, courageous priest of unwavering faith who inspired millions of Poles and earned the admiration of many in the West. While in danger of courting hagiography by the very nature of its subject, which may strike viewers as evocative of Jesus Christ's example, the film manages to skirt that category.

Mundane as Miraculous: Jasminum (2006), Jan Jakub Kolski

There is a manifestation and there is a mystery.

—St. Paul's Epistle to the Corinthians

Our ability to smell is exceedingly mundane and magical
at the same time.

—Nuri McBride

Jasminum (Latin for jasmine) by the director associated with magic realism garnered awards in Gdynia the year of its release and seven Eagles the following year, including for cinematography, music, sound, production design, and best actor (the outstanding Janusz Gajos).[27] A film of ineffable charm, *Jasminum* offers a seductive blend of binary phenomena: realism and fantasy, humor and seriousness, secular and religious, vulgar and elevated as it investigates what constitutes sainthood and the nature of love. Kolski has said of the film:

Krzysztof Kieślowski once sent me a few friendly words, among them these: "I value you for your seriousness and sense of humour." He was the first to notice this duality in which there is no contradiction. A sense of humour and attentiveness. A combination of these two elements can result in an extraordinary film. Those were my calculations when I wrote *Jasminum*. And, of course, one more calculation, the most important one: to enjoy the smiles of the audience leaving the cinema.[28]

Remarks by viewers suggest that they, indeed, smiled when exiting the cinema. Part of their pleasure may well have been stimulated by the appearance of a Polish matter-of-fact saint in a feature film—one that in unexpected ways recalls aspects of *Popiełuszko* and *Faustyna*, though *Jasminum* could hardly be more remote from the genre of a biopic and from full-fledged mysticism. On the contrary, viewers can understand quite easily why at the film's conclusion sainthood becomes conferred upon its unassuming protagonist.

All five senses are critical to *Jasminum*, though it somewhat slights *touch* and *taste*. Set in a poor monastery located in a small provincial town, the story opens with *sound*: dogs barking, wind howling, and thunder and lightning leading to the voice-over of the five-year-old Eugenia's narrative. In 1617, a young monk wakes up to the delivery of three coffins with the scent-generating bodies of the monks called Śliwa (Plum), Czereśnia (Sweet Cherry), and Czeremcha (Bird Cherry). This prehistory, punctuated by an overhead shot as God's perspective on earthly endeavors, which Kolski uses at key moments in the film, cedes to the contemporary period and the parallel *sight* of Zdrówko (Janusz Gajos), the monastery cook's, awaking. Thereafter the film starts to interweave four plotlines: Zdrówko's pursuit of his daily tasks against the background of the preoccupations troubling the monastery's residents: the expectation of Kleofas, the prior (Adam Ferency), and the three monks, Plum (Grzegorz Damięcki), Sweet Cherry (Dariusz Juzyszyn), and Bird Cherry (Krzysztof Pieczyński), named after their remote predecessors, that one of the three will be sanctified according to an old prophecy; the restoration of a religious painting by the visiting professional, Natasza (Grażyna Błęcka-Kolska), with her inquisitive daughter, Eugenia (Wiktoria Gasiewska); and the hairdresser Patrycja's (Monik Dryl) infatuation with the actor Zeman (Bogusław Linda). The lighter aspects of the film, such as the five-year-old's idiosyncratic narration, the musical motif of "la-la-la," and the situational and verbal humor, may distract the viewer from just how skillfully Kolski's film pulls the four plot threads together in a complicated knot that illuminates his themes of love and saintliness.

As Dostoevsky's *Brothers Karamazov* (1880) illustrates, Catholic mythology is not alone in positing the olfactive connection that contrasts the divine with the foul/human by identifying sanctity with posthumous pleasant scents versus the sinful body's *smell* of putrefaction.[29] "The Odor of Sanctity, formally known as Osmogenesia" elaborated by the film originated in the Middle Ages and held sway in the West for centuries, during which a saint's aromatic incorruptibility served as the transcendent ideal against which malodorous bodily remains presented "theological evidence of the transient and base nature of the material world."[30]

Knowledge of this centuries-long belief in such a miraculous distinction aids in understanding why scent is primary for Kolski's monks, whose exuded aromas Zdrówko collects on a daily basis, for they promise to identify which monk will merit sainthood.

In the secular (presumably irrational rather than miraculous) world, scent also plays a decisive role in Natasza's hobby of devising perfumes that allegedly influence human behavior. In the course of the film she discovers that her concoction of bird cherry and other ingredients lacks the element indispensable for stimulating love/desire—jasmine, a heavily scented flower traditionally associated with romantic love that is obligatory in wedding rituals in multiple countries.[31] When worn by Patrycja, the addition of jasmine to the perfume masterminded by Natasza not only results in passionate lovemaking with the actor Zeman (*touch*) but also prompts him to give her his car, gold watch, and avowal of unconditional love later substantiated by his rapturous description to Natasza of his feelings for Patrycja. Jasmine is also the scent that united the original seventeenth-century Bird Cherry and the woman in red who pined away for him waiting outside the monastery, was buried in the coffin that Zdrówko shows Natasza, and appears mysteriously at three junctures in the narrative as a symbol of undying love ("beyond the grave"). Miracles, in other words, may occur in the secular domain. Significantly, however, the inadequacy of romantic/sexual love—passionate and potentially destructive—is illustrated by the surprising revelation that the contemporary Bird Cherry betrayed his promise to Natasza some years ago and joined the religious order, just as subsequently he betrays his religious vows by fleeing from the monastery. Will Zeman prove faithful in the long run?

Christian love, contrasted to its romantic version, is what explains the film's concluding sequence, which reveals Zdrówko as God's chosen saint. The monk-cook's behavior corresponds to Christ's teachings, which Kolski presents unobtrusively and with humor as Zdrówko's everyday ritual of simple yet essential tasks, performed humbly and unquestioningly. Everything about the accurately named Zdrówko[32] makes him a saintly figure in the film's set of values: humility (he knows Latin better than Kleofas, but after thirty years in the monastery has not revealed that skill—"What for?" he asks); service (he dedicates all his days to feeding (*taste*) and taking care of everyone: as Eugenia notes, he first feeds the animals, then the humans at the monastery, and finally himself; all-embracing love (he sees every being as "God's creation," lifting pigs so that they can look up at heaven, leaving nibbles for a snail, and nurturing the ducks abandoned by their ambitious monk-owner); complete disinterest in benefit for himself (demonstrated when he reacts indignantly to Patrycja's offer of money to him and not the monastery); "suffering the little children" (specifically Eugenia, whom he feeds, for whom he creates a swing and whom he entertains with rhyming couplets, as well as accepting her terms of interaction, such as skipping along the monastery's corridors, hand in hand [*touch*]); a down-to-earth reverence for sainthood (as manifested in his relationship with the monastery's patron saint, Roch, whose statue he engages in dialogue, often mentioning the rundown condition of the monastery and its dearth of provisions.

Though formally the monastery's cook, Zdrówko is, in fact, its *spiritual* nurturer, utterly indifferent to self-promotion and uniquely appreciative of religious beauty, such as the sacred painting restored by Natasza. Always outwardly projected, he makes only one request for himself of St. Roch: namely, that Eugenia remain at the monastery, for she is the one female he has come to cherish—as he says, he makes sure never to look into a woman's eyes, presumably not to repeat the mistake of either the seventeenth-century or contemporary Bird Cherry. His love is reserved for wise innocence, embodied in Eugenia, who, upon meeting him, instantly sends him her version of a kiss and throughout the film seeks him out. Tellingly, when in the closing sequence of the film, which returns to the beginning via an overhead shot, a violent storm, and a monk's awakening, he incredulously discovers the stigmata that announce his sainthood, his response (which recalls Faustyna's) is a triple "Matko Bosko!" (Mother of God!), the rhetorical query whether God has gone mad, and the protest that he has to light the kitchen stove and begin his usual "daily work." But, as Eugenia sums up the concluding events in a rhyming couplet, he does become the monastery's saint: "It sometimes happens, if we look, / That a monastery has no cook" ("To się przecież czasem zdarza/ Żeby klasztor bez kucharza"). Sainthood, in short, consists of self-oblivious ministrations to others' needs, without regard for hierarchy or personal reward—a mode of religious service at odds with the seclusion and silence of the three self-involved monks optimistically awaiting sanctification.[33]

While recalling Faustyna in his sustained faith and regimen of constant work, Zdrówko never speaks of his belief but translates it into action. And he resembles Popiełuszko in his habit of catering to the well-being of everyone around him. Humility, compassion, and industriousness, as well as an alertness to the small but crucial details of everyday existence, mark him out from the other monastery residents. And the film's humor, which includes Zdrówko's use of vulgarities ("cholera," "psia krew," and "dupa"), enhances rather than belittling a captivating image of sainthood as a modest, righteous way of life, one promulgated by the Catholic Church. Whereas films such as Wojciech Smarzowski's later *Kler* (Clergy) lambast the church on the basis of its corrupt clergy, *Jasminum* may be said to dwell on what is admirable about at least one member of that currently beleaguered institution.[34]

THE DARKER SIDE

Possession, Salvation, and Sacrifice: **Matka Joanna od aniołów**
(Mother Joan of the Angels 1961), Jerzy Kawalerowicz

> Darkness can only be scattered by light, hatred
> can only be conquered by love.
>
> —Pope Paul John II

While *The Innocents* tackles nuns' violation, not by priests but by soldiers, the first significant Polish film of violence experienced by nuns, released more than a half-century ago, dramatizes their victimization by an unearthly enemy. Without question, the most famous twentieth-century Polish film about the Catholic Church is Kawalerowicz's risky 1961 feature (based on a 1942 novella with the same title by Jarosław Iwaszkiewicz), which has its Anglophone analogue in Ken Russell's disorderly, lurid *Devils* (1971). Both directors took up the purported possession by evil spirits of an Ursuline nunnery in Loudun (France) during the possession-obsessed seventeenth century, which resulted in a 1634 witchcraft trial culminating in the conviction of a local priest, Urbain Grandier, who was burned at the stake for alleged sorcery and a pact with the devil. The melodramatic incidents inspired several literary works, including Aldous Huxley's *Devils of Loudun* (1952), John Whiting's play *The Devils* (1961), indebted to Huxley's novel, Krzysztof Penderecki's opera, *Die Teufel von Loudun* (The Devils of Loudun 1969), based on Huxley's novel and Whiting's play, and Russell's film, which in a sensationalist vein likewise drew on both works.

Metaphysics, psychology, and sexuality lie at the heart of Kawalerowicz's black-and-white film, which, closely following Iwaszkiewicz, transferred the action from Loudun to the benighted Polish provinces during the eighteenth century, focused on events after Grandier's death, and starred his then-wife Lucyna Winnicka, who scored an impressive triumph in the titular role as the convent's abbess. Writing about the film many years later, the Reverend Professor Chrostowski hyperbolically, if predictably, declared the film "one of the most controversial works in Polish postwar cinema. Looking back after half a century, it must be said that there has never been a good time for that film. There are hundreds of reasons why it should not have been made." He proceeded to recall his visit with the director to the Vatican, where, he reports, Kawalerowicz remarked, "The Church is often accused of sweeping the weaknesses of its faithful under the carpet. That is true, but the carpet is woven with threads of mercy, goodness, and forgiveness. It is a carpet which does not crush, condemn or stigmatize."[35] *Mother Joan*, however, suggests otherwise. Though acclaimed abroad—it won the Silver Palm at Cannes and several other awards—the film was blacklisted in Poland, inasmuch as the Episcopate prohibited audiences from viewing it.[36]

The plot alone explains why the Catholic Church would find the film unsettling at best. It dramatizes the efforts of Józef Suryn (Mieczysław Voit), a priest summoned to exorcise the nuns in a convent headed by the titular Mother Joanna, reputedly the most possessed of all. During their exchanges, Father Suryn is increasingly drawn to the nun, who attempts to seduce him. Out of love for her, he takes upon himself the evil spirits possessing her and, believing that the sole means of delivering her from renewed possession is to "serve" Satan, he axes two men to death. A parallel plot, skillfully integrated into the Suryn/Joanna story, has the sole unpossessed nun, Sister Małgorzata (Anna Ciepielewska), abandon the convent for the squire Chrząszczewski (Stanisław Jasiukiewicz), whom she loves but who abandons her after a night of sexual intimacy. At Suryn's behest she returns to the convent, relaying to Mother Joanna how love prompted Suryn to sacrifice himself and save her through the homicide that damned him forever.

Kawalerowicz's priests and nuns are cast in an unambiguously heretical light: both are subject to possession by evil forces; both have strong sexual impulses (Suryn's love for Mother Joanna seems erotic as well as Christian in nature; Małgorzata betrays her religious vows for a carnal relationship with an unworthy object of her affections); when Father Suryn consults a rabbi, the latter points out that they are one and the same—an idea anathema to Catholic doctrine (Voit plays both roles);[37] a susceptible priest saves a "sinner" endowed with excessive pride by murdering two human beings—hardly a Catholic mode of salvation; a priest not only responds to a nun's sexual desire but also chooses her over God and voluntarily succumbs to Satan. Demonic possession occurs when religious belief is too weak to combat evil—and Janicka's performance manifestly psychologizes the persona of Joanna. Kawalarowicz's film underscores her towering ambition and lack of humility, which point to her worldliness, her failure to consecrate her life entirely to God, which Catholicism mandates. Similarly, while Father Suryn ultimately saves her, surely the cost of his soul and of two men's lives violates any and all precepts of the Catholic canon. Furthermore, Małgorzata's betrayal of her vow as the "bride of Christ" for a physically consummated amorous relationship suggests that women joining Catholic convents may be motivated, not by religious fervor, but by lack of amorous success in everyday life or other, less than admirable considerations.

Repressed sexuality lies at the core of the quandary faced by most of the film's religious figures—a dilemma that dominates the Catholic Church's contemporary battleground, and not only in Poland. Catholicism's prohibition against marriage and sexual activity for its representatives—not shared by either Eastern Orthodoxy or Protestantism—demands what many consider superhuman sublimation of deep-seated desires and drives that are natural and universal but that, without an outlet, become destructive, in tune with the theory of frustrated desires articulated (ahead of Freud) by Ludwig Feuerbach (1804–1872), who also deemed religious belief an illusory projection of human aspirations.[38] One may ask, and many have, why marriage and sexuality necessarily violate a love of God and the performance of Christian charity.

That question is explicitly tackled in Russell's politicized, "no hold barred" version of the Grandier story, which has the priest (Oliver Reed) challenge Catholic dogma in word and deed by arguing against celibacy as irrelevant to "God's plan" and enjoying not only sexual relations with two women but also a reputation as a serial fornicator.[39] Unfortunately, his reasonable rebellion, which poses a key challenge to the demands of Catholicism, drowns in the flood of Russell's flamboyantly stagy, graphic images patently intended to shock, including those dwelling on the sexual problems of Sister Jeanne. In this case, she (Vanessa Redgrave) appears as an onanistic hunchback fixated on Grandier and unwittingly instrumental in his downfall, which is masterminded by no less a figure than Richelieu (Christopher Logue). As customary in Russell's films, naked bodies, orgies, vile and violent characters, copious screams, and hyperbole rule. Called a "grand fiesta for sadists and perverts" by critic Judith Crist,[40] upon its final release *The Devils* was billed as a horror film, later appearing on the horror streaming service Shudder, chiefly because it is more hysterical than historical. Though a miniscule minority of critics consider/ed it original and even "a masterpiece,"[41] ultimately, it has sunk in Lethe. The fate of Kawalerowicz's film, by contrast, has proved to be precisely the opposite, its international reputation as a cinematic gem surviving to this day.

As one thoughtful critic noted, *Mother Joan* "is not an exposé but an exploration of human character" loosely based on historical events.[42] But, as its blacklisting and Rev. Professor Chrostowski's reaction indicated, Polish Catholic officialdom's perception was at radical odds with that view. Paradoxically, the film exerts a strong impact on audiences less through its intrepid questioning of Catholic principles and values than through its complex psychology, mirroring devices,[43] and sophisticated aesthetics—all analyzed and lauded by critics at home and abroad.[44] Throughout, Kawalerowicz turns to fine advantage not only the immemorial religious symbolism of contrasting black/darkness and white/light,[45] but also the intersection of the horizontal and vertical axes, which forms a cross, consistently deployed at critical moments[46] and captured in a stunning overhead shot of the nuns lying prone, arms extended wide, on the stone floor of the convent. Moreover, spatial categories and parts of the mise-en-scène, such as "grilles, heavy doors, barred windows, stone columns, [. . .] and the wooden grating" that Suryn has constructed to separate himself from Mother Joanna, create a sense of entrapment, of carceral confinement or "the human animal trapped in the meshes of his own ideas and ambitions."[47] By contrast to the self-indulgence of Russell's *Devils*, *Mother Joan* is formally disciplined, for in his films "Kawalerowicz consciously seeks strictness and constraints, so as to elicit maximum reflection through meticulously selective means."[48] Little wonder that Andrzej Wajda (1926–2016) in his memoirs singles out Kawalerowicz and Polański as "the two maniacs [in Polish film] of professional cinema" who succeeded in making "perfect" films.[49] Visual style unquestionably is Kawalerowicz's overriding preoccupation, and, by contrast to Russell, he achieves some of his most successful effects through minimalism and absence rather than proliferation, as in the famously original final sequence, where a bell above the weeping Joanna and Małgorzata rings but does so inaudibly—for the film's disastrous events have silenced "true religion."

Though controversial, Kawalerowicz's film not only won the Silver Palm at Cannes but also condignly received praise for its aesthetic rigor, unlike Andrzej Żuławski's (1940–2016) later *The Devil* (*Diabeł* 1972, released only in 1987), which has much in common with Russell's *Devils*.[50] Generally understood by its critical champions as an allegory of contemporary Poland,[51] the narrative traces the improbable actions of the young nobleman Jakub (Leszek Teleszyński), a purported Polish conspirator imprisoned in a cell within a convent under attack during the Prussian invasion of Poland (1793). Rescued, inexplicably, together with a nun (Monika Niemczyk) by a Satanic figure (Wojciech Pszoniak),[52] Jakub flees across a winter landscape marked by depravity, grotesque incidents of gory violence, and mayhem. As he travels with the nun, his mysterious savior goads him to commit a series of random, savage murders and to disintegrate into a state of complete insanity. Finally, after Jakub has served his purpose (naming fellow conspirators), the manipulative "devil," who proves to be a petty pragmatist of the sort that Dostoevsky ironized,[53] kills him before attempting to rape the nameless nun, who castrates him, whereupon he expires and unaccountably metamorphoses into a wolf (shades of vampirism).

As several reviewers have observed, the film, which was anathematized in Poland and led to Żuławski's emigration to France, is a macabre mess, its relentless bloody barbarity eventually losing impact and becoming merely tedious.[54] If Żuławski's goal is to expose the violation of Poland's citizens by its repressive government, then subjecting the film's audience to the same brute force is hardly the optimal mode of engaging that audience and prompting its reflection on the state of affairs in the country. Additionally, the superfluous presence of the nun as a constant witness to Jakub's homicidal spree seems mere *épatage*—an excuse to display a naked female body for much of the film and to annoy the Catholic Church. It certainly has nothing to reveal about Polish nuns or the church. Manifestly intended to shock, both the near-rape and the nun's revenge on the devil have little relevance to a philosophical struggle between good and evil that arguably ends in the latter's defeat.

Like Russell's film, *The Devil* operates by an aesthetic derived from the horror genre, which Western critics have theorized in terms of repression, nightmare, and apocalyptic monstrosity.[55] Arbitrariness governs the film's events, which perhaps explains why, despite considerable effort by the talented Pszoniak, his devil remains unconvincing in a narrative obdurately devoid of nuance, whereas the startling submission of Kawalerowicz's Suryn to Satan's blandishments is psychologically credible. While one can understand the strongly negative reaction of the Catholic Church, as well as that of many viewers, to *The Devil*, its aesthetic prevents/ed many from taking it seriously.

Power and Perversity: W imieniu diabła (In the Name of the Devil 2011), Barbara Sass

At first glance *In the Name of the Devil* by Sass (1936–2015) may strike one as an imitation of Kawalerowicz'a *Mother Joan* or a variation on it transposed to contemporary times. Like its predecessor a half-century earlier, it raises the question of demonic possession at a convent and boasts an egotistical Mother Superior, authoritative priests, and nuns who interact with the world outside their religious enclave. These materials, however, serve an appreciably different purpose from that of *Mother Joan*, for Sass, as she acknowledged in an interview, is concerned not with metaphysical issues but with the sociopolitical aspects of the church as an entity brazenly exercising unmonitored power.[56] What constitutes evil remains enigmatic in *Mother Joan*, but for Sass it clearly is the Catholic Church as one of the country's coercive institutions. Its regimentation and hierarchical order resemble the army—and to underline that analogy Sass has her protagonist, Anna, repeatedly run across the latter's obliviously marching soldiers when she ventures into town.

Whereas Kawalerowicz favored Father Suryn's perspective, Sass's focus is on the young nun Anna (Katarzyna Zawadzka), whose experiences and viewpoint structure the film. It opens with her racing and screaming along the convent corridor, shaken by a nightmare. The sequence instantly establishes what subsequently becomes explicit—that unspecified traumas at home drove her to the convent in search of shelter. Whereas the sympathetic local confessor, Father Stefan (Marian Dziędziel), believes that Anna should consult a doctor, the Mother Superior (Anna Radwan), who claims to have direct contact with God and the Virgin Mary, insists that Anna is in the grip of demonic possession. She bypasses Stefan and arranges the arrival of a priest more in tune with her thinking, Father Franciszek (Mariusz Bonaszewski), who essentially takes over the convent. As barbed wire around its walls suddenly transforms the convent into a concentration camp, Franciszek proselytizes the body as a significant part of divine worship and proceeds to brainwash the nuns, applying his hands to their bodies in a manner distinctly not spiritual.[57] Ultimately, the police arrive and liberate the nuns, while Anna decides that the ostensibly safe harbor of the church is not for her.

Sass envisions nothing to commend in convent life and, specifically, its "power structures and collective dynamics."[58] As in *Mother Joan*, repressed sexuality, as well as delusions of grandeur, finds its home among those claiming to worship God. It is difficult to credit the giggly, juvenile nuns with a solemn devotion to religion; the Mother Superior, a sadomasochistic self-flagellant, has an emotional and physical obsession with Anna that signals lesbianism; Father Franciszek's "laying on of hands" constitutes groping young women's bodies, and so forth. As Łucja, the most percipient of the nuns, early exclaims, "W tym nie ma Boga!" (There's no God in this!) In fact, God seems irrelevant in a closed environment where psychologically maimed overseers manipulate their passive and gullible victims.

Although a few critics greeted the film enthusiastically,[59] it failed to cause a stir. And though many welcomed Sass back to cinema after an eleven-year hiatus, ultimately the majority agreed that parts of the film were unconvincing or simply ineffective.[60] Indeed, the personae seem black and white, the narrative is fragmented, and despite fine acting (for her debut role Zawadzka won two awards), the film fails to portray the peccadillos of the Catholic Church, and particularly of the supposedly charismatic Father Franciszek, persuasively. Unfortunately, though no one would deny Sass's seriousness as a director, the film intermittently borders on Russell's *Devils* and nunsploitation.[61] The real challenge to Polish Catholicism, and one that attracted huge audiences, came several years later, in the form of Wojciech Smarzowski's implacably bleak *Clergy*.

A Devastating Indictment: Kler (Clergy 2018), Wojciech Smarzowski

> *Clergy* is a feature film, not a documentary.
>
> —Wojciech Smarzowski

> The most scandalous charges were suppressed; the
> Vicar of Christ was only accused of piracy, murder,
> rape, sodomy and incest.
>
> —Edward Gibbon[62]

Known for a hard-hitting realism evocative of exposés in such films as *Wesele* (The Wedding 2004), *Różyczka* (Little Rose 2010), *Drogówka* (Traffic Police 2013), and *Wołyń* (Volhynia 2016), Smarzowski (b. 1963)[63] in *Clergy* limns an annihilating portrait of the Polish Catholic Church through the lives of three priests and an archbishop. Collectively, the quartet violates every conceivable religious precept, constituting what one reviewer ironically called "a Cosa Nostra in cassocks."[64] The most controversial film of 2018, *Clergy* presents priests as drunken fornicators, petty thieves, and pedophiles, mired in cynical self-indulgence and indifferent to their religious vows as well as the spiritual needs of their flock. Neither charity nor chastity guides their behavior.

After surviving a fire caused by their inebriated heedlessness in the past, Fathers Andrzej Kukuła (Arkadiusz Jakubik), Leszek Lisowski (Jacek Braciak), and Tadeusz Trybus (Robert Więckiewicz) annually reunite amid copious alcohol and crude rowdiness to commemorate their bond. Their festivities recall the inanity of juvenile fraternity parties, preliminarily casting doubt on their devoutness. Worse soon follows. As the film unfolds, Kukuła reveals himself as a bribe-taker, Lisowski emerges as an ambition-driven, Machiavellian pedophile, and Trybus proves an alcoholic who impregnates his mistress, Hanka (Joanna Kulig), then tells her to have an abortion. Their unscrupulousness, however, seems petty when compared to that of the aptly named, foul-mouthed Archbishop Mordowicz (Janusz Gajos),[65] a monument to corruption and hypocrisy, who manipulates endlessly to enrich himself and conceal all wrongdoing within the church from the outside world. Smarzowski tars virtually all clergy at different rungs in the church hierarchy with the same dark brush.

Yet, the three priests whose blasphemous mini-orgy opens *Clergy* occupy distinct positions on the moral spectrum and ultimately resolve their problems in markedly contrasting ways. Smarzowski throws a couple of red herrings in the viewers' path and withholds information for much of the film so as to intensify the impact of delayed revelations.[66] Lisowski seems the "golden-haired boy" of the three, adept at foreign languages, living in a chic apartment, driving an expensive car, working closely with Archbishop Mordowicz, and expecting a glamorous transfer to the Vatican. We learn, however, that these are the rewards for criminal dealings and, close to the conclusion of the film, that he is the pedophile who violated Rysiek (Ignacy Klim)—an altar boy in Kukuła's church who collapses, is found by Kukuła and taken by ambulance to the hospital, where an examination discloses that he has been sodomized. Though Kukuła officially informs Mordowicz and others of Lisowski's actions, the high-level cover-up, aided by Lisowski's blackmailing of Mordowicz, results in his successful transfer to the Vatican. Our last glimpse of him as he is about to land in Rome shows venality triumphant and amply rewarded.

As events overtake the trio, the alcoholic Trybus suffers two weighty blows that alter his everyday world: Hanka leaves him and shortly thereafter he concludes that a man killed by a hit-and-run driver must have been the individual he ran down when drunk. Acknowledging that he loves Hanka, he manages to locate her, and after their reconciliation finally abandons his bottles of vodka. But the unexpected realization that he accidently killed someone torments him, prompting his confession to the police. Apparently, however, his deduction of guilt is inaccurate, and after his release he leaves the priesthood and sets up house with Hanka in a very modest apartment. Sobriety and a committed partnership reward his belated self-confrontation. Earlier in the film he delivers a sermon of which love comprises the center-piece, and, unexpectedly, the love shared with Hanka proves his salvation, promising a more honest and, significantly, secular life.

One of the most grueling aspects of the film is that in the perverse, topsy-turvy religious world of *Clergy*, the priest who comes to a bad end is Kukuła, who, despite his propensity to exact money for services that fall under his responsibilities, genuinely cares about his congregation. Hounded by some of the townspeople for wrongly imputed pedophilism, he comes to a hor-rified awareness of how Catholicism has become infinitely degraded by its most trusted practitioners. After unmasking Lisowski (though to no avail), he approaches Mordowicz from a distance during the archbishop's menda-cious speech to a crowd of thousands, and sets himself on fire. The film's final image of his burning body as a cruciform suggests martyrdom for a cause. With Kukuła's radical act Smarzowski ends the film on an interroga-tive note: will Kukuła's self-immolation initiate an inquiry or have any effect on the Catholic Church? The trajectory of *Clergy* militates against such an optimistic consequence, for there is no doubt that Mordowicz will continue his immoral, self-serving mode of life, which, we are given to understand, is long-standing. Virtue and justice, let alone devotion to religious values, has little place in the film, which sweepingly indicts the entire Catholic order as a hotbed of self-perpetuating iniquities.

Anyone tempted to ascribe the erosion of religiosity in today's Poland to the influx of Western phenomena after the disintegration of the socialist sys-tem—a kneejerk reaction to revelations of wrongdoing among conservative forces in the Slavic world today—would find no basis for such a hypothesis in the film. At a couple of key junctures, Smarzowski uses flashbacks not only to provide glimpses into Lisowski's and Kukuła's past but also and, more importantly, to establish a historical perspective. In a painful scene, Lisowki tearfully recalls being brutally flogged at the behest of a sadistic nun for wetting his bed as a child, then sodomized by his flogger. And at the retirement home for clergy, a distraught Kukuła shakenly confronts the priest who sexually abused him when he was an altar boy. Furthermore, Kukuła's

earlier exchange with a colleague at the home makes it clear that in the past
the now aged pedophilic priest subjected others to the same treatment. In a
deft interpolation, a video by a Dutchman presented to Mordowicz shows
one Pole after another facing the camera as s/he speaks of being abused by
clergy[67]—a journalistic device used subsequently by a documentary on the
topic by the Sekielski brothers, as discussed below.

What Smarzowski wishes to emphasize through these sequences is that
pedophilia in the Polish Catholic Church has existed for many decades, and
victims have become victimizers in a potentially endless legacy of violation. Moreover, the presence of women among those abused counters the
argument, advanced by some, that the problem is one of homosexuality.
At the conference initiated by Pope Francis summoning church personnel
to grapple with child sexual abuse, "some Catholic bishops and conservative church media outlets have continued to blame the clerical child sexual
abuse crisis on homosexuality," but more discerning participants, such as
Rev. Hans Zollner, "a member of the Vatican's child-protection commission
and president of the Center for Child Protection of the Pontifical Gregorian
University," sensibly identified power as the main issue in pedophilism.[68]
And the far-reaching power of the church and the population's acquiescence to that power are precisely what Smarzowski dramatizes, as did the
American film *Spotlight* (2015), which depicts the exposé by *The Boston
Globe*'s investigative journalists of pedophilism in the Catholic Church,
beginning with Massachusetts, a stronghold of American Catholicism, sec-
ond only to Rhode Island.[69]

Clergy broke all box-office records in Poland for the last thirty years.[70]
Gazeta Wyborcza reported that "a cinema in Zabrze, a city in the south of
the country, showed the movie up to 24 times a day to meet demand."[71]
Some viewers may have been drawn by the cast, which comprises several
of the most famous and award-laden actors in contemporary Polish cinema,
but the topic indisputably was a key attraction at a time when church abuse
in Poland was gaining ground as a legal issue. Moreover, Smarzowski's
reputation as a "maverick" director who tackles thorny issues may have
prompted fans of his previous films to view *Clergy* as a matter of course.
While breaking attendance records, however, the film simultaneously
earned the wrath and rejection of the government and, unsurprisingly, of
the very church whose ills it excoriates.[72] The ultraconservative nationalist
ruling party, PiS, pressured various cinemas to stop showing the film, on
the grounds that it is "contemptuous and hateful to Polish identity" and akin
to Nazi propaganda.[73] The right-wing weekly *Gazeta Polska* referenced
Clergy on the cover of an issue, but inside featured priests whom Poles ven-
erate as national heroes: Pope St. John Paul II, Cardinal Stefan Wyszyński,
Saint Maximilian Kolbe, and Blessed Jerzy Popiełuszko.[74] The paper also

reproduced the movie poster on billboards across Poland with images of those icons, accompanied by the uplifting if surreal words, "The clergy: our treasure in the fight against Nazism, communism, LGBT and Islamists."[75] Similarly, the PiS-allied chairman of public television, Jacek Kurski, dismissed *Clergy* as a "provocative, trashy" attack on the church that was "brutal and untrue."[76] Father Dariusz Kowalczyk, a Polish Jesuit teaching at Rome's Pontifical Gregorian University, told *Polska Times* that the film conveys a false image of the church and is merely "vulgar clergyphobia."[77] Other religious figures expressed kindred sentiments, though some insightfully suggested that heated negative reactions to the film merely served as unwitting advertisements for it. Regular audiences and film buffs, by contrast, reacted with enthusiasm and admiration. Its September premiere at the Gdynia Film Festival elicited an eleven-minute standing ovation, and in Warsaw cinemas it was met with "spontaneous applause."[78]

During interviews and conferences Smarzowski stated that he intended the film as a wake-up call to credulous Catholics and wished to see all pedophiles in cassocks placed behind bars ("Chcę, by wszyscy pedofile w sutannach trafili za kratki").[79] A self-confessed atheist, he intended to demythologize the institution of the church, not to disparage faith. He noted, "The church is present in our offices, on the street, and pushes us [sic] home and to bed. The church's failure to deal with child abuse, hiding paedophiles in [. . .] cassocks and transferring them from parish to parish, also needed discussion. This movie is addressed to Catholics [. . .]. I hope that after leaving the cinema, they will realise they are co-responsible for what they see on screen."[80]

The timing of *Clergy* could not have been more propitious. It appeared soon after a landmark legal decision in Poland, in which a court awarded a twenty-four-year-old woman in Poznań hefty financial compensation for abuse by a priest when she was thirteen—to be paid by his official religious affiliation.[81] And it anticipated by a few months the February 2019 meeting at the Vatican of nearly 200 Catholic leaders convened by Pope Francis to discuss and find solutions to sexual abuse of children by Catholic clergy. In May, the Pope "issued a groundbreaking new church law [. . .] requiring all Catholic priests and nuns around the world to report clergy sexual abuse and cover-ups by their superiors to church authorities, in a new effort to hold the Catholic hierarchy accountable for failing to protect their flocks."[82] Objections justly faulted the law for maintaining access to such reports solely within the church instead of also involving the police. But the public admission of such wrongdoings was a modest start that lent *Clergy* weight and that provided an international background for a Polish documentary that would shake the country a few months later and would reinforce the image of the Catholic Church at the center of *Clergy*.

CLERGY'S DOCUMENTARY COUNTERPART: TYLKO NIE MÓW NIKOMU (JUST DON'T TELL ANYONE 2019), TOMASZ AND MAREK SEKIELSKI[83]

Unprecedented crowds of Poles flocked not only to *Clergy* but also to a related documentary film completed soon afterward: *Just Don't Tell Anyone*, by the brother-journalists Tomasz and Marek Sekielski. Its appearance on YouTube in May 2019 instantly attracted hordes of viewers.[84] An unsparing examination of pedophilia in Poland, the documentary combines interviews with adults who were sexually violated by priests in their childhood and confrontations by the victims and the Sekielskis with bishops and priests about such activities. It also attempts to establish what measures, if any, have been taken to remove the sexual predators from their posts. What emerges unambiguously from such meetings is the automatic refusal of the Polish Catholic Church to acknowledge the frequency of pedophilia within its ranks, as well as its habit of sweeping the phenomenon under the proverbial rug. In an illustration of Oscar Wilde's quip that life all too frequently imitates art,[85] avoidance, disclaimers, and protests against accusations of wrongdoing (all part of *Clergy*'s narrative) are the church's reactions.[86] And, according to the documentary, a major force in safeguarding abusers was Pope John Paul II, whose decree ensured that reports of its occurrence would not be shared outside the church.

Numerous Poles have praised the Sekielskis for their courage and enter-prise, while reactions by the church have been mixed: Archbishop Wojciech Polak, the primate, has thanked the brothers, and Archbishop Salvatore Pennachio, the Vatican's ambassador to Poland, has expressed "sympathy and solidarity" with the victims on behalf of himself and Pope Francis. By contrast, Archbishop Leszek Sławoj Głódź of Gdansk has claimed that he has "better things to do than watch the film." And while Jesuit priest Jacek Prusak denounced the church as "a home for a herd of wolves in clerical collars,"[87] a viewer on YouTube counseled the need to distinguish between the church and "perverts" within it. After a critical response, Jarosław Kaczyński, the head of PiS and a practicing Catholic, declared that the country does not tolerate "pathology" within the Catholic Church and promised to back a commission to investigate sex abuse of minors not only in the church but also in other institutions. Accordingly, PiS pushed through parliament a law increasing the prison term for pedophilia from twelve to thirty years. It probably is no accident that these measures were adopted shortly before the country's par-liamentary elections in autumn 2019.[88]

Reportedly, "Poland's Prosecutor General has issued an investigation into the alleged crimes detailed in the film," but as a board member of the Polish foundation Nie Lękajcie Się (Have No Fear), which helps victims of child abuse committed by the Catholic Church, argued, implementation of sentences, not merely detection, is essential.[89] To predict the long-term effect on both the church and the Polish population—of the documentary and Smarzowski's feature—is impossible, but people's less reverent attitude toward the Catholic clergy seems most likely. And in May 2020, the Sekielski brothers released another community-funded documentary (*Zabawa w chowanego* [Hide and Seek]) about a specific priest, Arkadiusz Hajdasz, who molested boys in the various parishes to which he kept moving and who, after many years of attempts to bring him to justice, still eludes punishment.[90] As a character in *Clergy* points out, "The Church is holy, but it's made of sinful people" (Kościół jest święty, ale tworzą go ludzi grześni)—a sentiment echoed by Janusz Gajos in his brief YouTube commentary on the film and its importance.[91] Though evidence of the church's concealment is overwhelming, it would be reductive, at best, to make sweeping generalizations about all personnel within the Polish Catholic Church on the basis of individual cases that all three films spotlight.

History and Revelation: Ida *(2013), Paweł Pawlikowski*

The past is never dead. It's not even past.

—William Faulkner

In cinema, emotional truth and psychological truth is [*sic*] much more important [than history].

—Paweł Pawlikowski, in interview

Largely on account of being the first Polish feature to have won an Oscar for best foreign language film,[92] Pawlikowski's (b. 1957) highly original and compressed (82 minutes) *Ida* is internationally the most famous recent screen examination of a "bride of Christ" within the Catholic Church. Yet, it stands apart from European and American films about nuns insofar as it focuses less on the church or the young novitiate's vacillations about her chosen path, as instanced in Fred Zinnemann's award-winning *Nun's Story* (1959), than on the psychological impact of the past upon the present, to which the titular protagonist's religious identity seems secondary.

Set in 1962 Poland, the film unfurls an unusual and compelling plot. Young Anna (Agata Trzebuchowska), a convent-raised orphan readying to take her vows, is ordered by the Mother Superior to contact her sole surviving relative, living in Łódź, before doing so. The awkward meeting reveals that the novitiate is actually the Jewish Ida Lebenstein, placed in the convent by that very relative—her cynical, hard-drinking Aunt Wanda (Agata Kulesza), a former judge for the Soviets during World War II—who joins Ida in her search to learn what happened to their family. In the provincial village where the Lebensteins lived, they discover that three of its members were murdered by their neighbors (Adam Szyszkowski and Jerzy Trela), who had sheltered them until fear of Nazi discovery drove them to kill Ida's parents and Wanda's son, Tadzio.[93] Little Ida was spared because she did not look Jewish. After burying the trio's unearthed remains in a deserted Jewish cemetery in Lublin, the two return to their former lives, now experienced from a changed perspective. Haunted by her conscience, presumably for having left her son and for having cold-bloodedly condemned to death the victims of the Soviet system with which she collaborated, Wanda commits suicide. Self-contained by virtue of her convent training, Ida attends her funeral, then, dressed in Wanda's dress and shoes, visits the club where Lis (Dawid Ogrodnik), a young musician whom she and Wanda had met earlier, is playing in a jazz band. They spend the night together and he offers her marriage, family, and children. The following morning, however, Ida leaves the young saxophone player and, donning her nun's habit, departs—whether for the convent or elsewhere is uncertain, albeit most critics simplistically assumed that she rejects marriage and family for the religious alternative.[94]

While the final sequence shows Ida walking along the road that eventually leads to the convent, it bears remembering that her newfound identity and her earlier discoveries on the road prompted her, upon rejoining the nuns, to smile at convent rituals and to declare her unpreparedness for the serious step of taking final vows. Pawlikowski, in fact, opts for an open and imaginative ending, which introduces two novel elements: an unexpected camera placement and an equally unexpected aural component. The hymns, songs, and orchestral music throughout the film are strictly diegetic, the most startling being Mozart's magnificent Jupiter Symphony (his forty-first and last), which plays loudly on Wanda's gramophone as she leaps to her death. We also hear music on the radio and in performance by the young band and singer (Joanna Kulig) at the hotel club. Yet at the conclusion *extradiegetic music* accompanies Ida's brisk steps, which carry her *toward the viewer*, in a vocative camera mode that does not, however, breach the fourth wall.

Ferruccio Busoni's piano transcription of Bach's church cantata "Ich ruf zu dir, Herr Jesu Christ"/I call to You, Lord Jesus Christ (1732) may be viewed as Ida's decision finally to become "the bride of Christ," but just as easily may be a plea for understanding of her departure from the convent. In either event, the bipartite shift unequivocally signals a new perspective that, however, remains enigmatic regarding an individual schooled in discipline who consistently has embraced silence and impassivity.

For audiences familiar with earlier Polish cinema, the most fascinating aspect of *Ida* from a religious and aesthetic standpoint is, debatably, its rich relationship to Kawalerowicz's *Mother Joan*. Whereas the latter includes the puzzling sequence in which a rabbi tells the Catholic Suryn that they are one and the same (and both played by the same actor), Pawlikowski's *Ida* literalizes in a single persona the symbolic sameness of Jewish and Catholic that Kawalerowicz posits. Jewish by birth, Ida has been reared in a Catholic convent and prepares to take vows that will render her one of its official representatives. Yet the film's World War II narrative makes clear that in occupied Poland, Jews and Poles were treated very differently; that momentous difference determined whether one lived or died. Pawlikowski's noncommittal approach to his materials, like Kawalerowicz's in the pertinent meeting between the two men, offers no hint as to what such an anomalous identity as Anna's/Ida's implies within the context of the film's narrative.

Richard Brody, reviewing the film for *The New Yorker*, vehemently upbraided it because of what he condemned as its vagueness, its aesthetics, and Pawlikowski's refusal to "take sides" in Polish-Jewish issues. He reprehended the director for not spelling out motivation and for paucity of dialogue—precisely what I consider two of the film's substantial strengths.[95] Brody seems unaware that silence is a sine qua non of convent and monastery life, even though we see Anna/Ida and other novitiates work, eat, and interact in complete silence. And Trzebuchowska as Ida, especially in the scenes that contrast her with Kulesza's Wanda, most convincingly projects an inner strength that requires no words.[96] Possibly intended as a corrective, a short while later *The New Yorker* carried a diametrically opposite review of the film by David Denby, who called it "a compact masterpiece" and noted, "I can't recall a movie that makes such expressive use of silence and portraiture." Attuned to Pawlikowski's aesthetic choices, Denby appreciated Trzebuchowska's ability to convey "a preternatural calm and self-sufficiency" and an "opacity" that serves Pawlikowski's purposes.[97] Another critic similarly commended her onscreen persona as "a poised icon of luminous quietude and awakened curiosity."[98] And one of Poland's eminent film critics, Tadeusz Sobolewski, characterized *Ida* as "a quiet film posing the big questions that prey upon all of us: about evil, faith, our identity, and our country. *Ida* is one of the most mature films of the most recent period" ("cichy film wielkich pytań nurtujących nas wszystkich: o zło, wiarę, naszą tożsamość i kraj. *Ida*—to jeden z najdojrzalszych filmów ostatnich lat . . .").[99]

More than one reviewer noted Pawlikowski's revival of the aesthetics adopted by prominent Polish directors of the 1960s: preference for black-and-white over color, implication over explicitness, value-laden selection of music, and above all creative camerawork. While Brody's minority assessment was startling, the reaction of Polish audiences was sooner foreseeable. True to form, controversy arose regarding the film's purported lack of patriotism, lamenting "some Polish citizens' complicity in the Holocaust without mentioning that many Poles worked to save Jews during the Nazi occupation."[100] Such a reception had greeted virtually all films by Wajda depicting the Holocaust. Others felt that Pawlikowski soft-pedaled the Jewish question.[101] And the reaction of Polish Catholics and conservatives to the film could not have been more predictable, as "the resurgent Catholic far-right tried to get *Ida* banned or disqualified from prizes because of a perceived 'anti-Polish' sentiment."[102]

Yet *Ida* is no *In the Name of the Devil*. Scenes of the convent's rituals reflect an atmosphere of solemn dedication as the nuns and initiates perform daily duties, pray, sing hymns, and wordlessly consume their meals. An overhead shot of them prostrate before the altar specifically evokes a moment in *Mother Joan* when the camera likewise captures nuns' cruciform submission to a "higher power." Moreover, where Kawalerowicz relied on light and darkness for metaphysical polarities, Pawlikowski and his cinematographers, the talented Łukasz Żal and Ryszard Lenczewski, likewise invested natural light with meaning, but more frequently used space to communicate the film's values. In her perceptive review, Catherine Wheatley remarked:

> [The] detailed, painterly style of shooting is balanced by [. . .] use of natural light, which casts [. . .] sets in shadows. Wanda and Anna are literally boxed in by the unusual 1.37:1 aspect ratio and static camera, overwhelmed by the spaces they inhabit and the weight of history. Impassive grey skies and bulky cement blocks dominate the screen, consigning the characters to its lower corners. [. . .] The bare, brutal mise en scène is all right angles and parallel lines: window frames, doorways, railings, even the trees are unusually upright, as if the landscape itself is trying desperately to impose order on chaos. And of course there are the cruciforms that hang on wall after wall, and which a prostrate Anna will eventually form with her own body.[103]

Particularly in the sequences capturing Ida and Wanda's discovery and burial of their family's disinterred bones, the division of the screen into three parts, with the uppermost, largest, empty register showing white (the pure vault of heaven), adheres to the ancient tripartite concept of the cosmos as chthonic, earthly, and celestial.[104] Such a configuration, which reticulates throughout the film, is indissoluble from the spiritual questions raised by the convent and Ida's role within it, as well as the film's universalizing tendency. Evil here is associated with an implacable history, not the church (for a contrary view, see chapter 4). Though *Ida* has little to say explicitly about the Polish Catholic Church, it consistently installs an inscrutable realm that arches over human endeavors through its extraordinary photography.

CONCLUSION: SCREENING THE CHURCH

Portrayals of the Polish Catholic Church on screen run the full gamut from quasi-hagiographies to denunciations of its representatives' opprobrious practices. Reception of these cinematic offerings also varies appreciably, even within the church and the government, as well as among general movie audiences. Older generations and the government tend to object to non-heroic or what they consider demeaning images of Poland and its church, denying Polish collaboration with the Nazis. Though the church, unsurprisingly, favors positive narratives about its standing in Polish culture, some of its influential leaders acknowledge serious violations within its ranks. History retains its grip on Poland, though somewhat less on younger generations of Poles, who, in addition to their distance from the legacy of World War II and the subsequent Soviet stranglehold, are more attuned than their elders to popular culture, globalization, the internet, and fast-multiplying digital innovations.

Moreover, the very concept of national cinema has become complicated owing to cinematic transnationalism and such directors as, for instance, Pawlikowski and Małgorzata Szumowska, both remote from Polish Catholicism yet portraying it on screen, as in *Ida* and *W imię* . . . (In the Name of . . . 2013). Until his recent return to Poland, Pawlikowski released Anglophone documentaries and feature films as a British director, while Szumowska early in her career began seeking funding and collaboration outside of Poland. Yet these tendencies are not new, for even during the Soviet era Wajda, Jerzy Skolimowski, and others made films abroad and worked with foreign *Kulturarbeiter*.[105] Agnieszka Holland's professional biography, above all, demonstrates the directorial benefits of living, working, and collaborating with colleagues beyond Poland. At the same time, the Polish Catholic Church is a historically unique entity, and mass audiences' consistent enthusiasm for Smarzowski's films implies that Poles prefer Polish directors such as Smarzowski, who lives and works in Poland and whose straightforward films depend on domestic funds, as the appropriate individuals to engage specifically Polish issues or the Polish version of universal problems such as abuse by clergy—at least from a viewpoint with which Poles can identify. Yet, surely one can only be grateful that directors such as Pawlikowski philosophically extend what appear to be "quintessentially Polish issues" onto a metaphysical and universal level, particularly in a film such as *Ida*, which substantiates the inestimable value of retro aesthetics and retrospectively celebrates such sixties' films as Kawalerowicz's *Mother Joan*, as well as turning international attention to the riches of contemporary Polish film.

HG

NOTES

1. During the siege of Vienna in 1683, Catholic Poland's decisive defeat of the Turks is claimed as the salvation of Europe from Islam. See https://www.catholic-worldreport.com/2016/06/28/polands-history-is-a-story-of-resilient-catholic-faith/. Accessed March 12, 2020.

2. See Norman Davies, *Heart of Europe: The Past in Poland's Present* (Oxford: Oxford University Press, 2001), 245–311, particularly 278–311. Though the Commonwealth existed until the partitions, starting in the late seventeenth century its status as a haven of tolerance and diversity degraded owing to political and ideological discord and armed conflict.

3. Ibid., *passim.*

4. Polls and reports indicate that more than 80 percent of Poles identify themselves as Catholic, but in recent years attendance at Sunday Mass has fallen below 40 percent, and of attending it, 42 percent receive Holy Communion. See "Sunday Mass Attendance Falls Below 40% in Poland," Catholic World News, July 24, 2014, https://www.catholicculture.org/news/headlines/index.cfm?storyid=22111. Accessed October 15, 2019. One source cites Mass attendance today as standing at 36.7 percent, noting that "falling numbers combine with deeper commitment." Jonathan Luxmoore, "Poland's Catholic Church Takes on Its Critics," *National Catholic Reporter*, February 16, 2018, https://www.ncronline.org/news/world/polands-catholic-church -takes-its-critics. Accessed October 16, 2019.

5. See Marc Santora and Joanna Berendt, "Polish Women Protest Proposed Abortion Ban (Again)," *New York Times*, March 23, 2018, https://www.nytimes.com /2018/03/23/world/europe/poland-abortion-women-protest.html. Accessed March 21, 2019. The more recent draconian law that essentially prohibits all abortions likewise has sparked outraged protests. See Tomek Rolski, "Poland's New Abortion Law Triggers Broader Discontent as Women Lead Protests," October 27, 2020, https:// abcnews.go.com/International/polands-abortion-law-triggers-broader-discontent -women-lead/story?id=73853693. Accessed October 30, 2020.

6. For the current opposition to LGBTQ rights of the party in power, PiS (Prawo i Sprawiedliwość/Law and Justice), see Joanna Plucinska, Anna Wlodarczak-Semczuk, "Poland's ruling party picks LGBT rights as election battlefront," Reuters, March 15, 2019, https://www.reuters.com/article/us-poland-lgbt /polands-ruling-party-picks-lgbt-rights-as-election-battlefront-idUSKCN1QW0T7; "Poland's Ruling Chief Speaks Strongly against LGBT Rights," AP, March 16, 2019, https://www.foxnews.com/world/polands-ruling-chief-speaks-strongly-against -lgbt-rights. Both accessed March 21, 2019.

7. A stream of revelations about priests' sexual abuse of altar boys, as well as the weighty tome by Frédéric Martel, *In the Closet of the Vatican: Power, Homosexuality, Hypocrisy* (London: Bloomsbury Continuum, 2019), present bishops, cardinals, and sundry popes in at best a questionable light.

8. Joanna Berendt, "Catholic Church in Poland Releases Study on Sexual Abuse by Priests," *New York Times*, March 14, 2019, https://www.nytimes.com/2019/03/14

/world/europe/catholic-church-abuse-poland.html. Berendt places the percentage of self-identified Catholics at eighty-seven. For more on the issue of clergy's molestation of children, organizations that track such incidents, and more, see Berendt. Accessed March 21, 2019.

9. Originally published in *Cahiers du monde* (May 1951, no. 2), the year in which Bazin founded the journal, the essay in English appears as Cardullo, Bert and Bazin, André, "Cinema and Theology: The Case of Heaven Over the Marshes," *Journal of Religion & Film* 6, no. 2 (2016), Article 15, https://digitalcommons.unomaha.edu/jrf/vol6/iss2/15. Accessed January 23, 2020.

10. See Marek Haltof, *Polish Cinema: A History* (second edition) (New York and Oxford: Berghahn, 2019) and Ewa Mazierska, *Polish Postcommunist Cinema: From Pavement Level. New Studies in European Cinema*, Vol. 4 (Bern: Peter Lang, 2007), *passim*.

11. These include Krzysztof Zanussi's *Życie za życie: Maksymillian Kolbe* (A Life for a Life: Maximillian Kolbe, 1990), among others. See Haltof 2019, 282–83 and Mazierska, who concludes that feature films and documentaries about religious figures, which serve the same function, total almost thirty, though she does not list all of them. Mazierska, 2007, 116–22.

12. Stephen Holden, "Review: In *The Innocents*, Not Even Nuns Are Spared War Horrors," *New York Times*, June 30, 2016, https://www.nytimes.com/2016/07/01/movies/review-in-the-innocents-not-even-nuns-are-spared-war-horrors.html. Accessed February 2, 2017. Three of Poland's most talented actresses assume the film's major roles: Agata Buzek, Agata Kulesza (as formidable here as in *Róża* and *Ida*), and Joanna Kulig (of *Ida* and *Zimna wojna* fame).

13. "Sunday Mass attendance falls below 40% in Poland."

14. "Prominent Nun Says Polish Priests Must Stop Abusing Women Religious," CRUX/Catholic News Service, February 15, 2019, https://cruxnow.com/church-in-europe/2019/02/15/prominent-nun-says-polish-priests-must-stop-abusing-women-religious/. Accessed February 16, 2019.

15. Ibid.

16. Mazierska, *Polish Postcommunist Cinema*, 121.

17. James B. Anderson, "The Spanish Mystical Aesthetic," *Mystics Quarterly* 19, no. 3 (September 1993): 116.

18. Ibid., 117.

19. The film is based on Faustyna's diary, which her confessor advised her to maintain.

20. Segda's role here could not be more remote from the young alcoholic she plays in Barbara Sass's *Tylko strach* (Only Fear 1993).

21. The award was the Złota Kaczka (Golden Duck), pioneered in 1956 by the monthly *Film*, based on its readers' votes.

22. Anderson, "The Spanish Mystical Aesthetic," 122.

23. Popiełuszko's fate also inspired a documentary, *Ostatnia droga* (The Last Path), by Robert Wichrowski, a director who earlier worked for the SB—a startling paradox that rendered his film problematic for those familiar with his past. See

Krzysztof Derdowski, "Były eskek nakręcił film o ks. Jerzym Popiełusze," bydgo-szcz24.pl, November 18, 2014, https://bydgoszcz24.pl/pl/11_wiadomosci/9374_byly _esbek_nakrecil_film_o_ks_jerzym_popieluszce.html. Accessed October 11, 2019.

24. See *Twarze Agnieszki Holland/Faces of Agnieszka Holland* (Lodz: Muzeum Kinomatografii w Łodzi, 2013), 124–29.

25. For that analysis, see Coates, *Cinema, Religion and the Romantic Legacy* (London: Routledge, 2003), 138–42.

26. Roger Ebert, "To Kill a Priest," October 13, 1989, https://www.rogerebert .com/reviews/to-kill-a-priest-1989. Accessed July 3, 2019.

27. Instituted in 1999, Eagles are annual film prizes awarded by the Polish Film Academy since 2003, analogous to Hollywood's Academy Awards.

28. See *Jasminum*, Culture.pl, https://culture.pl/en/work/jasminum-jan-jakub -kolski. Accessed May 29, 2019.

29. In the novel, Alesha undergoes what initially seems a crisis of faith when his mentor Zosima's body fails to meet this canonical criterion for saintliness.

30. For a fascinating historical and psychological analysis of this topic see Nuri McBride, "The Odour of Sanctity: When the Dead Smell Divine," The Order of the Good Death, n.d., http://www.orderofthegooddeath.com/odour-sanctity-dead-smell -divine. Accessed March 2, 2020.

31. See https://flowermeanings.org/jasmine-flower-meaning/ and, somewhat idiosyncratically but relevantly, https://www.huffpost.com/entry/the-smell-of-jas-mine-the_b_3021273. Accessed March 2, 2020.

32. Translated into Latin as Sanitas, the name Zdrówko derives from the Polish word for healthy, *zdrowy*. Not accidentally, the Polish for "Hail Mary" is "Zdrowaś Mario."

33. The two contrasting modes of monasticism have a long history, and Russian Orthodoxy exemplifies the dualism in the two founding fathers of Russian monasti-cism—Antony (983–1073) and Theodosius (1035–1074). Whereas Antony favored ascetic isolation in the interests of self-perfection, Theodosius went "among the people" and aided the poor and ailing.

34. *Jasminum*'s citation from Federico Fellini's *Amarcord* (1973) supposedly is justified by its status as Prior Kleofas's favorite film. An award-winning comedy drama that features an adolescent boy as a protagonist, it likewise blends religion and sexuality, but does so to denounce Italy under fascism in the 1930s and the Catholic Church, both guilty of infantilizing the population. See Peter Bondanella, *The Cinema of Federico Fellini* (Princeton: Princeton University Press, 1992) and Bondanella's introduction to the film in the Criterion Collection, November 23, 1999, reproduced at https://www.criterion.com/current/posts/18-amarcord. Accessed April 5, 2006.

35. Rev. Prof. Waldemar Chrostowski, "He Hold His Story in Film," in *Jerzy Kawalerowicz: painter of the tenth muse* (Lodz: Muzeum Kinomatografii, 2012), 68, 70.

36. See Kawalerowicz's last interview in 2006–2007, with Stanisław Zawiśliński, reproduced in *Jerzy Kawalerowicz: malarz X muzy/painter of the tenth muse* (Lodz: Muzeum Kinomatografii, 2012), 230, 259. Also Jan Rek, *Kino Jerzego Kawalerowicza i jego konteksty* (Lodz: Wydawnictwo Uniwersytetu Łódzkiego, 2008), 109, ft. 14.

37. Paul Coates attempts to make sense of this enigmatic sequence in terms of Polish-Jewish relations. See Paul Coates, *The Red and the White: The Cinema of People's Poland* (London and New York: Wallflower Press, 2005), 186–87.

38. See Ludwig Feuerbach, *The Essence of Christianity* (Das Wesen des Christentums, 1841, 1843), translated by George Eliot in 1854.

39. In my judgment, *The Devils* belongs to the prolific subgenre of nunsploitation film, the chief goal of which is to titillate and shock through exposure of sexual antics, masochistic rituals, and other traits of both cheap vampire and horror films within a venerable institution. See Chris Fujiwara, "Convent Erotica," *Hermenaut*, December 22, 2000, https://web.archive.org/web/20110719183028/http://www.hermenaut.com /a48.shtml. Accessed November 18, 2019. See also Rosemary Curb and Nancy Manahan, eds., *Lesbian Nuns: Breaking Silence* (Tallahassee, FL: Naiad Press, 1985), republished in 2013, and especially the Introduction.

40. Jude Dry, "The Devils': Ken Russell's Banned 1971 Religious Horror Film Finally Gets Streaming Release," *Indie Wire*, March 15, 2017, https://www .indiewire.com/2017/03/devils-ken-russell-banned-horror-streaming-shudder-x-rated -1201793838/. Accessed November 18, 2019.

41. See, for instance, Deal Hudson, "Ken Russell's *The Devils* Is Badly Misunderstood," February 7, 2019, https://catholicherald.co.uk/magazine/ken-rus- sells-the-devils-is-badly-misunderstood/. Accessed November 19, 2019.

42. Ernest Callenbach, "*Mother Joan of the Angels* by Jerzy Kawalerowicz," *Film Quarterly* 17, no. 2 (Winter 1963–1964): 29.

43. Just as in *Pociąg* (The Train 1959) the lawyer's wife (Teresa Szmigielówna) is a vulgarized reflection of Marta (Lucyna Winnicka), so here Małgorzata (with her earthly love) mirrors Mother Joanna (and her angelic love) in a reduced and crude mode. Alicja Helman's fine discussion of the film addresses Kawalerowicz's pen- chant for this sort of differentiated, even contrastive doubling. Alicja Helman, "Jerzy Kawalerowicz—wirtuoz kamery," in *Kino polskie w dziesięciu sekwencjach*, ed. Ewelina Nurczyńsk-Fidelska (Lodz: Wydawnictwo Uniwersytetu Łódzkiego, 1996), 49. Under the same title but in slightly revised form the article appears in *Kino polskie w trzynastu sekwencjach*, ed. Ewelina Nurczyńsk-Fidelska (Cracow: Rabid, 2005), 79–91.

44. See, above all, Rek, 95–114. Also Haltof, *Polish Cinema: A History*, 153–56; Boleslaw Michalek and Frank Turaj, *The Modern Cinema of Poland* (Bloomington, IN: Indiana University Press, 1988), 102–4; Bartosz Staszczyszyn, "Speak of the Devil: Diabolical Plots in Polish Film," July 18, 2017, https://culture.pl/en/article/ speak-of-the-devil-diabolical-plots-in-polish-film. Accessed August 1, 2019.

45. Rek's astute commentary on the aesthetics of the film develops this observa- tion (100–101). Paul Coates believes that opposites are interchangeable in the film. See his *Cinema, Religion and the Romantic Legacy*, 106–107.

46. For specifics, see Rek *passim* and especially the incisive analysis by Seweryn Kuśmierczyk, "The Form of an Image: *Mother Joan of the Angels* and *Pharaoh*," in *Jerzy Kawalerowicz, malarz X muzy*, 92–100.

47. Callenbach, "*Mother Joan*," 29; also Rek, *Kino Jerzego Kawalerowicza*, 103–104, 112.

48. Kawalerowicz świadomie szuka rygorów i ograniczeń, by wydobyć maksimum refleksij ze starannie wyselekcjonowanych śródków. Helman, "Jerzy Kawalerowicz—wirtuoz kamery," 47.

49. Udawało się [. . .] tylko Kawalerowiczowi i Polańskiemu, naszym dwóm maniakam kina zawodowego. Andrzej Wajda, *Kino i reszte świata* (Cracow: Wydawnictwo Znak, 2000), 281.

50. On the censorship of the film, see Coates, *The Red and the White*, 100–103.

51. Żuławski explained the film as a political commentary on an incident in Poland during the 1960s, and various critics have taken him at his word, though the chaos depicted in and exampled by the film could reference any period or event devoid of reason, recognizable norms, and civilized conduct. See Jeremiah Kipp, "DVD Review: *The Devil*," *Slant*, October 4, 2007, https://www.slantmagazine.com/dvd/the-devil/ and Russ Fischer, "The Essentials: The 5 Best Andrzej Zulawski Films," *IndieWire*, February 19, 2016, https://www.indiewire.com/2016/02/the-essentials-the-5-best-andrzej-zulawski-films-268216/. Both accessed August 1, 2019.

52. In his survey of Żuławski's films, Michael Goddard puzzlingly identifies the actor playing the titular role as Michał Grudziński, who, in fact, plays Ezekiel/Ezechiel. See Michael Goddard, "Beyond Polish Moral Realism: The Subversive Cinema of Andrzej Żuławski," in *Polish Cinema in a Transnational Context*, eds. Ewa Mazierska and Michael Goddard (Rochester: University of Rochester Press, 2014), 240.

53. See, for instance, the unglamorous, shabby, psychologically projected demons of Stavrogin in *The Devils* (1872) and Ivan Karamazov in *The Brothers Karamazov* (1880).

54. See Ed Howard, "Diabel," *Only the Cinema*, January 19, 2011, http://seul-le-cinema.blogspot.com/2011/01/ diabel.html. Accessed December 1, 2018.

55. Robin Wood, "An Introduction to the American Horror Film," *Movies and Methods*, Vol. 2, ed. Bill Nichols (Berkeley: University of California Press, 1985), 195–220; Noël Carroll, *The Philosophy of Horror* (New York and London: Routledge, 1990); Bruce Kawin, "The Mummy's Pool," *Film Theory and Criticism*, eds. Gerald Mast, Marshall Cohen, Leo Braudy (New York and Oxford: Oxford University Press, 1992), 549–60; "The Horror Film," in *The Cinema Book*, 2nd edition, eds. Pam Cook and Mieke Bernink (London: British Film Institute, 1999), 194–208. The last contains an extensive bibliography on scholarship about the genre of horror (386–87).

56. See "Rozmowa z Barbarą Sass i Katarzyną Zawadzką," with Marta Sikorska, PISF: YouTube, June 8, 2011, https://www.youtube.com/watch?v=kWSjEBjJyLE. Accessed November 14, 2011.

57. The film is loosely based on the extraordinary events in a convent in Kazimierz Dolny (2005–2007), where a priest practiced "unholy" sexual acts on the nuns of the order Rodzina Betańska. See gazeta,pl, March 5, 2007, http://wiadomosci.gazeta.pl/wiadomosci/1,114873,3963488.html. Accessed November 16, 2011.

58. Shane Danielsen, "A Dour Exploration of a Nun's Descent," SBS, October 8, 2012, https://www.sbs.com.au/movies/review/name-devil-review. Accessed February 17, 2018.

59. See, for instance, "W imieniu diabła, czyli bliskie spotkania z nawiedze-niem," *Kurier poranny*, September 16, 2011, https://poranny.pl/w-imieniu-diabla-czyli-bliskie-spotkania-z-nawiedzeniem/ar/5397336. Accessed November 14, 2011.

60. See the thoughtful review by Piotr Śmiałowski in *Kino*, no. 9 (2011): 82–83.

61. See footnote 20.

62. Ironic comment by the anti-Catholic British historian Gibbon in his six-volume *History of the Decline and Fall of the Roman Empire* (1776–1788) about the trial and deposition of John XXIII in 1416.

63. For a compact summary of Smarzowski's screen oeuvre, see https://culture.pl/pl/tworca/wojciech-smarzowski. Accessed April 4, 2019.

64. Mike McCahill, "Counting the Sins of the Catholic Priesthood," *The Guardian*, October 11, 2018, https://www.theguardian.com/film/2018/oct/11/kler-review-wojciech-smarzowski-robert-wieckiewicz. Accessed April 4, 2019.

65. Mordowicz evokes both homicide (mordować = to murder) and animalism or crudeness (morda = muzzle or mug).

66. Though a shot of Rysiek removing his shirt in Kukuła's presence in the sac-risty suggests that Kukuła is the pedophile, especially because the other boys run up to spy on them, Lisowski turns out to be the one guilty of the boy's rape. Similarly, viewers believe, along with Trybus, that he has killed a man, though the police declare that both car and place of 'accident' clear his name. Smarzowski, however, leaves that question open. Additionally, he reveals that Lisowski saved his two col-leagues from the fire—a rescue of which Lisowski reminds Kukuła to dissuade the latter from reporting his pedophilic acts.

67. This disturbing segment apparently consists of real-life accounts.

68. See Jason Horowitz and Elisabetta Povoledo, "The Most Talked About Non-Topic at the Vatican? Homosexuality," *New York Times*, February 23, 2019, https://www.nytimes.com/2019/02/23/world/europe/vatican-summit-gay-priests.html?action=click&module=News pgtype=Homepage. February 23, 2019.

69. Many parallels exist between *Clergy* and Tom McCarthy's award-winning *Spotlight* (2015).

70. Even if the film were shown around the clock, given its length, it could not be shown twenty-four times in twenty-four hours, so the report must be exaggerated, unless it was shown at multiple movie theaters. During its first month of release almost 4.5 million people watched the film, more than the numbers for such nation-alistic adaptations of Polish literature as the megahits *Quo Vadis?* and *Pan Tadeusz.* Additionally, *Clergy* became an international hit, "earning 1.3 million US dollars in its first weekend in UK and Irish cinemas, the best ever opening weekend for a Polish film abroad." Shakhil Shah, "'I make films about things which cause me pain or heart-ache,'" EMERGINGEUROPE, December 1, 2018, https://emerging-europe.com/after-hours/i-make-films-about-things-which-cause-me-pain-or-heartache/. Accessed January 3, 2019.

71. Alex Marshall, "Movie about Church Sexual Abuse Is a Contentious Hit in Poland," *New York Times*, October 8, 2018, https://www.nytimes.com/2018/10/08/arts/poland-clergy-movie.html. Accessed January 3, 2019.

72. Anticipating problems with acquiring permission to shoot the film in Polish churches—it would have taken too long, he told the French TV channel Polandnnel Canal+—Smarzowski filmed most of *Clergy* in churches of the Czech Republic. Marcin Goclowski, "Movie about Corrupt Priests Outrages Politicians in Catholic Poland," Reuters, September 28, 2018, https://www.reuters.com/article/us-poland-religion-movie/movie-about-corrupt-priests-outrages-politicians-in-catholic-poland-idUSKCN1M82FR. Accessed January 3, 2019.

73. Dariusz Kalan, "Poland's Ruling Party Pressures Cinemas to Stop Showing Blockbuster Film about Catholic Church Abuse," *The Telegraph*, October 16, 2018, https://www.telegraph.co.uk/news/2018/10/16/polands-ruling-party-pressures-cinemas-stop-showing-blockbuster/. Accessed January 3, 2019.

74. Paulina Guzik, "Church in Poland Disturbed by Success of Anti-clerical Film," CRUX, October 6, 2018, https://cruxnow.com/church-in-europe/2018/10/06/church-in-poland-disturbed-by-success-of-anti-clerical-film/. Accessed January 3, 2019. Barbara Sass's *Pokuszenie* (Temptation 1995) draws on a key real-life episode during late Stalinism when the state attempted to discredit Wyszyński, venerated for his unshakable opposition to communism, by sending a female secret service agent disguised as a nun to seduce him. As in life, so in the film, temptation is overcome. On the film, see Ewa Mazierska, "Barbara Sass: The Author of Women's Films," in Ewa Mazierska and Elżbieta Ostrowska, *Women in Polish Cinema* (New York/Oxford: Berghahan, 2006), 179–80.

75. Christian Davies, "Polish Film The Clergy Sparks Hundreds of Allegations of Abuse," *The Guardian*, October 17, 2018, https://www.theguardian.com/world/2018/oct/15/polish-film-the-clergy-sparks-hundreds-of-allegations-of-abuse-kler-catholic. Accessed March 20, 2019.

76. Derek Scally, "Polish Clerical Abuse Film Turns Mirror on Audience," *The Irish Times*, October 10, 2018, https://www.irishtimes.com/news/world/europe/polish-clerical-abuse-film-turns-mirror-on-audience-1.3657382. Accessed March 3, 2019.

77. Guzik, "Church in Poland Disturbed."

78. Scally, "Polish Clerical Abuse Film."

79. Justyna Kobus, "'Kler' wzbudzil dyskusję, zanim ktokolwiek go zobaczył. Smarzowski dotknął tabu," Tvn24, September 19, 2018, https://www.tvn24.pl/kultura-styl,8/kler-smarzowskiego-zachwycil-i-oburzyl,869469.html. Accessed February 11, 2019.

80. Shah, "I Make Films" (adjusted for the sake of correct English), January 3, 2019.

81. He was a member of the Society of Christ Fathers for Poles Living Abroad. Reportedly, "The man, who imprisoned and raped the girl for more than 10 months, was arrested in 2008 and sentenced in 2010 to four years in prison, *Gazeta Wyborcza* daily reported." See "Polish Church Turns to Top Court in Pedophile Case," Reuters, October 3, 2018. https://www.reuters.com/article/us-poland-church-paedhophilia/polish-church-turns-to-top-court-in-pedophile-case-idUSKCN1MD1EM. Accessed January 3, 2019.

82. Nicole Winfield, "Pope Francis Issues New Church Law Regarding Clergy Sex Abuse. Victims Say It's Not Enough," *Time*, May 10, 2019, http://time.com/5587051/pope-francis-church-law-clergy-sex-abuse/. Accessed May 18, 2019.

83. "Tell No One," the 'official' translation of the title, is catchier, but not fully accurate.

84. Since May 11, 2019 the documentary has been available at https://www .youtube.com/watch?v=BrUvQ3W3nV4. After a mass reaction to the film, the brothers held a live "response to questions" on Facebook, which they called Sunday Night Live, https://www.facebook.com/Sekielski/videos/bracia-sekielscy-o-filmie -tylko-nie-m%C3%B3w-nikomu/350117622308486/. Both accessed February 24, 2020. By that time almost 6 million Poles had viewed the film, and twice that number of viewers were listed on YouTube. Before a week had passed since its appearance, a record-breaking 14 million people had watched it. The documentary was financed through a crowdfunding campaign, to which approximately 2,500 people contributed, and Tomasz insists that it therefore belongs to all of them and cannot be sold, but may be watched by anyone on YouTube. As of the most recent tabulation (October 27, 2020), the documentary has been viewed almost 25 twenty million times. See Antonia Mortensen, "Polish Priest Blames 'Devil' as He's Confronted by Alleged Victim Whose Life Was Ruined," CNN, May 26, 2019, https://www.cnn.com/2019/05/26/ europe/poland-catholic-church-abuse-intl/index.html. Accessed October 27, 2020.

85. In his essay "The Decay of Lying" (1889) Wilde asserted, "Life imitates Art Far More Than Art Imitates Life."

86. Of course, since Smarzowski consulted clergy and conducted research for his film, his film also reflects life.

87. Vanessa Gera, "Poland Shaken by Documentary about Pedophile Priests," The Associated Press, May 13, 2019, https://www.ctvnews.ca/world/poland-shaken -by-documentary-about-pedophile-priests-1.4419673. Accessed August 11, 2019.

88. "Poland's Leader Slams Church Pathology, Backs Sex Abuse Probe," CRUX, May 18, 2019, https://cruxnow.com/church-in-europe/2019/05/18/poland -leader-slams-church-pathology-backs-sex-abuse-probe/. Accessed May 27, 2019.

89. Antonia Mortensen, "Polish Priest Blames 'Devil' as He's Confronted by Alleged Victim Whose Life Was Ruined," CNN, May 26, 2019, https://www.cnn .com/2019/05/26/europe/poland-catholic-church-abuse-intl/index.html. Accessed May 27, 2019.

90. See https://www.youtube.com/watch?v=T0ym5kPf3Vc. Accessed June 2, 2019.

91. See https://www.youtube.com/watch?v=ojJyO0DMHuY. Accessed June 1, 2019.

92. At the annual film festival in Gdynia, *Ida* received the Golden Lion for best film as well as awards for cinematography (Łukasz Ża), set design (Jarosław Kamiński), and the lead female role—the formidable Agata Kulesza as Ida's complex Aunt Wanda, though many would argue that Agata Trzebuchowska as Ida/Anna qualifies as the film's female lead, she did receive the 'rising star elle award' at Gdynia and two prizes from organizations outside Poland. See Bartosz Staszczyszyn, September 18, 2013, https:// culture.pl/en/work/ida-pawel-pawlikowski. Accessed July 17, 2014.

93. In Poland, the punishment for harboring Jews during the Nazi occupation was execution.

94. A welcome exception is Catherine Wheatley, "Pawel Pawlikowski Condenses European (and cinematic) History into a 'Sad, Small,' Ineffably Potent Road Movie

of the Soul," *Sight and Sound*, November 28, 2014, https://www.bfi.org.uk/news
-opinion/sight-sound-magazine/reviews-recommendations/film-week-ida. Accessed
January 22, 2019.

95. Richard Brody, "The Distasteful Vagueness of *Ida*," *The New Yorker*, May
9, 2014, https://www.newyorker.com/culture/richard-brody/the-distasteful-vagueness
-of-ida. Accessed January 23, 2019.

96. Though the highly experienced Wanda outwardly seems the one in command,
it becomes clear that Ida's rich inner world provides a stable psychological anchor
lacking in her tormented aunt, and nothing dramatizes that contrast better than the
sequence in which the two spend the night in the same room at the hotel.

97. David Denby, "*Ida*: A Film Masterpiece," *The New Yorker*, May 27, 2014,
https://www.newyorker.com/culture/culture-desk/ida-a-film-masterpiece. Accessed
January 23, 2019.

98. "*Ida*," RogerEbert.com, May 2, 2014, https://www.rogerebert.com/reviews/
ida-2014. Accessed January 23, 2019.

99. Tadeusz Sobolewski, *Gazeta Wyborcza*, DVD of *Ida*, opusfilm, 2013. For
more of his comments on the film, see "Oscarowa 'Ida' po raz pierwszy w TV.
Pawlikowski: nadchodzi czas nacjonalizmu [ROZMOWA]," wyborcza.pl, November
19, 2015, http://wyborcza.pl/1,75410,19210750,oscarowa-ida-po-raz-pierwszy-w-tv
-pawlikowski-nadchodzi.html. Accessed January 23, 2019.

100. David Sims, "*Ida*'s Bittersweet Success: An Interview With [*sic*] Pawel
Pawlikowski," *The Atlantic*, February 12, 2015, https://www.theatlantic.com/enter-
tainment/archive/2015/02/pawel-pawlikowski-on-the-personal-and-the-historical-in
-ida/385568/. Accessed January 23, 2019.

101. See Karolina Wigura, "Dlaczego 'Ida' tak gniewa. Częściowe podsumowanie
dyskusji o filmie Pawła Pawlikowskiego," *Kultura liberalna*, no. 255 (48/2013),
November 26, 2013, https://kulturaliberalna.pl/2013 /11/26/wigura-dlaczego-ida-
tak-gniewa-czesciowe-podsumowanie-dyskusji-o-filmie-pawla-pawlikowskiego/.
Accessed January 23, 2019.

102. Tim Adams, "Paweł Pawlikowski: 'My Parents' Story Was the Matrix of All
My Stories," *The Guardian*, February 11, 2019, https://www.theguardian.com/film
/2019/feb/09/pawel-pawlikowski-poland-cold-war-ida. Accessed March 5, 2019.

103. Wheatley, "Pawel Pawlikowski Condenses."

104. That immemorial triadic concept typically is imaged as the Tree of Life,
which in one form or another is universal.

105. To appreciate just how extensively Polish directors collaborated with colleagues abroad even during the era of superimposed socialism, see Andrej Wajda's
fascinating memoirs, *Kino i reszta świata* (Cracow: Wydawnictwo Znak, 2000).

Chapter 2

Wandering Poles

Lost or Left in Migration

POLISH MIGRATION AND EMIGRATION IN THE LATE TWENTIETH AND EARLY TWENTY-FIRST CENTURIES

Since 2015, the world has grown accustomed to identifying Poland as one of the Central/East European countries determined to discourage, if not ban outright, the influx of immigrants of color, even if these refugees pass muster as Christians rather than Muslims. Such has been the rhetoric of Poland's Euro-skeptic, far-right nationalist ruling party, Law and Justice, reelected in 2020—which serves as the gatekeeper of the country's ethnic and Catholic homogeneity and successfully courts voters in small towns and the countryside with this platform. As Agnieszka Szpak, a scholar in political science and international studies, points out, "the Law and Justice Government is not against all migrations but attempts to attract only what it views as 'desirable migrants.' And the factors taken into account are not necessarily the skills of the migrants but their race or religion."[1]

Regardless of which party is in power, however, the political, social, and cultural context for recent Polish films on immigration and migration continues to reflect the experiences of *Polish immigrants* abroad.[2] This orientation is grounded in several layers of historical trauma. Many decades after the end of World War II, both Polish Catholics and the descendants of Polish Jewish survivors continue to live in its deep shadows—specifically, the joint German and Soviet invasion in 1939; Soviet mass murders of Poland's civic leaders and army officers and the deportation of roughly one million Polish citizens to the Far North, Siberia, and Central Asia from 1939 to 1941; the Nazi annihilation of almost all European Jewry on Polish territory; and the Nazis' persecution of Polish Catholics as subhumans and a source of slave labor in the Third Reich. After the war, the Western Allies' ceding of its

53

Central European partners (Poland and Yugoslavia) to the Stalinist sphere of influence doomed these countries to further political repression, isolation from the West, and regularly faltering command economies. Polish citizens seeking work in the West after the fall of the Berlin wall in 1989 were acutely aware of their second-class status as *Gastarbeiter.*

Following Poland's 2004 acceptance into the European Union, by 2013 the number of Polish immigrants and migrants to Western Europe had ballooned to 2.3 million.[3] These migrants, mostly young, well-educated Poles, sought better employment opportunities and higher wages than they could find at home, and they gravitated particularly to the UK, Ireland, Germany, France, Sweden, and the Netherlands. Like migrant workers the world over, these Poles chose the hard road of adapting to a foreign culture, becoming proficient in a second language, and usually accepting work for which they were overqualified in order to advance their family's prospects, whether that family relocated with them or, more often, had to be left behind in Poland. In short, from 1939 to the present, citizens of Poland have been conditioned not to see themselves as a host country for the less fortunate but to perceive *themselves* as put-upon immigrants and migrant laborers. Though the EU ostensibly offers Poles the choice rather than the necessity to relocate, Poles feel keenly their reception and demotion as "backward" Eastern Europeans employed by their Western European betters. The Poles function as those white-skinned laborers who, in historian David Roediger's analysis, still have to "work toward white-ness" through their "civilized" behavior and industry, whether they live in Western Europe or the United States.[4]

This highly condensed historical background is offered to help viewers better understand the four films selected here for analysis: Dariusz Gajewski's 2015 *Strange Heaven (Obce niebo)*; Urszula Antoniak's 2017 *Beyond Words (Pomiędzy słowami)*; Anna Jadowska's 2017 *Wild Roses (Dzikie róże)*; and Piotr Domalewski's 2017 *Silent Night (Cicha noc)*. In contrast to the approach that Kris van Heuckelom pursues in his major monograph on Polish migrants' representation in primarily Western cinema, this chapter focuses exclusively on Polish films that explore the experience of Polish migrants and their families from their diverse points of view.[5] Only *Beyond Words*, a Polish-Dutch collaboration, might be construed, according to Yosefa Loshitzky's definition, as a "film of minority discourse . . . created by a member of the minority community itself in Fortress Europe."[6] All four, helmed by Polish-born and educated directors, appeared at least a decade after Poland's EU entry, and consequently highlight either the experience of Poles working in northern and western EU nations or the fraught existence of Polish families in Poland attempting to cohere and thrive despite the absence of their (usually male) breadwinner.

The first pair of films, *Strange Heaven* and *Beyond Words*, were shot in seemingly desirable destinations outside of Poland—*Strange Heaven* in a small community on Sweden's Baltic coast and *Beyond Words* in Germany's capital city of Berlin. *Wild Roses* and *Silent Night* play out in different parts of the Polish countryside, economically depressed places where the families depend on the money sent them by male heads of households working abroad. *Wild Roses* is located near the town of Oleśnica in southwestern Poland (lower Silesia). *Silent Night* is set in the picturesque, cheap farmland surrounding the northeastern Polish city of Olsztyn. Here, as the film quickly discloses, Poland itself is up for sale to rich EU buyers.

POLES ABROAD: *STRANGE HEAVEN* (2015)

The decision to emigrate is rooted
in not accepting some part of yourself.

—Dariusz Gajewski

When Gajewski's *Strange Heaven* premiered in the autumn of 2015, Polish reviewers noted the various ways it seemed formulaic in terms of genre or message. Grzegorz Fortuna read the film as "an ordinary thriller" that riffs on the theme of emigration as a near-tragic mistake.[7] Others categorized *Strange Heaven* as a real-life horror film, a black-and-white drama that they championed for its critique of authoritarian Swedish policies on child welfare. Łukasz Adamski claimed that the film was "transfixing in its authentic rendering" of a Huxley-esque anti-utopian nightmare.[8] Kacper Szulecki prefaced his film review in *Kultura Liberalna* with a report on how child protection services in Sweden (BRIS), Norway (Barnevern), and Germany (Jugendant) have been transformed into "inhuman machines of terror," farming out a disproportionately large number of allegedly "abused" immigrant children to foster families who are ethnically Swedish, Norwegian, and German.[9] In this Polish film, it would seem, the ghosts of Aryanization are not so easily exorcised. The English translation of its title as *Alien Heaven* would better convey the clash between bureaucratic and immigrant sensibilities.

Gajewski's film does not go so far as to accuse the Swedes of nationalizing Polish immigrant children. After all, *Strange Heaven* is a Polish-Swedish coproduction featuring Swedish as well as Polish actors. But Gajewski does claim that the film's pivotal drama about a Polish child's involuntary placement with Swedish foster parents is based on stories he had heard from Swedish Polonia. He typecasts the Swedish protagonist, a school social worker named Anita, as a humorless villain. Played in monotone by Ewa

Fröling (known best for her role as the mother in Ingmar Bergman's 1982 film *Fanny and Alexander*), Anita is a stickler for bureaucratic rules and militaristic uniforms. In a October 21, 2015, interview for *Magazyn Viva!*, Gajewski packages his pro-Poland message in more general terms: "People emigrate to Sweden because they want to live in a more orderly and affluent country. And Sweden is certainly that. But instead of emigrating, maybe it is more important to put things in order where you already live? In *Strange Heaven* I wanted to show that emigration is not a way out, that the decision to emigrate is rooted in not accepting some part of oneself. In the most profound sense, emigration is always a rejection of who you are."[10] Gajewski reinforces this view by linking it with his private life; we learn from the interview that the director's wife, actress Agnieszka Grochowska, gave birth to their son during Gajewski's work on this film and appears in *Strange Heaven* as its leading lady. Gajewski strongly implies that his happy new status as a family man and his belief in Grochowska's fundamental honesty, shining through every role she plays, shaped the film's final moral.

In fact, *Strange Heaven* screens a story that, regardless of Gajewski's explicit or implicit intention and Grochowska's undisguisable "honesty," is much more complicated than an exposé of Sweden's "nanny state" or the touching tale of one Polish family's journey from self-alienation to honest self-acceptance. As the opening scene demonstrates, the family of three who "chose" Sweden is fractured and unhappy. The camera tracks their car as they drive through a seemingly endless forest until they reach a dock at the water's edge. There the rakish father Marek (Bartłomiej Topa) surprises his wife and daughter with his purchase of a modest motorboat in lieu of a house. The nine-year-old Ula (Barbara Kubiak) is thrilled: the boat bears her name and Marek immediately begins teaching her how to operate it. The wife Basia, whom Grochowska plays as a moody woman who shifts abruptly between anxiety and anger, is visibly irritated by Marek's choice. Basia automatically lights a cigarette as she watches the little boat's progress into the harbor, a Swedish flag snaps in the wind, and the title *Strange Heaven* appears on the screen like a storm warning.

The scenes immediately following juxtapose the family members' individual experiences of entrapment. First Ula appears in her classroom, speaking Swedish easily but otherwise unwilling to accept what she perceives as the injustices dealt her. She argues with the teacher who wants to change her name to "Ursula" for convenience's sake (two other "Ula's" are already on the class roll), and she lashes out at a classmate who makes fun of her. After Ula impulsively sweeps the offender's things off his desk, she exits the room. The cut to Basia frames her in the family's small apartment, where she draws on a cigarette and listens to an African man in an apartment building opposite shout from the balcony that he has the right to be master in his home. Her reverie is interrupted by the arrival of a client. Basia works part-time as a masseuse and the camera shoots her joyless face in close-up as she begins the session. She is not mistress in her home but at the beck and call of apparently male customers. In contrast to Ula and Basia, Marek appears outside, gainfully employed as a school soccer coach and seemingly in charge. Yet, while he is drilling his team on the field, a Polish-speaking woman (Magdalena Boczarska) accosts him, angry that he wants to end their affair. This quick canvass of the family by day shows Ula and Basia's profound alienation and loneliness in their new life and intimates that Marek's desire for gratification and validation tempts him away from the family itself, at best a fragile oasis.

Strange Heaven never lays out the reasons why Marek and Basia chose to emigrate. Their lone tie with Poland consists of a Skype call with Basia's mother during which the couple, temporarily reconciled after Marek's betrayal, brush off the older woman's questions and stern advice like snarky teenagers. Earlier in the film, Basia attributed Ula's "anti-social behavior" in school to the girl's missing her grandmother. During the Skype call, however, Ula ignores her grandparent, eager to imitate her immature parents as they laugh and deflect advice. Yet recurring shots of the girl sitting alone on a creaky swing outside the family apartment warn of a child mostly in limbo, longing for play with her unreliable father or peace away from her mother's turbulent company. Though the camera involves us most sympathetically with the Poles, it does not screen their flaws in soft focus—especially vis-à-vis Ula. As Tadeusz Sobolewski observes, *Strange Heaven* not only confronts Polish viewers fearful of alien immigrants with the problematic behavior of Polish immigrants abroad but also indicates that Ula may need someone like the grim Anita, who promises her safety, stability, and comfort.[11]

The film sets in motion the battle over Ula's custody almost from the beginning, though Basia, Marek, and Ula—cut off from other immigrants—have no way of knowing what to fear. Ula's angry flight from the classroom lands her in Anita's office, where the social worker gives her an orange (Swedish plenty) and then plies her with questions about her parents' arguing and her father's behavior (Swedish intervention). The ten-year-old Barbara Kubiak's incarnation of a nine-year-old Ula is extraordinary: she deftly conveys the wariness and deceptive gratitude of a child accustomed to dangerously unpredictable adults.[12] The viewer, like Anita, Ula's parents, and, eventually, her foster parents, must constantly scan Ula's face for clues—is she afraid, content, sad, dissembling? Ula keeps mum in Anita's office but accepts the social worker's card printed with the hotline for BRIS, a phone number that Anita assures her she can call if she is ever afraid, without anyone knowing who she is. Ula's trap is cleverly baited.

From this point on, Anita swoops down on the Polish family's home, openly treating the parents as suspects. She seems a bit of a cardboard villain, her presumption outrageous and her English almost comically stilted, especially in comparison with Basia's much more idiomatic command of the language. For Western European and North American viewers, however, Anita's judgments are altogether familiar and perhaps not so unreasonable. The Poles should have paid the rent on time. Basia should not be smoking. Ula's problems with concentration and aggression should be worked out through therapy. Basia alternately apologizes and resists under interrogation, while Ula remains outside, alone on the swing or practicing soccer moves by herself. Later that night, when Ula is awakened and then frightened by the noise and glimpse of her parents having sex, she calls BRIS from the bathroom and accidentally falls into the tub, bruising her back. The police arrive that night in response to her call, Anita returns the next day and surreptitiously photographs Ula's injury, and the Swedish system prepares to move Ula into a foster home.

The film then shifts into the generic plot of a thriller, pitting loving parents against a punitive bureaucracy, though all the characters, with the exception of Anita, retain some complexity. Basia's response to her daughter's kidnapping evolves from aggression and despair into more disciplined conspiratorial action. Marek similarly sobers up from drunken brawling—he tries to beat up Ula's Swedish foster father in an attempt to see Ula—and cobbles together a rescue plan with his wife, their lone friend (a Ukrainian), and an august Polish lawyer (a cameo by Jan Englert, whose star presence momentarily overwhelms the screen with Polish patriotic luster). The Swedish foster parents, Björn and Harriet, are carefully nuanced within a narrow emotional register. A well-heeled older couple still grieving for the biological child they lost, they prove eager to please Ula, naturally placid, and therefore shocked by Basia's high emotions—especially the tantrum she feigns as cover for Marek so he can instruct Ula quietly about their escape plans. Björn and Harriet do hide the fact that Ula nearly killed herself in their care. Ultimately, however, the Swedish couple agree to help Basia, Marek, and Ula flee their country. As Harriet later explains to a furious Anita: "We wanted to help a child, not steal one from her parents."

The one possible hitch in the Polish couple's rescue effort, however, is Ula's exposure to life with Björn and Harriet. The girl is initially biddable: Anita lies to her about the terms of her stay, explaining that Ula will remain with Björn and Harriet until her parents work things out. For the first time in the film, Ula's face glows with interest as she wakes up in a lovely room, spies a playhouse in the backyard, hums as she trips downstairs, and breakfasts on hot chocolate. She is positively transported when her foster parents show her their lovely wooden motorboat, a fairy-tale improvement on Marek's rubber dinghy, and present her with Lupo, the family dog, a beautiful Husky who immediately becomes her sidekick and pupil. *Strange Heaven* risks a glorious Swedish temptation for a Polish immigrant girl longing for calm and companionship.[13]

Yet once Ula discovers that she must remain in paradise forever without her mother and father, her reaction echoes that of her parents—extreme willful action curbed into deceptive obedience. Ula first attempts to run away from Swedish paradise by fancy motorboat. When the frantic Björn and Harriet catch up with her before she reaches the open sea, Ula simply jumps into the water and must be saved by Björn. In the aftermath, she mimics acquiescence and even affection, strategically calling Harriet "mama." Though the film never depicts Ula's regret over her lost paradise, Gajewski intersperses a heart-tugging scene of Lupo racing through the woods after his fleeing playmate. At least one Swedish character is filmed to evoke the viewer's unambivalent sympathy and respect.

Strange Heaven concludes much as it begins, with the camera tracking Marek, Basia, and Ula in their getaway car, though their direction is reversed and their drive ends on the side of the road, where Marek pulls off to sleep after a near head-on collision with a truck. A radio broadcast in Polish conveys to the viewer that they are "home" and Ula now legally belongs with her parents; the Swedes' bureaucratic reach cannot cross the border. Nevertheless, the three exit the car separately, a series of shots that emphasizes their voluntary reconciliation. Ula, feeling ashamed, confesses to her mother that she was the one who called BRIS; Basia embraces Ula and rocks her in her arms, and at last extends her hand to Marek when he finally catches up with mother and child. (figure 2.1) As the camera pulls up and away, the three cavort in an open field and finally lie down together, pointing upward to a presumably "familiar" heaven. In this final shot, the Polish family may be acting out Gajewski's message—that repatriation has restored them to their true selves. Yet, given that viewers still do not know why Basia, Marek, and Ula emigrated in the first place (i.e., their presumably unhappy predicament at home) and cannot guess how long the "conversion" of these three volatile people will last, this final shot reads as a momentary truce.

POLES ABROAD: *BEYOND WORDS* (2017)

> You are a totally different person when you are speaking Polish. Like a little boy.
>
> —Franz in *Beyond Words*

Beyond Words films the story of a single Polish emigrant who strives to pass as a successful young German. The ambitious Michał (Jakub Gierszał) never wants to seem out of place in Berlin, the homeland of his choice.

Urszula Antoniak, the film's director and author of its screenplay, had her cinematographer Lennert Hillege shoot *Beyond Words* in a rich black and white, thereby intimating that this film is partly a stylish homage to Berlin, the entity that reviewer Krzysztof Połaski identifies as a "third protagonist" in the film. Połaski likewise describes Gierszał's character as "elegant, a walking cover photo from [the journal] *GQ*."[14] What he does not remark is how Gierszał's Michał, with his shock of blond hair and tall, slender frame, instinctively grooms and carries himself as a fashion model when he strolls down famous city streets or stands against the backdrop of a Berlin landmark. The Polish protagonist uses his modern "Aryan beauty" and carefully chosen costumes to fit into the most stylish sections of the city.[15] The Berlin he frequents professionally and socially mainly features white Europeans, high-rise office buildings, and high-end stores and restaurants. It is not the hybridized, unglamorous, deconstructed cityscape depicted in other contemporary European migrant and diasporic films.[16]

It is interesting that Antoniak, a successful crossover artist born and raised in Poland, yet professionally based in the Netherlands (her adopted home), concentrates in *Beyond Words* on the dilemma of a high-functioning Polish immigrant. Her decision to cast Gierszał in this role likely stemmed from his rare combination of bilingualism and stereotypically German good looks. Gierszał himself has pursued a binational acting career, incarnating both Polish and German characters in films and on television. Unlike Antoniak's created protagonist, however, Gierszał, the performer, easily projects a fluid identity, perhaps because he absorbed the German language and behavior during his childhood in Hamburg, where his Polish family lived when his father worked there as a theater director.[17] In contrast to Gajewski, who depends on his leading actress to deliver a "truth" that her complex performance actually renders ambiguous, Antoniak relies on the completely bicultural Gierszał to act out rather than articulate the tensions between his inherited and acquired identities—a strategy that ultimately fails.

As stunning as Michał's performance of an iconic Germanness looks and sounds, the film initially offers us glimpses into the anxiety he feels and the exercises he undertakes to ensure this impression. The film's first shot trains on as-yet-unidentified Michał standing before a pockmarked wall, perhaps of prewar construction, and accentuates his meticulously styled hair, immaculate white shirt, and dark suit and tie. Yet this young man's face is vigilant, pensive, his mouth twitching with possible anxiety, as if he is preparing in the wings before he steps out on the stage of the city. A subsequent early sequence in the film admits us into Michał's tidy, sparsely decorated apartment, where he stands stripped naked, using the space as the workshop where he refines his Germanness. We listen as Michał painstakingly (and unerringly) repeats the German legal terms being pronounced on a recording and we watch as he irons one of the many identical white dress shirts that he hangs on a clothes rack beside him.[18]

Michał's behavioral role model—and the only German with whom he seems to be on close terms—is his contemporary and, more importantly, his boss, a lawyer named Franz (Christian Löber). Antoniak's screenplay conditions us to infer a great deal in *Beyond Words*, given its reserved protagonist, often deflective dialogue, and minimal exposition of its characters' histories. The ambiguity of Michał's relationship with Franz, his professional superior, initial idol, and friend, is demonstrated in the pranks that Franz orchestrates on the job and after hours. For example, Franz summons Michał as his "clerk" in order to spy on participants during a negotiation, after which they exit and laugh at their dupes in the hallway. In another instance, the two young lawyers share lines of coke and taunt older men with foul language and simulated farts in the executive men's restroom. Franz, a brunette German who cannot compete with Michał's good looks, is coaching his disciple to be snidely condescending to his opponents and inferiors, to behave as a slick lawyer with his eye on promotion, the right sort of good life, and the cultivation of "German" manliness. Michał seems eager to be part of this elitist fraternity of two, though his forced banter and laughter suggest his still subordinate position.

Two plotlines disrupt the progress of Michał's successful, if superficial and unexplained, assimilation. The first, introduced early in *Beyond Words*, involves Michał's potential legal defense of an African poet seeking to resettle in Germany. During Michał's preliminary interview of the poet, conducted face to face across a desk with a disembodied interpreter speaking through the telephone, the disdainful young white man and the haughty middle-aged black man are pitted against each other on visually equal terms, mid-shot for mid-shot, close-up for close-up. Michał insists that the poet state a compelling reason for resettlement: "war, repression? Torture, maybe?" The poet refuses to comply and deliberately goads Michał with his condescension: "I'm not like you. But you are like me." He implies that the white man who would be his lawyer is also an immigrant, but neither as talented nor as powerful as he. Michał, furious at this ungrateful black man who presumes to be superior, later tells Franz that he will not take the case, confident that his "friend" will not force him to do otherwise.

This plotline surfaces again much later, forcing the film into a misguided, literally white-against-black conclusion. The second disruptive plotline proves more intriguing, in large part because it plugs in the star power of the talented Polish actor Andrzej Chyra. In keeping with Antoniak's practice of minimal disclosure, we suddenly discover that Michał is expecting a visit from his father, with whom he had had little contact after his parents' divorce and whom he long had presumed dead. Chyra usually stars in Polish films as the charismatic, attractive lead; in *Beyond Words*, he is deliberately cast to dazzle less than the tall blond Gierszał, but to command equal attention through his self-confident, often provocative observations. As Stanisław, Michał's father, Chyra is scruffily dressed, balding, thickening, and significantly shorter than his on-screen offspring.[19]

The two are juxtaposed before their agreed-upon meeting in Michał's apartment. Ever the methodical student, Michał scouts out the man who says he is his father in advance. The camera tracks the suit-clad Michał as he ventures into one of the gathering spots for Berlin's Polish immigrant community, where the storefronts are less posh and the crowds more raucous. The sound of someone shouting "fuck off" to a pair of young women alerts Michał to a man who looks like his parent. He follows him into a packed bar, where Stanisław regales drinkers with the same anecdote he just had told outside, a tale in which two Polish immigrants are confronted by a German policeman asking about their work permits. One of the two, Józek, who has a permit, vouches for his friend Franek, who does not, and when the policeman calls Franek over for confirmation, Józek warns him away, shouting "Spierdalaj się!" (Get the fuck out of here!) Michał smiles at the predictable joke and is about to cut in and introduce himself, when his father moves off to another audience, oblivious to his presence.

Stanisław's unprepossessing appearance, tired anecdote, and easy circulation in Berlin's Polonia (a space that Michał has either moved "beyond" or always avoided) initially tag him as just another Polish immigrant reduced to working-class status, at ease with his similarly undistinguished compatriots. Michał's first glimpse of his father could decide him to cancel their reunion chiefly on the grounds of preserving his own carefully cultivated image. But he is too angry and needy, or so we must infer. The next day Michał faces off with Stanisław across the threshold of his apartment, slipping easily into unaccented Polish. His jockeying for power in this scene erupts from his father's neglect, not shame over their relationship. "You look good for someone who is dead," he quips to his father. Stanisław, clearly taken aback at the sight of his tall, handsome son, allows the insult to pass: "You look super." Michał asserts himself once more: "Because I am super." Then courtesy and curiosity kick in, and Michał invites his father inside.

Thereafter, the balance of power between "super" son and life-worn father keeps shifting in terms of what is said and what remains "beyond words." Chyra does not let his character lapse into a caricature of the embarrassing Polish country cousin in Western Europe.[20] Stanisław is well aware of his failures, but he brandishes his tastes and judgments without hesitation. After their awkward introduction, he swiftly takes charge, interrogating Michał about his choice of profession (he is disappointed that his son has become a lawyer instead of the musician he himself wanted to be) and criticizing him for the absence of any memorabilia from Poland in his apartment, which he likens to a mausoleum. Under this assault, Michał is surprised into becoming more vulnerable, child-like, and interested. He reveals to his father what a loyal son he has been to his "mama," visiting her grave in Poland every All Saint's Day and refusing to show his faithless father her pictures. While Stanisław showers, Michał rummages through his clothes, smells them as a bereft child would, and finds a photo of himself as a little boy. By the time father and son leave the apartment for a luncheon with Franz, Michał has forestalled feeling embarrassed by his father's casual dress by loaning him one of his snowy white ironed shirts.

At the meal that Michał likely planned so as to rely on Franz's support, the young Pole instead becomes more attracted to his long-lost parent. Expecting his father to be awed by Franz, he is surprised when Stanisław frankly states (in Polish) that he does not like his friend and chooses to walk down the stairs instead of sharing an elevator with them down to the street. Stanisław brings the Polish language and a Polish worldview into the film, and Michał must play at once translator and diplomat between increasingly antagonistic parties. His father's worldview predictably includes an anti-German bias rooted in Polish suffering during World War II. As Franz grills Stanisław about his work and drops a remark about Polish refugees in Germany after the war, Stanisław asks whom Franz has to defend as a lawyer "to get so stinking rich" and warns the German not to dig too deeply into a wartime past "in which there are very different stories." Michał translates deftly—one might say ambi-culturally—not conveying the animus of their actual words. But his interest in his iconoclastic, sardonic father clearly grows. The young man becomes more expressive and animated as he speaks with Stanisław in Polish. The rapport between father and son is not lost on Franz, and he is offended when Stanisław breaks their language barrier with this hostile question to his son: "How can you say Übermensch without him understanding?" Sensing that he is losing his disciple, Franz haughtily dismisses Michał's Polishness as infantilizing: "You are a totally different person when you speak Polish. Like a little boy."

Michał's fascination with Stanisław and any likeness between them builds through much of the film, on poignant display as he studies his father's enjoyment of a classical guitar concert or struggles to discern any similarity between his face and his parent's as he watches Stanisław sleep. Even when Stanisław deflects questions about his absence in his son's life or his failure to answer letters, Michał does not retreat. Instead, the young man starts to reconceive himself in his father's supposed image. After Stanisław laments the fact that Michał chose to study German instead of French ("we could be in Paris now!"), he digs deeper, asking his son whether the Germans accept him. Michał replies, somewhat defensively, that they cannot ignore him, and then wonders out loud if he inherited his quest to become German from his father:

"I've always wanted to swap new adventures for old friends. That's probably from you." When Stanisław at last gives Michał the parental seal of approval that he craves, admitting that his son "had the balls" to achieve his life goal and he is proud of him, Michał's face, featured in a front close-up, beams with satisfaction. It evidently does not disturb him that this approval is bestowed in a noisy bar featuring topless exotic dancers where Michał must pay the tip his father wants to offer a particularly talented "mademoiselle" (figure 2.2). Nor does Michał ponder the sharp distinction between his father's antagonism toward the Germans and his own uncritical embrace of them. He seems to assume that Stanisław can blot out "those very different stories" about the war and champion his son's twenty-first-century Aryanization.

At the point of seeming triumph, however, Michał blunders, Stanisław admits an ignoble reason for their sudden reunion, and Antoniak forces her protagonist into a clumsy melodrama. After father and son leave the bar, Michał teases Stanisław by repeating the "fuck off" punch line of his anecdote, and Stanisław, taken unawares and apparently offended, disappears for several days. When Stanisław finally returns to his son's apartment, he tells Michał the story of how his own father ultimately embarrassed and alienated him, implying that he and Michał have reached the same impasse. This story, functioning as assumption or pretext, leads to Stanisław's abrupt announcement that he must leave and needs a large sum of cash to be on his way. It seems that Michał's good relations with his thin-skinned, restless, improvident father rely entirely on his abiding boyish awe and financial support. Antoniak, alas, leaves her protagonist to process this painful revelation in silence once Stanisław leaves. In this scene, as in the scenes in which Michał misconstrues his father's acceptance, too much is left "beyond words" for the protagonist's satisfactory character development.[21]

After Stanisław abandons him a second time, Michał quickly tries to restore his friendship with his former mentor Franz, calling him to volunteer as the African poet's defense attorney because, as he hastily explains, he appreciates the savvy optics of using one immigrant to save another. Michał also rewrites Stanisław's disturbing visit into a palatable vignette for Franz's consumption—the tale of the experienced German host squiring his out-of-town father to the usual tourist sites. Despite Michał's efforts to please him, Franz is no longer willing to be his friend on the same terms. Franz informs Michał that he not only will serve as the poet's defense attorney, since the African's wealthy backers demand experienced representation, but he also has got tired of playing along with Michał's presumption of their shared Germanness: "You can try every day to take my place, but you can't."[22]

In *Strange Heaven*, Basia briefly registers that her immigrant family shares the same socioeconomic status as that of their African neighbors, but she targets Swedish bureaucrats as the enemy. In *Beyond Words*, an affluent young

Pole, betrayed by an opinionated, parasitic Polish father and a competitive, mean-spirited German friend, reacts, oddly enough, by scapegoating Berlin's African immigrants for what is presumably his identity crisis. Perhaps Michał's self-perceived failure as a "white" German or an "almost white" Pole compels him to test his racial "superiority" among black immigrants, who in his mind include the well-supported poet entitled to Franz's services and the talented street drummers whom his musical father so admires.[23] After Franz cuts short their conversation, Michał follows a random African man from the city train into an underground enclave of African-patronized clubs, bars, and arcades. Feeling trapped and conspicuous as he conducts reconnaissance on these "inferior" immigrants, Michał ultimately picks a fight with two men and gets a thorough beating.[24] His story concludes in transit as he rides home, bloodied *and* bowed, in a taxi. When he murmurs out loud how much he loves Berlin as the city slips past the car windows, the driver asks him if he is a native. Michał's subsequent admission that he is from Poland elicits the kind of compliment he would have relished a few days before: "I wouldn't have thought that." By the end of the film, Michał is aware that he must remain a man between—irrevocably estranged from Poland and incapable of being the German he thought he had nearly become. Nevertheless, the very flawed role models from whom Michał failed to receive approval and acceptance reduce his in-between state to the grotesque rather than the tragic. In Michał's case, the dilemma of the high-functioning immigrant was his pursuit of a twisted, blinkered elitism.

POLES LEFT AT HOME: *WILD ROSES* (2017)

When you were gone, things were
different here. We were happy.

—Marysia in *Wild Roses*

Two recent films that examine the Polish families "left behind" anchor their plots in what seem to be conventional gender roles. In both, the long-absent migrant worker is the male head of household (with his oldest son in one case following in his footsteps). Care for the family and home falls on the shoulders of the mother and, depending on their ages, the daughters and sons. In writing and directing *Wild Roses*, filmmaker Anna Jadowska highlights the most stressful of family separations—when the migrating husband leaves behind a young wife with small children in her care and little support. Several of the film's reviewers (all of them male) contend that this choice of protagonist and scenario naturally transforms *Wild Roses* into "a woman's picture";

after all, they point out, this film, unlike the vast corpus of Polish cinema, was created almost exclusively by women. Apart from Jadowska filling double roles, Małgorzata Szyłak served as its cinematographer, Anna Mass edited the film, Anna Anosowicz and Marta Ostrowicz were, respectively, production and costume designers, and the score was composed by Agnieszka Stulgińska.[25] Łukasz Maciejewski, observing how the film seems to evoke events from burgeoning emotions in lieu of quickly paced and scripted plotting, concludes that Jadowska "has created one of the bravest and most interesting films in recent years" through "the unique duet played out between the director Jadowska and her leading actress, Marta Nieradkiewicz."[26]

Rather than invoke essentializing generalizations about women's experience and "womanhood," the emotion-steeped rollout of *Wild Roses* can best be deciphered through close viewing and basic knowledge of a woman's physical ordeal during and immediately after childbirth. The film does not spell out the fact that Ewa, the protagonist, has just had a baby until it concludes. She—and we—need to return to this fact after the ordeals that transform her. But the opening scene, which takes place in a maternity ward, provides the viewer with a generous hint. A quiet, deathly pale Ewa (played flawlessly by Nieradkiewicz) sits on a bench in a hall next to a weeping woman who is momentarily out of the frame. Both are waiting for the doctor to discharge them. A very pregnant woman paces in the background. When an unseen infant begins wailing in a room down the hall, Ewa instantly turns her head in its direction. The next shot shows her rushing toward a waiting tram, carrying only a cumbersome overnight bag. Ewa has either lost a baby by miscarriage or abortion or, more likely, given her attention to the infant's cry, has left a baby in the ward's care. Whatever has happened to her cannot be brought back to the situation in which she lives. Indeed, Ewa duplicates this act of abandonment when she inadvertently leaves her overnight bag on the tram. A helpful young man restores it to her as she is walking away.

Jadowska's opening is ingenious: even if the viewers have not deduced what may have happened, they are conditioned to empathize with the exhausted, distracted Ewa as she repeatedly demonstrates her inability to cope. We can clock how long the journey home is for the weary Ewa, both physically and psychologically. When she catches the tram after leaving the maternity ward, night is falling. When Ewa gets out of a car in the far distance and proceeds to walk slowly down a gravel path between vast flat fields, covering the last part of her journey on foot, the sun is bearing down and bees are buzzing among the tall weeds. Ewa leads an at once isolated and claustrophobic life in a Polish village—alone in an unfinished house with two small children, yet surrounded by relatives and neighbors who know or are avid to find out everybody's business. The village's single communal center is the parish church, where appearances before everyone in the village must be maintained and real-life problems taken outside.

Making a film about a Polish village is a tricky business in Poland, since most filmmakers, reviewers, and viewers hail from big cities and easily can be faulted for romanticizing or, more often, disparaging provincial life. Yet, as Maciej Kowalczyk points out at the beginning of his review, the village portrayed in *Wild Roses* is where (or near to where) director Anna Jadowska grew up, in Mała Ligota, near the town of Oleśnica. This background, Kowalczyk states, ensures that Jadowska, "unlike many filmmakers before her, does not have to study up on village life or look down on its residents from on high."[27]

Jadowska's film also implies that her heroine grew up in the same place where she now raises her family. Ewa's first stop off the gravel path is at her mother's apartment, where her no-nonsense, sharp-tongued parent (veteran actress Halina Rasiakówna) is caring for her grandchildren—the seven-year-old Marysia and toddler Jasiek—and complaining that they are spoiled. After Ewa reinstalls her brood at home, the camera tracks how every normal chore or minor irritation overwhelms her. Her daily walk with her children, which involves pushing Jasiek's stroller over rough gravel to a grim makeshift playground, so exhausts her that she collapses midway to rest. When the over-dramatic Marysia (Natalia Bartnik), aggrieved at being left so long with her grandmother, declares that she has "shitty parents" and wishes that Ewa had died in the hospital, her mother can only muster a mild reproach. The most eloquent image of Ewa's helplessness unfolds in a long shot with diegetic sound and no dialogue: when she tries to air out a blanket on the second-story balcony of her house, it slips from her hands onto the dirt below.

Filmed up close, Ewa's domestic circumstances appear in disarray, literally under construction. Inside the house, all the rooms, with the exception of the kitchen, remain barely furnished or empty; long, hanging strips of clear plastic substitute for doors; and the children sleep on mattresses on the floor. Outside, a small stream trickles across the property and children's bright plastic toys lie abandoned on its sandy bank, while bricks and sacks of cement are scattered all over the unlandscaped lot. Kowalczyk argues that Ewa's "unfinished house projects dissolution and degeneration."[28]

This house in progress, which Ewa has been charged to transform into a home, is the pride and joy of her husband, Andrzej, who works in Norway. It is never clear why Andrzej leaves his young family for such long periods of time. Reviewer Krzysztof Połaski infers that the father disliked at-home parenting from the start.[29] In sharp contrast, Ewa has established a close rapport with her children, even the fractious Marysia. Her rare smiles in the film are reserved for her daughter and son. Andrzej (whom Michał Żurawski incarnates effectively as community bigwig and at-home bully) dictates his family's goals and behavior, despite his visiting status. As it turns out, Ewa has managed to return home just before Andrzej flies in to oversee Marysia's First Communion and the obligatory family dinner. Ewa seems apprehensive about their reunion, due to guilt, fear, and possibly distaste. She cedes her seat in the car to Marysia when her mother and brother drive out to the local airport. We therefore watch Andrzej arrive from Ewa's point of view. While Andrzej plays the overly hearty, generous paterfamilias, waking up Jasiek to impress his son with a huge toy firetruck and gratifying Marysia with a beautiful First Communion dress, his interaction with Ewa is tentative and distracted.

Andrzej's return marks the beginning of Ewa's siege—by her husband, her teenaged lover Marceli, an interfering "friend," and a sworn enemy. Instead of celebrating the homecoming of the wandering Pole, *Wild Roses* deploys the returning husband on a collision course with his waiting wife, a clash that may result in the break-up of the marriage or, as seems more likely, Andrzej's punishment of a "sinful" Ewa. Her prospects at first look grim. The patriarchy of the parish church seems to move in lockstep with the band of male villagers. After husband and wife attend the rehearsal for children preparing to receive First Communion, during which Marysia forgets the lyrics of the song she is supposed to perform, Andrzej catches up with his gathered "bros," who will fill him in on local gossip as he regales them with tales of Norway. The lone indication that Ewa might find sympathy rather than blanket condemnation among the group comes from a friend whom Andrzej offers a job overseas. The man declines for the sake of his marriage: "My wife says if I left for even one week, she'd divorce me."

While her husband socializes with his buddies, the people with whom he feels most comfortable, a wary Ewa follows Marysia into the distance where a group of younger men are playing soccer. There she spies her adolescent lover, shirtless, driving the ball toward the goal. Though Ewa retreats quickly before Marceli notices her and Andrzej notices Marceli, her escape is temporary. Later that night, which Andrzej naturally decides to spend with his male friends gathered around a Playstation, Marceli slips up to the house, as he has done for at least the last nine months. Protesting his love, he assures Ewa about her husband's whereabouts and then asks her what Andrzej knows and "what she has done." Ewa rebuffs him, offering no answers and calling him a child. She uses this dismissal line several times in the film, reminding them both of the substantial age difference between them and perhaps hoping to offend him into a retreat.

That the otherwise sympathetic Ewa has taken up with such a young man might shock viewers, rendering her "sin" irresponsible and perhaps criminal. Most reviewers place Marceli in high school and intimate that Ewa is perhaps ten years his senior. But Jadowska tempers impressions of Ewa as a predator by scripting Marceli to be the passionate aggressor in their relationship, a six-teen- or seventeen-year-old who refuses to relinquish his older, married lover even after she has borne their child. Moreover, when Marceli is depicted with boys nearer his own age, he behaves and is obeyed as a leader. Though it is likely that Marceli and Ewa's romance erupted as a doubly forbidden passion, its endurance seems to reflect the idiosyncratic mesh of their personalities: Marceli's boisterous strength and Ewa's quiet meekness, the boy's relative maturity and Ewa's need for adoration in lieu of oppressive control.

Ewa finds temporary respite from Marceli's successive attempts to renew their romance and Andrzej's ever more threatening questions (he wants to see her hospital discharge papers) when she goes to harvest the wild roses named in the film's title. In this Edenic space, a lush forest crisscrossed by rushing creeks and tranquil ponds, Ewa can work with Jasiek (and sometimes Marysia) beside her, the children parked on a blanket with food and toys. The natural beauty, rhythmic harvesting, and noninvasive company of primarily women workers soothe Ewa. This is the place where she evidently feels most at home, earning her own money, however modest a sum, and temporarily eluding the obligations of keeping house in Andrzej's unfinished showcase. The first time we see Ewa and Marysia together in this setting, they talk like confederates, frankly and earnestly. Marysia wants to make sure that Ewa is not "contagious" after her hospital stay and will not infect Andrzej, and Ewa reminds Marysia of her solemn promise not to tell her father what happened while he was away.

Indeed, in the following sequence, which focuses on the day of Marysia's First Communion, mother and daughter seem more closely intertwined, complementing each other in their resistance—Marysia to the church and Ewa to her accusers. While Ewa becomes more stubborn in her silence and refusal to behave as others expect her to, the voluble Marysia blurts out her doubts, emotions, and memories, regardless of the consequences. As the procession of children is being organized, Andrzej decides to go to confes-sion and pointedly asks Ewa if she will go. Ewa instantly says no, as if she is denying the need or the efficacy of doing so. In general, Jadowska represents the village church as an amateur stage set for ritualistic exercises that have nothing to do with the congregants' spiritual and social welfare.[30] Marysia, in particular, probes its limitations: she tells her mother that she does not want to make her First Communion because she has no idea what this rite of pas-sage means and fears what will happen to her due to her "terrible sins." Ewa comforts her daughter with a smile, but once she files into the church pew after her husband, she falls down in a dead faint, adding her own drama to the proceedings and alarming the already spooked Marysia. Andrzej swiftly carries Ewa outside, reacting to her mishap with rage instead of comfort. His wife has committed a cardinal sin in his eyes—ruining the family's public image: "You fuck everything up. I thought at least this communion would be normal. But you can even fuck this up." The exchange bares the toxic pattern of their marriage: Andrzej's tyrannical control and Ewa's invariably subpar performance.

Andrzej must rush back to deal with a now weeping Marysia, and Basia, the wife of his friend Marek, kindly offers to drive Ewa home. Yet this favor quickly morphs into a fishing expedition. The cagey Basia, from whose point of view we eye Ewa in her rear-view mirror, wants Ewa to unburden herself and trust in prayer, the more so since Andrzej is plying everyone with questions about her conduct. When Basia finally discloses that she and her husband fed Andrzej the local gossip about the boy Ewa was seen with and the rumors of her pregnancy, Ewa insists that Basia stop the car so that she can walk home alone. After her literal "fall," spousal abuse, and voyeuristic inquisition, Ewa's feelings are hardening into self-preserving anger. Within seconds, however, she faces true road rage, as Marceli's mother has been following Basia. The crazed woman hurls insults and threats at Ewa through her car window and comes close to hitting her: "Stay the fuck away from my kid and take care of yours. You probably drowned him."

A shaken, but resolute, Ewa reaches home on foot after the dinner guests have assembled, and even manages to shower and dress in time to pose for a happy family portrait, literally enacting the old Polish proverb that "families look best in photographs." Her mother, for once, treats her charitably as she helps her behind the scenes, telling her that she has done no evil, advising her to handle Andrzej with tact, and frankly promising her relief when her husband returns to Norway. In the meantime, Marysia, despite her promise, has divulged the most important information about the past to her father and the viewers. Upset that her mother has gone missing most of the day, Marysia wheels on Andrzej and wants to know "what he's done to her": "When you were gone, things were different here. We were happy." In rare concord, Ewa's mother and daughter have replaced intimations of Ewa's "sin" with assertions of her goodness and her restructured family's happiness while her husband was away. Marysia's testimony reinforces the impression that her mother's romance with a teenager was benign, and perhaps even beneficial.

The final act of *Wild Roses* wholly liberates Ewa from fear and guilt and enables her to act on her family's behalf after a glimpse into the abyss—in this case, the terrifying possibility of losing (another) child. The scene shifts back to Ewa's chosen home among the wild roses, where she naps in the sun with Jasiek and is awakened by Marceli's advances. Ewa moves away from her toddler and yields to her lover's caresses for a few moments before she breaks away, but by then Jasiek has disappeared. The desperate search for Jasiek, in which Ewa must enlist Andrzej and Andrzej commandeers his squadron of male friends, stretches from afternoon until nightfall, when the news reaches them that the boy was found by a local woman and is safe. During and immediately after this terrible ordeal, Ewa not only rebels against her husband but also rethinks what sort of family she wants to have. During the search, when an enraged Andrzej orders Ewa to stand up and shout for Jasiek, to act the way he thinks a loving mother should, Ewa counterattacks him as a sham father: "You are not here. Do you have any idea how it is to be here alone with two kids? Do you hear what I'm saying?" (figure 2.3). When Andrzej protests that he works "fucking hard" so his kids will have "a normal home," Ewa scornfully dismisses him as a provider: "I want to vomit when I look at that house. I can't even sleep there." Andrzej refuses to listen, but Ewa has spoken her truth at last.

Once Jasiek is brought home and Andrzej is treating the searchers to drinks and ordering his wife to "drink to Jasiek," Ewa leaves in disgust, intent now on making a life with those she loves. She finds Marceli, who, unlike Andrzej, disperses his pack of male (and female) friends so that they can talk in private, and tells him what she is about to do. For the first time, Ewa treats Marceli as a partner, though his future role remains unclear. The film's last scene takes place in the maternity ward where Ewa's story began. At this point, Ewa is no longer afraid to do and say what she wants. She tells a nurse that she has come to take back the child she bore there and left for adoption. The ensuing blackout prevents a certain happy end. Yet in this film about a Polish migrant and the family he left behind, the mother entrusted with children and home intends to remake both without her husband. Whether Andrzej's migration was the cause or the result of his ambition and control, Ewa aims to replace him as the head of *her* household. The "how" and "where" of her plan remain a mystery, yet Jadowska's closing dedication of the film "to the memory of Mama" hints at a real-life role model for this changed Ewa's courage and determination.

POLES LEFT AT HOME: *SILENT NIGHT* (2017)

Let's be frank, because emigration is not truly a flight FOR Poland, but FROM Poland, from graves, unhappiness, endless futile labors. A flight from endless trouble, endless work without reward, an enthusiastic death.

—Andrzej Bobkowski

In Polish as well as English, the title of *Silent Night* refers to the famed Christmas carol (establishing the film's seasonal resonance), while waxing ironic about the disruptive, secret-spilling, increasingly violent Christmas Eve that rocks an extended family gathered together in the northeastern

Polish provinces. Like *Beyond Words* and *Wild Roses*, *Silent Night* was written by its director, the well-known actor Piotr Domalewski, an especially remarkable achievement given that this movie was Domalewski's feature film debut and won him first prize at the 2017 Polish Film Festival in Gdynia.

Of greatest importance to his Polish reviewers, however, are Domalewski's knowledgeable, empathetic portraits of the residents of Warmia and Mazury, a region in northeastern Poland of "inherited poverty" where the locals have depended on migrant providers since the nineteenth century, when Poland was partitioned under three occupying empires.[31] The concern for Domalewski's experiential pedigree and good intentions resounds more sharply in this film's critical reception than it did in the case of *Wild Roses*. The reviewers of *Silent Night* not only want to defend the decency of this northeastern version of "Poland B," the poor, supposedly complex-ridden and alcohol-soaked provinces, but also to distinguish Domalewski's character studies from those of filmmaker Wojciech Smarzowski (b. 1963), whose provocative work accentuates the brutal suffering, corruption, and inhumanity visited on or manifest in his provincial subjects, be they a rich villager caught up in crime when he bribes a man to marry his pregnant daughter (*The Wedding*) or Mazurian women being gang raped by Soviet partisans during World War II (*Róża*). The critics point out that Domalewski was born in Łomża, a town even *farther* east than Olsztyn, and bred in the sort of small-town environment depicted in *Silent Night*.[32] Or, as Łukasz Adamski frankly assures his readers, Domalewski knows better than those "smartasses from European Warsaw" to subject their beloved Warmia and Mazuria to Smarzowski-style smear tactics.[33]

That written, *Silent Night* does seem to ride into the Polish east with a local version of a Warsaw smartass. As noted above, the film's plot poses the conventional gender pairing of the male migrant worker and the Polish woman/girl left behind. But, unlike *Wild Roses*, *Silent Night* never quite abandons traditional male conceptions of wielding power and achieving success. Tensions play out mainly between father and son, older and younger brothers, not husbands and wives. As Goscilo's chapter 3 on the family demonstrates in detail, the strongest woman in *Silent Night* is portrayed as an all-seeing, all-suffering caretaker. The Ewa figure in this film appears only as text messages on the small screen of another character's smartphone.

We enter this family's orbit in the extroverted company of its ambitious oldest son, fittingly named Adam, who has planned a surprise visit home on Christmas Eve to negotiate with his family for his own inevitably better future. Adam (the excellent Dawid Ogrodnik) is a migrant worker, like his father Zbyszek (the versatile character actor, Arkardiusz Jakubik) and grandfather (Paweł Nowisz) before him. News of his Polish girlfriend's pregnancy has inspired him to marry her and relocate all three to Holland, where, after an infusion of family cash, he knows that he can open his own business and live happily ever after. In sharp contrast to Andrzej in *Wild Roses*, who relishes his reputation as a big-shot visitor, Adam intends to do nothing less than break the family curse of absentee fathering, raising his child to enjoy the better economic prospects of the West *in* the West.

From the film's outset, Adam seems confident that he has all the facts, knows all the angles, and can depend on his wits and charm to seal the deal quickly. Though he is traveling in a bus filled with other Polish migrant workers making the long holiday trip from Holland to eastern Poland, he rides equipped with a new handheld camera, a device that literally gives him power over his narrative, as he chats with his child-to-be, comments on and judges everyone he sees, and records the lot for posterity. We are quickly reminded, however, that Domalewski and his cinematographer, Piotr Sobociński, Jr., wield a larger, more authoritative camera when Adam exits the bus for the last "comfort stop" before the workers reach home. This sequence of shots foreshadows the limitations of Adam's power and vision, though it does so with a fillip of humor reminiscent of filmmaker Stanisław Bareja's blend of the satirical, crass, and absurd. As Adam checks to see if he can spare the change to use the indoor facilities, the camera frames him in a medium shot and then pulls back and pans a long line of migrant laborers urinating outside with their backs to the viewer. The title of *Silent Night* appears against this backdrop of Polish fathers, husbands, and sons relieving themselves on Polish ground before they come home for the holidays.

As Adam transfers from the bus to a rental car, which he intends to show off as his own to his family, the film further unpacks his character and agenda. He is a success story and an operator, a *Gastarbeiter* on whom his family relies and a native son who is beginning to calculate the euros that Polish land might be worth. As much as Adam loves his family and automatically acts the parts of a helpful son and a partisan sibling—fixing the stalled ignition in his father's car, helping his brother Paweł steal a Christmas tree from a neighbor's property, roughing up his brother-in-law for abusing his sister—he returns to Poland on this trip with an *emigrant*'s vision and values. He primarily bought his camera as a marketing tool for a potential property buyer back in Holland. As he drives the rental car through Olsztyn, he narrates a video tour of the town's historic sights and completes his pitch with footage of his grandfather's old house nestled by a picturesque lake, a place he pitches as "your private paradise" with a salesman's final flourish.

Planning his arrival on Christmas Eve day, Adam is sure to find his extended family gathered under one roof, the women and girls busy preparing the twelve traditional dishes that a Polish *Wigilia* (Christmas Eve) supper requires, the men, most of them older, shooting the breeze in the garage, doing a few odd jobs, and starting their holiday drinking early. Nevertheless,

Adam's appearance comes as a surprise or, in the case of his stern-faced, perpetually vigilant mother Teresa (the formidable Agnieszka Suchora), a shock:
"Jesus Maria! What happened? Did they fire you?" As the one who necessarily assumes responsibility for keeping the family peace, Teresa senses that
Adam's unannounced visit means trouble, though she does not yet know the
particulars. In several of the pithy one-on-one dialogues that Domalewski
uses to maintain the brisk pace of his ever-branching plot, Teresa telegraphs
her concern about Adam's relations with his younger brother Paweł (Tomasz
Ziętek), who left his job in Holland abruptly and has been in a bad way
ever since.[34] Her other sotto voce remarks warn Adam not to encourage
his father's drinking, because Zbyszek has managed to stay sober for two
months. "We will save the holiday," Teresa announces to her eldest as she
efficiently removes bottles of vodka from their hiding places and pours the
liquor out the window.

Yet Teresa cannot guess that Adam intends to upset the family peace in
a much more profound way. Nor, to his credit, does Adam quite grasp how
hurtful his proposal will be to the people he loves. Once his buyer in Holland
emails him enthusiastically, having received the sales video and the photograph of the deed, Adam at last decides to mention his scheme to his father.
Their subsequent exchange spells out two diametrically opposed visions of
what family and life in Poland mean. (figure 2.4) Zbyszek presumes that
Adam will sell his grandfather's house in order to build a business at home,
employing family members. Adam counters that he will use the money to
found a business in Holland, where he "knows builders and suppliers" and
intends to move his own little family for good. The son's rejection of his
father's model becomes painfully clear:

Zbyszek: So you'll drop everything and run away?
Adam: I don't want to be like you. I want to be there for my children.
Zbyszek: Did I raise you all so badly?
Adam: You didn't have the chance.
　　　　Pause as Zbyszek stares at Adam, at once pained and resigned.
Zbyszek: You'll have to convince Paweł and Jola. But the house is yours.

Zbyszek does not admit his anguish, guilt, and worry about Adam's decision
until the film nears its conclusion. In the meantime, *Silent Night* registers how
two generations of absent fathers working overseas have shaped the current
extended family. Zbyszek's father, who lives with his son, is an unabashed,
foul-mouthed drunk left primarily under Teresa's care, and functions as a
source of irritation and amusement to his grandchildren. When the grandfather
gets his hands on Adam's camera, he videotapes the once high-tech goods
that he and his son brought back from abroad, objects that once represented

the good life in the socialist era and now are laughably obsolete. Then Kasia, Adam's youngest sibling, the "surprise" baby of the family, aims the camera at a wall covered with family photos in which Zbyszek is noticeably missing. When Kasia asks why, Adam tempers his explanation: "He wasn't always gone, just when we took pictures." But a few scenes later, Teresa speaks frankly about how devastating the situation was for her and her husband: "All I've ever done is take care of you and worry about you kids. I know it wasn't ideal and your father was always gone. But I tried. Being apart ruined our lives."

Though Adam abides by his father's wishes and manages to obtain his siblings' consent to sell the house with the proviso that he will pay back their shares quickly, their agreements come at personal costs none of them could have foreseen. Jola (Maria Dębska) assents readily, because her professional disappointment in the local job market echoes Adam's. As she comments wryly, her master's degree "entitles" her to work as a cashier, babysitter, or sales clerk. But Jola's husband, the sullen alcoholic Marcin (Tomasz Schuchardt), gives his wife a black eye for excluding him from these financial deliberations. Paweł ultimately agrees but is first enraged by Adam's proposition, in part because he had hoped to transform the grandfather's house into his own workshop, in part because he deeply resents Adam's presumed superiority as the older brother and his successful adaptation to working abroad. By loaning their share in the house to Adam, both Jola and Paweł tacitly commit themselves to make do in Poland—Jola because she has resigned herself to her loutish husband and local prospects, Paweł because he could not acclimate to life and work abroad due to as-yet-undisclosed attachments at home.

After a day of wheeling, dealing, boasting, and cajoling, Adam is stunned to find his plan scuttled in a suddenly tragic climax. He has just announced his Christmas miracle to those assembled—that he and Asia will marry, have a child, and move on—when his family's fragile ecosystem starts to crumble. Zbyszek has gone missing and Teresa, alarmed, dispatches her sons to find him. Zbyszek's earlier talk with Adam has nudged him off the wagon and into the house earmarked for sale, where he proceeds to drain a bottle of vodka. When Adam discovers him there, a drunk Zbyszek admits his failure as a father but volunteers a very sobering insight to his emigrating son:

> You know why I was afraid of going abroad? Because, at that time I thought I could feel like a human being there and not some Polack. Only years later I realized that it was exactly there that I felt most like a Polack. And only here in Poland can I be a human being. That's what this country is for. That here we can feel like human beings.[35]

Perhaps Adam has the courage and self-confidence to flourish as a human being abroad, but Zbyszek cannot prevent himself from warning his son.

At this tipping point, Adam also stumbles onto the fact that his inspiration for making the trip and carrying out his plan is a mirage. All day he has avoided answering Asia's incessant calls, arrogantly assuming that she will be thrilled when he presents her with a new life abroad neatly arranged for them both. But the texts that Adam spies on Paweł's phone and Paweł's belated confession reveal that his brother is the actual father of Asia's baby and the man whom she loves. The brothers consequently come to blows in the house they both had wanted to appropriate, knocking down an oil lantern that engulfs the building in flames. The two manage to save themselves and their father, but thereafter Adam stalks off into the night. All seems lost—the woman who would be his wife, the baby who would establish their family, the property that would jumpstart their good life in a country "better" than Poland. After his high hopes and big talk, Adam has no family other than the flawed one that he was determined not to emulate.

In the muted aftermath, the one family member with whom Adam can talk is Kasia, the child who has been most indulged, growing up with both parents in Poland and receiving special attention from a father who buys her a violin, takes her to lessons, and praises her awful playing. By virtue of being the youngest, Kasia enjoys an observer status, insulated against the family rivalries and crippling obligations that beset the adults. Even when her grandfather is utterly intoxicated or her brothers are arguing bitterly, they smile or make faces for her as she films them with Adam's borrowed camera. Late that night Adam falls asleep on the kitchen bench, exhausted by his trip, hard drinking, and failure, and he wakes up to Kasia as the only one still at home, for there was no room in the car for her when the family left to attend midnight mass. Ever the big brother, Adam drives her to church, and after Kasia wishes him a merry Christmas and kisses him goodbye, she hands him his camera, assuring him that she "has recorded everything just as you told me to."

The final scene of *Silent Night* depicts Adam back on the bus, heading west 24 hours after he set out on his cleverly planned, yet terribly thoughtless mission. In complete contrast to the opening scene, a very weary Adam chooses to view what Kasia filmed for him instead of filming and narrating himself. "Kasia's film" opens with the Polish Christmas Eve ritual of wishing family and friends all good things in the new year. Kasia wishes her big brother "prosperity, a nice life in Holland," and the request that he bring them back nice clothes. Prosperity and generosity are what any Pole would wish a family member working abroad. Yet Domalewski keeps "Kasia's film" rolling along with his film's closing credits, sharing with Adam and us the random footage she recorded of a family in holiday mode—one of the girl cousins doing splits on the kitchen floor, the incorrigible grandfather "exercising" with his vodka bottle as weight while the young people laugh and keep count of his "lifts," and Adam receiving hearty congratulations after his big announcement. As

Adam and we watch this film, no resolution is reached and no verdict about where and how a Pole can live best is revealed. But we all have the opportunity to enjoy the experience of being there with the extended family, an experience that Adam's drastically instrumentalized point of view missed.

CONCLUSION

Strange Heaven and *Beyond Words*, the two films about immigrant Poles analyzed above, deliver no new revelations about working and living in the EU's north and west. The interactions that take place between Western and Eastern Europeans in both films evoke familiar national and regional stereotypes: law-abiding, bland, or supercilious Swedes and Germans condescending to and provoking rule-skeptic, ironic, and emotionally volatile Poles. Both films cut off their protagonists from any local Polonia or broad network of friends and acquaintances in the host country. In *Strange Heaven*, the isolation of Basia, Marek, and Ula encourages viewer attachment as well as critical scrutiny of the flawed relations between two mercurial parents and their bewildered, lonely daughter. But when this headstrong, clueless family stumbles against Sweden's highly invasive child protection laws, their isolation transforms them into desperate victims in an unexpected thriller. Basia, Marek, and Ula, at last disciplining themselves to work as a united team, flee the West as enemy territory. For these Polish immigrants, life in Sweden was an initially seductive hell. Yet their giddy escape at the end of the film does not prove that Poland will be heaven.

Beyond Words at first seems to promise a psychologically richer tale of an immigrant who is mastering the German language and upper-middle-class behavior and thoroughly familiar with the laws of Germany and the EU. Indeed, Michał is perfectly qualified to defend immigrants in court, though he prefers to do so for clients least comparable to himself—for example, refugee women of color with small children. For this young, talented, upwardly mobile Pole in the early twenty-first century, Germany will never become the hell that his grandparents' and parents' generations remember from World War II.

Yet the impetus driving Michał to duplicate his German boss's elitist, nationalist professional and private life is unsettling and never explored. When the film brings Michał's long-lost Polish father to his gated apartment building, we could infer that his zeal to assimilate in Germany derives from the lack of a strong male role model during his adolescence in Poland. Once Stanisław arrives, Michał's admiration does shift temporarily from German to Pole, from controlling friend to parent-provocateur. The young man's evident desire for his father's love and approval momentarily opens up his character to the viewers as well. Yet Michał specifically wants Stanisław to bless his "adventurous" choice to become a wealthy German lawyer. Just as Michał never explains why he emulates his boss and loves Berlin, so he is never allowed to articulate what his father and being Polish mean to him after Stanisław's exploitative visit. Michał's silence and subsequent tangle with African immigrants in Berlin may indicate his need to rid himself of what he perceives to be a stigmatizing Polishness. Unfortunately, Antoniak's screenplay leaves her potentially intriguing protagonist a stylish blank.

In comparison with the formulaic *Strange Heaven* and inchoate *Beyond Words*, the two films focused on stay-at-home Polish protagonists are far more nuanced in their portraiture and surprising in the final plot twists. According to relieved Polish reviewers, *Wild Roses* and *Silent Night* pass the test of screening Poland B both accurately and respectfully, ostensibly because both directors grew up in or close to the places they represent. Neither Jadowska nor Domalewski masks the poverty, shabbiness, and lack of modern amenities in their respective provincial locations. In *Wild Roses*, the camera dwells on Ewa's half-built home, unlandscaped lot, and the endless gravel paths that she is forced to traverse by foot. She must rely on car rides from family or strangers to reach the local church or the hospital. *Silent Night* mainly takes place in the family's ramshackle farmhouse and the muddy yard between the house and the garage. Adam knows that the best way to impress his family is to pass off his bright red rental car as evidence of "his good year."

At the same time, both films point out the beauty in their provincial surroundings—the extensive wild rose plantation, the old peasant house situated near a pretty lake—and, above all, privilege their provincial subjects, whose desires and plans eventually upend the visions that their visiting migrant "providers" intend to realize. In *Wild Roses*, the most innovative of the films presented here, the main protagonist's sensibility elides with the natural paradise in which she works and where she feels most at peace and in control. In contrast to the young adults featured in *Silent Night*, Ewa expresses no discontent about being left behind professionally or economically in Poland B. Rather, Jadowska allows her exhausted sinner to gradually reveal her heretical worldview—her hatred of her husband's tyrannical bourgeois patriarchy; aversion to the village's stifling status quo; desire for a teenaged boy who is an obliging playmate rather than a pompous ass; and determination to be a mother and head of the household for all her children, regardless of their paternity. Against the tremendous obstacles of village, marriage, and economic dependence, the film tracks Ewa's slow, stubborn advance toward a modest kind of matriarchy.

Domalewski's deftly scripted *Silent Night* succeeds in articulating the views of a strong ensemble of characters; Adam's handheld camera serves as both symbol and mechanism for shared narrative perspectives. This film "rides home" with Adam, initiating us into his emigrant plan to cash in on his family inheritance and relocate his money, labor, and new family (girlfriend Asia and baby-to-be) to the West. We infer that he, as the eldest child in his family, felt most keenly the burden of his father's absences as a migrant worker and his mother's reliance on him to watch out for his younger siblings and follow in his father's footsteps. Most recently, that burden included Adam's covering his younger brother Paweł's work shifts in the Netherlands because Paweł, apparently incapable of adjusting to life abroad, had returned home months before.

Yet as Adam informs his family about his master plan—born out of ingenuity, resentment, audacity, and joy (the new baby)—he overlooks their sacrifices and seemingly more modest ambitions at everyone's peril. In consequence, Adam and his siblings' inheritance is destroyed, his wounded father breaks his promise to his wife and returns to the bottle, and Asia and the brother whom he underestimated turn out to be the expecting parents. In *Silent Night*, as in *Wild Roses*, a baby determines the main protagonist's complicated progress or devastating failure. In both cases, too, the baby binds its parents to Poland.

Interestingly enough, both films share one other significant character. Regardless of their youth, Marysia in *Wild Roses* and Kasia in *Silent Night* figure as observant truth-tellers in their respective worlds of fumbling adults. As such, they function as allies to and scouts for the protagonist. Marysia voices the heretical notions about church, male bonding, and family happiness that Ewa feels too guilty or afraid to express. The older Kasia strives to make sense of family history and relationships in dialogue with her big brother Adam and records the family's Christmas Eve at his behest and to his surprise. Marysia and Kasia may not prefigure a feminist future in Poland B. But Jadowska and Domalewski's assignment of important speaking parts to feisty, questioning, smart girls in their films is a phenomenon worth celebrating.

BH

NOTES

1. Agnieszka Szpak, "How to Deal with Migrants and the State's Backlash—Polish Cities' Experience," *European Planning Studies* 27, no. 6 (2019): 1160. Szpak also notes the covert contradiction between the rhetoric and practice of the Law and Justice party, for while it "declares its hostility to migrants, especially from the Middle East to North African countries (many of them Muslim and as such seen by the Government as a security threat) . . . it quietly accepts more and more of them

(for example the Nepalese obtained 9200 work permits, the Byelorussians 7600 and the Moldavians 2500 [in 2018]": 1160.

2. Dorota Lubińska notes Poland's distinctive and experientially grounded self-perception in her overview of Polish migrant workers in Sweden. Whereas "Sweden has always been a country which has rather received immigrants . . . Poland has a history of shifting borders and of both voluntary and involuntary migration, and is considered as one of the most important emigration countries in modern times." "Polish Migrants in Sweden: An Overview," *Folia Scandinavica* 15 (Poznań 2013): 73.

3. For more information on what has been called the post-2004 "Polish exodus," see Anne White, *Polish Families and Migration since EU Accession* (Bristol: The Policy Press, 2011) and Joanna Rostek and Dirk Uffelman, eds., *Contemporary Polish Migrant Culture and Literature in Germany, Ireland, and the UK* (Frankfurt am Main: Peter Lang, 2011).

4. David R. Roediger, *Working Toward Whiteness: How America's Immigrants Became White, The Strange Journey from Ellis Island to the Suburbs* (New York: Basic Books, 2005). See also Matthew Frye Jacobson, *Whiteness of a Different Color: European Immigrants and the Alchemy of the Poor* (Cambridge, MA: Harvard University Press, 1998).

5. Kris van Heuckelom, *Polish Migrants in European Film, 1918-2017* (Cham, Switzerland: Palgrave Macmillan, 2019). Van Heuckelom thus defines his approach and identifies the movies that he analyzes, "most of the films that will be dealt with are West or North European (and, to a lesser extent, South European), whereas Central and Eastern European cinemas will play no role of significance" (6).

6. Yosefa Loshitzky, "Screening Strangers in Fortress Europe and Beyond," *Crossings: Journal of Migration and Culture* 5, nos. 2/3 (2014): 195.

7. Grzegorz Fortuna, "*Obce niebo*—Gdynia 2015)*, film.org.pl, September 23, 2015, https://film.org.pl/r/recenzje/obce-niebo-gdynia-2015-68781/. Accessed December 12, 2019.

8. Łukasz Adamski, "*Obce niebo*. Polska rodzina vs. 'szwecjalizm.' Czy naprawdę chcemy takiego autorytaryzmu w Polsce?" wPolityce.pl, October 13, 2015, https://wpolityce.pl/kultura/268357-obce-niebo-polska-rodzina-vs-szwecjalizm-czy-naprawde-chcemy-takiego-autorytaryzmu-w-polsce-recenzja. Accessed December 11, 2019.

9. Kacper Szulecki, "Nordycka czarna wołga porywa polskie dzieci. Recenzja filmu *Obce niebo* Dariusza Gajewskiego," *Kultura Liberalna*, October 27, 2015, https://kulturaliberalna.pl/2015/10/27/nordycka-czarna-wolga-porywa-polskie-dzieci -recenzja-filmu-obce-niebo-dariusza-gajewskiego/. Accessed December 20, 2019.

10. Magdalena Żakowska, "Dariusz Gajewski znalazł swoje niebo. 'Ciekawi mnie nasze życie z Agnieszką.' " *Magazyn Viva!*, October 21, 2015, https://viva.pl/kul-tura/film/dariusz-gajewski-opowiada-o-swoim-nowym-filmie-obce-niebo-i-o-zonie -93408-r1/. Accessed December 12, 2019.

11. Tadeusz Sobolewski, "*Obce niebo*—film podstępny. Zimne piekło Szwecji, gorąco piekło Polski." *Gazeta Wyborcza*, October 15, 2015, https://wyborcza.pl /1,101707,19024829,obce-niebo-film-podstepny-zimne-pieklo-szwecji-gorace.html. Accessed December 11, 2019.

12. Reviewer Bartosz Staszczyszyn declares that Kubiak's emotionally intense performance is the film's "greatest discovery." *"Obce niebo, reż Dariusz Gajewski."* culture. pl https://culture.pl/pl/dzielo/obce-niebo-rez-dariusz-gajewski. Accessed December 12, 2019.

13. Reviewer Alex Ramon finds these scenes "subtly chilling," as they demonstrate easily Ula can settle in a new family and "a nicer house," with "a much loved dog and even a substitute Grandmother figure." *popmatters*, September 24, 2015, https://www.popmatters.com/gdynia-film-festival-2015-new-world-strange-heaven -the-here-after-2495486324.html. Accessed December 20, 2019.

14. Krzysztof Połaski, *"Pomiędzy słowami:krótka opowieśćo Polaku, który chciał stać się über Niemcem,"* *Telemagazyn*, February 14, 2018, https://www.telemagazyn.pl/artykuly/pomiedzy-slowami-recenzja-krotka-opowiesc-o-polaku-ktory-chcial -stac-sie-uber-niemcem-63094.html. Accessed December 12, 2019.

It bears noting here that Antoniak locates her protagonist in Germany, not the Netherlands, where she lives in emigration. Germany better serves her purposes in having Michał be "educated" by his father, who judges German influence through his generation's memories of World War II.

15. Reviewer Piotr Guszkowski coins Michał's looks as "Aryan." *"Pomiędzy słowami:* studium emigracji," *Gazeta Wyborcza*, February 15, 2018, https://wyborcza.pl/7,101707,23028516,pomiedzy-slowami-studium-emigracji-recenzja.html. Accessed December 20, 2019.

16. Yosefa Loshitzky, *Screening Strangers: Migration and Diaspora in Contemporary European Cinema* (Bloomington and Indianapolis: Indiana University Press, 2010), 45–46.

17. Van Heuckelom (2019): 250.

18. Reviewer Przemysław Dobrzyński remarks that Michał "doffs his mask" at home. "O Polaku, co Niemcem chciał zostać. *Pomiędzy słowami—recenzja,"* *Rozrywka.blog*, February 15, 2018, https://www.spidersweb.pl/rozrywka/2018/02/15 /pomiedzy-slowami-recenzja-filmu/. Accessed December 12, 2019. Van Heuckelom maintains that Michał's mastery of legal terms in German forms part of his rite of passage as a functionary in EU, a European body that privileges Western over Eastern European nations (2019): 221.

19. Guszkowski describes Chyra as Gierszał's "counterweight," an "unkempt, unruly man whose face reflects life's hard knocks" (op. cit. footnote 12). According to van Heuckelom, within the narrower context of films about Polish migrants and immigrants, "Chyra has come to replace [Zbigniew Zamachowski] as the most prominent male face of Polish migration," though the roles he has played mark his as "morally more ambiguous" than that of Zamachowski (2019): 239.

20. Reviewer Marcin Kempista praises Antoniak for the way she deftly renders the relations between father and son and commends Gierszał and Chyra for their "especially well-matched duet." *"Homo viator—recenzja filmu Pomiędzy słowami,"* *Pełna sala*, October 17, 2017, http://pelnasala.pl/pomiedzy-slowami/. Accessed December 20, 2019. Reviewer Sara Ward designates Chyra as "the overtly Polish cheese" to Gierszał's "German-assimilating chalk." *Screendaily,* September 8, 2017, https://www.screendaily.com/reviews/beyond-words-toronto-review/5121719 .article. Accessed January 2, 2020.

21. Reviewer Guy Lodge criticizes the filmmaker for leaving her character in limbo: "Antoniak's spare script doesn't probe too deeply into his ruptured psyche, meaning much of *Beyond Words* falls in a curious tonal middle ground between earnest and ersatz," *Variety*, September 27, 2017, https://variety.com/2017/film/reviews/beyond-words-review-1202574984/. Accessed January 2, 2020.

22. Of note here is Antoniak's utter waste of the talented actress, Justyna Wasilewska. Wasilewska plays a Polish barmaid whom Michał knows and Stanisław finds attractive. Połaski suggests that this character represents another face of immigration in *Beyond Words* (op. cit. footnote 11). But Wasilewska's recurring image as a glum, resigned passenger on the Berlin tram is a motif that Antoniak never spells out in the film.

23. My analysis here markedly differs from van Hueckelom's reading of Michał's going "underground . . . in order to physically experience what it means to be 'other' " (2019): 223.

24. While Połaski interprets this descent into an underground Berlin as a powerful sequence in which Michał "struggles with his demons," reviewers Guszkowski and Kempista complain that it presents a "cliched" and "disastrous" conclusion to an otherwise subtle, beautifully filmed movie.

25. Bartosz Staszczyczyn, "*Dzikie roże*—Anna Jadowska," Culture.pl, December 29, 2017, https://culture.pl/pl/dzielo/dzikie-roze-rez-anna-jadowska. Accessed December 22, 2019; Tadeusz Sobolewski, *Wyborcza.pl, "Dzikie róże:* Jeden z najlepszych polskich filmów 2017 roku opowiada o dziejach grzechu," December 27, 2017, https://wyborcza.pl/7,101707,22831667,dzikie-roze-jeden-z-najlepszych-polskich-filmow-2017-roku.html. Accessed December 22, 2019.

26. Łukasz Maciejewski, "*Dzikie róże:* jedyny taki duet w polskim kinie," *Narodowe centrum kultury,* April 12, 2018, https://nck.pl/projekty-kulturalne/projekty/kultura-dostepna/aktualnosci/dzikie-roze-kultura-dostepna-w-kinach. Accessed December 23, 2019.

27. Maciej Kowalczyk, "W potrzasku—recenzja filmu *Dzikie róże,*" *Pełna sala,* January 9, 2018, http://pelnasala.pl/dzikie-roze/. Accessed December 22, 2019.

28. Ibid.

29. Krzysztof Połaski, "*Dzikie róże:* Z rodziną najlepiej wychodzi się na zdjęciu," *Telemagazyn*, May 12, 2018, https://www.telemagazyn.pl/artykuly/dzikie-roze-z-rodzina-najlepiej-wychodzi-sie-na-zdjeciu-recenzja-59479.html. Accessed December 20, 2019.

30. Staszczyczyn astutely observes that Jadowska represents social, religious, and family rituals as "acts of symbolic violence against women" (op. cit.).

31. Tomasz Rachwald-Rostkowski offers this historical context in "Polak-koczownik: Recenzja filmu *Cicha noc* Piotra Domalewskiego," *Kultura liberalna,* November 18, 2017, https://kulturaliberalna.pl/2017/11/28/tomasz-rachwald-rostkowski-polak-koczownik-cicha-noc-recenzja/. Accessed January 4, 2020.

32. Ibid. Tomasz Zacharczuk, "Mądry, dojrzały, poruszający. Recenzja filmu *Cicha noc,*" *Trójmiasto.pl,* November 24, 2017, https://rozrywka.trojmiasto.pl/Zwyciezca-Zlotych-Lwow-juz-w-kinach-Recenzja-filmu-Cicha-noc-n118787.html. Accessed January 4, 2020.

33. Łukasz Adamski, "*Cicha noc.* Polska *Sieranevada.* Przenikliwe i mądre dzieło," *WPolityce.pl*, September 21, 2017, https://wpolityce.pl/kultura/358868 -adamski-z-festiwalu-w-gdyni-cicha-noc-polska-sieranevada-przenikliwe-i-madre -dzielo-recenzja. Accessed January 5, 2020.

34. A number of reviewers praise Domalewski's crisp, emotionally on-point dia-logues—Zaharczuk, *op cit.*; Janusz Wróblewski, "Cicha niemoc. Recenzja filmu *Cicha noc*," *Polityka*, November 21, 2017, https://www.polityka.pl/tygodnikpolityka/kul-tura/film/1727932,1,recenzja-filmu-cicha-noc-rez-piotr-domalewski.read. Accessed January 5, 2020; Krzysztof Połaski, "*Cicha noc*: Mocny cios w nasze polskie mordy," *Telemagazyn*, November 24, 2017, https://www.telemagazyn.pl/artykuly/cicha-noc -mocny-cios-w-nasze-polskie-mordy-recenzja-61616.html. Accessed January 4, 2020; and Amber Wilkinson, "*Silent Night* (2017) Film Review," *Eye for Film*, April 26, 2018, https://www.eyeforfilm.co.uk/review/silent-night-2017-film-review -by-amber-wilkinson. Accessed January 6, 2020. Przemysław Dobrzyński smartly observes that all of the characters in the film, major and minor, are written with their own "microhistories." "Nasze wspaniałe polskie święta. *Cicha noc* recenzja," *Rozrywka blog*, November 24, 2017, https://www.spidersweb.pl/rozrywka/2017/11 /24/cicha-noc-recenzja-filmu/. Accessed January 5, 2020.

35. See https://www.spidersweb.pl/rozrywka/2017/11/24/cicha-noc-recenzja -filmu/. Accessed January 5, 2020.

The Polish word "polak" means "a Pole," but given the context and tenor of the father's pained statement, the derogatory "Polack" seems a more suitable translation, for which the English subtitles also opt.

Chapter 3

All in the Family

The Ties That Bind and Blight

MYTHS AND MYTHOLOGIES

Aristotle in his *Poetics* identified the emotional core of Greek tragedy as familial conflict—"situations in which sufferings arise within close relationships, e.g. brother kills brother, son father, mother son, or son mother—or is on the verge of killing them, or does something else of the same kind."[1] The action of the genre coincided with that of ancient myths, which narrated kindred murderous clashes, as well as marital betrayals, incest, and murder or abandonment of offspring. Since plays by Aeschylus, Euripides, and Sophocles entertained no illusions about familial relations, in modern times Sigmund Freud famously turned to Oedipus for his paradigm of filial rivalry and ascribed the majority of human psychological turmoil to a childhood maimed by family dynamics, especially in the area of sexuality. At the same time, universal belief holds that "the family is the nucleus of civilization and the basic social unit of society"—a notion of kinship that renders political recourse to the rhetoric of nation as family so effective, as illustrated above all by Stalin.[2] His canny, hollow proclamation of the nation as the Big Family, with the biological family as its lesser, Small Family unleashed a series of deaths and betrayals, for the naïve population failed to perceive the murderous nature of The Father's, that is, Stalin's politics.[3] Particularly if they are courting listeners' approval, public figures from various walks of life, their behavior to the contrary, like to proclaim that their families supersede all else in their lives. The affective appeal of family rhetoric also influences discourse by sundry institutions, such as businesses, universities, clubs, and a host of organizations with similarly implausible qualifications for kinship. Nowadays spousal, parental, and filial homicides persist, as do incest, infanticide, and molestation of children, but their recurrence does not discourage the bracing, though manifestly spurious, concept of the family as an impregnable haven of safety, love, and trust.

As elsewhere, such an unfounded exaltation of the family has thrived in Poland, partially owing to the cult of the mother as Matka Polka/Boska (Divine Mother Poland)—a pedestaled identity, which casts motherhood "in its fullness and perfection"[4] inextricable from the Catholic country's durable kenotic self-image. The Mother writ large is synonymous with the persona of a stoic, all-forgiving icon of nurturing femininity capable of withstanding all travails and ever ready to offer comfort, support, and self-sacrifice for her loved ones.[5] Devoid of sexuality and subjective desires, such an indomitable paragon of passive endurance lives to serve others, who depend on her, yet relegate her to subservience, for male melodrama tends to dominate the country's most memorable narratives. Recent films in Poland, their skepticism about the Panglossian view of the family notwithstanding, have reinvigorated that image within a somewhat bleak context, while a minority of directors have limned a few startling antipodes.

DOUBLE EXPOSURE: *CICHA NOC* (SILENT NIGHT 2017), PIOTR DOMALEWSKI

There are no secrets that time alone does not reveal.

—Jean Racine, *Britannicus*

We all know that your kin look nice only in photographs.
I wanted to tell a story about why, despite of [*sic*] everything,
we do pose for pictures with them.

—Piotr Domalewski re *Cicha noc*

Anyone interested in what one critic dubbed a naturalistic portrait of a family, devoid of sentimentality and rosy hues, could hardly do better than watch Domalewski's (b. 1983) debut feature, *Silent Night*, for which he also authored the screenplay. Set in rural Poland, it opens with the optimistic visit of Adam (Dawid Ogrodnik), an enterprising young Pole working in the Netherlands, who returns to his ancestral home on Christmas Eve; it ends with his disillusioned departure late that evening. Why he suddenly appears after a lengthy absence and why his younger brother, unlike everyone else in the household, seems unhappy to see him constitute the two mysteries that Domalewski skillfully paces. He reveals the first motivation early on, for it drives the film's actions, and the second considerably later, as a means of radically altering Adam's happy assumptions and the image he projects of all-around success in the West, such as passing off as his possession the car he has rented.

That image originally contrasts with the defeatist picture of the other family members: the cousins indentured to their iPhones; the grandfather (Paweł Nowisz), drunk even before the Yule festivities start; the grandmother, who is largely ignored (Elżbieta Kepinska); the father (Arkadiusz Jakubik), an unemployed recovering alcoholic all too aware of his failures; the younger brother, Paweł (Tomasz Ziętek), who apparently could not retain the job that Adam arranged for him in Holland and now avoids Adam; the sister Jolka (Maria Dębska), married to the abusive Marcin (Tomasz Schuchardt); an aunt and an uncle attached to tasteless jokes (Adam Cywka), plus the teenage sister, Kasia (Amelia Tyszkiewicz), more mature and receptive than her elders and the sole individual with whom Adam has a common language. Finally, bringing up the rear, we see the "sainted figure" so often encountered in film and in everyday life, the battle-fatigued mother, Teresa (Agnieszka Suchora), an unappreciated caregiver who prepares meals, attempts to defuse volatile confrontations, and holds the family together.

All male family members, including Adam, drink to excess, while the females tend to cater to their frailties and aggression. When Teresa urges her husband not to fall off the wagon, he hurls his glass across the room, then proceeds to consume an entire bottle of liquor in the privacy of the grandfather's separate dwelling. A far from sober Marcin beats up Jolka to teach her that decisions about family property need to involve him. Adam, as Teresa notes, is "just like" his father: and not only his imitative employment abroad, but also his secret indulgence in the alcohol that he brings with him—which he denies to his mother—suggest that her observation is accurate. Given that from start to finish the grandfather appears at various stages of blithering intoxication, the viewer may be excused for assuming that alcoholism is a patrilinear or simply male disease.[6]

As the film develops, the puzzling sequence preceding its introduction, which shows Adam joyfully speaking to a sonogram in his hand, becomes explained. The anticipated birth of his child has prompted Adam's visit to the family, not to share their celebration of Christmas, but to persuade his two siblings to transfer to him their share of the grandfather's property. Adam's ambitious plan entails its sale to found a new business that will support his new family and yield profits that he will use to repay his brother and sister. The revelation of this secret stimulus for his unexpected visit also confirms that he will continue to live abroad—news that shocks and dismays most of his listeners, but that becomes irrelevant with the film's second revelation, that not he, but Paweł fathered "his" future child. The duo's ensuing fight accidently results in the destruction of the very property Adam wished to sell to a foreign buyer. His hopes for "success in the West" based on Poland's rich yet cheap-selling land, in other words, literally go up in smoke.

Upon Adam's chastened departure, two questions confront the viewer: First, is the Polish family a disabling rather than enabling entity in today's world? Though violence, betrayal, and resentment underlie superficially cordial familial relations, the family still cleaves together and strives to overcome its profound inadequacies. After all, following the bout of fisticuffs with his brother, Adam seems resigned to the latter's duplicity: he simply returns the keys to the apartment that he has shared with his fiancée/girlfriend, Asia (the precise nature of the relationship is never defined), and leaves, his future a question mark. Indeed, he directs his greater physical anger against his abusive brother-in-law for maltreating the docile Jolka, who makes no protest or complaint about being battered. One reviewer concluded that "in all this gloominess, there is a ray of bright light: family love, however imperfect and toxic, which keeps everyone together."[7] How Domalewski's depiction of the group dynamic can be interpreted as indicative of familial affection may be difficult to imagine for someone unfamiliar with the traditional refrain of Russian women, "If he beats me, he loves me." Acceptance of the men's primitive conduct will never prompt changes in the interests of a more civilized mode of behavior that, at the very least, would free women from their tiresome, thankless role of endlessly tolerant domestic custodians. As Artur Zaborski notes in his review, after the defused, low-key ending, everything will go back to "normal," and aspirations and experience count for naught, for the spirit of fatalism, manifested in repetition, prevails in the film.[8] While the ending is inconclusive, it hardly sounds an upbeat note.

Second, what is Poland's relationship to a West with which it has partnered through the European Union (2004) and numerous intellectual and socioeconomic initiatives, yet by comparison with which Poland remains both poor and dependent on finding emigrant work that requires separation from family? At a poignant juncture in the characters' efforts to elucidate their behavior, Adam's ineffectual father declares himself proud of his son and confesses that he feared going abroad because prior to his departure he believed that he could be a human being there, and not just some Polack.[9] Subsequently, he realized that such was exactly his identity there, whereas he could be a human being in Poland: "That's what this country is for. So that we can feel human." According to him, he ruined his health working in German construction. Yet, though Teresa tells Adam that he is just like his father, his initiative, the film suggests (especially in light of the grim Polish setting), can be realized productively only abroad (see chapter 2 on immigration). After all, he has a regular job in the Netherlands, entrepreneurial ambitions, and a command of English—all of which, presumably, his father lacked during his younger years. Though Adam shouts at his father that "For people like us the times are always the same," if one examines the three generations of men within the family, then a moderate degree of Europeanization appears to have taken place with each generation, whereby the modern Adam's situation could hardly be more remote from his grandfather's and, to a lesser degree, is unlike his father's. Notably, his uncle, who also worked abroad, is not an alcoholic, so the disillusionment of emigrant employment does not lead automatically to uncontrollable drinking.

The film soft-pedals the historical dimension, which, moreover, is complicated by the younger brother's betrayal of Adam and the conflagration of the latter's hopes along with his grandfather's property. Fatalism on the men's part, however, throttles possibilities, for their actions facilitate the negative repetition inhering in the notion of "people like us." Ultimately, though the religious and cultural significance of Christmas Eve is the celebration of the momentous start of a fundamentally new era—one that will eventuate for Adam in dramatically different terms from those he anticipated—*Silent Night* essentially casts the occasion as an excuse for inebriation and eruption of ill-concealed frustrations and resentments, along with various degrees of implied but embattled affection.

Two female characters rise above the dysfunctional family relations. One is the harried but persevering mother, who strives to preserve a modicum of civilized behavior among the assembled relatives and who organizes all aspects of the festivities apart from the Christmas tree, which the two brothers steal from a neighbor. When in the process Adam is bitten by a dog, it is Teresa, of course, who tends to his wound. She also proves a steadying influence on her husband, her words preventing him, however resentfully, from indulging in alcohol at the communal table. In short, she fulfills the traditional role of resilient, ever-forbearing mother.

The other exception is Kasia, the youngest family member, who plays "Silent Night" on the violin and who, at Adam's request, films the entire proceedings on his small digital camera. Her quiet demeanor, tranquil observation of the evening's circumstances, and honest exchanges with him imply a greater maturity than possessed by any of her older relatives apart from the kenotic mother. And her self-possession throughout the evening also suggests that this particular Christmas Eve with all the assembled relatives repeats previous ones in its alcohol-infused clashes. Domalewski underscores the remoteness of the familial gathering from the spiritual meaning of "Silent Night" by having Kasia play the violin badly, chiefly off-key.

Astonishingly, in light of what the scenes reveal about family dynamics, most Polish critics commenting on the film called it a mirror of contemporary society with which they could identify—a somewhat dispiriting viewpoint that no Western reviewer shared. For instance, commending the film as "intelligent, mature, and moving" (mądry, dojrzały i poruszający), Tomasz Zacharczuk asserted, "we feel natural and as though at home with Domalewski's screen

family" (z filmową rodziną Domalewskiego czujemy się naturalnie i jak u sie-
bie).[10] A similar sense of recognition emerged in Adam Siennica's endorsement
of the film as "simply a good, intelligent film about ordinary Polish life" (po
prostu dobry, mądry film o polskiej codzienności).[11] Characterizing *Silent Night*
as a film about love, Bartosz Staszczyszyn claimed that it "creates a picture into
which a Polish audience can gaze as in a mirror" (tworzy obraz, w którym polska publiczność może przejrzeć się jak w lustrze).[12] A dissenting voice among
Polish reviewers was that of Artur Zaborski in *Kino*. According to him, the
film is basically an extension of Wojciech Smarzowski's cinematic world, with
ubiquitous darkness and silence, and vodka flowing on all sides. Everything we
see on the screen, he complains, is disquieting: the personae's conversations,
the dearth of light that tirelessly reinforces the battle with a metaphorical darkness, and the outfits selected to emphasize the fatalism of the depicted world,
which are either poor or shoddy. There is no middle ground, Zarborski concludes, and the director has no distance from his materials, unlike Smarzowski
in *Wesele* (The Wedding 2004).[13] This scathing assessment of a film that won
the Golden Lion (Złote Lwy, for best film) at Gdynia and nine other awards
swims against the current of Polish reactions and strikes me as partially valid
but somewhat ungenerous regarding Domalewski's debut effort. While it is
not far-fetched to compare Domalewski cinematic *style* with some features of
Smarzowski's, the young director tends to avoid Smarzowski's extremes, especially the caricatured personae of *The Wedding*, in favor of a relatively low-key
atmosphere and characters who struggle to preserve their affection for one
another, with uneven results. Consequently, the ultimate image of the family
is appreciably less disheartening than in *The Wedding* and Smarzowski's *Dom
zły* (The Dark House 2009), discussed in chapter 6. One Western reviewer of
Silent Night encouragingly remarked, "family can sometimes be poisonous but
it usually proves to be its own antidote."[14] Whether the film actually posits such
an antidote is, at best, debatable.

"L'ENFER C'EST LES AUTRES": *OSTATNIA RODZINA* (THE LAST FAMILY 2016), JAN MATUSZYŃSKI

Family life isn't always sunshine and a rainbow.

—Poster advertising the film[15]

nowhere is it implicitly said that a family is
anything but a group of people who like and dislike
each other in equal measure.

—Zdzisław Beksiński in *The Last Family*

Whereas Domalewski shot *Silent Night* from his own original script, Jan Matuszyński's (1984) debut feature, *The Last Family*, was based on materials documenting the actual life of Zdzisław Beksiński (b. 1929), a successful Warsaw artist who worked in photography, painting, and sculpture until his murder in 2005. With a screenplay by Roberto Bolesto, known for his work on Agnieszka Smoczyńska's *Córki dancingu* (The Lure 2015), the film charts the last twenty-eight years (1977–2005) in the life of the surrealist (Andrzej Seweryn), his wife, Zofia (Aleksandra Konieczna), and their profoundly disturbed, suicidal son, Tomasz (Dawid Ogrodnik).

Although the film also features Beksiński's mother (Zofia Perczyśka) and mother-in-law (Danuta Nagórna), their roles are largely passive, included as part of the focus on the omnipresence of death within the family. The only other significant character is Piotr Domochowski (Andrzej Chyra), an art dealer residing in France, who, as an interviewer (and Beksiński's biographer), is the sole individual with whom Beksiński shares his unhealthy inner world. Other minor roles are those of young women whose presence as Tomasz's girlfriends highlights his impotence and inability to forge relations with anyone outside the family. And since the trio of Zdzisław, Zofia, and Tomasz occupy center stage throughout and, moreover, rarely appear outside the artist's apartment, the claustrophobia generated by their closed environment and intensified by the camerawork (Kacper Fertacz) reflects the terminal self-preoccupation of the family's two men. As one reviewer put it, "thanks to inventive camerawork, mesmeric performances and incisive yet elliptical editing and storytelling, the claustrophobia becomes a feature [of the portrayed lives] instead of a liability."[16] We witness the problems of the Beksińskis' "heated, hermetic existence."[17]

As in *Silent Night*, so here the woman is the glue, the go-between, the cook, cleaner, and comforter. In fact, she learns to drive only to transport her self-absorbed husband and is the sole parent to struggle for meaningful interaction with, and understanding of, their self-destructive son. In a telling episode she asks Tomasz why he feels compelled to treat as he does those who love him, whereas her husband merely contents himself with ironic and irrelevant comments in response to his son's physical violence, loud ranting, and overwrought raving. Adam Kruk in his review for *Kino* notes that "the entire life of the family is organized around the men, their needs, their shifts in mood, and their obsessions" (całe życie familijne organizowane jest wokół mężczyzn, ich potrzeb, wahań nastrojów, obsesji).[18] His astute critique accurately pinpoints the mother's role in the film, the gender politics of which may be generalized across multiple Polish films released in the last two decades:

> For extinguishing smaller and larger conflagrations—let alone laundering, cooking, and even driving—the one responsible is Zofia, [. . .] who endures

everything submissively. Only occasionally does a grimace of tiredness and pain appear on her face. One can say that she carries her cross with dignity— why, she's the only one of the trio to display evidence of religiousness. But she's not in a position to influence either her husband or her son with it, for their attention is directed at their own egos. As the title puts it,

Tomek [Tomasz] will not continue the family line—this will be the last family.[19]

Remarking on the mysteries in the film, Tadeusz Sobolewski lists Zdzisław's art and his murder, Tomasz's psychology, and finally his marriage to Zofia—a "placid, positive [religious] believer," so radically different from him as to make one wonder how they ever came together.[20] Another reviewer notes how she is a "shadow carrying the entire family on her shoulders."[21]

Zofia, in fact, is convenient for the artist: gulping down antidepressants, she performs all household tasks, including in Tomasz's apartment, drives her husband wherever necessary, and when Tomasz cannot cope with a young woman who is interested in him but whom he cannot satisfy, calms him down by taking care of the problem. Mariology and martyrology unite in Zofia. Tellingly, after her death, which precedes Zdzisław's by seven years, nothing changes in the widower's routine; simply, paid professionals replace his wife in cleaning the apartment as he continues producing his artworks. What does one make of a husband whose immediate response upon discovering his spouse dead on the kitchen floor is to film her body with the camcorder that he constantly uses to document his life and surroundings? Not grief, but the desire to augment materials for posterity that will eventually feed into his biography and published interviews takes precedence over all else.

At first glance, Tomasz seems the more neurotic of the two men, given to hysterical outbursts, unprovoked violence (at one point he trashes the kitchen that his mother has just spent hours putting it in order), shouting and screaming instead of speaking. His huge success as a DJ and translator from English, as well as his critical sensitivity to his father's art, does not influence his psychological disorder, which leads to unbridled fits of frenzy and repeated attempts at suicide. Yet Zdzisław's temperament may strike many viewers as a potent, albeit unacknowledged, factor in his son's chronic mental upheaval. Outwardly calm, given to ironic quips, and seemingly disturbed at nothing around him, Zdzisław shows no evidence of caring about anything but his art and himself. Physically present, he is psychologically absent, intent on the classical music that inspires his art, his projects, and his future in the annals of creativity. His international reputation and unchallenged status in the family as the patriarchal "Important Man"[22] may well account, if only partially, for his son's impotence. Moreover, the sadomasochistic fantasies—of rape and being pleasurably brutalized by a female less than half his age—revealed during the interview that opens and closes the film, suggests that he entertains deranged scenarios but, unlike his son, controls his noxious desires instead of succumbing to them. Two of the most repellent sequences in the film, however, underscore their similarity. In the first, we witness Zdzisław, "an inelegant, frequently boorish type,"[23] sitting at the kitchen counter, messily and greedily shoving food into his mouth, accompanied by his breezy, nonchalant admission, "I eat like a pig." The second takes place after Zofia's death, when the two men wolf down their food in an identical fashion. Whereas Tomasz's epic egotism combines with a death wish, however, Zdzisław's creates an impenetrable, self-protective shell. Nothing seems to disturb him, including Tomasz's obsession with suicide: he merely requests that his son delay the next attempt until after Zofia's death, does not discourage him, and makes no effort to thwart Tomasz's finally successful self-administered death by reaching him in time to save him. Opaque, indifferent to everything but his art, and grotesquely cheerful regardless of ominous events at his very side, Zdzisław remains inaccessible not only to his family but also to the film's viewers.

What does emerge clearly in what some commentators have interpreted as an apocalyptic narrative is the dark omnipresence of death in the Beksiński family, ever hovering over them.[24] While Tomasz's genuine efforts to kill himself repeatedly fail, in a sequence based on real experience, he is one of the few people to walk away unharmed from a disastrous airplane crash landing that leaves one person dead and several seriously injured. Otherwise, all genuine fatalities, which, given the temporal compression in the film, seem to pile up rapidly, belong to the Beksiński clan. Accompanied by Zdzisław's caustic, unemotional wisecracks, his mother-in-law and mother (both living with the family and, of course, tended to by Zofia) die in quick succession, followed by Zofia (1998), Tomasz (1999), and last of all, the artist himself, who is mysteriously murdered in his own home. All but Tomasz expire in the apartment that serves as a psychological prison of sorts for all but the artist, who thrives in his "study cum studio," equipped with stereo, camera, computer, canvases, camcorder, and all the accoutrements that appear to mean more to him than the human beings living with him. If the family appears blighted, then its cynosural figure of the artist may well be the source and sustenance of that blight, which appears as the family curse.

It requires little effort to align the function of maternity in *Silent Night* and *The Last Family* with the clichéd paradigm of the Polish Matka Polka/ Boska and the dolorous model of gospels-based motherhood proposed by Julia Kristeva in her essay "Stabat Mater" (1977). Relegated to reproduction and passivity, the divine mother, according to Kristeva, lives outside of language (subjectivity), while the son obeys his father and calls upon him, not the mother who bore him, at his life's end. According to Kristeva, "there is an abyss between the mother and the child"[25] to whom she gave birth and subsequently lost to "social circumstances" that are part of what Jacques Lacan has called the Symbolic Order—a male domain. In both films, sameness and economic endeavor or cultural creativity ally the father and son, to which the biological capacities of the mother, mired in domesticity, are subordinated and rendered irrelevant once he reaches adulthood. Such a scenario, however, represents only one of many and more differentiated portrayals of motherhood in recent Polish films.

LIFE AS PSYCHODRAMA OR MATERNAL DEATH AS FAMILIAL DEMISE: *33 SCENY Z ŻYCIA* (33 SCENES FROM LIFE 2008), MAŁGORZATA SZUMOWSKA[26]

Whereas Teresa's death in *The Last Family* finally prompts her son to acknowledge her importance to him and to mourn her, while her husband accepts it with startling external equanimity, Szumowska's (b. 1973) breakthrough fourth feature examines the devastation wrought by loss of the mother for both spouse and offspring in a similarly creative family. Perhaps the difference in perspective springs from the gender of the two directors. By contrast to Matuszyński's male-focused narrative, Szumowska's is thoroughly gynocentric. Loosely based on the female director's own struggle with the loss of her famous parents,[27] the film spotlights the centrality of the mother and the significance of her death for her two daughters as well as her husband. Unlike *The Last Family*, *33 Scenes from Life* starts by showing the loving conviviality of a two-generational, close-knit family of artists in Kraków: the mother-writer, Barbara (Małgorzata Hajewska); the father, Jurek, a documentary filmmaker (Andrzej Hudziak); their favored daughter, Julia, a successful photographer (Julia Jentsch); her sister, Kaśka (Iza Kuna), and her fiancé-priest, Tomek (Rafał Maćkowiak). Also present are Julia's husband, Piotr (Maciej Stuhr), a composer much in demand and therefore often abroad. While not a blood relative, Julia's technologically savvy coworker, Adrian (Peter Gantzler), is integrated into the collective, thus a regular at such gatherings. Bonded by affection and responsiveness to one another's work, the talented group enjoys lively dinners as they share reminiscences and their latest news amid laughter, teasing, and the sort of fond interplay common within intimate circles.

This happy image of a supportive, flourishing family, which regularly convenes at the parents' country home, suffers a fatal blow when Barbara is diagnosed with cancer and soon requires hospitalization. To communicate the dire significance of this event for her spouse and offspring, Szumowska dwells for a prolonged period on often grotesque humor as a defense mechanism beside her hospital bed that indexes the shock and disorientation of her family at the inevitable eventuality of her death. Briefly allowed home for Christmas, she and her worsening condition prompt Jurek's highly emotional, inebriated response to the awkwardly placed Christmas tree onto which he displaces his fear and anger at what is all too obviously a terminal illness. That hysterical sequence foreshadows his total collapse after her funeral.

Barbara, however, is no Teresa. A highly successful author of detective fiction, she is opinionated, stubborn, and not noticeably domestic (not she, but Julia prepares the meal for the large family gathering). Barbara's relationship with her spouse, daughters, and their partners seems strong but not dependent on any qualities identified with the Matka Polka/Boska stereotype of maternity. Even on what clearly will be her deathbed she exhibits a mordant wit and a formidable will; significantly, despite her cancer, she takes a long time to die, for, a doctor notes, she possesses a strong heart.[28] Remote though her image is from that of diffident mother-as-nurturer-and-peacemaker unambiguously installed in *Silent Night* and *The Last Family*, her crucial role in the family is equally unassailable and stems from her intellectual vigor and staunch self-confidence.

Just as death attends the Beksiński family, here it analogously is introduced early, with the disappearance of Barbara's beloved dog, Mrówa—a moment that sounds a dissonant note in the carefree happiness as the assembled dinner group in the countryside stroll and delight in nature. Mrówa's sudden, unexpected death soon afterward[29] prefigures Barbara's, all too quickly followed by that of her shattered, alcoholic husband from heart failure after he returns from the detox procedure to which Julia and Adrian commit him. Editing ensures the rapidity with which these three deaths seem to succeed one another. Indeed, Tadeusz Sobolewski in his review remarks, "they had just been sitting at table in the countryside and watching the falling stars, when immediately afterwards they meet in the hospital" (dopiero co siedzieli przy stole na wsi i oglądali spadające gwiazdy, a zaraz potem spotykają sie w szpitalu).[30] Not immediately, in fact, because Szumowska inserts the motif of mortality between those two episodes via Mrówa's death. From the start both Barbara and Mrówa experience a lack of appetite; in her argument with Jurek about her health, the dog's death and the possibility of Barbara's having cancer are linked by their inclusion in the same sentence as Barbara strenuously resists Jurek's worried insistence that she consult a doctor. Once Jurek returns home from his detoxification, editing again suggests that he dies almost immediately afterward.

All these irretrievable losses demolish the psychological bulwark of Julia's world and mark the end of her childhood, marriage, and sense of self. The photographs that she devises for the biennale—a computer-generated redesign of her mother's tumors—get rejected. Though Piotr flies back home during emergencies, he continues to work with an orchestra in Cologne for lengthy periods. On a larger scale, the mother's death provokes the disintegration of the family and the degradation of moral values: Jurek drinks uncontrollably, Kaśka disappears, Julia, unable to cope, turns to Adrian, the family friend about whose sexual orientation she and Piotr had laughingly speculated during happier times. With Piotr abroad and both parents gone forever, the anchorless Julia, ironically, ends up having sex with Adrian and essentially burying her marriage, for at film's end she chooses the ever-present and reliable Adrian (a father figure) over the loving but frequently absent Piotr.[31] Yet Julia's tragedy, as in Greek drama, vouchsafes anagnorisis (ἀναγνώρισις)—the decisive insight to which the action has moved. Here, in the final sequence, she admits to Adrian that she wished to remain forever a child vis-à-vis her father, mother, and Piotr—and the final shot is of Julia alone on the bed she has just shared with Adrian, glimpsed through large windows, facing an uncertain future in which life has forced her to become an adult. As Konrad Zarębski points out, she feels the need for a completely new beginning.[32] *33 Scenes* essentially documents what the ethnographer Arnold van Gennep defined as a rite of passage structuring one's development from birth to death, with the transition from one status to another frequently entailing a psychological crisis.[33] The funerals of the parents in the film mark Julia's belated passage from child to adult.

The film emphasizes the mother's significance by means not only of plot, whereby the mother's death leads to the unraveling of other family members' lives, but also of two scenes linked through verbal repetition. Shortly before Barbara dies, she whispers, "Mummy, Mummy" (*Mamusiu, Mamusiu*), the identical words uttered by Julia after her death. That parallelism suggests the trauma universally entailed in loss of the mother, to which pertain Adrian's frequent responses to Julia's questions, which also are the last words he speaks and which close the film: "I don't know" (*Nie wiem*). Though Adrian is replying to her query whether he will wait for her if she manages to cope psychologically by moving into her parents' apartment, taking care of the (second) dog, and traveling abroad, in a more profound sense he articulates the existential uncertainty vis-à-vis life, death, and the wholly unpredictable consequences of losing forever those who originally gave us life—mothers. It is no coincidence that Szumowska in an interview accentuated the universality of her story, for the rite of passage through which Julia suffers awaits everyone.[34]

THE FRAGILE MALE EGO: *MILOŚĆ*
(LOVE 2012), SŁAWOMIR FABICKI[35]

In all of my films, the men are weaker than the women. Even the
mayor's wife [in *Miłość*] is stronger than her husband.

—Sławomir Fabicki in interview

Daring in its choice of a long-tabooed topic and its absence of extradiegetic
music, Fabicki's (b. 1970) second feature, *Love*, does not center on maternity, yet is notable for contrasting three strong mothers with three ineffectual
fathers—ineffectual in appreciably different ways.[36] Inspired by a bona fide
case in Olsztyn that came to court, *Love* dramatizes the devastating aftermath
of a rape committed by Adam (Adam Woronowicz), the popular mayor of an
unspecified town. The victim is his pregnant junior colleague, Maria (Julia
Kijowska), with whom he is obsessed, and transpires in the apartment she
shares with her architect-husband, Tomek (Marcin Dorociński). Maria delays
telling Tomek of the violation until after their baby, Ilona, is born, and does
so under duress, after which most of the film traces his evolving reactions to
what has happened. At the same time, Tomek has to confront the fact that
his mother (Dorota Kolak), undergoing chemotherapy for cancer, is fading.
Her death occurs shortly before Ilona's christening at the film's conclusion.

Parental and spousal roles are inextricable in the film. That the mayor's
wife (Agata Kulesza), who remains nameless, stays with her husband after
learning of the rape defies explanation until Tomek calls upon the couple at
their home. During his uninvited visit to Maria and Tomek's apartment, while
pleading with her to marry him, Adam vows to divorce his wife, claiming that
their marriage has been empty for a long time. Yet he clearly has confessed to
his wife about the rape and it is she who deals with the enraged Tomek, while
Adam retreats to his study. Handing Tomek the 100,000 złoty (approximately
$25,000) intended to compensate for the rape, she requests that thereafter he
leave them alone. Above all, what greets Tomek upon entering the house
clarifies the difficulty of her situation: the couple's handicapped son instantly
races up to him, throws his arms around him, and keeps hugging him, resisting his mother's efforts to separate him from their visitor, while the mayor
plays no part in the awkward scene. In short, she takes care of not only her
husband's problems but also their son's, and though it may be excessive to
interpret this sequence as the boy's longing for a father other than his own, it
is telling that no interaction occurs between Adam and his offspring throughout Tomek's brief stay. Responsibility for the uncomprehending boy and for
ensuring the family's well-being remains solely hers, not unlike Zofia's in
The Last Family and Teresa's in *Silent Night*.

Though in a dissimilar mode, Maria also demonstrates maternal concern under harrowing circumstances. Immediately after the assault, she calls her gynecologist to ensure that nothing has imperiled her baby's viability. Once Ilona is born, she concentrates on (breast)feeding her, taking her for walks, and providing all the care that the baby might need. Initially, Tomek offers loving support to both, but once his suspicions about Maria's complicity in the rape take hold, he starts sleeping in his office, and she alone remains the constant parent. Tomek prefers to forget that when, at the film's start, Maria tells him that Adam's appreciation of her is not purely professional, he brushes her unease aside, for her job facilitates his acquisition of contracts. His dismissal of her disquiet now transforms into resentment of her relations with her boss, which he increasingly interprets as her betrayal of their marriage. As his outrage at Adam modulates to rage and suspicions directed at Maria and displaced onto others, he enacts the Inquisitor with her, moves out, comes and goes as he pleases, questions Ilona's paternity, engages in a one-night stand with a stranger he picks up at a bar, and, at one point, strikes Maria. As Tadeusz Sobolewski incisively sums up the situation, "The husband nurtures a jealousy that springs from his inferiority complex. He assumes the mask of a macho whose honor has been wounded, but his uncertainty manifests itself in the unexpected admission of weakness: 'I couldn't believe that you wanted to be with me.' "[37] Irrational, insecure, and wallowing in self-pity, Tomek views the rape as an attack on him, and offers his wife scant comfort and understanding, informing her that he possibly no longer loves her. As one reviewer succinctly puts it, he acts "like the victim and the hangman."[38] Only toward the end does he reveal the underlying cause of his behavior: when he proposed, he found it difficult to believe that she would accept him as a husband. "Tomek [. . .] doesn't understand why his beautiful wife could actually love him. He's not at home in his own skin," Fabicki noted.[39] In another interview, he described Tomek as "introverted, insecure . . . a very unlikeable, egoistic guy," whereas his wife possesses "emotional wisdom" (mądrość emocionalną) and maturity of character.[40] In other words, she bears the burden of his self-doubts.

Again, the viewer may well ask why Maria not only stays with him but also makes several generous overtures that ultimately lead to their tentative reconciliation. The title provides the answer, albeit an incomplete one. Throughout, the film corroborates Maria's superiority to Tomek in various contexts: her professional success outstrips his; she copes with the rape better than he; unlike him, she never resorts to violence as a mode of misplaced retaliation; and when his father (Marian Dziędziel) telephones to announce his wife's imminent death, Maria not only insists that all three of them go to her, but upon their arrival, unlike Tomek and his father, soothes the dying woman by lying beside her, softly humming and murmuring words of reassurance. Where Tomek crumbles under pressure, she shows resilience and constancy as wife and mother, and it is probable that, quite apart from loving Tomek, she accepts the diminished nature of their marriage so that in the future Ilona will have the benefit of two parents.

Not unlike Domalewski's *Silent Night, Love* exposes weakness as a patrilinear flaw. The three sequences consisting of Tomek's visits to his parents' apartment establish the mother as the insightful, down-to-earth spouse all too aware of how little time she has left in this world. When Tomek first stops by, she instantly deduces by his appearance that he is not living at home, and sends her husband to make tea so that she can have a frank conversation alone with their son. Rightly dismissing the latter's meaningless words of pseudo-comfort regarding her terminal illness, she is even capable of indulging in humor. As Fabicki commented in an interview, "Tomek is feeble. His mother has the power over him, she takes care of him and she makes the decisions."[41] By contrast, the father seems at sea, as also during the deathbed scene, when he simply stands by helplessly as his wife of many decades lies moaning weakly during her last moments until Maria takes control. Above all, after her death, instead of turning up at Ilona's christening, he sits at home until Tomek is forced to fetch him, whereupon he declares himself incapable of joining them in church. Yet the next minute he confesses his happiness that his wife finally died, without adding that he experiences relief because her sufferings are over. Is he glad, then, because *his* sufferings have ended? Does his reaction to her cancer parallel his son's to Maria's rape?

As in the reversal dominating *Mother to Her Own Mother*, discussed below, the offspring takes care of the parent, or, rather, Tomek takes care of his father, persuading him to accompany him to church, where Maria has been waiting in uncertainty. Presumably, as a widower, hereafter he will play a greater role in the life of Tomek's family, though he will not demonstrate the perspicacity and emotional empathy that his wife showed to their son. By contrast, the matrilinear continuity in *Love* operates in a strikingly positive mode. A daughter-in-law rather than a daughter, Maria has no hesitation, despite the deterioration of her marriage, in easing her mother-in-law's last minutes, and her ministrations prove effective. Moreover, as in *33 Scenes from Life*, the dying woman calls, not upon God or her husband, but upon her mother, with the iteration of "Mamusiu . . ."—the exact words uttered by Teresa in Szumowska's film.

THE BIOLOGY TRAP: *MATKA SWOJEJ MATKI* (MOTHER TO HER OWN MOTHER 1996), ROBERT GLIŃSKI

> Duty is what one expects from others, it is not what one does oneself.
>
> —Oscar Wilde

Anyone familiar with Simone de Beauvoir's watershed feminist tract, *Le Deuxième sexe* (The Second Sex 1949), translated into Polish (*Druga płeć* 1972) and published in two editions,[42] would be struck by its delayed influence on (or convergence with) the progressive line in post-socialist Polish cinema. For the purposes of my discussion of recent films delving into maternity, I find it productive to analyze the relevance of her chapter titled "The Mother" in Part V of her book, under the subtitle "Situation," to three contentious films about motherhood that dramatically depart from the officially promulgated Polish stereotype rooted in the legacy of the Virgin Mary. One of the numerous entrenched clichés that have ruled precepts of maternity is the sanctity of the unquestioned biological tie between mother and daughter. Collectively, the three films I analyze below demolish such a bromide in no uncertain terms.[43]

One of the several reversals dramatized in *33 Scenes from Life* is the standard situation of offspring becoming their parents' caretakers or "parents" when age, disease (Barbara), or drunkenness (Jurek) incapacitates the older generation. Gliński's (b. 1952) entire *Mother to Her Own Mother*, as the title conveys, explores such a *volte-face*, though in unusual circumstances that generate additional complications. By now the discovery that propels most of the film's actions has become hackneyed through numerous dramatizations on the big and little screen: an aspiring nineteen-year-old violinist, Alicja (Maria Seweryn),[44] who idolizes her veterinarian-mother, Barbara (Joanna Żółkowska),[45] with whom she enjoys a sunny, loving relationship, accidently comes upon an official document attesting that she was adopted. Shocked, enraged, and curious, she seeks out her biological mother, Ewa (Krystyna Janda), an amoral "down and out" alcoholic deadbeat given to casual sex and living in what is essentially a hovel. Ewa takes material and psychological advantage of Alicja's naïve generosity, financially facilitated by the mother who reared her. A singer cum swinger, the damaged, volatile Ewa exploits Alicja, who keeps returning to her and trying to "help" her, while also wondering why she gave her up for adoption. Finally, the neglected and jealous Barbara, determined to reclaim her beloved adopted daughter and save her from Ewa's relentless machinations, shoots her. The last sequence shows the adoptive mother and now restored, appreciative daughter, bonded as before, meeting in the prison where Barbara is in custody. Intertitles that follow inform the viewer of the three women's subsequent fates: Barbara receives a two-year suspended sentence, Ewa survives and after three months is released from hospital, while Alicja is accepted (presumably at Julliard) in New York, where she continues her studies.

Mother to Her Own Mother amply illustrates de Beauvoir's conviction that "no maternal 'instinct' exists."[46] If the film wishes to comment on offspring's conflict between an adoptive and a biological mother, then it blatantly stacks the cards in favor of the adoptive mother in an overly simplistic fashion. Barbara is wealthy, successful, balanced, extremely affectionate, and ready to sacrifice herself for her beloved daughter. And scene after scene hyperbolically contrasts the unbalanced, suicidal, embarrassingly raucous Ewa to this icon of maternity. If a biological mother beckons straightforwardly through the body, Ewa's is the abject body in Julia Kristeva's sense, for she repeatedly violates its borders through hysterical tears and "disrupts the wish for physical self-control and social propriety"—nowhere more vividly than in her unruly, scandalous behavior at Alicja's graduation party (an event structured by social conventions) and at the beach, where she draws her biological daughter into her sphere of uncontrolled physicality.[47] Not only her body but also her clothes convey Ewa's violation of propriety, which is why Barbara's disconsolate realization of her daughter's confusion of loyalties prompts her briefly to mimic Ewa's image—drinking and sitting in an inviting, challenging position, sporting a gaudy outfit and cheap jewelry instead of her habitual low-key suits. Ewa's abjection is as visible as Barbara's tasteful restraint. On both visual and characterological levels, a less primitive treatment of the choice between the two mothers would have endowed Ewa with at least some redeeming traits instead of reducing her to a near-parody of a self-obsessed, parasitical, (self-)destructive hysteric with an intransitive mode of interaction. The facile disparity between a mother willing to do anything for her daughter and one prepared to do anything *to* her out of selfishness hardly yields a thoughtful, let alone complex, treatment of a genuine dilemma.

Furthermore, despite excellent acting and the bravura performance of Janda, who recently has assumed several maternal roles (in *The Reverse* and *Elles*) and appeared as a grandmother in Jacek Borcuch's *Dolce fine giornata* (2019), the scenario suffers from a number of unconvincing turns in the plot. Notably, it is difficult to credit Alicja's overly rapid withdrawal from the woman who brought her up in seemingly ideal circumstances for nineteen years in favor of an obnoxious, capricious drunk. Secondly, the marriage proposal of Roman (Jerzy Stuhr), an old acquaintance of Ewa's from whom she parted decades ago, almost immediately upon their chance encounter at a cemetery, challenges credulity. So does Alicja's claim that she and the young guitar player, whom Ewa calls her boyfriend but who dubs her a monster (*potwór*), are in love, having spent the night together on the beach? Finally, Barbara's violent attempt to eliminate her sponger-rival culminates in the roster of implausible developments. According to Gliński, he intended to investigate emotional vandalism in "a story about stealing feelings." Responding to this characterization of the film by its director, Jacek Szczerba justifiably objects, "The triangle of daughter, adoptive mother, and biological mother is awkwardly put together, so to extricate themselves from the situation somehow, in the finale the filmmakers had to reach for a completely incongruous pistol which goes off like Chekhov's gun."[48] Chekhov argued something else, however: that a weapon on the wall early in the action should go off by a work's conclusion, whereas Ewa's gun materializes with a startling suddenness as a *prop ex machina* shortly before the film ends.

A regrettable aspect of *Mother to Her Own Mother* is its poor use of Wanda Wiłkomirska (1929–2018), a formidable world-renowned violinist, pedagogue, and cosmopolitan recipient of many international awards. That she agreed to assume the role of Alicja's music professor was quite a coup for Gliński. How puzzling, then, that the script has her articulate a predictable cliché: Alicja's violin-playing early in the film elicits from her the trite comment that she plays correctly, but without soul and especially heart. Countless such situations encountered in cinema and on TV lead the viewer to anticipate that after all her travails with the two mothers, Alicja's performance toward the film's end will prompt her teacher's endorsement of her playing now as— yes, "from the heart." And that is precisely the judgment that Wiłkomirska delivers. Such bathos does little to rescue the film from its replay of familiar situations and avoidance of all complexity.

Ultimately, the film embraces the consoling formula of "all's well that ends well." Rather than tackling the complicated relationship between a biological mother and one who adopts a child because of her inability to have one (which Barbara identifies as her case), the narrative via Alicja facilely opts for the "good mother" (a Matka Polka/Boska for the first three-quarters of the film) instead of the "bad mother" (insufferable throughout). Since the birth mother here, as the young guitarist on the beach remarks, is a "monster," biology ultimately falls by the wayside. Perhaps the best that may be said of the film is that it rejects an essentialist (biological) concept of positive motherhood while trying to install it, if in modified form, in the self-sacrificing and ever-loving adoptive mother, who embodies the Polish cliché of ideal maternity.

MURDEROUS MATERNITY: *SYN KRÓLOWEJ ŚNIEGU* (SON OF THE SNOW QUEEN 2017/2018), ROBERT WICHROWSKI

If *Mother to Her Own Mother* demythologizes the sanctity of biological maternal love by dramatizing parental abandonment and subsequent instrumentalization, Wichrowski's (1966) *Son of the Snow Queen*, which received deservedly blistering reviews,[49] surpasses the previous film by its uncompromising annihilation of the Polish Marian paradigm. Based on real events that shook Poland in 2001, the plot revolves around the single mother Anna (Michalina Olszańska) and the titular son, Marcin (Maciej Bożek). A normal boy who not only lacks a father but also wears large glasses that alienate him from other children in his kindergarten, he yearns for affection and unwittingly proves a hindrance to her. While Anna leaves the house to work or simply to enjoy herself, her kind landlady, Zofia (Anna Seniuk), from whom she rents a room, and Kazimierz, the old, retired writer next door (Franciszek Pieczka), take care of Marcin. Frustrated and narcissistic, Anna finally loses patience, not to mention all sense of morals, and has Kamil (Rafał Fudalej), the long-suffering young man smitten with her, and a new acquaintance (Robert Czebotar) kill the boy.

The title's reference to the Hans Christian Andersen's famous tale of "The Snow Queen" (1844) and Kazimierz's reading from it at the film start prepare one for the bleakness of the narrative, but Wichrowski fails to make the most of the prior text.[50] The Danish writer's Snow Queen is not a mother but a cold-blooded evildoer associated with remoteness and snow who spirits away to her icy palace children whom she essentially abandons to eternal isolation. Andersen's tale focuses on two orphans—the boy Kay, whom she carries off to her kingdom, and Gerda, his neighboring closest friend, who rescues him after sundry encounters on route to the Snow Queen's domain. Finally, the couple safely return home, unexpectedly matured into adulthood. Essentially the tale certifies the power of warmhearted love and fearless loyalty.

Wichrowski's dispassionate, self-involved Anna shares the Snow Queen's emotional indifference, and one could argue that Kazimierz, whose backyard recreates an Andersen fairytale world into which he initiates the impressionable boy, approximates Gerda's role, inasmuch as he is fond of Marcin and after the murder joins him posthumously in the Andersen paradise that is his attic. That fantastic conclusion, as well as a glimpse of Anna decked out as the Snow Queen preceding it, however, seems arbitrary and tacked on to a narrative that develops in a strictly realistic key. Moreover, as one reviewer objected, Marcin functions "merely as an object that catalyzes Anna's toxic emotions" (pełni on [. . .] funkcję przedmiotową. Jest wyłącznie katalizatorem toksycznych emocji Anny),[51] and rarely appears as a bona fide living and breathing being, for the director's primary interest lies in Anna.

Anna perfectly demonstrates de Beauvoir's argument against the preconception that "maternity is enough in all cases to crown a woman's life," and Anna harbors not "an unavowed hostility," but an explicit dislike of her son, who "by no means provides that happy self-fulfillment which has been promised her since her childhood."[52] According to Anna, Marcin is the result of rape, though, as a chronic liar, she also offers another version of his paternity, and what the film reveals about Anna's character might well elicit viewers' surprise that she carried the resultant pregnancy through to term. Why she decided to have the child remains a question not only unanswered but not even asked. "Neither the director nor the screenwriter even tries to fathom the protagonists' motivations,"[53] for the film prefers to remain on the surface, tracing actions without delving into what lies behind them. Quite simply, the dishonest, manipulative Anna finds her seven-year-old son nothing but a burden that she endlessly criticizes and habitually passes on to Zofia and Kazimierz, who care for him and strive to compensate for her neglect. Early in the film, Kamil's religious mother calls Anna "ambulatory evil" (*chodzące zło*), and whereas at that point her judgment seems exaggerated, ultimately it proves accurate. What engages bottle-blonde Anna is window-shopping, her "romance" with Kamil, and undressing for photograph sessions with her new acquaintance—the cynical pedophile who assists in Marcin's murder and burial in the woods.[54] Presumably, Anna-mother as "a discontented woman"[55] envisions a more exciting life of irresponsible pleasure without the boy, who at one stage pathetically asks permission of Kamil to call him Dad (*tato*) occasionally when Kamil picks him up at kindergarten (something Anna never condescends to do) so that his classmates will believe that he belongs to a "normal" family.

Yet one sequence shows the usually callous Anna being kind and affectionate with Marcin. After their visit to the optometrist, who explains that the myopic boy needs stronger glasses before he undergoes laser surgery, mother and son appear to have a genuine exchange as they start heading homeward. She smiles, reassures him, and even ruffles his hair. Wichrowski's inclusion of this unique illustration of Anna's maternal potential is inconsistent and puzzling, all the more because soon afterwards she simply announces to Kamil that they need to get rid of her son ("Musimy jego się pozbyć"). And after taking him to a fairground and ensuring that he enjoys himself, that is precisely what they do: while Anna sits in a van determinedly gazing straight ahead and Marcin cries out, "Mamo!" Kamil and the photographer strangle and suffocate him in the rear of the vehicle, then bury him once darkness falls. As the credits begin to roll, an intertitle informs viewers that between 2007 and 2016, 215 children were murdered in Poland, while the English subtitle states that 143 children's homicides occurred between 2011 and 2016.

Poland, of course, is not unique in this regard, and the numbers in the United States are significantly higher.[56] The Polish statistics may be accurate, but, unlike American reports, they do not specify who committed the tabulated murders—strangers? relatives? parents? Whatever the case, in a Catholic country that for centuries has deified the mother as both family custodian and symbol of the nation, a woman's calculated, pitiless extermination of her own child must have shocked viewers. Bold in his decision to dramatize such a heinous act, Wichrowski, who cowrote the script with Paweł Sala, unfortunately, fell short of exploring the intricate psychological motives that could lead to it.

À LA RECHERCHE DU TEMPS PERDU: *FUGA* (FUGUE 2018), AGNIESZKA SMOCZYŃSKA

Fugue: a state or period of loss of awareness of one's identity, often
coupled with flight from one's usual environment, associated with certain
forms of hysteria and epilepsy.

Nothing could be more remote from Smoczyńska's (b. 1978) likewise Andersen-indebted cinematic debut, *The Lure* (2015), than her psychologically intense, realistic *Fugue*, which shares the earlier film's gynocentrism. Fueled by the dissociative disorder called fugue from which the female protagonist, Alicja (Gabriela Muskała), suffers, the film dramatizes her inability to access the past and establish a meaningful connection with her family, comprising her husband, son, and parents.[57]

Few films open with a sequence that matches *Fugue* in the capacity to startle viewers and pique their curiosity—hence reviewers' sundry labels of "mystery," "psychological thriller," "psychodrama/melodrama," "a Scandinoir inflected drama," and "a relationship drama" for the film's genre.[58] A blonde with shoulder-length hair, well-dressed and in stiletto heels, is filmed from the rear within a dark tunnel. In a noticeably discombobulated state, staggering along unidentified railroad tracks, she arrives at a Warsaw station, then proceeds to scramble up onto the platform, crouch, and urinate. Two years pass, and, having assaulted a policeman, she reappears as a casually dressed brunette with a rough manner, questioned unavailingly by a psychiatrist-case worker, Michał (Piotr Skiba), at a hospital. As we subsequently learn, her identity remains unknown, for she has no memory until a TV talk show publicizes her photograph, urging viewers to call in if they recognize her. A man claiming to be her father (Zbigniew Walerys) responds, identifying her as Kinga, a married woman with a son. Why, one may wonder, has her spouse not tried to find her or answered the appeal? When Michał drives her from Warsaw to Wrocław, where she lives, Smoczyńska's long tracking shot on the highway suggests the psychological distance Alicja has traveled in the last two years, which the following sequences confirm.

At her parents' dinner, supposedly arranged to welcome her back, we encounter her husband, Krzysztof (Łukasz Simlat), her mother (Halina Rasiakówna), her grandmother, Hanka (Lucja Burzynska), whose dementia peculiarly allies her with Alicja, and the sympathetic Michał, clearly invited to ease the occasion. Krzysztof's brother and sister-in-law have joined the group. Once the awkward meal is over, Krzysztof drives Alicja home, which is utterly alien to her, as are her husband and preschooler son, Daniel (Iwo Rajski). Indeed, Alicja's very name speaks of her alienation from her surroundings, as is true of her namesake in Lewis Carroll's *Alice in Wonderland*

(1865) and *Through the Looking Glass* (1871). That the boy calls Ewa (Malgorzata Buczkowska)—Kinga's best friend and teaching colleague— "Mother" indicates that Kinga's maternal role has been usurped and not very subtly points to Ewa's intimacy with Krzysztof. The rest of the film tracks Alicja's gradual attempts at integration into her household, at first with aggressive aversion, then with a more conciliatory attitude. Yet, even when she and Krzysztof overcome their initial mutual intolerance and go dancing after their dinner with his brother and sister-in-law, it is to Michael Gurevich's conspicuously titled "Lovers Are Strangers."[59] So are the two spouses.

As the denouement eventually reveals, Alicja's trauma-induced condition resulted from the automobile accident that occurred two years ago when she fled with Daniel upon reading the divorce papers that indicated Krzysztof's intention to keep their son with him. The accident ejected Daniel through the windshield, and examining his body led her to believe that she had killed the boy. Hence her traumatic amnesia. For most of the film, however, Alicja dwells in limbo, while both husband and son have no idea how to cope with her. After all, as Krzysztof explains to her, for him and Daniel she was dead, and as evidence he shows her the gravestone erected in her memory at the spot where she could have been killed. That revelation triggers Alicja's recovery of her memory and, in a sense, liberates her. The film concludes with her departure, for the fugue has transformed the housewife Kinga into an independent woman presumably intent on pursuing her own destiny instead of fitting into a traditional family paradigm.

Kinga and Alicja could hardly diverge more categorically. Our first glimpse of Kinga and the videos of her that we watch along with Alicja upon her return leave no doubt that she was a typically good, conventional wife and mother as deconstructed by de Beauvoir. She dressed "properly," breastfed and played with her son, smiled for the camera, and enjoyed her parents' approval, even though, as the direct, unaccommodating Alicja senses and confirms, she never loved Krzysztof. By contrast, Alicja sports short, spiky hair to match her demeanor, dresses carelessly, wears flat shoes, pants (and before she discovers them, nothing on her lower body), swears, smokes incessantly, is offhand, rough, and uninterested in pleasing anybody. Though her well-to-do parents, to whom she seems indifferent, strive to accept her, during one exchange her mother announces that she does not recognize her—a remark of which the irony in light of her daughter's circumstances escapes her, but which Alicja's riposte emphasizes.

If Alicja's frequently abrasive manner makes her unsympathetic on a number of occasions, Smoczyńska inserts two shots that elicit viewers' insight into the amnesiac's psychological dilemma. And here the camerawork plays a key role. Jakub Kijowski, who collaborated on Tomasz Wasilewski's *Płynące wieżowce* (Floating Skyscrapers 2013) and Smoczyńska's first feature, shoots most of the film in what one review accurately called "washed-out, faded colors" (w spranych, wypłowiałych kolorach)—mainly blues and browns.[60] That choice is both effective and unobtrusive, for most of the film's action takes place during a snowy winter in what for the protagonist is the dreariness of the Wrocław countryside. At one juncture those colors shift to a vivid aquamarine when we see Alicja, who is in bed, as if emerging from a watery grave—clearly, an expressive metaphor for her situation. And immediately prior to this moment an unusually bold visual of her MRI transforms into a lovely, colorful profusion of wildflowers, purple, red, pink, bright green—an extraordinary way of troping her vibrant inner world. And the introverted music of the Czech composer Filip Mišek reinforces the film's focus on Alicja's interiority.[61] Given the contrast between Kinga's bleak environment and Alicja's newly found, vivid freedom, her decision to leave the Słowik house for good seems inevitable, and it is abetted by the onset of spring, which signals resurrection, a new beginning.

In a surprisingly uncomprehending review of the film, the senior critic Andrzej Kołodyński referred to *Fugue* as "a woman's film" (film kobiecy)—a confusion of gynocentrism with a specific Hollywood genre that had its heyday in the 1930s and 1940s, on the brink of which Ewa Mazierska also teeters when discussing female directors.[62] While psychological trauma signaled by the title characterizes the protagonist, the masochism, de-eroticization, and the male gender of the director that scholarship on the genre has pinpointed simply are absent here.[63] Moreover, the association between women and home, fundamental to the genre, could hardly be more remote from Smoczyńska's film.

Fugue purposely leaves a couple of questions suspended: namely, how Alicja spent the two years in Warsaw and what her plans for the future entail. At the same time, it poses several questions to which the answers are implicit: Guy Lodge in his review asks whether Kinga was really happy, and the revelations at the film's end suggest not. Citing Hegel's dictum, "The birth of children is the death of parents," de Beauvoir notes that a woman may dread childbirth because "she fears that it will mean the loss of her own life."[64] Alicja makes that equation late. According to Artur Zaborski, the film queries whether it is possible to stop being a mother, and answers by concluding yes, if one matures into a strong, independent and self-determining woman who dispenses with the myth of "Mother Poland" for good ("wyrasta na silną, niezależną i samostanowiącą o sobie kobietę, raz na zawsze rozprawiającą się z mitem o matce Polsce"). Doubtless, even among those critics greeting the film enthusiastically at Cannes and elsewhere, some found Alicja's leaving her son a problematic choice. Smoczyńska, however, includes a sequence at the film's end of the two at play that shows Alicja's decision as hard won.

Upon preparing to depart, she seems regretful and authentically fond of the boy, having succeeded in forging an emotional link with him through play. Yet, she also knows that, having forgotten her once, he can do so again, particularly with Krzysztof's help and the "maternal" presence of Ewa as a familiar, stable substitute. Released two decades earlier, *Mother to Her Own Mother* illustrates the viability of such a scenario, in which love and steadfast support instead of biology constitute the primary prerequisites for motherhood. And, having lived for years with a man she never loved and having subordinated her life to the coercive social strictures derived from the Matka Polka/Boska ideal, Alicja opts for a potentially more fulfilling alternative.

CONCLUSION

Why do expiring women, even strong ones, in their fifties or older summon up the presumably long-vanished presence of their mothers? Of course, one may view this phenomenon as rooted in religion, specifically the thirteenth-century Christian hymn, "Stabat Mater," of Christ's sorrowful mother contemplating his death on the cross, a frequent subject of iconography. Set to music by Karol Szymanowski (1882–1937) and more than a dozen notable composers, the medieval hymn, from which Kristeva derived the title of her essay, was suppressed in the sixteenth century (by male church authorities), but restored two centuries later. It bears remembering Christ's words before he expires, according to Mark and Matthew: "My God, my God, why hast thou forsaken me?"—the ultimate Father as a model for men's inability to confront the death of their sons and mortality in general, while the Virgin Mother's presence at the crucifixion set the terms of human maternity. Such a hymn, of course, ties in with the Matka Polka/Boska paradigm embraced by Catholic Poland. Dying women's appeal to their mothers may be viewed as a secularized reclamation of the maternal mourning (Mater Dolorosa) that in the religious canon inheres in Christ's crucifixion.

Beyond that explanation, it bears remembering that over the centuries, women have been responsible for administering to the sick and dying, for supervising and enacting funeral rituals and grieving over the deceased.[65] Funeral parlors may be owned by men, but in cultures lacking such businesses, the functions attendant upon death have been shouldered by women, who wash and dress bodies, then mourn over them. Alternatively, one may ascribe women's call to the mother as an impulse to unite, at death, with the one who gave them birth. And, finally, whereas sons tend to compete with fathers, daughters identify with their mothers, as the title of the feminist Nancy Friday's *My Mother/My Self* (1977) stresses in its argument that separating themselves from their mothers is a gargantuan task for women: the subtitle of the volume reads *The Daughter's Search for Identity*. What distinguishes the three mothers in *Love* from the indomitable paragons of maternity acceding to dwell in the background is their articulate recognition of their own worth and their spouses' deficiencies, as well as their principled commitment to their children. In the case of Maria, the immemorial misogynistic identification of men with culture/mind, and women with nature/body breaks down, for she is a highly successful executive with outstanding professional skills in a competitive field.

Polish film over the last two decades has dwelled on family relations in a variety of genres: melodramas, psychological dramas, historical epics, crime narratives, and comedies.

Whereas some of the narratives have relegated the traditional self-effacing mother—the unacknowledged backbone of the family—to the background or cast her as an appendage to her spouse, in recent years, especially in films by younger directors, she has emerged at the forefront, and not always as an uncomplaining model of selflessness or even a benevolent caretaker. Such a shift implies that contemporary screen examinations of the family are no longer straitjacketed by a secular version of Matka Boska presiding over the kitchen but are willing to extend her domain to broader realms, where she may find not only self-fulfillment but also a multifaceted life that complements or even substitutes for her interactions at home.

HG

NOTES

1. Aristotle, *Poetics*, trans. Malcolm Heath (London: Penguin Books, 1996), 23.
2. William Bennett, "Stronger Families, Stronger Societies," *New York Times*, April 24, 2012, https://www.nytimes.com/roomfordebate/2012/04/24/are-family-values-outdated/stronger-families-stronger-societies. Accessed January 30, 2014.
3. One of the most infamous incidents involved Pavlik Morozov, a youth who informed on his father so as to demonstrate loyalty to the Big Family and its goals, only to be killed subsequently by his own family.
4. Marina Warner, *Alone of All Her Sex: The Myth and the Cult of the Virgin Mary* (New York: Vintage, 1983), 192.
5. On the perpetuation of this image, see Elżbieta Ostrowska, "Filmic Representations of the 'Polish Mother' in Post–Second World War Polish Cinema," *European Journal of Polish Studies* 5 (1998): 419–35 and Joanna Szwajcowska, "The Myth of the Polish Mother," in *Women in Polish Cinema*, eds. Ewa Mazierska and Elżbieta Ostrowska (New York/Oxford: Berghahn Books, 2006), 15–33. Russia likewise embraced such an iconography, which proved highly convenient for a male-centered society. For the sundry hypostases of such a religious gendered icon in

Russian culture, see *Framing Mary: The Mother of God in Modern, Revolutionary, and Post-Soviet Russian Culture,* eds. Amy Singleton Adams and Vera Shevzov (DeKalb, IL: Northern Illinois University Press, 2018).

In addition to Warner's superb study of the Marian cult (see ft. 4), which examines the subject's status as virgin, queen, bride, mother, and intercessor, a shorter thought-provoking examination is the article by Julia Kristeva, "Stabat Mater," in *The Portable Kristeva,* ed. Toril Moi (New York: Columbia University Press, 1986), 160–86.

6. And, as numerous other films evidence, a national problem.

7. Ola Salwa, "Silent Night: All Is (Not) Calm," CINEUROPA, November 23, 2017. https://cineuropa.org/en/newsdetail/342933/. Accessed December 7, 2017.

8. Artur Zaborski, *Cicha noc, Kino,* no. 11 (2017): 68.

9. The Polish word "polak" means "a Pole," but given the context and tenor of the father's pained statement, Polack seems a more suitable translation, for which the English subtitles also opt.

10. Tomasz Zacharczuk, "Mądry, dojrzały i poruszający. Recenzja filmu 'Cicha noc,' " trojmiasto.pl, November 24, 2017, https://kino.trojmiasto.pl/Zwyciezca -Zlotych-Lwow-juz-w-kinach-Recenzja-filmu-Cicha-noc-n118787.html. Accessed December 7, 2017.

11. Adam Siennica, "Cicha noc—recenzja filmu," naekranie.pl, November 24, 2017, https://naekranie.pl/recenzje/cicha-noc-recenzja-filmu-festiwal-polskich -filmow-fabularnych-gdyni. Accessed December 7, 2017.

12. Bartosz Staszczyszyn, "'Cicha noc,' reż. Piotr Domalewski," culture.pl, n.d., https://culture.pl/pl/dzielo/cicha-noc-rez-piotr-domalewski. Accessed December 7, 2017.

13. Zaborski. For a discussion of *Wesele,* see Ewa Mazierska, *Polish Postcommunist Cinema: From Pavement Level* (Bern: Peter Lang, 2007), 163–67; for brief comments on the film, see Marek Haltof, *Polish Cinema: A History* (New York and Oxford: Berghahn, 2019), second, updated edition, 405–407.

14. Amber Wilkinson, "*Silent Night,*" eyeforfilm, April 26, 2018, https://www.eye-forfilm.co.uk/review/silent-night-2017-film-review-by-amber-wilkinson. Accessed July 19, 2018.

15. The sentiment is articulated by Beksiński in an exchange with his wife late at night.

16. Leslie Felperin, "The Last Family Review—Mesmerising Portrait of a Battling Brood," *The Guardian,* December 3, 2018, https://www.theguardian.com/film/2016 /nov/03/the-last-family-review-jan-p-matuszynski-polish-film. Accessed February 4, 2019.

17. Danny King, "In Poland's 'The Last Family,' an Artist's Clan Unravels Over Decades," *The Village Voice,* January 26, 2018, https://www.villagevoice.com/2018 /01/26/in-polands-the-last-family-an-artists-clan-unravels-over-decades/. Accessed February 4, 2019.

18. Adam Kruk, "Ostatnia rodzina," *Kino,* no. 9 (2016): 69, http://kino.org.pl// index.php?option=com_content&task=view&id=2567&Itemid=1729. Accessed July 19, 2018.

19. Za gaszenie mniejszych i większych pożarów—nie mówiąc już o praniu, gotowaniu, a nawet prowadzeniu samochodu—odpowiada Zofia, która znosi wszystko z pokorą. Czasem tylko na jej twarzy pojawi się grymas zmęczenia i bólu. Można rzec, że godnie niesie swój krzyż—wszak ona jedyna w tej trójcy wykazuje oznaki religijności. Nie jest jednak w stanie zarazić nią męża czy syna, ci zwróceni są w stronę własnego ego. Jak chce tytuł, Tomek rodu nie przedłuży—to będzie ostatnia rodzina. Ibid.

20. Tadeusz Sobolewski, "Sobolewski o filmie 'Ostatnia Rodzina': To nie kryminał, tylko opowieść o miłości i depresji. Wyborcza.pl, August 5, 2016, http://wyborcza.pl/7,101707,20501550,sobolewski-o-filmie-ostatnia-rodzina-to-nie-kryminal-tylko.html. Accessed June 12, 2017.

21. Monika Małkowska, "Ostatnia rodzina. Mit wciśnięty w banal," RZECZPOSPOLITA, September 27, 2016, https://www.rp.pl/Film/309279859 -Ostatnia-rodzina-Mit-wcisniety-w-banal.html. Accessed July 19, 2017.

22. King, "In Poland's 'The Last Family.' "

23. Ibid.

24. The concept of apocalypse stems, no doubt, from the title, but also from the nature of Beksiński's Surrealist paintings and, possibly, the photographs that recently appeared online in a brief "exhibition." See "The Photography of Zdzisław Beksiński," https://culture.pl/en/video/the-photography-of-zdzislaw-beksinski-video. Accessed July 1, 2019.

25. Julia Kristeva, "Stabat Mater," in *The Portable Kristeva*, ed. Kelly Oliver (New York: Columbia University Press, 2002), 324.

26. I borrow the subtitle "Life as Psychodrama" from Tadeusz Sobolewski's review of the film in *Gazeta Wyborcza*, November 7, 2008, http://wyborcza.pl/1 ,75410,5892199,33_sceny_z_zycia_i_smierci.html. Accessed July 19, 2018.

27. Even when arguing that the autobiographical connection had no relevance for the film, critics nonetheless kept mentioning it.

28. Just as significantly, Jurek's death is attributed to his (presumably weak) heart.

29. The parallelism contains a contrast, inasmuch as Mrówa goes off to die far from her owners, whereas Barbara relies on the constant presence of the family.

30. Tadeusz Sobolewski, "33 sceny z życia i śmierci," Wyborcza.pl, November 7, 2008, http://wyborcza.pl/1,75410,5892199,33_sceny_z_zycia_i_smierci.html. Accessed July 19, 2018.

31. An American reviewer detects "an overt father fixation" in Julia, but if her investment in him may be called a fixation, then she also suffers from a mother fixation. The point is that she loves both parents and, for an adult, overly relies on them for her sense of identity and security. At the same time, he is the sole commentator to note (accurately) that "Piotr's melodic yet dissonant compositions are nicely incorporated into the soundtrack." See Jay Weissberg "33 Scenes from Life," *Variety*, August 19, 2018, https://variety.com/2008/film/reviews/33-scenes-from-life-1200507656/. December 3, 2018.

32. Konrad Zarębski, "33 ceny z życia," *Kino*, no. 11 (2008): 76, http://kino.org.pl/ /index.php?option=com_content&task=view&id=266&Itemid=214. Accessed July 19, 2018.

33. See Arnold van Gennep, *Les rites de passage* (1909).

34. Magdalena Lebecka, "Prawie psychodrama," *Kino*, no. 9 (2008): 17, http://filmotekaszkolna.pl/dla-uczniow/materialy-filmoznawcze/prawie-psychodrama. Accessed July 19, 2018.

35. For puzzling reasons translators of the English subtitles on the official DVD rendered the title as *Loving*, which Anglophone reviewers perpetuated, whereas the Polish simply means *Love*.

36. For Fabicki's life and career in cinema, see Jacek Wakar, trans. Gabriela Łazarkiewicz, Directors Guild of Poland https://polishdirectors.com/en/member_post/fabicki-slawomir/. Accessed August 18, 2018.

37. Mąż hoduje w sobie zazdrość wynikająca z kompleksu niższości. Przyjmuje maskę macho, którego honor został urażony, ale jest w nim niepewność przejawiającaja się w niespodziewanym wyznaniu słabości: "Nie mogłem uwierzyć, że chcesz być ze mną." Tadeusz Sobolewski, "'Miłość' Fabickiego: Nie wiem, czy jeszcze cię kocham," Wyborcza.pl, March 16, 2013, http://wyborcza.pl/1,75410,13570522,_Milosc__Fabickiego__Nie_wiem__czy_jeszcze_cie_kocham.html. Accessed August 18, 2018.

38. Marta Jazowska, "Loving—Sławomir Fabicki," Culture.pl, https://culture.pl/en/work/loving-slawomir-fabicki. Accessed August 18, 2018.

39. Interview with Moritz Pfeifer, *East European Film Bulletin*, 38 (February 2014), https://eefb.org/interviews/slawomir-fabicki-on-loving/?pdf=2091. Accessed August 18, 2018.

40. "Sławomir Fabicki—Loving—Video Interview," Culture.pl, https://culture.pl/en/video/slawomir-fabicki-loving-video-interview. Accessed August 18, 2019.

41. Ibid.

42. Translated in 1972 by Gabryela Mycielska and Maria Leśniewska, de Beauvoir's book underwent a second Polish edition in 2003 (pub. Jacek Jantorski & Co.).

43. Sylwia Karolak has written insightfully about Polish women's prose that confronts the "complicated, often difficult and painful relations between mothers and daughters." All the mothers are Jewesses and Holocaust survivors in families without fathers. See Sylwia Karolak, "Utwory o matkach i córkach: kobiece narracje postmemorialne," *Politeja*, no. 35 (2015): 171–88.

44. She is the real-life daughter of Krystyna Janda and Andrzej Seweryn.

45. Żółkowska is the film's screenwriter and the director's wife. In other words, *Matka swojej matki* is a true behind-the-scenes family affair.

46. Simone de Beauvoir, *The Second Sex*, trans. H.M. Parshley (New York: Vintage Books, 1989), 511.

47. See Julia Kristeva, *Powers of Horror: An Essay on Abjection*, trans. By Leon S. Roudiez (New York: Columbia University Press, 1982). Specific citation from Sara Beardsworth, *Julia Kristeva: Psychoanalysis and Modernity* (New York: SUNY Press, 2004), https://www.sunypress.edu/pdf/61009.pdf. Accessed November 1, 2007.

48. Jacek Szczerba, *Gazeta Wyborcza*, October 23, 1996, cited in Małgorzata Fiejdasz, "Robert Gliński," culture.pl, August 2007/May 2011, https://culture.pl/en/artist/robert-glinski. Accessed March 2, 2018.

49. The accompanying material to the DVD quotes from the few positive reviews, by Jacek Cieślak, Anna Krajkowska, and Maciej Misiorny.

50. As one reviewer put it, "Where's the Fairy Tale?" (Gdzie jest baśń?). See Martyna Halbiniak, "Okruch lodu w sercu. 'Syn Królowej Śniegu'—recenzja filmu," *Ostatnia Tawerna*, January 31, 2018, https://ostatniatawerna.pl/okruch-lodu-w-sercu -syn-krolowej-sniegu-recenzja-filmu/. Accessed March 2, 2018.

51. Marcin Pietrzyk, "Matka-szmatka i inne bajki," FILMWEB, January 22, 2018, https://www.filmweb.pl/review/Matka-szmatka+i+inne+bajki-20986. Accessed March 2, 2018.

52. de Beauvoir, *The Second Sex*, 521, 514–515.

53. Ani reżyser, ani scenaryszta ne próbują nawet wniknąć w głąb motywacji bohaterów. Pietrzyk, "Matka-szmatka."

54. Adrian Luzar, January 16, 2018, https://film.interia.pl/recenzje/news-syn -krolowej-sniegu-recenzja-zimno-coraz-zimniej,nId,2508882. Accessed March 2, 2018.

55. de Beauvoir, *The Second Sex*, 513.

56. UNICEF reported in 2016 that approximately four annual child homicides for every 100,000 people occur in the US. Cameron Norsworthy, "How Many Children Are Victims of Homicide Each Year? The U.S. Has High Numbers," ROMPER, August 23, 2016, https://www.romper.com/p/how-many-children-are-victims-of -homicide-each-year-the-us-has-high-numbers-17008. Accessed March 2, 2018.

57. Muskała authored the script, on which she reportedly worked for six years. See the review at https://culture.pl/pl/dzielo/fuga-rez-agnieszka-smoczynska. Accessed February 1, 2020. As one reviewer observed, there exists "a current, albeit small trend for actresses in their forties and fifties" to write scenarios for themselves. Mirjana Karanovic for *A Good Wife* and Karen Teles for *Loveling*. Muskala and Joanna Żółkowska obviously belong to this small contingent. See Amber Wilkinson, "Fugue," May 20, 2018, https://www.eyeforfilm.co.uk/review/fugue-2018-film -review-by-amber-wilkinson. Accessed February 1, 2020. Apparently, the persona of Alicja "was inspired by a true story." See Maggie Gogler, "Fugue," VIEW OF THE ARTS, May 16, 2018, https://viewofthearts.com/2018/05/16/71st-cannes-film -festival-fugue-review/. Accessed February 1, 2020.

58. The official DVD of the film calls it a mystery characteristic of David Lynch, while the site Culture.pl tags the film as a psychological thriller. See https://culture .pl/pl/dzielo/fuga-rez-agnieszka-smoczynska. See also Guy Lodge, "Film Review: 'Fugue,'" VARIETY, May 16, 2018, https://variety.com/2018/film/reviews/fugue -review-1202812117/, Wilkinson, and Jason Pirodsky, "'Fugue' an Intriguing Polish Mystery," *The Prague Reporter*, July 15, 2018, https://www.praguereporter.com/ home/2018/7/5/kviff-2018-review-fugue-an-intriguing-polish-mystery. All accessed February 1, 2020.

59. Anton Bitel, "Fugue (Fuga 2018)," April 13, 2019, https://projectedfigures .com/2019/04/13/fugue-fuga-2018/. Accessed February 1, 2020.

60. Culture.pl (ft. 58); Guy Lodge, "Film Review: 'Fugue.'"

61. Artur Zaborski, *"Fuga,"* *Kino*, no. 12 (2018): 77, http://kino.org.pl//index .php?option=com_content&task=view&id=3124&Itemid=2184. Accessed February 2, 2020.

62. Andrzej Kołodyński, *"Fuga,"* *Kino*, no. 6 (2019): 89. See the chapters on Barbara Sass and Dorota Kędzierzawska in Ewa Mazierska and Elżbieta Ostrowska,

Women in Polish Cinema (New York and Oxford: Berghahn Books, 2006), 166–84, 205–20.

63. See M.A. Doane, *The Desire to Desire: The Woman's Film of the 1940s* (Bloomington, IN: Indiana University Press, 1987) and Tania Modleski, "Time and Desire in the Woman's Film," in *Film Theory and Criticism*, eds. G. Cohen et al. (Oxford: Oxford University Press, 1992).

64. de Beauvoir, *The Second Sex*, 497.

65. For instance, laments over the dead in the Russian, Greek, and Chinese countryside have been the exclusive province of professional female mourners (moirologists) for centuries. See Iurii Sokolov, *Russian Folklore* (Hatboro, PA: Folklore Associates, 1955), 225–234 and Margaret Alexiou, *The Ritual Lament in Greek Tradition* (Cambridge: Cambridge University Press, 1974), 10.

Chapter 4

Rescreening Christian-Jewish Relations in Interwar, Wartime, and Postwar Poland

THE TWENTY-FIRST-CENTURY CULTURAL CONTEXT: THE JEWISH REVIVAL

The number of Polish citizens who identify as Jewish is minuscule (an estimated 4,500 to 50,000) vis-à-vis Poland's overwhelmingly Catholic population of approximately 38 million. Yet current relations among Polish Christians, Polish Jews, and the many scattered descendants of Polish Jews killed in the Holocaust or deported in the government-sponsored purge of so-called Zionists in 1968, have improved and worsened in strange ways since the emergence of an independent post-communist Poland.[1] The passing of the People's Republic of Poland in 1989 at last allowed citizens to state and publicly mourn the Nazis' decimation of 90 percent of Polish Jewry (3 million people)—this in lieu of the generic "enemies of fascism" inscribed as victims on Soviet-era monuments and plaques. The communist government's demise put an end to what film scholar Marek Haltof calls the "years of organized forgetting (1965–1985)," when "party propagandists emphasized the image of Poland as a one-nation state."[2]

In terms of improvement, the new government's attention to the Holocaust and, consequently, the terrible loss of the largest and most influential ethnic minority in interwar Poland (10 percent of the Polish population nationwide and roughly 33 percent of the residents in major Polish cities) has prompted many Poles to learn about the Ashkenazi Jews' thousand-year presence on Polish territory. The first Polish program devoted to Jewish Studies was established at Kraków's prestigious Jagiellonian University in 1986, three years before the change in government.[3] Over the next two decades, similar departments and institutes emerged at the Universities of Warsaw, Wrocław, Poznań, and Lublin. Because the city of Kraków, unlike Warsaw, was not demolished in World War II by the German army, its once-Jewish majority district of Kazimierz remained more or less physically intact, and became the site of the first and now world-famous Festival of Jewish Culture. The brainchild of local impresarios Janusz Makuch and Krzysztof Gierat in 1988, this annual festival has expanded over the last three decades into a ten-day event featuring lectures, exhibits, workshops, films, and concert performances by Jewish musicians from all over the world.[4] Other Polish cultural activists have followed in Makuch and Gierat's footsteps: Since the early 2000s, over forty different Jewish festivals are held each year in Poland.[5]

Non-Polish foundations and philanthropists—most affiliated with supporting the Jewish diaspora—also made major contributions to what has come to be known as the "Jewish revival" in Poland. Since the late 1980s, the Ronald S. Lauder Foundation has sponsored educational Jewish summer camps, youth clubs, and schooling for Polish children.[6] Other foundations have helped underwrite the establishment of formal social spaces, such as the Jewish Community Centre in Kraków, and institutions that educate and engage Polish visitors in Jewish history and culture—the largest of which is Warsaw's Polin: The Museum of the History of Polish Jews, opened in 2013.[7] In an extensive number of Polish cities and towns, foreign and local donors and organizations have worked together to restore Jewish heritage sites such as synagogues, prayer houses, and, especially, cemeteries that long have been neglected due to the death or emigration of Jewish descendants.[8]

Many Poles have been drawn into Jewish heritage stewardship on their own, perhaps because they stumbled on a half-ruined Jewish cemetery during a camping trip or were interested in contacting the descendants of the former Jewish residents in their hometowns.[9] Younger Poles have sought information about Jewish life and culture when they discovered that they have Jewish ancestry, whether or not their blood relations qualify them as Jewish according to halachic law.[10] Until quite recently, Poland has been one of the few places in the world where it has become safe and even fashionable to claim one's Jewish heritage openly.

Over the last decade, an array of documentary films, primarily made by non-Polish directors, attest to Jewish descendants' surprise at a welcoming climate for Jewish visitors in Poland. These include Simon Target's 2014 *A Town Called Brzostek*, which tells the story of Professor Jonathan Webber, an Orthodox Jew from England who decides to restore the Jewish cemetery of the town in which his grandfather was born.[11] Target's observation underscores what thousands of Jews from the United States and Israel have discovered on Jewish heritage tours in Poland: "I think if you are a Jew who has been told all your life that Poles are anti-Semitic, you have to walk through the rynek [marketplace] of Kraków, Wrocław or Brzostek today, wearing your kippah or yarmulke, to realize the opposite is in fact the case."[12] *Raise the Roof* (2015), a fascinating documentary by Cary and Yari Wolinsky ten years in the making, details how Handshouse Studio, an American nonprofit specializing in educational building projects, reproduced—with the help of scholars, artisans, and students from Poland and elsewhere—the gorgeous ceiling and *bimah* [prayer podium] of the eighteenth-century wooden synagogue of Gwoździec, a work of art installed in the Polin Museum's permanent exhibition.[13] The most difficult questions about the future of Jewish life in Poland are posed in Adam Zucker's 2015 *The Return*, which tracks the journeys of four young women (three Polish, one Slovak) who either discover their Jewish ancestry or elect to be Jewish in twenty-first-century Poland.[14] The film unveils the complexity each woman faces in creating her life as a Jew after she has embraced that choice: "What does it mean to be Jewish in a country with the richest of histories, yet almost no living presence? . . . Ultimately, is Judaism in Poland truly viable?" The four-year span of Zucker's documentary allows viewers to see how these young women's very different responses unfold, as one chooses marriage to an Orthodox Jew and conversion to Orthodoxy, while others build a transnational life and identity, moving between Poland and the United States or Poland and Israel, where one can simply relax and "stop thinking about being Jewish."[15]

THE TWENTY-FIRST-CENTURY CONTEXT: JEDWABNE, NEW HOLOCAUST SCHOLARSHIP, AND DOCUMENTARIES

> Over a half-century has passed since the hell of the Holocaust, but its spectre still hangs over the world and doesn't allow us to forget.
>
> —Irena Sendler

In tandem with the Jewish revival, which has strived to celebrate 1,000 years of Jewish life and improve the possibilities of a Jewish presence in Poland, scholars now researching the Holocaust are unearthing specifically Polish Christian crimes against humanity. The painstaking recovery of Polish-Jewish relations during the war presents an ever grimmer, more complicated not-so-distant past. Most Polish Christians are keenly aware of their own families' wartime victimization and have been assured, in the worst case, of their parents', grandparents', and great-grandparents' passivity vis-à-vis the Jews. But more evidence confirms the fact that many Polish Christians, with or without German orders and provocations, murdered and stole from their longtime Jewish neighbors.

To better understand the waves of shock, mortification, and fury this hor-rific revelation has caused in Poland, some contextualization is in order. First, the Second Republic of Poland (1919–1939) was a Western ally dur-ing World War II; its government was never allied with Nazi Germany and rightly feared the sudden implementation of the Molotov-Ribbentropp Pact between Germany and the USSR in August 1939 as a military trap. Second, Nazi Germany decided to locate the largest concentration and death camps for the extermination of European Jewry in Poland because the vast major-ity of Ashkenazi Jews already lived there. An estimated three million Polish Jews were murdered in this killing zone. Third, though Polish Christians were not targeted for extermination by the Reich, Nazis judged them to be racially inferior; in consequence, Polish resistance was to be destroyed, and other Polish Christians used as slave labor. During the war, the Nazis killed an estimated 1.9 million Polish Christians and deported 1.5 million for forced labor in Germany.[16] Fourth, as the US Holocaust Memorial Museum posts, aiding or hiding Jews "in much of German-occupied eastern Europe . . . were deemed capital offenses"; if Polish Christians dared to help Polish Jews and were exposed, they and their families were executed.[17] The dangers of informing "neighbors" plagued Polish Jews and any Polish Christians who were moved to help them.

Polish Christians suffered enormously during the war, the well-organized Polish resistance and its Home Army fought valiantly against the German occupiers, and individual Polish Christian helpers form the largest eth-nic group honored by Yad Vashem as the Righteous Among the Nations. Nevertheless, historians both in and outside Poland have been accruing disturbing data of Polish Christians' "intimate violence" against the Jews.[18] The first bombshell that rocked the national conscience was historian Jan T. Gross's book, *Sąsiedzi: Historia Zagłady żydowskiego miasteczka* (2000) [Neighbors: The Destruction of the Jewish Community in Jedwabne, Poland (2001)], an analysis of the massacre of, at the very least, 400 Polish Jews in Jedwabne, most of whom a local gang of Polish Christians beat, stabbed, and herded into a large barn, which they then locked and set on fire.[19] Gross subsequently published two more works of historical scholarship about Polish Christian atrocities against their Jewish neighbors: *Fear: Anti-Semitism in Poland after Auschwitz* (2007), and, with Irena Grudzińska Gross, *Golden Harvest: Events on the Periphery of the Holocaust* (2012).

Gross has come to be identified by different Polish administrations as chief hero or villain in revising Polish Holocaust history, but he is by no means alone in this important critical inquiry.[20] Other trailblazers include Poland-based and foreign scholars, including Barbara Engelking, Jacek Leociak, Jan Grabowski, Dariusz Libionka, Natalia Aleksiun, and many more. As sociolo-gist Geneviève Zubrzycki attests, their work has "invalidated key tenets of a national mythology" and led to an enduring division between right-wing Poles, who perceive any critical discussion of Polish Christians' role in the Holocaust "as defamation of the Polish nation," and "many [Poles] on the political left and center [who] actively seek to recover the memory of Jewish presence and its tragic destruction."[21] Under the Law and Justice-dominated government, this debate spawned the "Amended Act on the Institute of National Remembrance" signed into law on February 6, 2018, which essentially forbids and potentially punishes scholars and journalists who claim "collective Polish support" of the Holocaust.[22] Regardless of the political and professional consequences, the aforementioned trailblazers, plus a new generation of Holocaust scholars trained in Poland, have persisted in their research and publishing, intent on uncovering evidence-based truth.

It is also imperative to recognize that courageous Polish documentary filmmakers had launched their own investigations into Christian violence against the Jews during and after the Holocaust over a decade before Gross's *Neighbors* appeared in Poland. These films contrast sharply in atmosphere and objective with the largely foreign-produced documentaries of the Jewish revival and its consequences, yet the two bodies of work importantly complement each other in their respective quests for local justice and international understanding. Marcel Łoziński's 1988 *Świadkowie* [Witnesses] records the testimony of those who watched the especially violent 1946 pogrom against surviving Jews unfold in Kielce, a postwar atrocity about which the world still knows very little. Łoziński's 1991 documentary *Siedmiu Żydów z mojej klasy* [Seven Jews from My Class] films his reunion with seven former classmates who were subsequently deported from Poland in 1968 as part of government's "anti-Zionist" campaign, another important tragedy in Christian-Jewish relations that nonetheless demonstrates a Poland more openly divided by the government's outrageous action. Łoziński's son, Paweł, following in his father's footsteps, filmed the important *Miejsce urodzenia* [Birthplace], which documents Polish-Jewish writer Henryk Grynberg's return to Poland—specifically, to the villages near which he and his family hid during the Holocaust. Grynberg talks with the peasants (all previously contacted by Łoziński) who remembered his family and, in some cases, gave them food and temporary shelter. Through these often difficult revelatory conversations, the writer learns the grim truth about the missing members of his family: how his two-year-old brother (he himself had been four) was abandoned, turned over to the local German authorities, and summarily shot, while his father was murdered by two Polish villagers, who coveted his dairy cows. *Birthplace* concludes with an iconic scene that several later feature films quote. A group of villagers unearth the remains of Grynberg's father for him, and the writer is left overwhelmed by this terrible reunion with his parent's skull and bones.

Documentarians also paved the way, on the scale of their necessarily smaller viewing audience, for Gross's internationally explosive book. Before *Neighbors* was ready for the press, Agnieszka Arnold, a filmmaker and TV reporter, screened her first film on the Jedwabne massacre. Her 1999 *Gdzie jest mój starszy syn Kain?* [Where is my older son, Cain?] features the testimonies of Jedwabne survivor Szmul Wassersztajn and the daughter of the Christian who owned the barn where the massacre was carried out. Arnold's second film, *Sąsiedzi* [Neighbors], presents an extensive series of her interviews with Jedwabne residents who had scattered all over the postwar world. According to at least one source, Arnold was sanguine about letting Gross use her second film's title for his history and lent him the transcripts of her interviews.[23] Gross attests, in turn, that it was only when he viewed Szmul Wassersztajn giving testimony in *Where Is My Older Son, Cain?* "that he absorbed the reality of what had occurred" at Jedwabne—the atrocity committed by longtime neighbor against neighbor.[24] Film realized for Gross the horrifyingly interhuman complexity of the intimate prosecution of the Holocaust.

TWENTY-FIRST-CENTURY RESCREENINGS OF THE POLISH JEWS

The four films I have selected and analyze in this chapter constitute the most ambitious attempts to rescreen Christian-Jewish relations in this bold new era of Polish film, in each case utilizing the advantages of improved technology and the objective, evidence-based historical research being conducted in the twenty-first century. All four have evoked strong student reactions in my courses; their responses have ranged from uneasy sentimentality to confused outrage, and my analyses owe much to our frank class discussions. I present the quartet of films here in the chronological order of the historical periods that the films target. Jolanta Dylewska's *Po-Lin: Okruchy pamięci* [Po-Lin: Scraps of Memory] (2008) strives to recreate—through moving images and interviews—an interwar Jewish world made up of film footage presenting the residents and townscape of different shtetls. Dylewska, a cinematographer by training, achieves a minor miracle in piecing together a mosaic of home movies made by visiting Jewish relatives from overseas. Agnieszka Holland's feature film, *W ciemności* [In Darkness] (2011), focuses on a complex network of Christian-Jewish interactions in wartime Lwów, a Polish city occupied by the Germans with the help of a Ukrainian nationalist militia. The plot of *In Darkness*, based on a true story, moves from aboveground to the sewers below, where a group of Jews survive the Holocaust with the help of a Polish Catholic sewer worker, Leopold Socha, one of the least known of the Righteous Among Nations.

Paweł Pawlikowski's *Ida* (2013) and Władysław Pasikowski's *Pokłosie* [Aftermath] (2012), both fiction films, address the horrors of Poland's local Holocaust in the countryside, though their protagonists inhabit a postwar world. In *Ida*, set in the early 1960s, the eponymous protagonist, a Catholic novice about to take her vows, learns that she is a Jew from her lone living relative, an aunt once feared as a Stalinist-era prosecutor. Aunt and niece set out to find out where their relatives are buried and how they were killed during the war. In *Aftermath*, director and screenwriter Pasikowski draws extensively on Gross's revelations about the Jedwabne massacre in a strangely imbalanced mix of thriller and historical film. Two brothers, long alienated after the elder (Franek) moved to America, reunite in 2000 because the younger brother (Józek) is carrying out his own variation of the Jewish revival on their family's farm. The village's angry reaction to Józek's collecting and displaying Jewish *matsevah*, or headstones, misappropriated by both Germans and Poles, has so frightened his wife and children that they seek refuge in Franek's home overseas. The brothers consequently join forces to discover—through doctored documents and the bones of victims—that their father and older Christian neighbors killed Jewish neighbors and stole these Jews' more valuable farms without the Nazis' help.

THE MANIPULATION OF MOVING IMAGES: *PO-LIN: SCRAPS OF MEMORY* (2008)

The longer I spent with my grandfather's film, the richer and more fragmentary its images became.

—Glenn Kurtz[25]

When Jolanta Dylewska's *Po-Lin: Scraps of Memory* was released in 2008, almost all of its reviewers hailed it as beautifully made and of great educational value in representing interwar Jews living in the shtetls as happy, industrious, *living* people. Janusz Wróblewski enthuses about the documentary's "angelic, almost fairy-tale-like perspective" and its painstaking descriptions of the Jews' everyday activities and observance of religious holidays.[26] Tadeusz Sobolewski applauds the fact that Dylewska has made a movie about Jewish life and not the Holocaust, yet oddly likens the subjects' emergence from dark interiors toward the camera as a variant on the old Slavic pagan ritual of *Dziady* [Forefathers' Eve], when the dead visit the living once a year: "[These Jews] accuse no one and want nothing from us. Rather, they are somehow necessary to us."[27] Clearly, the juries at different festivals likewise felt moved and cheered. *Po-Lin* received the Gold Teeth Award at Chicago's

Polish Film Festival, the Golden Reel Award from the San Francisco Film Writers' Circle, and the Golden Phoenix from Warsaw's International Film Festival of Jewish Motifs.[28]

In his fine book on Polish film and the Holocaust, Marek Haltof singles out Dylewska's work as "the best-known" among other contemporary documentary films and television programs striving "to recreate Jewish life in prewar Poland."[29] Dylewska, who studied both directing and cinematography at the Łódź Film School, works primarily as a cinematographer.[30] In making *Po-Lin*, she worked with challenging materials—an extensive number of home movies made by relatives from the United States and Palestine visiting kin in the old country. These movies had been donated, along with photographs, to the Shalom Foundation in the mid-1990s. In addition to restoring and sequencing these aging, grainy amateur films, Dylewska decided to match their subjects and buildings, whenever she could, with what was written about them in the Books of Memory produced for each Jewish community after the Holocaust. The Books, in turn, furnish the voiceover text for the black-and-white interwar footage. According to Haltof, Dylewska also traveled to the nineteen towns where the home movies were made to contact and interview elderly residents who remembered their Jewish neighbors and to shoot contemporary landscapes corresponding to those featured in the interwar films.[31] In consultation with Hanna Krall, a well-known Jewish journalist and writer, Dylewska was persuaded to enhance the reality of the black-and-white world she was building, changing the verbal tense of the Books of Memory from past to present and adding close approximations of diegetic sound to the silent film, from bird song and murmuring voices to horses' hooves clattering over cobblestones.[32]

The result of what Wróblewski praises as her "Benedictine labor" is extraordinary.[33] Dylewska herself has defined the camera as "a kind of transcendental corridor" that intensifies the viewer's experience of the subject filmed, and her reviewers marvel at her achievement of that intensity in *Po-Lin* through meticulous restoration, editing, addition of a soundtrack, and linking of the verbal to the visual.[34] The moving images of healthy, welcoming, confident Jews likely evoke such an intense reaction because they boldly contrast with the more familiar Holocaust representation of Jews as starved, tortured, terrified victims in documentary and fictional films. Such images are perhaps what Sobolewski thought Polish viewers "needed." Dylewska renders this projected black-and-white world more authoritative by using a single narrator as its chronicler—in this case, the actor Piotr Fronczewski, whose sonorous baritone deftly reassures, ennobles, and sometimes seems to tremble with a righteous Jew's belief in the religious passages that he reads.[35] The inserted color footage of the elderly Polish neighbors temporarily disperses the intensity, but their memories (evoked by an invisible interviewer) surround these Jews with gentile approval, ranging from friendships shared to (more often) scattered impressions of Jewish kindness, industry, and *forgiveness*.

The color footage unveiling how time and loss have changed important places in the shtetl underscore how spaces designed with meaning and used with purpose have been overrun by haphazard town planning and car-oriented culture after the war. If one were to extrapolate from the then-and-now juxtapositions *Po-Lin* presents, one can see how the Holocaust and its aftermath left emptiness in towns bereft of their Jewish communities, an emptiness never satisfactorily redesigned or, in the case of mass graves, appropriately marked. Gone are the dominant synagogues, the prayer houses, ritual baths, hospitals, orphanages, and occasional libraries, as well as the marketplaces lined with shops. Gone are the female shopkeepers and stall keepers, the men strolling in pairs and deep in discussion, the clusters of boisterous schoolboys, and the young ladies trying out lipstick (likely gifts from the relative behind the camera).

One wishes that Dylewska had dwelled more on these stark contrasts of past *versus* present and, by extension, had contextualized more specifically and repeatedly how the archival films were made and *for whom*. As Elżbieta Janicka and Tomasz Żukowski systematically trace in their sharp critique of *Po-Lin*, the "angelic, almost fairy-tale-like structure" that Dylewska painstakingly constructs was never intended to meet Polish gentiles' "needs," nor did it represent Jews interacting with gentiles or coping with Polish nationalist policies and economic strictures in the interwar period. These movies were made by Jews for Jews in a familial holiday atmosphere (figure 4.1). The relatives involved in filming may have perceived the shtetls as shabby or exotic, but they were pleased to see their extended families and wanted to make a happy moving picture that they could share with relatives and friends at home. Hence the subjects in these films approach the camera with smiles, dressed in their best, sometimes coaxing hesitant elders and children to move forward in a welcoming line. Their happy greeting was extended to family, not as a display designed for curious gentiles. Yet, in Janicka and Żukowski's analysis, Dylewska implicitly presents "these archived pictures by Jewish amateur camera operators as the materialization and guarantee of the Poles' true memories of them," as the self-representation of a minority culture that must necessarily oblige a dominant majority culture.[36] Ironically, Dylewska's major contribution to the Jewish revival here is her manipulation of inter-familial communications to advertise "good and contented Jewishness" for Polish consumption. In lieu of her virtuosic synthesis, she could have restored some Jewish agency and differentiation here if she had included the filmed commentaries of Jewish Studies scholars knowledgeable about shtetl life or the specific interwar histories of the identified towns—Kaluszyn, Kolbuszowa, Zaręby Kościelne, Borysław, and others.

Janicka and Żukowski identify Dylewska's approach as an example of
"philosemitic violence," admitting that such violence can be perpetrated
with the best intentions. They argue that the Polish Catholic witnesses, all of
whom remember their Jewish neighbors fondly, articulate one "good Polish
Jew" stereotype after another—the acculturated Jew who proudly teaches
love for "our homeland"; the Jew who lends a Christian money when no one
else will in order to keep the peace; and the Jew who forgives Christian customers when they apologize for observing a right-wing boycott by the powerful National Democrat party of their shops.[37] Dylewska's witnesses definitely
represent much more benign and articulate alternates to those interviewed
in Holocaust documentaries such as French filmmaker Claude Lanzmann's
Shoah or Łoziński's *Birthplace*. As Wróblewski writes with seeming relief,
the neighbors assembled in *Po-Lin* do not resemble the neighbors portrayed
in Gross's books.[38] Yet, as Sobolewski admits, even these well-disposed
Christian witnesses convey how alien the Jewish world was to their own.[39]

I disagree with Janicka and Żukowski's assertions that every witness in
Po-Lin deals in Jewish stereotypes. At the very least, these participants are
brave enough to commit their sometimes close relationships and generally
impressed memories of their Jewish neighbors to the "permanent" record
of film. But the two critics' fundamental objection to the documentary correctly targets its most painful omission. Perhaps to protect her carefully
reconstructed vision of interwar Jewry, Dylewska delays any mention of the
Holocaust until late in the film, and treats it as a wholly external catastrophe.[40]
The Polish Catholic witnesses are not asked to remember it in front of the
camera. That task is assigned to one of the very few Jewish survivors from
Kaluszyn, Cwi Kamionka, now an Israeli citizen, as he stands on a grassy
meadow that is suddenly revealed to be a mass grave for 2,000 Jews, including 80 members of his maternal and paternal families. Kamionka delivers
this painful testimony with remarkable self-possession, and then walks back
toward town as the camera rises to provide an aerial/crane shot of the mass
grave while different voices utter the names of the dead in ever more rapid,
less intelligible succession. As moving as this final scene is intended to be,
Janicka and Żukowski take Dylewska to task for Kamionka's token appearance and the film's continuing silence, for *Po-Lin* never raises the burning
questions about Christian assistance in this massacre and possible appro-
priation of Kaluszyn's Jewish property after thousands of Jews were shot in
town, starved in work details, or deported to Treblinka.[41] Perhaps Kamionka's
imprimatur as a survivor sufficed for Dylewska; perhaps the answers to these
questions were not yet known in 2008. In any event, according to a witness
account posted on the website www.cmentarze-żydowskie.pl [Jewish cemeteries in Poland], Germans ordered the local firemen to restrain those waiting to be executed, an order that the Poles carried out but may have abhorred

rather than embraced, because between the wars the Kaluszyn fire department had integrated Catholic and Jewish volunteers.[42]

In sum, Dylewska's *Po-Lin: Scraps of Memory* treats viewers to a wonderfully restored series of exclusive interwar films. Though one shtetl blurs into another and Fronczewski's narrated Books of Memory identify only a few of the individuals shown, *Po-Lin* amasses an impressive array of fascinating people, buildings, and local scenes that we are privileged to view. We see Hasidic Jews in traditional garb and acculturating Jews distinguished by their choice of modern clothing, hair and beard styles, and experimentation with cosmetics. We glimpse standard marketplaces, substantial synagogues, and at least one new library dedicated to Isaac Leib Peretz, the great Yiddish writer (1852–1915). We are admitted into well-kept, ornately decorated Jewish cemeteries in which living Jews dutifully attend to their dead.

But missing in *Po-Lin* are the essential facts of interwar Polish politics, which was constantly nationalized in favor of "true Poles" by the National Democrats; the economic crises exacerbated by Christian boycotts of Jewish businesses; the nonreligious Jewish organizations (the Bund, Zionism) that recruited and often lured young people away from the shtetl to the city; and, of course, the complicated betrayals, atrocities, and inexorable mass murder of the Holocaust. Rather than accuse Dylewska of "philosemitic violence," I would characterize *Po-Lin* as the work of a dedicated illusionist, a gifted cinematographer in thrall to her mesmerizing subjects, who utilizes the Books of Memory, Fronczewski's baritone, and obliging Polish witnesses to authenticate the interwar Jews as she sees them. Unfortunately, this packaging reduces the intensity she feels to anodyne advertisement for the Polish viewing public. It would be so interesting if Dylewska could screen these individual silent films for those who live in their tagged locations today, for local citizens there might better understand the rich bicultural foundations of their hometowns.

DE-THEATRICALIZING THE HOLOCAUST: HOLLAND'S *IN DARKNESS*

At [Socha's] funeral, someone said, "It's God's punishment for helping the Jews."
As if we need God to punish each other.

—End credits, *In Darkness*

Agnieszka Holland, one of the best and best-known Polish filmmakers working today, early experienced the difficulties of being Jewish in Poland. Her

paternal grandparents perished in Auschwitz; her father, a high-profile communist activist after the war, was arrested for treason in 1961 and committed
suicide in jail. Labeled a political persona non grata, Holland could not be
admitted into the Łódź Film School and consequently pursued her studies at
the Film Institute of the Academy of Performing Arts in Prague during the
heyday of the Czech New Wave. When she returned to Poland in 1970, she
worked as an assistant director for Krzysztof Zanussi and was accepted into
Wajda's famed Production Unit X. With the Polish government's imposition
of martial law in 1981, Holland emigrated to France and thereafter has pursued her career as a filmmaker and TV director in the United States, Western
Europe, and Poland.

Before beginning production on her 2011 *In Darkness*, Holland had
directed or played a central role in making several Polish Holocaust films.
Her credits include the 1985 *Bittere Ernte* [Angry Harvest], a feature that
portrays the tormented relationship between a Jewish woman seeking refuge
and a Silesian farmer who is both her rescuer and rapist; the international
award–winning *Europa, Europa* (1990), based on the true story of a Jew who
succeeded in passing as a charismatic member of the Hitler Youth; and her
screenplay for Wajda's 1990 *Korczak*, a film portrait of the last years of the
assimilated Jew Henryk Goldszmit (known by his Polish pseudonym Janusz
Korczak), the pediatrician and great specialist on children's health and education, who chose to live with his charges in the Warsaw Ghetto's Jewish
orphanage and die with them in the Treblinka death camp.

At least two reviewers of *In Darkness*, one American and the other Polish,
wonder openly why Holland bothered to add one more "Holocaust film" to
what they perceived as a conventionalized or exhausted "genre." A. O. Scott
opens his unusually tone-deaf review in the *New York Times* by declaring
that *In Darkness* "provides the latest evidence that the Holocaust movie has
become a genre of [*sic*] its own right. Even a true story can follow the familiar
conventions of film narrative, and this tale of the righteous gentile selflessly
assisting in the survival of a handful of persecuted Jews is no exception." Scott
oddly dismisses Holland's film as "touching, warm and dramatically satisfying.
But that, given the subject matter, is exactly the problem."[43] Given the spatial
limitations of a film review, Scott does not locate his "genre" in the burgeoning, multifaceted scholarship on representing the Holocaust on film.[44] What
he implies instead are the pragmatic narrative building blocks of a popular
Hollywood genre film—a seeming blend of the thriller (terrible danger, narrow
escapes) and melodrama (clear projections of good and evil in the hero, victims,
and enemy), the happy end of a Jewish group's rescue, and the commemoration
of a loving relationship between hero and those s/he saved.

Sebastian Adamkiewicz, the Polish reviewer whose views coincide with
Scott's, writes with more awe and less *ennui*, admitting that he cannot

imagine how any film—in this case, Holland's *In Darkness*—could disclose more about the Holocaust experience in the wake of Steven Spielberg's *Schindler's List* and Roman Polański's *The Pianist*, though both of these movies could be faulted for entrenching the very conventions that Scott implies.[45] Nonetheless, Adamkiewicz has stumbled onto the two best popular benchmarks to elicit the distinction of Holland's film. In contrast to the hero's empowered vantage point and the transcendent conclusion of *Schindler's List*, on the one hand, and, on the other, the protagonist's ordeal by isolation, salvation through his public performance of Chopin before postwar Poles, and final tribute to the triumph of art over the extermination of millions in *The Pianist*, *In Darkness* remains in the trenches of interhuman misery, exposing in shadowy close-up flawed, desperate people squabbling with each other as they cope with the dangerous, exhausting marathon of wartime survival.

Indeed, Holland stubbornly eschews the "familiar conventions" of a popular Holocaust film by insisting on such authentic representation that Western viewers may at first be frustrated by its dreary realism and contingent moral decisions. *In Darkness* is based, more or less, on Krystyna Chiger's *The Girl in the Green Sweater: A Life in Holocaust's Shadow* (2008), a real-life account of the fourteen months during which she, her parents, younger brother, and eight other Jews hid in the sewers of Lwów with the help of a Catholic sewer worker.[46] Holland may not have been so interested if the memoir had functioned as the screenplay. Screenwriter David F. Shamoon radically changes the young Krystyna's glowing portrait of her father, Ignacy Chiger, whose reckless bravery and physical resourcefulness he reassigns to the younger character of Mundek Margulies (Benno Fürmann). In his stead, Shamoon constructs an older, more scholarly, and introspective paterfamilias (Herbert Knaup). Shamoon also purposefully dispenses with Krystyna's worship of the Catholic sewer worker, Leopold (Poldek) Socha (a masterfully phlegmatic incarnation by Robert Więckiewicz), who shines throughout her memoirs as a savior with a soft spot for children. The only character sweetened in Shamoon's screenplay is Socha's wife, Wanda (a zesty, warm performance by Kinga Preis), who in Chiger's account remains deeply suspicious of her spouse's contract with the Jews.

Holland, in turn, tackles the film's technological challenges and historical complexity in pursuit of integrity rather than thrills and mass appeal. In an interview with Piotr Śmiałowski for *Kino*, the director explains that she had no wish to duplicate the visually stunning, stark black-and-white contrasts used by Carol Reed in the exciting, iconic chase scene through the Viennese sewers at the end of his 1949 classic, *The Third Man*.[47] Instead, she relied on the talented Dylewska to solve the problem of lighting the sewer sets realistically. The cinematographer ingeniously used the large lanterns that the characters raised up before them as they sloshed through the muck.[48] This means that the title's darkness literally shadows most of the main events, not as film noir effects, but as a realist representation of the city's literal underside. The mise-en-scène's naturalism is further assured by close-ups of curious rats and make-up effectively mimicking raw sewage on the actors' skin and clothes.

Holland likewise refuses to resort to English as the film's lingua franca, rejecting the popularizing path taken by Polański in *The Pianist*. An experienced director in the United States, she nonetheless resisted the use of the non-diegetic sound of English and English-speaking actors when she commenced work on *In Darkness*: "The English language is one of the elements that most irritates me in films about the Holocaust. English theatricalizes everything. Its use makes reality on the screen seem artificial, and once that happens, this reality becomes more bearable."[49] The characters of *In Darkness* speak and shift between the sizable number of languages used in a multicultural wartime Lwów (postwar the city Lviv in Ukraine): German, Yiddish, Ukrainian, Polish, and the local Polish dialect called *bałak*. The switching of languages will likely mean little to English-speaking audiences, yet, as historian Timothy Snyder points out in his immensely helpful contextualization of the film, "Holland assumes that viewers will have some sense of where Lwów was, what it had already suffered, who its peoples were, what languages they spoke."[50] This means that viewers need to bear in mind the racist wartime hierarchy extending downward from Germans to Ukrainians to Poles to Jews and to infer from characters' clothing, situation, and behavior what is going on and what is at stake. It helps somewhat to know that the men wearing black uniforms represent members of a Ukrainian nationalist militia (not *all* Ukrainians) serving as police for the German Army and SS.

Building on this authenticity, *In Darkness* maintains a careful balancing act between its representations of Jews and Christians, specifically in terms of plot building and complex character and group development. As Elżbieta Ostrowska astutely argues, Holland challenges the superior power and privileged perception normally attributed to the Christian "helper" by decentering the film's vantage point and devoting equal time and attention to the double narratives of Socha's small circle and the group of Jewish survivors. In Ostrowska's estimation, *In Darkness* devotes 40 minutes, respectively, to the Jews' frantic responses to the ghetto's liquidation and Socha's ever-changing fortunes before it screens an hour of their interactions. Such strategies force "the viewer to constantly realign his/her spectatorial perspective and consequently his/her emotional attachment."[51]

The strong cast further enhance and complicate their characters as they navigate the hazards and opportunities of the wartime plots. Więckiewicz takes great pains to portray Socha as a petty crook, a thick-skinned operator, and a run-of-the-mill anti-Semite, whose capacity for kindness seems restricted to his family circle. *In Darkness* opens with Socha and Szczepek

(Krzysztof Skonieczny), his younger friend and accomplice, ransacking a posh apartment. The return of the apartment's tenant, a young Polish woman, and her Nazi lover, takes the thieves by surprise, yet the moral high ground tilts crazily from crime victims to criminals as Socha shames the girl for consorting with the enemy, seizes the German's jammed gun, and knocks him to the ground. During their getaway through the forest, Socha and Szczepek stop in their tracks as they spy, in a long shot, Nazis driving naked Jewish women of all ages to their death, like some mad apparition of devils chasing forest wraiths. Thereafter, Socha slips back into his one-room apartment as the sun rises, and he behaves as a loving father and husband, checking on his daughter, Stefcia, as she sleeps, and persuading his wife, Wanda, to have sex before morning mass. By the time Socha happens upon the Jewish men from the ghetto who have managed to dig their way through to the sewers, we are no longer surprised that this ever-mutating "helper" smiles slyly and bargains hard with them for his services, agreeing to what he thinks will be lucrative extortion with little effort. Holland early on weans her viewers from assuming Socha's heroism.

The Jewish characters in the film are no less changeable than Socha and manifest little group solidarity. Though Ignacy, Paulina (Maria Schrader), Krystyna (Milla Bankowicz), and Paweł (Oliwer Stanczak) Chiger present a sympathetic upper-class family, prudent enough to have escaped with a stash of valuables, others in this motley assortment of refugees resent the Chigers' wealth, class condescension, and power, and eventually rob them in order to attempt an escape from the sewers. The same Janek Weiss (Marcin Bosak) who leads the mutiny against the Chigers is an adulterer, whose open affair with Chaja (Julia Kijowska) decides his wife and daughter to remain aboveground in the ghetto. Janek subsequently abandons Chaja in the sewers, leaving her pregnant with their child. Other Jewish characters specifically challenge Socha's authority and anticipate his treachery. Mundek Margulies bears the nickname *Korsarz* [Pirate], reflecting a predilection for violence and petty crime that matches Socha's. At several points, he threatens or tries to kill the Pole who, he presumes, will sell them out. The macho Jew and macho Catholic bond relatively late in the film when they must join forces to kill a German soldier who threatens to expose the Jews' hiding place. Thereafter, Mundek admits that Socha, "the Polack Moses," is decent, and Socha admits that Mundek, "the Jew," is brave.

In addition to fleshing out Catholic and Jewish characters, the film tracks the daily challenges confronting both hiding Jews and their Polish go-between. The scenes in the sewers mainly detail the group's attempt to normalize their life, despite the filth, stench, damp, cold, and darkness. Someone makes the long trek for fresh water, meals are cooked, men shave (or do not), Chiger keeps a diary, Jacob Berestycki, the lone Orthodox Jew (Jerzy

Walczak), prays aloud in a corner, and the Chiger children do their lessons
and draw pictures. At night Janek and Chaja have noisy sex, prompting some
to disapprove and others to watch with longing. The Jews' plotline branches
out to accommodate a budding love affair between Mundek and Klara (a
forthright Agnieszka Grochowska), and this in turn steels Mundek to enter
the Janowska work camp (a holding place for the Jews after the ghetto's liquidation), where he voluntarily exposes himself to the caprices and savagery
of the Nazis in a vain attempt to save his true love's sister.

Socha's plotline demonstrates step by step how fleecing the Jews in fact
wreaks havoc with his life. During the ghetto's destruction, he has to work
hard and fast to move his group into the sewers (he struggles most with a
Krystyna afraid of the dark and stench), and then risk execution from the
Ukrainian militia when he emerges from a manhole in the territory they
patrol. In this instance, Socha's life is saved because he is vouched for by a
certain Lieutenant Bortnik (played with alternating malice and geniality by
Michał Żurawski), a Ukrainian with whom Socha once shared a jail cell. In
assuming a job with life and death consequences for his clients, Socha finds
that he, too, is run ragged in the marathon to survive. He can no longer frequent his usual grocery because the clerk there automatically charges him a
sizable bribe to ensure her silence about his extra money and bulk purchases.
Bortnik, with Socha in his debt, leans on him twice to ferret out the Jews
rumored to be living in the sewers. The second search luckily ends with
Bortnik's accidental, providential death.

What ultimately redeems the gruff, suspect Polish sewer worker in his clients' eyes is his kindness toward their children—not only Krystyna and her
little brother, Paweł, but also the baby that Chaja bears. This attachment is
declared at the outset in Chiger's memoir, in which the historical Socha admitted that the vision of Mrs. Chiger and her two children moved him to offer his
services. Krystyna's Socha, also a petty thief who had been in jail, was a man
seeking atonement for his sins, hoping that his work rescuing Jews would be
his salvation. Holland's film obviously rejects the historical Socha's quest for
absolution but renders this love of children plausible for her fictional Socha
through his evident respect for Wanda and devotion to their daughter. The character of Wanda is mercurial, quick to anger and forgiveness, but she is consistent in her sympathy for the Jews. She resists Socha's proposal to abscond with
the Chigers' jewelry, make her a lady of leisure, and leave the Jews to perish.

Socha's attachment to the children and, in consequence, the Jews' increasing trust in him begins when he happens on the lost Krystyna and Paweł
after he decides to check on the group's welfare one last time. Mrs. Chiger
hugs him—the group's first gesture of physical affection. Their interaction
intensifies after Chaja gives birth to her son. When Socha describes the
baby's "beautiful little mug" to Wanda as they lie in bed that night, his wife

impetuously suggests that they adopt the boy. Socha returns to the sewers, smiling happily for the first time in the film, only to discover that Chaja has smothered the infant. He is thunderstruck, and when Klara, distraught, snaps that the baby's death will make things easier for him, Socha at last bares his feelings without snarling: he had come to adopt this child as his own, and he will not dump the baby into the river, but give him a proper burial. Klara apologizes, and she, Chiger, and Berestycki accompany Socha through the sewers to the river bank. In this beautifully shot scene, Holland risks evoking normal grief: Socha's black form labors against a white backdrop of snow, Berestycki chants a memorial prayer, Klara's eyes fill with tears, and Socha genuflects over the tiny grave after he has patted down the dirt.

Socha completes his transformation into a sometime good man, but not a haloed hero, when he is allowed to play with Krystyna and Paweł, a liberating act that brings all three of them joy. After a worried Mrs. Chiger tells him that Krystyna no longer speaks or eats, Socha responds by carrying the girl to a manhole cover, lifting it up, and urging her to breathe the fresh air and look at the world. The poverty of that world, shot from Krystyna's street-level point of view, would dismay someone less deprived—a few strutting pigeons, a stray dog hunting for food, and the sound of an accordion playing—but it cheers Krystyna, and she smiles as Socha dances with her in his arms. At this pivotal moment, the other three Chigers surround Socha, the parents confessing that they have no more money to pay him while Paweł begs for a piggyback ride. Socha first accedes to Paweł's request, according to his suddenly changed set of priorities, and to the boy's delight. Then Socha cuts a deal with the Chigers that would have been unthinkable months before: he will slip them the money with which they will pretend to pay him, so that no one dismisses him as some pushover. As Socha leaves their hiding place and walks home, his conscious goodness registers in the close-up of his usual poker face. Whereas Socha the operator wore a sly, cynical smile, Socha the pushover looks disgusted with himself, though one side of his mouth twists up, conveying pleasure and self-irony.

An audience familiar with the assumed "conventions of the Holocaust film genre" would likely expect that Socha's shift in expression would build to a happy ending. But Holland's conclusion most pointedly renounces the "touching, warm and dramatically satisfying" ethos that Scott claims for the film. The director aims instead for the authentic. We initially experience the Jews' liberation from their traumatized physical and psychological point of view. They sit anxiously in the sewers, waiting for the Soviet bombing and shelling of German-occupied Lwów to stop, and listening for Socha's all clear. As the Pole lifts each of them up and out through the manhole, they are blinded by the sunlight and must be reminded to breathe deeply at last. Once aboveground, the camera, framing the main characters in mid-shot,

moves deftly among the slowly recovering Jews and a now exuberant, lively
Socha playing host as Wanda comes bearing cake and a bottle of vodka on a
tray. Outside this inner circle, passersby stop, some with interest, most with
looks of consternation. One or two intrude with questions and then withdraw
as Socha barks at them to "move along." He is happily intent on introducing
"my Wanda" to "my Jews" and distributing refreshments. There are no medical personnel, waiting ambulances, and cheering crowds. The Socha family
constitutes the Jews' lone welcoming committee and defensive cocoon. The
onlookers gradually form an ambiguous darker human border in the background, while Socha treats "his people" as a private party that he is bound to
protect (figure 4.2).

Holland leaves us with this unsettled, intimate, low-key "liberation."
Adamkiewicz admits his disappointment in the film's anti-climax and suggests that "it would have been more interesting if *In Darkness* had ended with
the planting of trees for Leopold Socha and his wife in the garden of Yad
Vashem"[52]—that is, with a flourish out of *Schindler's List*. Instead, printed
information begins scrolling down the screen, and before we are gratified
to read that "Leopold and Wanda (Magdalena) Socha are among more than
6,000 Poles honored by Israel as the Righteous Among the Nations," we are
sideswiped by an unexpected tragedy and relentless anti-Semitism:

> On May 12, 1945, Leopold Socha was killed, saving his daughter from an
> out-of-control
>   Russian army truck.
>   At his funeral, someone said: "It's God's punishment for helping the Jews."
>   As if we needed God to punish each other.

In sum, Holland has not created what some critics dismiss as "just another
[popular] Holocaust movie" in *In Darkness*. She has produced the most realistic Polish feature film on the *Shoah* to date, maintaining a dreary, dispirited
mise-en-scène in the sewers, systematically blurring conventional black-and-
white contrasts in the mentality and actions of Jews and Christians in wartime
Poland, and underscoring their overlap in agency, morality, solidarity, fear,
and social ostracism in a postwar Poland.

THE BLANK OF POSTWAR JEWISHNESS
IN PAWLIKOWSKI'S *IDA*

People are trapped in history and history in them.

—James Baldwin

In chapter 1, Goscilo provides an extremely useful introduction to Pawlikowski's award-winning *Ida* (2013), summarizing its plot, delineating its austere aesthetic approach, and noting Polish right-wing objections to its alleged misrepresentation of Christians as complicit in killing and robbing Jews during and after the Holocaust. Goscilo also locates Pawlikowski's work within the key context of other Polish films about the Catholic Church, indicating that this director's retrospective view on the institution in the 1960s is more individualized than revisionist. While Goscilo asserts that "*Ida* has little to say explicitly about the Polish Catholic Church," her analysis, like that of other perceptive reviewers, appreciates how the strict silence of convent life and cinematographer Łukasz Żal's painterly attention to the nuns' rituals and their church's spare, light-filled interior inform, in large part, what the film conveys as the sacred and the beautiful.

How, then, does *Ida* represent the two Jewish protagonists in communist, Catholic Poland less than two decades after the war? These female characters—the communist judge Wanda Gruz (Agata Kulesza), once a ruthless Stalinist-era prosecutor, and her niece, Anna/Ida Lebensztajn (Agata Trzebuchowska), a Catholic novice required by her Mother Superior to learn about her Jewish identity before taking her vows—have provoked strong criticism from historians of Polish Jewry and feminist critics in Poland. Helena Datner, a prominent scholar at the Jewish Historical Institute, dismisses both protagonists as schematically drawn marionettes that variously incarnate pernicious anti-Semitic stereotypes such as the decadent Jewess, the avenging Jewish communist, and the blessed Jewish convert.[53]

In lieu of a film review, feminist journalist and activist Anna Zawadzka delivers a blistering caricature of Wanda as one of the countless communist prosecutors who crop up in postwar Poland—all of them, of course, Jewish women. In Zawadzka's sketch, Wanda not only drinks and fornicates but also prosecutes others out of revenge (a Jew), guilt (a bad mother who has abandoned her child), and audacity (a bad Jewish *communist* woman who dared to join the partisans and fight against the Nazis).[54] In accord with Datner and Zawadzka, feminist scholar Agnieszka Graff points out that the title character in Pawlikowski's film emerges as the best possible Jew for a Polish Christian audience, a convert, who—once she has experimented with her older relative's wicked ways—can overcome a vengeful, traumatized Jewishness in herself through her belief in Jesus Christ, or, in Datner's formulation, "can wash away her non-Catholic origins in the convent."[55] The three reviewers clearly read the film's final scene as Ida's return to the convent to become a "bride of Christ."

Graff argues more generally that Pawlikowski's film "escapes from the threat of history into the beauty of images, music, and human faces." *Ida*, she maintains, refuses to engage with the specifics of history: "This film explains nothing, values nothing, aestheticizes everything, and makes everything a private matter."[56] Most other Polish critics avoid such sweeping generalizations but point out factual mistakes in the plot. Henryk Grynberg, the original returning Jew onscreen in *Birthplace*, lists several errors that Pawlikowski and Rebecca Lenkiewicz (the coauthor of *Ida*'s screenplay) did not register in their research. First, Wanda's refusal to have any postwar contact with her surviving niece would be unlikely. A Jewish communist would be sure to retrieve any young relatives who had been given sanctuary in a convent, an "enemy" institution. Whatever their personal hesitations, their party comrades would have persuaded them to do so. If that persuasion failed, there existed competing Jewish organizations seeking and paying to adopt saved Jewish children after the war. Second, a prosecutor would have been free to investigate the murders of her child and sister immediately after the war, an action that Wanda does not pursue until after she has lost her prosecutorial power. Third, Wanda would have been empowered to evict the Skiba family (their son Feliks is revealed as her relatives' murderer) and take back the house they appropriated—for her niece, if not for herself.[57] Grynberg's corrections are not nitpicking. As sociologist Karolina Wigura remarks in summing up these the contradictory reviews of *Ida*, if one makes a movie about 1960s Poland starring a Jewish novice and a former Stalinist prosecutor who happens to be a Jewish woman, "then it will be hard to sidestep history."[58]

That *Ida* at once spellbinds most reviewers and infuriates some scholars more familiar with Polish-Jewish history stems, I submit, from Pawlikowski's elliptical references to history and blend of real-life referent with his highly controlled dramatic and aesthetic vision. In a 2015 interview with Terry Gross, host of National Public Radio's show *Fresh Air*, Pawlikowski talks about the genesis of his two female protagonists. The seed for Anna/Ida came from "a story of a Polish priest who discovered, a little like my heroine, that he was of Jewish origins."[59] It seems very likely that Pawlikowski is referring to the famous case of Romuald-Jakub Weksler-Waszkiniel (b. 1943), who was adopted as an infant by Polish Christians (his Jewish parents died in the camps) and subsequently studied for the priesthood and became a professor of philosophy at Poland's Catholic University in Lublin. Weksler-Waszkiniel learned of his Jewish roots when he was thirty-five, and thereafter started studying Judaism and eventually moved to Israel. Director Ronit Kertsner released a documentary about his life, titled *Torn*, in 2011.[60] Pawlikowski was attracted to this man's complicated biography not as a subject or even a template but as "a good starting point for a story."

Indeed, Anna/Ida's story begins when her Mother Superior orders her to visit her lone living relative, despite the girl's reluctance, before she can take her vows. The nun tells the girl nothing about her relative or her origins. She leaves this enormous task to Wanda Gruz, the delinquent aunt. Wanda, who lives in a spacious apartment in Łódź (her compensation as a one-time party luminary), pitches Ida the facts of her Jewish identity like a hardball, perhaps to distance herself once more from too painful an association, perhaps to shake the seeming self-assurance of the Catholic novice with her sister's face sitting in her kitchen. During Ida's intense journey to familiarize herself with her roots, she must weather her aunt's initial animus, put up with a priest's dissembling, and consent to an odious deal with the Catholic who killed her mother and cousin. When Ida asks the priest in her parents' hometown if he knew any Jews during the war, he feigns ignorance, implicitly blaming the Jews for the gap that kept the religious communities apart: "The Jews stuck together" [Żydzi utrzymali się razem]. We later realize that this priest was the man who delivered her, an abandoned Jewish baby, to the convent. When Ida asks her mother's murderer why he did not kill her, he explains that she could live because she did not look like a Jew.

Thus, while Ida's revealed secret does offer a tantalizing starting point, Pawlikowski and his coauthor Lenkiewicz do not follow through, denying her possible positive ways to learn what it means to be a Jew. Ida's Jewishness seems to be a taboo topic for her Catholic elders, was the reason her mother and cousin were killed, would have led to her murder if she had a "Jewish look," and must be hidden once more if she wishes to take her vows. Any positive representation of her Jewishness remains a blank. The Jewish priest who had piqued Pawlikowski's interest had the means to study his Jewish heritage, learning Hebrew to read Torah, albeit almost two decades after Ida's "reveal." But, in provincial Poland of 1962, Ida has no access to mentors or materials. We can assume that she has never laid eyes on a self-identifying religious Jew, and certainly no Jewish religious dress could compete with the spiritual and social power that her novice's habit and headpiece bestow on her. Nor in the early 1960s can a camera linger over the beautifully austere or ornate interior of a synagogue in the eastern provinces of Poland, where Ida's convent is located. Almost all of these places of worship had been destroyed, along with the shtetls that surrounded them.[61]

Ida's only resource about her Jewish origins is her aunt, who left her family during the war to fight as a partisan in the communist-aligned People's Army. According to his interview on *Fresh Air*, Pawlikowski had an acquaintance in mind as the model for Wanda's character, a historical figure whom he only observed as a charismatic woman in postwar exile. When the director taught at Oxford University in the early 1980s, he socialized occasionally with Professor Włodzimierz Brus and his wife, Helena Wolińska-Brus (1919–2008). He remembers the latter as "a very charming older lady . . . who was warm, witty, ironic, [and] very wise about the world," a generous hostess who invited him over "for dinner and drinks occasionally because there were not many Polish speakers in Oxford at the time."[62] Wolińska-Brus's persona gave the director no clue to her past as a ruthless Communist Party careerist, who, as Pawlikowski was shocked to learn, was accused of crimes against humanity by the Polish government and eluded extradition to Poland for trial three times. This Jewish Varsovian, born Fajga Mindla Danielak, had joined the Communist Party as a young woman, and was the sole member of her family to escape death in Treblinka during the war. In the early 1950s, Wolińska-Brus rose to the rank of military prosecutor. Her illegal work in this position led the post-communist Polish authorities to accuse her "of fabricating evidence that led to the execution of General Emil Fieldorf [a Home Army leader who refused to collaborate with the People's Army] and the wrongful arrest of 24 others."[63]

As in the case of Weksler-Waszkiniel, Pawlikowski had no intention of recreating Wolińska-Brus on the screen. But the woman's notoriety, coupled with the general antipathy of post-1989 Polish audiences to early Communist Party leaders in the 1950s, meant that he and cowriter Lenkiewicz had to belittle Wanda's political backstory and, in consequence, her biography as a young Jewish girl who strived to be a hero. Wanda never explains why she became a communist and an atheist, a rebellious choice for a young middle-class Jewish woman in interwar Poland. She only mentions her flight to join the partisans as she openly mourns the deaths of her son and sister, disparaging her decision as abandoning family instead of fighting a monster. When Ida directly asks her aunt who she is, having observed how the local police fawn on her, Wanda's reply is succinct, harsh, and self-erasing. She once was a ruthless prosecutor nicknamed "Bloody Wanda" and now is a nobody. In early 1960s Poland, being a vigilant Stalinist is no longer possible, and being a decorated veteran of the Communist Party is passé, as the stiff line-up of bureaucrats at Wanda's graveside demonstrates, with their boilerplate eulogy and tinny recording of *The Internationale*.

What remains of the ardent partisan and Bloody Wanda is nevertheless a star character, more riveting than charming, thanks to Agata Kulesza's brilliant performance as a keenly intelligent, tough-talking, good-looking, damaged dame. Rather than reject her as a stereotype of the sensual Jewess, British reviewer Catherine Wheatley relishes her as the transposed Hollywood type of "an old-school noir broad," who plugs "the emotional dam with booze, sex, cigarettes, and sharp lines."[64] To be sure, Kulesza's Wanda is not boxed into either type. She suffers more profound trauma, and she offsets her self-destructive behavior with a mordant wit, classy clothes, and the undiminished instincts of a hunter. She persists as a woman accustomed to command, to interrogate, and to mete out justice, regardless of her status as a "nobody."

This Wanda is still moved by her love for Róża, her kid sister, and, to her shock, Ida seems to reincarnate Róża in flesh and spirit. After initially dismissing her niece, Wanda brings her home again after work, and provides her with much more than her name, birthplace, and the names of her parents. She shows the girl photographs of their Jewish family, including those of Róża and her "coarse" husband, who consigned them to a poor life on a small farm (figure 4.3). Wanda also implicitly teaches her naïve niece about the Holocaust. As she dryly explains, there are no tended graves where Ida can pray for her parents. Instead, Wanda the hunter spontaneously devises their road trip together in order to find out who murdered their family members and where their bodies might be dumped. Over the course of that trip, Ida visits her first home, meets the father, Szymon Skiba (Jerzy Trela) and the son, Feliks Skiba (Adam Szyszkowski), who had pledged to hide her family, and witnesses her aunt's fierce interrogation of both. Wanda's sharp questions at first upset her niece, but soon train Ida to ask her own of the local priest and Feliks. Ultimately, Ida alone does business with the murderer as he proposes to trade family bones for the rights to the family house.

Ida also learns from her aunt what it is like to be a member of a biological, secular family. Wanda's teasing of her niece runs the gamut from playful blasphemy (hiding Ida's picture of Jesus, insisting that they read the Bible together) to a few worldly temptations (spritzing her with cologne, offering her a party dress for a night on the town). These antics annoy and eventually anger the cloistered girl. But Wanda's greatest, rather conventional, worry about her niece's plans to pledge soul and body to a nonexistent god is that Ida would be deprived of the romance and fun she deserves. Fortunately, the older woman's decision to pick up Lis (Dawid Ogrodnik), a hitchhiking saxophone player bound for their destination, yields happier dividends. Lis not only opens Ida's eyes to her (and his) physical attractiveness but also remains her only friend outside of the convent after her aunt's death.

Wanda imparts perhaps the most important family facts to Ida in describing her mother's character. The film's initial shots of Ida depict her intently painting the face of a statue of Jesus that will occupy a prominent position in front of the convent; this scene's significance only resonates when Wanda reminisces about her sister. Wanda characterizes Róża as a dreamer and an artist, her opposite given her preference for "adventures." Wanda singles out the stained-glass window that Róża created with leftover materials and installed in their cow barn as an example of her sister's artistic, impractical nature. Yet when aunt and niece meet later in that barn and Wanda repeats her story, Ida stares at the window, mesmerized by her mother's work. (figure 4.4). The suggested mother-daughter resemblance raises an interesting question: Perhaps Ida is not so much a converted Jew who longs to be a bride of Christ, but an artistic soul who finds immense gratification in the convent's beauty and her role in adorning it. Perhaps Ida is not unlike her creator, Pawlikowski.

After a rugged road trip, capped by the 24-hour ordeal of finding the family remains, reinterring them in the Lublin family plot, and driving back to the

convent, the young protagonist has accrued only jagged fragments of family
lore—photos she has perused, a confession about how and why her mother
and cousin were murdered, intimate handling of her family's bones, and fond
stories Wanda has told her about her mother. But Ida has witnessed firsthand
the horror of and silence about local anti-Semitism and the Holocaust. And
she has come to know, love, and even like her teasing, godless, audacious
aunt. Though Wanda declines to watch Ida take her vows, the two come
together in an intense hug. Wanda wishes aloud that Róża could see her as
she is (her version of a family blessing), and Ida wipes away a tear.

Thus, the trip that Ida first resisted taking, balking at her Mother Superior's
order, has rattled Ida's worldview and literally disquieted her. The once
dedicated novice breaks the vow of silence, laughing softly at some memory
during a convent meal. She watches her fellow novices' clumsy intimate
moments from a detached perspective, perhaps feeling her own newly
acquired difference, perhaps wondering at their naïveté. Thinking intrudes on
her praying, though none of her thoughts are revealed in close-up or communication. The film includes no soul-searching dialogue between Ida and her
Mother Superior, only Ida's simple words addressed to her own work of art,
the statue of Jesus that she herself has painted: "I am not ready. Forgive me."
It is as if Ida has displaced the Jesus of the Catholic Church, her groom-to-be,
with a more personable idol-interlocutor.

Then Wanda's sudden suicide deprives Ida of her aunt's love and untapped
knowledge and forces her to see whether she can content herself with what
she clumsily reconstructs as her aunt's way of life. Back in Wanda's extrava-
gantly empty apartment, Ida does what she thinks her aunt would do: listens
to her records, puts on her evening dress and high heels, tries smoking a cigarette, drinks vodka, and eventually goes out with Lis, her saxophone-playing
admirer, to listen to him play, dance with him, and go to bed with him. When
Lis invites her to travel with his band, Ida interrogates him quietly, repeatedly
asking, "And then?" [*I potem?*]. Put on the spot, Lis guesses out loud how
their life together would unfold: a dog, marriage, children, a house, troubles.
Before Lis awakes, Ida has redonned her habit and seems to be heading back
to the convent.

We can infer that Ida is frightened by the two life blueprints that she
barely knows: her aunt's "adventures" and Lis's simplified sketch. But the
scene of her walking does not suggest, as Datner and Graff maintain, that
she is off to atone for her aunt's sins or "to wash away her Jewishness." Her
expression conveys anxiety rather than resolution. For the first time, Żal uses
a handheld camera, framing Ida from the front in a medium shot with no
anchoring visual connection to the convent building in the background. Ida
faces a steady series of vehicles driving in the opposite direction, giving her
a wide berth, yet disrupting her progress. Perhaps, in Ida's calculation, the

convent offers her the most peaceful life in which no loved one will abandon her and no troubles disturb her. But, taking her vows (a concluding scene that Pawlikowski and Lenkiewicz did not insert) means leading an entire life in a silence she no longer seems able to keep and a solitude that will not satisfy her new craving for connection. For, if Ida remains silent and cloistered, her complicated identity will petrify into a permanent blank, like disconnected bones hastily reburied in an unfamiliar graveyard. The film leaves us face to face with a young woman who seems, above all, "not ready."

POLES AGAINST POLES: DIGGING UP THE HOLOCAUST AT HOME IN PASIKOWSKI'S *AFTERMATH*

You mustn't forget that we filmmakers are always trying to persuade the audience that the picture on the screen is something real, and I'm also trying to get them to believe they are alongside the hero, looking into a small village on the Eastern border of Poland.

—Władysław Pasikowski[65]

Director Władysław Pasikowski, primarily famed for successful crime thrillers informed by the action-packed plots and psychopathic portraiture of Francis Ford Coppola and Martin Scorsese's mafia pictures, started work on a very different sort of movie in 2005.[66] He wrote a screenplay titled *Kaddish* after reading Gross's first monograph on Jedwabne, a book that he found both revelatory and shaming: "Until I'd read *Neighbors*, I had no idea about what went on in Jedwabne and other towns in the areas that the Red Army had abandoned after June 1941."[67] Controversy surrounded Pasikowski's project from the outset; investors worried about funding what was perceived to be an anti-Polish film, and *Kaddish* was shelved for six years and reworked under the new title of *Aftermath*.[68] Since its 2012 release, the film provoked right-wing nationalist outrage ranging from name-calling ("anti-Polish propaganda") to a ban on its screening in some cinemas to online death threats and verbal attacks on its star, Maciej Stuhr, in which he was "degraded" from "Pole" to "Jew."[69] At the same time, Pasikowski's film won accolades from his professional peers—the Critics' Prize at the 2012 Gdynia Film Festival and the Yad Vashem Award at the 2013 Jerusalem Film Festival.[70]

Though *Aftermath* debuted a year before *Ida*, I analyze it last in this series for several reasons. This film moves its retrospective point of view on the local Holocaust forward to 2000, when one might expect a less deafening silence and more acknowledgment of Polish Christian complicity. *Aftermath* demands that acknowledgment. As Polish reviewer Barbara Hollender aptly observes, *Aftermath* departs from other screen representations about Polish participation in the Holocaust—both documentaries and features—by delivering its message "with a sledge hammer."[71] Other reviewers echo both her approval of the film's topic and ambivalence about its simplifications, redundancies, and heavy-handed symbolism. As Mikołaj Mirowski shrewdly states in his review title, *Aftermath* "is a very important, though not a great film."[72] Above all, in contrast to the films analyzed above, the importance of Pasikowski's film lies in its concern for how post-Holocaust generations of Polish Christians *must* respond to the atrocities committed by their parents, grandparents, and great-grandparents. As Janusz Wróblewski asserts, *Aftermath* does not tell the history of Jedwabne, for there is no doubt that those horrors took place. Instead, the film "speaks about the moral hangover, burning shame, and terrifying inherited memories that burden everyone's conscience. What should be done, what stance Poles should adopt—not only those who will do anything to jettison the sins of the past (the film mainly targets them), but also young people who have nothing to do with those crimes?"[73]

Pasikowski constructs this serious film as a thriller, a genre he knows well, though virtually all his reviewers foresee the plot's inevitable collapse into hyperbolic horror. Even a reviewer for *Variety*, who describes *Aftermath* as "a fast-paced 'backwater burg with a dark secret' quasi-horror film," recognizes that the final secret "looms too large to fit within the plot's parameters, creating strange disconnects between form and content."[74] Yet, for the first half of the film, the thriller's standard features—stalked and harassed protagonists, ominous non-diegetic soundtrack, escalating violence, and an increasingly fruitful and dangerous investigation—keep the plot humming. We watch as Franciszek (Franek) Kalina (played with admirable stubbornness by Ireneusz Czop), a Pole who spent the last twenty years in Chicago, first returns to the eastern fields of Poland B to find out why his younger brother, Józef (Józek), whom Maciej Stuhr interprets as sensitive, slow, and obdurate, has frightened his wife and kids into relocating to Chicago as well. Guilt and resentment still fester between the two siblings. Franek is sorry for emigrating and not risking return trips for his parents' funerals, and Józek cannot quite forgive him for his disappearance and long absence. The hard work of maintaining the family farm has fallen entirely on Józek's shoulders. But the theft of Franek's meager luggage, a rock thrown through the window of Józek's farmhouse, and the villagers' surly advice to Franek to get his brother out of town convince the older brother that Józek is in danger and needs his unconditional support, come what may.

Franek quickly takes on the requisite role of investigator in the thriller, trying to understand how his brother has riled the village and researching why their father's property title for their farm is not in order, a fact that blocks the bank from giving Józek a loan. In the first case, Franek is stunned to learn that Józek has been "rescuing" *matsevah* from the road where Germans had denigrated them for use as paving material during the war. Somehow Józek has managed to re-erect them in their "mother's field" [*matczyne pole*] and learned enough Hebrew to decipher their inscriptions. As Józek explains to his consternated brother, he had to save these tombstones "because they [represented] human beings after all," and he could not do otherwise (figure 4.5). Though some reviewers, along with Franek, find Józek's "hobby" incomprehensible, others, most notably Elżbieta Janicka, point out Józek's resemblance to the real-life Zbigniew Romaniuk who appears in Marian Marzyński's 1996 *Shtetl* (a series prepared for the American WGBH program, *Frontline*).[75] Janicka notes that both the historical Romaniuk and the fictional Józek are straightforward, uncomplicated, brave, and sensitive loners, whose experience in restoring *matsevah* realigns their worldview.

Franek's second case proves more complicated and, ultimately, more dangerous. In keeping with the thriller's dependence on unbelievably speedy resolutions of intricate problems, Franek discovers, over the course of a single afternoon, a suspicious collective wartime transfer of properties from Jewish to Christian villagers, a major clue that somehow has eluded the aged documents clerk (Stanisław Brudny) for decades.[76] The Kalinas's father and all their surviving Christian neighbors had managed to swap their marshy, flood-prone holdings for the Jews' more arable land on high ground two months before the Red Army liberated Poland from the Nazis. Franek and Józek had assumed that the family obtained the new property as a result of the agrarian reform conducted in the communist era. This news leads Franek to the most shocking phase of his investigation: figuring out the logistics and parties involved in the land transfer by questioning surviving witnesses. As unseen hostile neighbors mount ever more threatening attacks on the brothers—killing Józek's watchdog, painting anti-Semitic graffiti on his house, and setting fire to his "mother's field" filled with *matsevah*—Franek interviews an elderly woman in the hospital and old Sudecki (Ryszard Ronczewski), the codger who had warned him his first day to take Józek back with him to America. Before the younger males in Sudecki's family run Franek off their property with pitchforks, the old man angrily spills a clue: "How do you know the Germans deported the Jews? You can't say what didn't happen. Look to your own house."

At this point the fast-paced thriller plot derails, devolving into one hyperbolic scene after another. Pasikowski pulls out all the stops to convince viewers that a Jedwabne-like massacre of Polish Jews took place here and implicates almost all the remaining families as perpetrators. Franek drags Józek to the burned-down structure of their parents' first house to dig for

Jewish bodies in a raging thunderstorm. Over the course of one night, the brothers recover large piles of skulls, femurs, and pelvises—the bones of many of the 100 Jews who once lived in their native village. As if this two-person excavation of a mass grave is not enough, come dawn a local hermitess (a star turn by the famed elderly actress, Danuta Szaflarska) happens upon the exhausted duo at the site. She not only bears witness to the atrocities perpetrated by Christians against Jews that fateful night (without direct German involvement) but also states that "everyone saw . . . the entire village" drive the Jews into the Kalinas's house, set it on fire, and guarantee that all of them perished in the inferno, even small children.

Pasikowski has conjured up a nearly perfect eyewitness for Franek, but the hermitess herself was not a perpetrator and has the head injury to prove it. Therefore, the brothers immediately decide to confront old Malinowski, then head of the village, about his actions. The ninety-year-old Malinowski (played by Robert Rogalski with frightening verisimilitude) quickly morphs into a monster before their eyes, descending from lies to threats ("hey, Kalina, be careful the truth doesn't choke you") to an enraged, in-the-moment recounting of their father's bestiality. While Malinowski lit the deadly fire on one side, he shouts, the elder Kalina ignited it on the other, hacked his Jewish neighbors with a saw, and beat a Jewish woman who had resisted his sexual advances with such fury that she cried out repeatedly for her mother as she died from a partial decapitation. Janicka remarks that the actor Rogalski himself had witnessed the liquidation of the ghetto and, with Pasikowski's permission, doubled the length of his written monologue by drawing on the horrors that he had seen.[77]

Malinowski's chilling confession-defamation plus the material evidence of scores of bodies provide the Kalina brothers ample grounds to demand a federal investigation, albeit far from their village of the damned. Instead of sending his protagonists off on a bus to Warsaw, Pasikowski prefers a climax in which a spectacular act of atrocity warns the viewers how covering up a crime against humanity must erupt in evil in the "aftermath." To the befuddlement and chagrin of almost all of the film's reviewers, a group of villagers kill Józek offscreen, beating him, cutting his throat, and hanging his bruised body on wooden supports high up on a large barn door. The camera reveals this mock crucifixion ominously, with a high angle shot on the door as it slowly swings open. In the absence of any Jews, the descendants of the original mob settle for a "Jew lover" as their substitute target, perhaps the most grotesque, idiotic way of keeping the village's dread secret. Janicka, the outlier among the critics, argues that the symbolism works well: the Polish Christians in *Aftermath*, who long have perceived themselves as martyrs like Christ in the world, literally and symbolically "out" themselves as the cruci-fiers.[78] In contrast, *Variety*'s Scheib recoils from the crucifixion scene as "a denouement straight out of the Middle Ages."[79] Hollender diplomatically wishes that Pasikowski had had more faith in his viewers' intelligence and avoided such excesses.[80] Wróblewski deplores the heavy-handed symbolism in this and other scenes as irritating and unnecessary.[81] Grynberg does not mince words, condemning this "unbelievable crucifixion" for undercutting the real horror and suffering of the Jews killed in the local Holocaust sixty years before (according to timeline of the film).[82]

By the film's end, Czop as Franek must haul *Aftermath* back into the twenty-first century. His character has grown through the brothers' ordeal, gaining viewer empathy without losing its believability. Stuhr as Józek plays a doomed symbol, a loving son who tended the family farm only to find that his patrimony is stolen property, his parents' former home the site of a massacre, and his father a patriarch-turned-beast. This knowledge undoes him, and a village alarmed by his modeling of a more inclusive notion of Polishness makes an example of his execution to frighten off those who might share his views. Franek, in contrast, returns to Poland only because he must, expresses neither sentimentality nor nostalgia for the fields of "home," and broke with his father long ago. Strangely enough, Franek has turned into an unabashed anti-Semite in America, directing his anger at the "Jews of Chicago," who, he attests, exploit cheap Polish immigrant labor for dangerous jobs even as they badmouth Polish intolerance.

Yet, as soon as Franek realizes that Józek is under attack, he responds with absolute loyalty and concrete plans of action. Despite his anti-Semitism, he helps his brother haul away more *matsevah* to their "mother's field," and fights beside him against a group of angry villagers. Most important, Franek will not back away from the ugly truth, no matter how much it tarnishes his family and proves "the Jews of Chicago" right in their claims against the Poles. Franek opposes a suddenly terrified Józek, who thinks that they should rebury the bones where they found them, insisting instead that they give their Jewish neighbors a decent burial: "In twenty generations they'll remember about our village, Malinowski, and our father. And that's their right. And maybe the likes of our father won't show up again."

In the final scene of *Aftermath*, Franek has achieved that goal. He looks on as Jews from overseas visit the newly created Jewish graveyard and lay memorial stones atop the *matsevah* that his brother had saved, while a rabbi reads Kaddish. Franek figures as the only Pole in the frame, implying that he is the single descendant from the village who openly supports commemorating the local Jews whom the villagers had murdered. True to his character, his expression is grim and he chooses to honor the dead in his own way—with a Catholic votive candle rather than a stone. Yet Franek, the stubborn anti-Semitic Pole who could not prevent himself from doing the right thing, remains the lone living tolerable protagonist beside whom we viewers can stand.

CONCLUSION

As each new generation of Polish citizens moves roughly twenty years further away from the experience of the Holocaust and its highly censored representation under the PRL, Polish screening of Christian-Jewish relations in the twenty-first century, in most cases, has become more nuanced in terms of characterization, plot development, and stylistic approach. The umbrella of the Jewish revival encouraged the historical study of Jewish life across its broad, diverse spectrum—from Hasidic communities in the shtetls to Bundists and Folkists who sought to create a modern Yiddish-language society throughout Poland to acculturated Jews who retained connections with the metropolitan Jewish community even as they advanced in Polish-language professions and the arts. Within this spectrum, Dylewska's *Po-Lin: Scraps of Memory* undertakes the difficult challenge of projecting moving, positive images of shtetl Jews who counter interwar anti-Semitic caricatures of Jews as poor, exoticized, and "backwards," on the one hand, and, on the other, the terrible wartime photographs of starved, terrorized Jews on the verge of deportation to a death camp. Dylewska succeeds in restoring and sequencing a wonderful cache of home movies, privileging all those who view her film with glimpses of Jewish families striving to look their best before the cameras of their emigrated relatives or the emigrated relatives of their Jewish neighbors. The footage that Dylewska has fit together constitutes a revealing, valuable resource on Polish *Jews*, but it is of no relevance for gauging interwar Christian-Jewish relations, despite the included testimony of Polish Christian witnesses, and a supposedly authenticating narration.

In the wake of intrepid documentarians in the 1980s and 1990s and equally determined scholars since the 2000s, feature film directors have cracked open the Pandora's box of the Holocaust in Poland in assorted ways. Focusing on the Holocaust in progress, Holland chose for *In Darkness* a screenplay based on a true story set in Lwów, perhaps Poland's most ethnically and linguistically complicated city. The filmmaker takes advantage of this extraordinarily diverse location to blur multiple binary oppositions—between heroes and villains, patriots and collaborators, criminals and "upright" citizens, greater and lesser victims. Holland and Shamoon, her screenwriter, juxtapose a thieving, brutish Christian with a small group of varied Jewish characters—secular, religious, sympathetic, repugnant, overwhelmed, and audacious. Relations between Poldek Socha and his clients remain mutually suspicious and business-based until late in the film. There are several instances where Socha, himself under surveillance, can only pray that the Jews are savvy enough to hide themselves without warning (they are). The grossly naturalist setting of the sewers challenges and victimizes them all, especially when spring flooding nearly drowns or crushes them. By the conclusion of *In Darkness*, a single

Christian family and a small contingent of Jews have come to trust each other, but the uneasy anti-climax conveys what sort of welcome all of them will receive in postwar Poland.

The ending of *In Darkness* casts a pall also palpable in the two postwar films analyzed above. In Pawlikowski's *Ida*, a novice who grew up in a convent is either denied or spared the knowledge that she was born a Jew until she has decided to take her vows as a nun. Given communist Poland's acceptance of the Catholic Church aboveground, this young woman could lead an untroubled life as a nun, respected as a spiritual intercessor by the vast majority of Poles. Yet, by forcing Ida to meet her aunt, Wanda Gruz, Pawlikowski and Lenkiewicz open the Pandora's box for both women as well as Polish viewers in 2013 still absorbing the facts of Polish Christian complicity in murdering and robbing Jews. Wanda, a former prosecutor, does not doubt this possibility and, to her niece's surprise, ultimately wrings a confession out of the Polish farmer who killed Ida's mother and Wanda's young son. For Wanda, the turmoil of encountering her beloved sister in her niece reconnects her to the pain of long-buried grief and guilt and the bittersweet joy of a new family attachment. This she does not survive. Ida's world is blown wide open by the revelation of her Jewish heritage, her encounters with a murderous, but publicly silenced, anti-Semitism, and her growing attachment to her aunt, who introduces her to her first romantic admirer and to tales about and at least one work of her artistic mother, Róża. By the film's end, we still have no idea how Ida will navigate her life, given these revelations and experiences, because we last see her on the run.

By contrast, Pasikowski's bold judgment is painfully clear, but his film without innovation or reflection on the broader consequences of its action. As soon as Franek Kalina arrives at the family farm in *Aftermath*, the director lights the fuse to blow the box apart, releasing the demons, but unconcerned about how future generations can put them to rest. Józek Kalina has been striving to honor the local Jewish dead sixty years after they were murdered, not knowing who killed them or how. There are a few other villagers sympathetic to his cause—the police chief, his young deputy, the elderly village priest, and a female doctor—but their response is merely palliative, protecting him from being lynched or patching him up after inevitable fights. The rest of the village lurks as an evil mob, pledged to keep the secret that their Christian parents or grandparents massacred the Jews and then reaped the spoils. When Franek flies in from America, his investigations solve both mysteries and reveal the key role that his and Józek's father played in both. But when Józek is executed in a mock crucifixion, viewers learn nothing about this second crime's aftermath. The final scene portrays Franek, the outsider, surveying the model Jewish graveyard that his brother had wanted. Yet the Christian perpetrators and their accomplices, insofar as the film is concerned, remain offscreen, apparently unpunished, and unmoved toward any admission of guilt or pursuit of reconciliation.

BH

NOTES

1. The low estimate is taken from the World Jewish Congress website, which cites Hebrew University demographer Sergio DellaPergola's figures of between 4,500 and 10,000 Jews in 2002 https://www.worldjewishcongress.org/en/about/communities/PL. Accessed May 2, 2020. According to Sasha Vasiljuk, "We're Here: Polish Jews Today," culture.pl, August 1, 2017, https://culture.pl/en/article/were -here-polands-jewish-community-today. Accessed May 2, 2020. According to Sasha Vasiljuk, "We're Here: Poland's Jewish Community Today," current estimates range from 30,000 to 50,000.

2. For more on these Soviet-era policies (during the periods of high Stalinism and Edward Gierek's rule) that purposefully did not delineate "special victims," see Marek Haltof's *Polish Film and the Holocaust: Politics and Memory* (New York: Berghahn Books, 2012): 34–35, 37, 48, 117–18, 134, 135.

3. An extensive history of the development of Jewish Studies at Jagiellonian University can be found on its Institute website, http://www.judaistyka.uj.edu.pl/instytut/historia. Accessed May 3, 2020.

4. See the official website for the Jewish Culture Festival in Kraków, https://www.jewishfestival.pl/en/. Accessed December 11, 2020.

5. Geneviève Zubrzycki, "The Politics of Jewish Absence in Contemporary Poland," *Journal of Contemporary History* 25, no. 2 (2017): 258.

6. Maciej Pawlak, "30 Years of the Ronald S. Lauder Foundation in Poland, 1987-2017," *Scripta Judaica Cracoviensia* 15 (2017): 155–67.

7. Major benefactors of Polin—including the Koret Foundation, the Taube Family Foundation, Irene Kronhill Pletka and Kronhill Pletka Foundation, and many others—are listed here, https://www.polin.pl/en/support/donor-list. Accessed December 11, 2020. The Jewish Community Centre, opened in 2008, was founded by Britain's World Jewish Relief and the Joint Distribution Committee.

8. Jewish Heritage Europe, a web portal funded by Rothschild Foundation (Hanadiv) Europe and coordinated by Ruth Ellen Gruber, serves as a very useful resource on the broad scope of these projects and activities in Poland. See https://jewish-heritage-europe.eu/. Accessed December 11, 2020.

9. For at least two examples of such stewards, see Beth Holmgren, "Holocaust History and Jewish Heritage Preservation: Scholars and Stewards Working in PiS-ruled Poland," *Shofar: An Interdisciplinary Journal of Jewish Studies* 37, no. 1 (2019): 96–107.

10. For more information on this fascinating phenomenon, see Katka Reszke's *Return of the Jew: Identity Narratives of the Third Post-Holocaust Generation of Jews in Poland* (Boston: Academic Studies Press, 2013).

11. For an informative interview with the filmmaker, see Greg Archer's "A Town Called Brzostek Among the Compelling Documentaries at the 27th Polish Film Festival in America," *Huffpost*, November 11, 2015; updated December 6, 2017, https://www.huffpost.com/entry/a-town-called-brzostek-am_b_8535638. Accessed December 11, 2020.

12. For a fascinating study of the Jewish heritage tourist industry in post-communist Kraków, see Erica Lehrer's *Jewish Poland Revisited: Heritage Tourism in Unquiet Spaces* (Bloomington, IN: Indiana University Press, 2013).

13. For more information on this lovely film, see Penny Schwarz, "The Intrepid Couple Who Restored a Gem of a Polish Synagogue," *The Times of Israel*, September 30, 2015, https://www.timesofisrael.com/the-intrepid-couple-who-restored-a-gem-of-a-polish-synagogue/. Accessed December 11, 2020.

14. *The Return* (edited, directed, and produced by Adam Zucker), 2014. Accessed December 10, 2020.

15. Cited from Tom Tugend, "Five Years in the Making: 'The Return' Takes New Look at Polish Jewish Revival," *Jewish Telegraphic Agency*, January 21, 2015, https://www.jta.org/2015/01/21/culture/five-years-in-the-making-the-return-takes-new-look-at-polish-jewish-revival. Accessed December 11, 2020.

16. These estimates are taken from the website for the U.S. Holocaust Memorial Museum, https://encyclopedia.ushmm.org/content/en/article/polish-victims. Accessed December 11, 2020.

17. The US Holocaust Memorial Museum notes this punishment for Polish Christians hiding Polish Jews on this web page: https://www.ushmm.org/learn/timeline-of-events/1942-1945/german-poster-announces-death-penalty-for-aiding-jews. Accessed December 12, 2020.

18. On the Yad Vashem website, the individual honored Poles number 6,992; the next largest group are the Dutch at 5,778. From the Yad Vashem website—yadvashem.org—"Statistics" page listed under organizing page "The Righteous" and subsequent page "About the Righteous": https://www.yadvashem.org/righteous/statistics.html. Accessed December 12, 2020.

19. See, among many others, Dariusz Stola's essay, "Jedwabne: Revisiting the Evidence and Nature of the Crime," *Holocaust and Genocide Studies* 17, no. 1 (Spring 2003): 139–51; and Anna Bikont's *The Crime and the Silence: Confronting the Massacre of Jews in Wartime Jedwabne*, trans. Alissa Valles (New York: Farrar, Straus and Giroux, 2016), 18, where one of the eyewitnesses estimates that 1,000 Jews were forced into the barn. This number is less than the 1,600 that Gross cites in his book. The exhumation of the bodies on the site was limited to five days, because of the objections of Orthodox Jews. The Polish original of Bikont's book is titled *My z Jedwabnego* [We from Jedwabne] (Wołowiec, PL: Wydawnictwo Czarne, 2015).

20. For example, in 2016 "in response to the 2,000 letters that had been received by the president's office calling for a renunciation of the honorary title," the current Polish government, under the leadership of the right-wing "Law and Justice" Party, wanted to strip Gross of the "Order of Merit" he was awarded in 1996. See Ofer Aderets, "Historian Who Shed Light on World War II Massacres Goes from Honoree to 'Pole Hater,'" *Haaretz*, March 1, 2016, https://www.haaretz.com/jewish/.premium-the-pole-who-is-breaking-the-silence-1.5410809. Accessed December 12, 2020.

21. Geneviève Zubrzycki, "The Politics of Jewish Absence in Contemporary Poland," *Journal of Contemporary History* 25, no. 2 (2017): 257–258.

22. On June 27, 2018, the Polish Parliament amended this law, "remov[ing] parts that imposed jail terms on people who suggest the nation was complicit in Nazi crimes." Herb Keinon, "Poland Changes Its Controversial Holocaust Law," *Jerusalem Post*, June 27, 2018, https://www.jpost.com/diaspora/poland-changes-its -controversial-holocaust-law-561025. Accessed December 10, 2020.

23. Deborah Sklar, "Polish Filmmaker Put WWII Massacre on the Map," *Jewish Telegraphic Agency*, July 8, 2001, https://www.jta.org/2001/09/18/lifestyle/polish -filmmaker-put-wwii-massacre-on-the-map. Accessed December 10, 2020.

24. Marci Shore, "Conversing with Ghosts: Jedwabne, *Żydokomuna*, and Totalitarianism," *Kritika: Explorations in Russian and Eurasian History* 6, no. 2 (Spring 2005): 345–374.

25. Glenn Kurtz, *Three Minutes in Poland: Discovering a Lost World in a 1938 Family Film* (Farrar, Straus, & Giroux, 2014). Kurtz's book focuses on how the author managed to identify the Polish Jews who happened to appear on his grandfather's home movie made in Poland between the world wars.

26. Janusz Wróblewski, "Recenzja filmu *Po-Lin: Okruchy pamięci*, reż. Jolanta Dylewska," *Polityka*, November 10, 2008, https://www.polityka.pl/tygodnikpolityka /kultura/film/273316,1,recenzja-filmu-po-lin-rez-jolanta-dylewska.read. Accessed December 12, 2020.

27. Tadeusz Sobolewski, "Film z tamtego świata," *Gazeta wyborcza*, November 8–9, 2008, https://wyborcza.pl/1,75410,5896960,Film_z_tamtego_swiata.html. Accessed December 12, 2020.

28. Konrad Zarębski, *"Po-Lin: Okruchy pamięci,"* Culture.pl, 2009, https://culture.pl/pl/dzielo/po-lin-okruchy-pamieci. Accessed December 12, 2020.

29. Marek Haltof, *Polish Film and the Holocaust: Politics and Memory* (New York: Berghahn Books, 2012), 223.

30. Konrad Zarębski, "Jolanta Dylewska," culture.pl, November 2009, https:// culture.pl/pl/tworca/jolanta-dylewska. Accessed December 12, 2020.

31. Haltof, *Polish Film and the Holocaust*, 223.

32. Konrad Zarębski, *"Po-Lin: Okruchy pamięci,"* culture.pl, 2009; Sobolewski, "Film z tamtego świata" . . .; and Elżbieta Janicka and Tomasz Żukowski, "Przemoc filosemicka [Philosemitic violence]," *Studia Litteraria et Historica* 12, no. 1 (2012): 9.

33. Janusz Wróblewski, "Recenzja filmu *Po-Lin: Okruchy pamięci*, reż. Jolanta Dylewska."

34. It is interesting that Dylewska phrases this as an intense connection between herself and the subject, which mistakenly implies that the screened subject itself is animate. Zarębski, "Jolanta Dylewska," culture.pl, November 2009.

35. In their deeply critical reading of *Po-Lin*, Elżbieta Janicka and Tomasz Żukowski compare Fronczewski's vocal effect to that of the famed Russian tele-hypnotist, Anatolii Kashpirovskii. "Przemoc filosemicka" 2012: 5.

36. Ibid. 5, 2.

37. Ibid., 27, 29, 31.

38. Janusz Wróblewski, "Recenzja filmu *Po-Lin: Okruchy pamięci*, reż. Jolanta Dylewska."

39. Tadeusz Sobolewski, "Film z tamtego świata."

40. Janicka and Żukowski, "Przemoc filosemicka": 17–20.

41. Ibid., 32–35.

42. This information was recovered from a website about Jewish cemeteries in Poland, http://cmentarze-zydowskie.pl/kaluszynhistoria.htm. Accessed June 13, 2020.

43. A. O. Scott, "Unlikely Hero in an Underground Hideout, Away from the Nazis," *New York Times*, December 8, 2011, https://www.nytimes.com/2011/12/09/movies/in-darkness-from-agnieszka-holland-review.html. Accessed December 13, 2020.

44. For a few selected examples of this scholarship, see, for example, Annette Insdorf, *Indelible Shadows: Film and the Holocaust*, 2nd edition (Cambridge: Cambridge University Press, 2002); Omer Bertov, *The "Jew" in Cinema: From The Golem to Don't Touch My Holocaust* (Bloomington, IN: Indiana University Press, 2005); and Aaron Kerner, *Film and the Holocaust: New Perspectives on Dramas, Documentaries, and Experimental Films* (London and New York: Continuum, 2011).

45. Sebastian Adamkiewicz, "*W ciemności*, reż. Agnieszka Holland –recenzja," *Histmag.org*, January 10, 2012, https://histmag.org/W-ciemnosci-rez.-Agnieszka -Holland-recenzja-filmu-6261. Accessed December 13, 2020.

46. Krystyna Chiger and Daniel Paisner, *The Girl in the Green Sweater* (New York: St. Martin's Press, 2008). The first English-language account of these Jews' wartime ordeal appeared in Robert Marshall's *In the Sewers of Lwów: A Heroic Story of Survival from the Holocaust* (London and New York: Bloomsbury Press, 2013, reprinted edition).

47. Piotr Śmiałowski, "A przecież mógł ich wydać," *Kino*, 2012, 1, pp. 15–19.

48. Jedrzej Dudkiewicz, " 'W ciemności'—recenzja," *Magazyn Kontakt*, January 9, 2012, https://magazynkontakt.pl/w-ciemnosci-recenzja/. Accessed December 13, 2020.

49. Konrad J. Zarębski, " 'W ciemności'—reż. Agnieszka Holland," culture.p l, December 2011, https://culture.pl/pl/dzielo/w-ciemnosci-rez-agnieszka-holland. Accessed December 13, 2020.

50. Timothy Snyder, "The Overwhelming Realism of 'In Darkness,' " *New York Times*, *Culture Desk*, February 22, 2012, https://www.newyorker.com/culture/culture -desk/the-overwhelming-realism-of-in-darkness. Accessed December 10, 2020.

51. Elżbieta Ostrowska, " 'I Will Wash It Out': Holocaust Reconciliation in Agnieszka Holland's 2011 Film, *In Darkness*," *Holocaust and Genocide Studies*, 79, no. 1 (Spring 2015): 58, 63.

52. Sebastian Adamkiewicz, "*W ciemności*, reż. Agnieszka Holland—recenzja," *Histmag.org*.

53. Zofia Rojek, " 'Ida' pełna antysemickich stereotypów? Krytyka najnowszego filmu Pawlikowskiego," *naTemat.pl*, November 5, 2013, https://natemat.pl/80843,ida -pelna-antysemickich-stereotypow. Accessed December 14, 2020.

54. Anna Zawadzka, *"Ida," Lewica.pl,* October 25, 2013, http://lewica.pl/blog/zawadzka/28791/. Accessed December 15, 2020. Richard Brody's review of *Ida*—as Goscilo points out, the first to appear in *The New Yorker*—likewise criticizes the film's emphasis on Wanda's "bad behavior": "Ultimately, the movie legitimizes resentment of the very Jews who were murdered on Polish soil—even at the hands of Poles. "The Distasteful Vagueness of 'Ida,' " *The New Yorker*, May 9, 2014, https://www.newyorker.com/culture/richard-brody/the-distasteful-vagueness-of-ida#:~:text=It%20tells%20the%20story%20of,family%2C%20and%20was%20named%20Ida. Accessed December 2, 2020.

55. Agnieszka Graff, "'Ida'—subtelność i polityka," *Krytyka polityczna*, November 1, 2013, https://krytykapolityczna.pl/kultura/film/graff-ida-subtelnosc-i-polityka/. Accessed December 14, 2020; Rojek, 2013.

56. Agnieszka Graff, " 'Ida'—subtelność i polityka," *Krytyka polityczna.*

57. Henryk Grynberg, "Powodzenie 'Pokłosia' i 'Idy' w Nowym Jorku [Fragment 'Pamiętnika II']," *Kultura liberalna*, July 8, 2014, https://dzismis.com/2014/07/18/powodzenie-poklosia-i-idy-w-nowym-jorku-fragment-pamietnika-ii/. Accessed December 14, 2020.

58. Karolina Wigura, "Dlaczego Ida tak gniewa. Częsciowo podsumowanie dyskusji o filmie Pawła Pawlikowskiego," *Kultural liberalna*, November 26, 2013, https://kulturaliberalna.pl/2013/11/26/wigura-dlaczego-ida-tak-gniewa-czesciowe-podsumowanie-dyskusji-o-filmie-pawla-pawlikowskiego/. Accessed December 15, 2020.

59. NPR show, *Fresh Air*, hosted by Terry Gross, " 'Ida' Director Made Film to 'Recover the Poland of His Childhood," February 12, 2015 interview with Paweł Pawlikowski, https://www.npr.org/2015/02/12/385742784/ida-director-made-film-to-recover-the-poland-of-his-childhood. Accessed December 13, 2020.

60. Mark Pattison, "Movie Tells Story of Polish Priest Born a Jew during the Holocaust," *The Forward*, December 6, 2011, https://thedialog.org/featured/movie-tells-story-of-polish-priest-born-a-jew-during-holocaust/. Accessed December 13, 2020. See also the fascinating interview that Karol Dzięciołowska conducted with Weksler-Waszkiniel in May 2009, Lublin, posted on https://sprawiedliwi.org.pl/en/stories-of-rescue/your-stories/interview-pr-romuald-jakub-weksler-waszkinel. Accessed December 13, 2020.

61. The impressive fortress synagogue in Szydłów, the town where Wanda and Ida stay, was destroyed by the Nazis, but renovated as a library and cultural center in the 1960s.

62. Terry Gross, " 'Ida' Director Made Film to 'Recover the Poland of His Childhood," February 12, 2015 interview with Paweł Pawlikowski.

63. Robert Booth, "Widow, 88, Faces Arrest Warrant over Death of Polish Hero," *The Guardian*, November 20, 2007, https://www.theguardian.com/uk/2007/nov/21/secondworldwar.ukcrime. Accessed December 8, 2020. Nick Hodge, "Helena Wolińska-Brus: 1919-2008," *The Kraków Post*, December 31, 2008, http://www.krakowpost.com/pdf/Krakow_Post_issue_51.pdf. page 7. Accessed December 8, 2020. One of those wrongfully arrested was Władysław Bartoszewski, one of the great heroes of liberal Poland—an Auschwitz prisoner, "a key member of the Polish

Underground's Council to Aid Jews," and, after the fall of communist Poland, an elected member of the Polish Senate, and an honorary Israeli citizen.

64. Catherine Wheatley, "Film of the Week: 'Ida,' " *Sight and Sound: The International Film Magazines*, November 28, 2014, https://www2.bfi.org.uk/news -opinion/sight-sound-magazine/reviews-recommendations/film-week-ida. Accessed December 10, 2020.

65. Leonard Quart, "Breaking National Taboos: An Interview with Władysław Pasikowski and Dariusz Jabłoński," *Cinéaste* 9, no. 31 (Winter 2013): 22–25, 60.

66. Michał Przeperski, " 'Pokłosie'—reż. Władysława Pasikowskiego, recenzja i ocena filmu," *Histmag.org*, November 15, 2012, https://histmag.org/Poklosie-rez. -Wladyslaw-Pasikowski-7296. Accessed December 12, 2020.

67. Leonard Quart, "Breaking National Taboos: An Interview Władysław Pasikowski and Dariusz Jabłoński"; Barbara Hollender, " 'Pokłosie'—recenzja filmu," *Rzeczpospolita*, November 9, 2012, https://www.rp.pl/artykul/950085 -Poklosie—recenzja-filmu.html. Accessed December 12, 2020.

68. Barbara Hollender, " 'Pokłosie'—recenzja filmu," *Rzeczpospolita*. In Quart's interview, producer Dariusz Jabłoński states that "[m]ost of the funding came from the Polish Film Institute, private Polish funds, and from three other countries— Holland, Russia, and Slovakia."

69. Denise Grollmus, "In the Polish Aftermath," *Tablet*, April 17, 2013, https:// www.tabletmag.com/sections/arts-letters/articles/in-the-polish-aftermath. Accessed December 13, 2020.

70. Beth Hanna, "Critics Get Behind Controversial Polish Drama 'Aftermath,' " *IndieWire*, November 15, 2013, https://www.indiewire.com/2013/11/critics-get -behind-controversial-polish-drama-aftermath-trailer-195063/. Accessed December 14, 2020.

71. Barbara Hollender, " 'Pokłosie'—recenzja filmu," *Rzeczpospolita*.

72. Mikołaj Mirowski, "Bo to bardzo ważny, choć niewybitny film jest. Recenzja filmu 'Pokłosie,' " *Liberte.pl*, March 28, 2013, https://liberte.pl/bo-to-bardzo-wazny -choc-nie-wybitny-film-jest-recenzja-filmu-poklosie-wladyslawa-pasikowskiego/. Accessed December 14, 2020. See also Michał Przeperski, " 'Pokłosie'—reż. Władysława Pasikowskiego, recenzja i ocena filmu," *Histmag.org*.

73. Janusz Wróblewski, "Recenzja filmu: 'Pokłosie,' reż. Władysław Pasikowski. Paląca spuścizna," *Polityka*, November 6, 2012, https://www.polityka.pl/tygodnikpol- ityka/kultura/film/1532003,1,recenzja-filmu-poklosie-rez-wladyslaw-pasikowski .read. Accessed December 12, 2020.

74. Ronnie Scheib, "Film Review: 'Aftermath,' " *Variety*, November 1, 2013, https://variety.com/2013/film/reviews/aftermath-review-1200783281/. Accessed December 13, 2020.

75. Those puzzled include Michał Przeperski, " 'Pokłosie'—reż. Władysława Pasikowskiego, recenzja i ocena filmu," *Histmag.org*, and Ella Bittencourt, who identifies "Józek's sense of guilt" as "the film's clumsiest narrative device," inserted as "a handy motor to unravel the conspiracy," "Review: *Aftermath*," *Slant*, October 28, 2013, https://www.slantmagazine.com/film/aftermath/. Accessed December 14, 2020. Elżbieta Janicka develops an impressive, extensive analysis of *Aftermath* in

"*Corpus Christi, corpus delicti*—nowy kontrakt narracyjny. 'Pokłosie' wobec kompromitacji kategorii polskiego świadka Zagłady," *Studia Litteraria et Historica*, 2018 (7): 1–93; see page 6 for her identification of Romaniuk.

76. In his review of *Aftermath*, Jan Pelczar ridicules the belief-defying feats of Józek—moving the heavy, unwieldy *matsevah* by himself—and Franek, whose perusal of deeds and maps is filmed like a thriller within a thriller. " 'Pokłosie'—Recenzja filmu," *Radio RAM*, December 3, 2012, https://www.radioram.pl/articles/view/23144/POKLOSIE-Recenzja-filmu. Accessed December 15, 2020.

77. Elżbieta Janicka, "*Corpus Christi, corpus delicti*—nowy kontrakt narracyjny": 3.

78. Elżbieta Janicka, "*Corpus Christi, corpus delicti*—nowy kontrakt narracyjny": 28.

79. Ronnie Scheib, "Film Review: 'Aftermath,' " *Variety*.

80. Barbara Hollender, " 'Pokłosie'—recenzja filmu," *Rzeczpospolita*.

81. Janusz Wróblewski, "Recenzja filmu: 'Pokłosie,' reż. Władysław Pasikowski. Paląca spuścizna," *Polityka*.

82. Henryk Grynberg, "Powodzenie 'Pokłosia' i 'Idy' w Nowym Jorku [Fragment 'Pamiętnika II']."

Figure 1.1. Faustyna ruminates on bread as a divine gift, evoking the Biblical passage in which Jesus Christ breaks bread that he gave to the apostles, saying, "this is my body." 1 Corinthians 11:24. Source: *Faustina*. 1995. Jerzy Łukasiewicz.

Figure 1.2. Popiełuszko with his friends from Solidarity, devoid of his priest's vestments and committed to quotidian "good deeds." Source: *Popieluszko: Freedom Is within Us*. 2009. Rafał Wieczyński.

Figure 1.3. Faithful to his conviction that all live beings should be able to "see God," Zdrówko lifts the pig up to heaven. Source: *Jasminum*. 2006. Jan Jakub Kolski.

Figure 1.4. Instantly intuiting Zdrówko's unassuming saintliness, Eugeniusza sends him her version of a kiss, for the two are joined in earthly innocence. Source: *Jasminum*. 2006. Jan Jakub Kolski.

Figure 1.5. An overhead shot of nuns in the conventional Catholic prostrated pose that symbolizes humble worship of God. It reverberates in Pawel Pawlikowski's *Ida*. Source: *Mother Joan of the Angels*. 1961. Jerzy Kawalerowicz.

Figure 1.6. The three priests share a toast during one of their debauched, drunken evenings in dramatic violation of the spiritual values they publicly profess to uphold. Source: *Clergy*. 2018. Wojciech Smarzowski.

Figure 1.7. The supreme hypocrite, Archbishop Mordowicz, delivers an address at utter odds with his self-serving goals and vile machinations. Source: *Clergy*. 2018. Wojciech Smarzowski.

Figure 1.8. Having experienced secular pleasures, Ida makes her steady way to a destination that Pawlikowski leaves unidentified as she moves toward the viewer. Source: *Ida*. 2013. Paweł Pawlikowski.

Figure 2.1. Once Basia captures and soothes her fleeing, frightened daughter, she extends a hand to Marek in a gesture of reconciliation. Source: *Strange Heaven*. 2015. Dariusz Gajewski.

Figure 2.2. A happy Michał at last receives his errant Polish father's approval of his life choices as the two drink together in a Berlin club. Source: *Beyond Words*. 2017. Urszula Antoniak.

Figure 2.3.   As they frantically search the rose plantation for their missing son, Ewa rebels against Andrzej's self-aggrandizing vision of her wifely and maternal duties. Source: *Wild Roses*. 2017. Anna Jadowska.

Figure 2.4.   Adam talks with his father about selling their family's inheritance and stuns him with the announcement that he, in contrast to his father and grandfather, plans to work and live abroad. Source: *Silent Night*. 2017. Piotr Domalewski.

Figure 3.1. The entire family gathers at the table in celebration on Christmas Eve after a cascade of startling revelations and emotional conflicts among its members. Source: *Silent Night*. 2017. Piotr Domalewski.

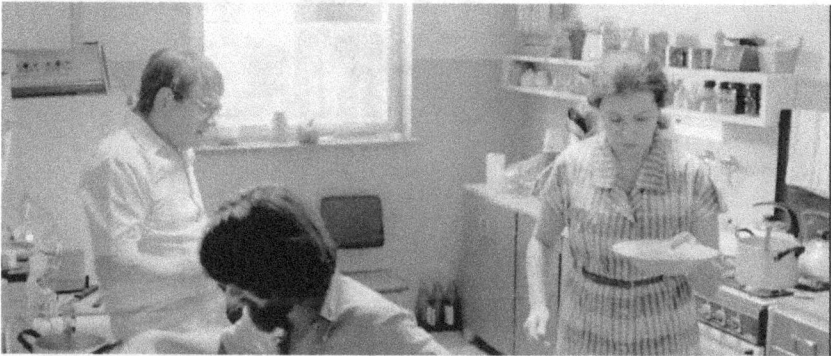

Figure 3.2. Eternally serving both self-preoccupied husband and volatile son, the tireless mother accepts her kenotic role. Source: *The Last Family*. 2016. Jan Matuszyński.

Figure 3.3. Morally and psychologically unmoored after her parents' deaths, Julia leans on Adrian, who, however, fails to reassure her. Source: *33 Scenes from Life*. 2008. Małgorzata Szumowska.

Figure 3.4. Though inconclusive, the ending of *Love*, with the three remaining family members gathered in church for the baby's christening, adumbrates a new, potentially better, beginning. Source: *Love*. 2012. Sławomir Fabicki.

Figure 3.5. Alicja hysterically rails at her loving adoptive mother from the doorway of her selfish and unstable biological mother's apartment house, thereby revealing her immaturity. Source: *Mother to Her Own Mother*. 1996. Robert Gliński.

Figure 3.6. As her two male coconspirators murder her son in the back of the vehicle, Anna determinedly stays silent, literalizing the trope of "turning her back on him." Source: *Son of the Snow Queen*. 2017/8. Robert Wichrowski.

Figure 3.7. The traumatized Kinga urinates on the platform of a Warsaw train station. Source: *Fugue*. 2018. Agnieszka Smoczyńska.

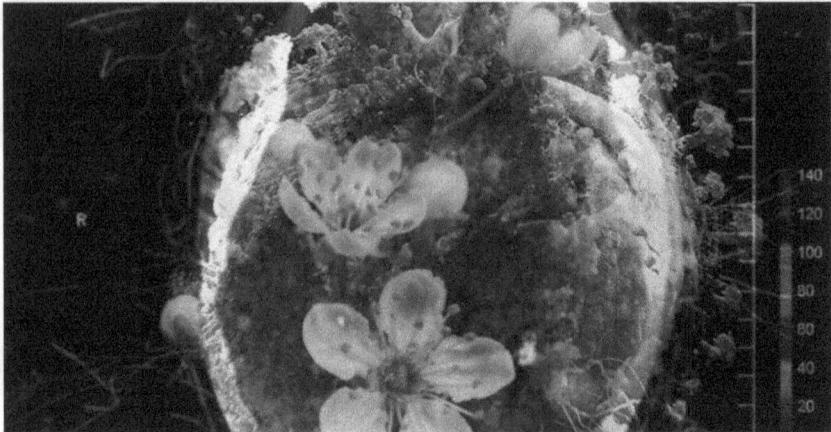

Figure 3.8. Alicja's MRI, in fantastic terms, symbolizes the richness blossoming in her inner world. Source: *Fugue*. 2018. Agnieszka Smoczyńska.

Figure 4.1. In this snippet from a home movie, a Polish Jewish family comes forward towards viewers whom they assume are family members living overseas. Source: *Po-Lin: Scraps of Memory*. 2008. Jolanta Dylewska.

Figure 4.2. With the Soviet army's liberation of Lwów, Socha happily plays host for "his Jews," treating them to vodka and cake even as he attempts to protect them from curious or hostile spectators on the street. Source: *In Darkness*. 2011. Agnieszka Holland.

Figure 4.3.   Having invited her niece Ida back to her home, Wanda familiarizes the Catholic novice with her Jewish family by showing her photographs. Source: *Ida*. 2013. Paweł Pawlikowski.

Figure 4.4.   Ida absorbs more of her family's inheritance as she gazes on the free-form stained-glass window that her mother had created for the cow barn. Source: Ida. 2013. Paweł Pawlikowski.

Figure 4.5. Franek is shocked by the many *matsevah* that his brother Józek has recovered and displayed in their "mother's field." Source: *Aftermath*. 2012. Władysław Pasikowski.

Figure 5.1. The clue that the police ignore and trample on, though it could have led them to one of the murderers. Source: *The Debt*. 1999. Krzysztof Krauze.

Figure 5.2. An earlier celebration of Mazurkiewicz's birthday that reveals Olszowy's and Anna's connection with him. Source: *The Lullaby Killer*. 2017. Krzysztof Lang.

Figure 5.3. Julia Brystygier's guilt-inspired hallucination of the soldier from the Home Army whom she sadistically whipped in her official position as Soviet interrogator. Source. *Blindness*. 2016. Ryszard Bugajski.

Figure 5.4. The three young entrepreneurs happily welcome the guests at the fête marking the success of Navar, their electronics company. Source: *Closed Circuit*. 2013. Ryszard Bugajski.

Figure 5.5. The district prosecutor, Kostrzewa, plays the overbearing host to his two fellow schemers at his country home. Source: *Closed Circuit*. 2013. Ryszard Bugajski.

Figure 6.1. In Kraków's main market square, Lieutenant Jerzy stumbles upon the Soviet screening of their falsified newsreel of the Katyń massacre, in which the Nazis are "proved" to be the executioners. Source: *Katyń*. 2007. Andrzej Wajda.

Figure 6.2. The final scene in *The Dark House* displays the sweeping degeneration of the Polish police force, its honest leader murdered and abandoned in the snow, officers scattering with bribes in hand, and one drunken policeman hurling an empty vodka bottle at the camera above. Source: *Dark House*. 2009. Wojciech Smarzowski.

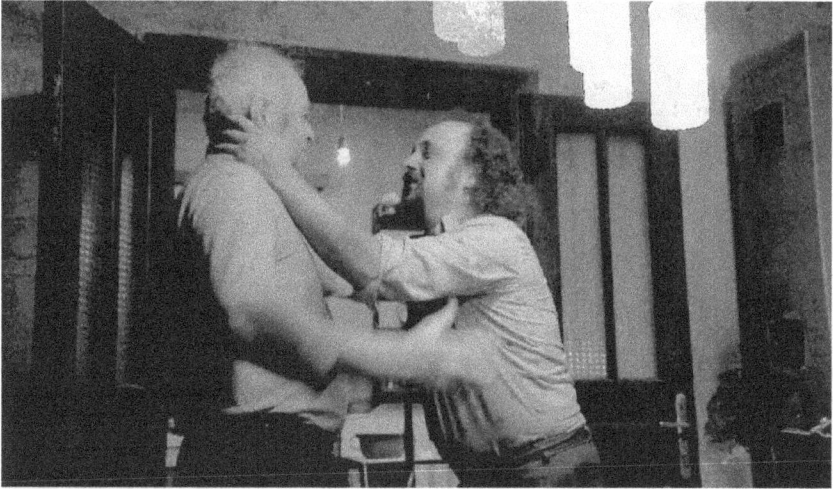

Figure 6.3. After an evening of heavy drinking and scheming, Środoń and Dziabas seal the deal about their planned moonshine operation with a bear hug. Source: *Dark House*. 2009. Wojciech Smarzowski.

Figure 6.4. Bronisław Falski, the secret policeman, is staged to enter Sabina's life as her film noir savior, a Polish Humphrey Bogart. Source: *Reverse*. 2009. Borys Lankosz.

Figure 6.5. Studying her carefree lover lying in the grass, Zula feels compelled to confess that she is informing on him. Source: *Cold War*. 2018. Paweł Pawlikowski.

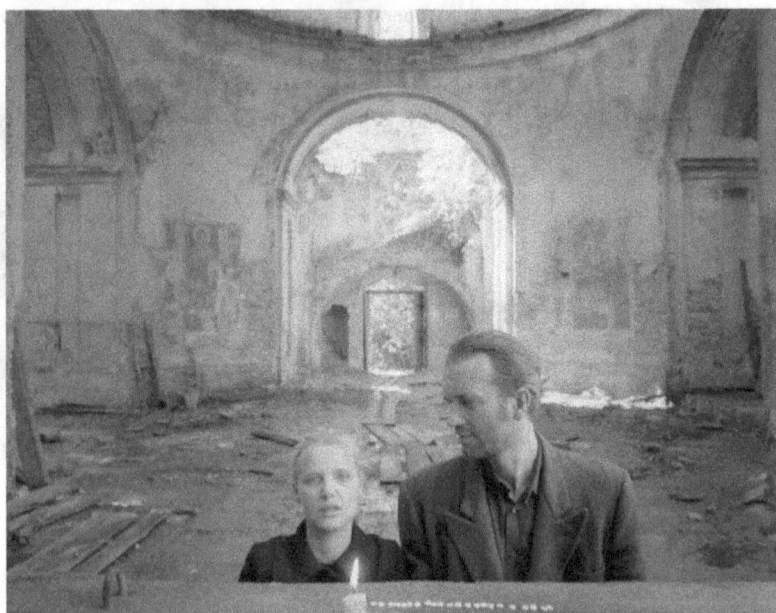

Figure 6.6. Once they are reunited in Poland, Zula orchestrates her one true marriage to Wiktor, and Wiktor meekly complies. Source: *Cold War*. 2018. Paweł Pawlikowski.

Figure 7.1. Kamila and Rożek enjoy one of their more tranquil trysts, soon to be joined by Warczewski. Source: *Little Rose*. 2010. Jan Kidawa-Błoński.

Figure 7.2. The unofficial family unit of Kamila, Dorotka, and Warczewski ostensibly enjoy an outing as they relax on the bench where, however, he regularly passes on his subversive articles to a colleague. Source: *Little Rose*. 2010. Jan Kidawa-Błoński.

Figure 7.3. Despite his awareness of Kamila's betrayal, Warczewski nonetheless marries her, and his mother, presumably ignorant of Kamila's work for the security forces, attends the ceremony. Source: *Little Rose*. 2010. Jan Kidawa-Błoński.

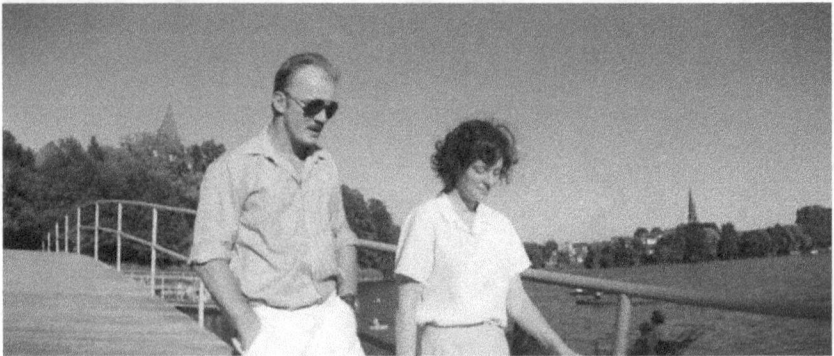

Figure 7.4. Wisłocka unexpectedly finds "the love of her life" in the provinces, where Jurek initiates her into the joys of sexual intercourse. Source: *The Art of Loving*. 2016/7. Maria Sadowska.

Figure 7.5. As the bourgeois Anne discovers, the prostitute Alicja seems freer than her married, conventional interviewer. Source: *Elles*. 2011. Małgorzata Szumowska.

Figure 7.6. Though elegant and well-appointed, Anne's family home reeks of sterility and absence. Source: *Elles*. 2011. Małgorzata Szumowska.

Figure 7.7. Contrary to his hopes and expectations, Tadek's visit to his half-sister Anka meets with irritated impatience rather than a pleased welcome. Source: *Shameless*. 2012. Filip Marczewski.

Figure 8.1. Janek's faith in Arek's promise to take care of his family after Janek's death is based on their longstanding friendship and Arek's all too obvious erotic love for Janek. Source: *The Lovers from Marona*. 2005. Izabella Cywińska.

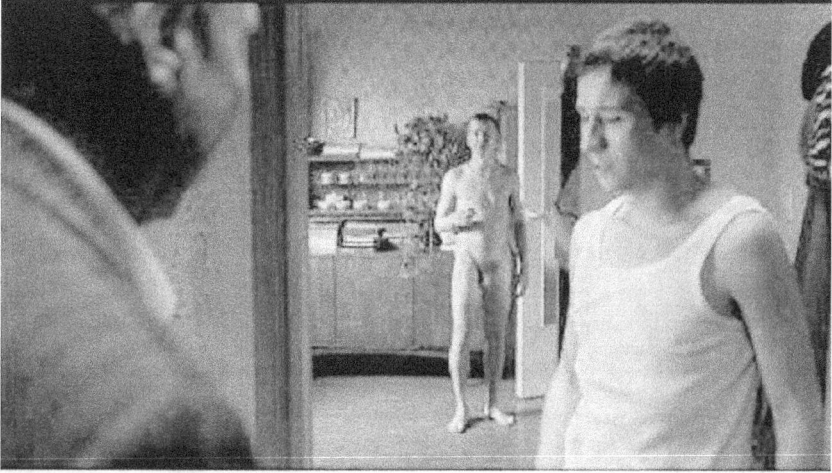

Figure 8.2. Unsurprisingly, upon a surprise visit to Adam's apartment, his father is shocked to discover there the revealing presence of a naked Bystry. Source: *Drowsiness/ Torpor*. 2008. Magdalena Piekorz.

Figure 8.3. Adam responds to the primitive call of his sexual instincts in a revised, transgendered version of Eden. Source: *In the Name of....* 2013. Małgorzata Szumowska.

Figure 8.4. In the classic "morning after" sequence, Adam and Łukasz enjoy a loving moment, with no regrets expressed by either man. Source: *In the Name of....* 2013. Małgorzata Szumowska.

Figure 8.5. The closing shot of the film captures Łukasz in his new role. Source: *In the Name of....* 2013. Małgorzata Szumowska.

Chapter 5

Crime à la Carte
Death and Double-Dealing

ON THE STREET AND ON THE SCREEN

Crime conventionally is defined as "an illegal act for which someone can be punished by the government" and a "grave offense especially against morality."[1] Infractions of the law cover a broad spectrum, ranging from exceeding the speed limit or stealing cough drops to rape and murder. Like all countries, Poland has its share of criminals, and during the era of socialism the most notorious was arguably "the Silesian vampire," who from 1964 to 1970 murdered fourteen women and attempted to kill six more.[2] Identified by the police as Zdzisław Marchwicki (b. 1927), he was executed in 1977. Doubts about his guilt and reservations about the authenticity of some damning evidence were quashed by a state intent on preserving its touted reputation as an upright order free of the West's moral turpitude.[3] The vast media attention accorded the case indexed the infrequency of such occurrences in that period. Janusz Kidawa captured the terror occasioned by the serial killer in the film *"Anna" i wampir* ("Anna" and the Vampire 1981)—a rare and rather idiosyncratic example of a nonpolitical police procedural that incorporates some documentary footage.[4] After the dissolution of the Eastern Bloc, however, organized crime grew into an alarming national problem when the notorious Pruszków gang launched its activities: drug dealing, theft, money laundering, kidnapping, and assassinations of those obstructing their machinations. Betrayed to the authorities by one of their own, Jarosław "Masa" Sokołowski, the members were tried, incarcerated—though for only a couple of years—and upon release professed their intention to lead "normal" lives in the future.[5]

Though the crime rate in Poland has fluctuated during the twenty-first century, the country increasingly has adopted stringent laws, both national and international, to curb illegal activities. In general, major legal violations have entailed corruption and bribery rather than violent assault and homicide, which explains the government's focus on the former. Whereas in 2011, Poland had a homicide rate of 1.2 per 100,000 population, with a total of 449 murders, by 2014 that rate had shrunk to 0.7 per 100,000, accounting for 283 murders.[6] The steady decrease has led the U.S. Department of State Travel Advisory to issue reassuring statistics for visitors to Poland, which indicate that travelers need exercise nothing beyond "normal precautions" abroad, for "Poland continues to be one of the safest countries in Europe."[7] Corruption, however, remains a worrisome issue, though multiple official initiatives have been undertaken to check it: "Poland has signed and ratified the OECD Convention on Combating Bribery, the United Nations Convention against Corruption, the Council of Europe Civil Law Convention on Corruption and the Criminal Law Convention on Corruption." Moreover, penalties for criminal corruption include imprisonment of up to twelve years for individuals and/or a fine.[8] And the government does not hesitate to investigate even influential officials. For instance, the Central Anti-Corruption Bureau (CBA), established in 2006 primarily to detect and prevent corruption in the public domain, in December 2017 initiated proceedings involving Stanisław Kogut, a PiS (ruling party) senator alleged to have made "improper use" of his public powers in exchange for donations to a foundation of which he chaired the board.[9] Such concerted efforts have resulted in today's ranking of Poland as "the 36th least corrupt nation out of 175 countries, according to the 2018 Corruption Perceptions Index reported by Transparency International," after having reached "an unprecedented high of 70th place in 2005 and a record low of 24th in 1996."[10]

Crime makes for exciting celluloid narratives, which sophisticated directors from Tod Browning and Fritz Lang to Alfred Hitchcock recognized as early as the 1920s and 1930s. In Poland during those decades, the two directors known for the genre were Wiktor Biegański and Michał Wyszyński, who released such films as *Vampiry Warszawy* (Vampires of Warsaw 1925), *Kobieta, która grzechu pragnie* (The Woman Who Desires Sin 1929), *Niebezpieczny romans* (A Dangerous Romance 1930), and *Czarna perla* (The Black Pearl 1934).[11] Obviously, during and immediately after World War II, the country had other priorities, and the subsequent Soviet stranglehold discouraged forays into a genre that suggested inadequate governmental oversight. Accordingly, the genre never enjoyed popularity among Polish directors and became invigorated only after the Soviet Union imploded. Action films featuring crime proliferated, the best known and most lucrative of which were directed by Władysław Pasikowski, essentially imitated conventions of the American genre, and revitalized Bogusław Linda's halting career as the "cool, sharpshooting, honorable killer" disposing of nefarious elements in post-socialist Poland.[12] Pasikowski's *Psy* (Pigs 1992), *Psy 2* (1994), and

Psy 3 (2020),[13] plus sundry variations on an all too familiar formula, identified above all with Sylvester Stallone's *Rambo* and Bruce Willis's *Die Hard*
series, continue to attract audiences who prefer uncomplicated action films
with predictable outcomes. Patryk Vega, currently the director of choice
for scenarios of mafioso excesses churned out in rapid succession, inherited
the mantle from Pasikowski, as evident in his customary fare: the *Pitbull*
(2005–2016) and *Kobiety mafii* (Mafia Women 2018–2020) series, as well as
Botoks (2017) and more of the automated same.

Other, more complex examples of the genre, however, appeared in the
new millennium, spanning sundry modes of both individual and collective
criminality and raising thought-provoking issues central to an unfamiliar
sociopolitical order with new economic rules. The possibilities of the genre
had been explored at the century's turn, in what is probably the most unusual
and certainly the best crime film of the late nineties: the award-winning *Dług*
(The Debt 1999).

THE NEW POLAND'S CRIMINAL CONT(R)ACTS: *DŁUG* (THE DEBT 1999), KRZYSZTOF KRAUZE

The Debt's simplicity of plot notwithstanding, its psychology is commendably nuanced, unlike in many "shoot 'em up" crime films of the nineties,
such as Pasikowski's *Kroll* (1991) and Maciej Ślesicki's *Sara* (1997). Krauze
(1953–2014) based his scenario on an authentic Polish criminal case of 1994
involving two ambitious businessmen who disposed of their blackmailers by
beheading them and throwing them into the Wisła/Vistula River to escape
detection. Indeed, *The Debt* opens with two decapitated bodies fished out
of the water by the Polish police, who automatically assume that internal
conflict within the Russian mafia accounts for the murders and therefore is
of scant importance ("Let them kill one another"). In an extended subsequent
flashback that forms the core of the film, however, we learn the real identity
of the killers and their motivation.

Capturing the tense, exhilarating atmosphere of nascent entrepreneurship
that dominated the decade, the film shows young Adam Borecki (Robert
Gonera) and Stefan Kowalczyk (Jacek Borcuch) intent on importing scooters from Italy but unable to launch their business for refusal of a bank loan.
During a chance meeting, a seemingly sympathetic Gerard Nowak (Andrzej
Chyra)—Stefan's former upstairs neighbor—volunteers to help, but the two
find the outrageous interest rate he cites unacceptable and reject his proposal.
To their amazement, Gerard presents a bill for his "services," warning that
each day's delay in payment will incur additional exorbitant fees, and the
remainder of the film tracks his unremitting, brutal efforts to enforce what he

calls their contract (the debt of the title).[14] Unable to escape his increasingly vicious harassment, Adam masterminds his murder, and the two kill and behead both Gerard and his enforcer, Młody (Przemysław Modliszewski), consigning them to a proverbial watery grave. As one insightful reviewer phrased it, "All moral reference points are gradually eroded" and "persecutor and victim swap places within a matter of three months."[15] Unable to live with his conscience, however, Adam confesses to the police and receives a prison sentence of twenty-five years, as does Stefan, while their friend Tadeusz, likewise persecuted by Gerard and hiding in Copenhagen after the murder, is sentenced to six years.[16]

As Michael Stevenson's wide-ranging review accurately noted, the introductory sequence instantly establishes the incompetence of the law and its irrelevance to Poles' everyday life.[17] As well as jumping to unwarranted conclusions and carelessly trampling on a key clue that remains undetected (a silver elephant on a chain dropped by Adam), the police and forensic experts have no interest in uncovering the real circumstances of the crime, since the process would require effort. Moreover, Adam's urgent appeal to the police regarding Gerard's terrorizing tactics yields nothing helpful, for genuine aid would necessitate an investigation and bring no material benefit to the police force.[18] Młody can enforce Gerard's monstrous demands, but the police are incapable of enforcing the law. The film's poster pithily summarizes the partners' dilemma: "Nobody wants to help you" (*Nikt nie chce ci pomóc*).

Necessary changes in the country's infrastructure (laws regulating business, the banking system, and the police force) did not accompany the announced transition to a market economy, which was mired in criminal activities. If during the Soviet era law enforcement agencies "overfulfilled their plans" (at least on paper), in the film's new capitalist Poland they merely go through the motions of doing their duty. Stevenson argues that though "the hope of building a Polish life on the Western model emerged after the collapse of communism," the film exposes the illusionary nature of that hope and "implies that without a secure civil society, the personal is threatened in Poland." To a large extent, such is the case, but the overriding problem during the nineties (and in Russia to an incomparably greater degree)[19] was the desire "to get rich quickly," to take risks, and to compromise one's morals for the sake of instant monetary gain. That goal ineluctably entailed some form of interaction with mobsters or marginal figures, many of them unscrupulous representatives of the law also eager to acquire "easy money." Impatient, ambitious, and inexperienced, Adam and Stefan do not pursue a range of alternatives to a bank loan, and when Adam follows his father's belated advice and presents his prospectus for the Italian scooters to the Polish-Italian Fund, its director readily approves funding, but by then Gerard has set his coercive plan in motion.

Ironically, the murder of Gerard and Młody (recently released from prison) is solved only when Adam, the chief perpetrator of the murder—under normal circumstances, a law-abiding Polish citizen—owns up to the deed by telephone on Savior's Square (Plac Zbawiciela). Neither Adam nor Stefan is a criminal by nature, and only desperation drives them to the fatal act, which, however, reveals the potential for homicide in those who consider themselves incorruptible, decent citizens. Tadeusz Sobolewski observed that in the film "the anatomy of murder—blackmail, persecution, bloody revenge and what comes next—is terrifyingly ordinary. [. . .] The criminal is no different from us in terms of appearance and behavior. But worst of all, we turn out to be the criminal ourselves!"[20] Polish reviewers accurately emphasized how Adam and Stefan's meetings with Gerard launch the process of their own moral corruption. Precisely that aspect of the film is most disturbing to audiences, and certainly to Poles who felt threatened by the criminal extremes ushered in by the shift to a capitalist socioeconomic model that promised so much. And, needless to say, the ugly revelation of crime as a communicable virus threatened the better life supposedly made attainable by jettisoning the Soviet grip on the Eastern Bloc.

In many ways Gerard differs little from Adam, Stefan, and Tadeusz. At first glance, his appearance and manner seem utterly innocuous, even charming, and he is a family man, with a pleasant wife and a daughter, Kasia, to whom he is attentive and affectionate.[21] A loving fiancé and uncle, Adam similarly is supervising the construction of a house in which he and his pregnant fiancée, Basia (Joanna Szurmiej), plan to live as a family; Stefan enjoys an intimate, domestic relationship with his girlfriend, Jola (Agnieszka Warchulska), as does Tadeusz with his. Pursuit of money, however, takes a toll on all these ties and pushes the three naïfs to silence their nemesis through an act they earlier would have deemed inconceivable. All the women remain ignorant of their partners' schemes but suffer the consequences when they misfire. Basia miscarries after a disturbing telephone conversation with Adam, and the unsuspecting Jola is roughly ordered by Stefan to stay away from him.

Reviewers astutely perceived the influence of a Russian literary classic—Dostoevsky's *Crime and Punishment* (1866)—on the last segment of the film. Like the novelist's killer, Adam falls ill with a fever after the homicide, cannot focus on anything but the murder, and experiences a profound sense of isolation. He confesses to Basia, as Dostoevsky's Raskolnikov does to Sonia, and though a shocked, incredulous Basia first dismisses him, she ends up seeking him out and pleading with him to flee abroad. Only an official confession, however, brings Adam a degree of psychological relief, as is the case of Dostoevsky's Raskolnikov. Temporarily silenced, Adam's conscience after the homicide gives him no rest, though the degree to which he abhors or regrets the murder remains unknown, for the film omits the specifics of his conversation with the police, which ends the film.

Fascinatingly, *The Debt* may have had a direct, if delayed, impact on the fate of Artur Bryliński and Sławomir Sikora, the criminal businessmen on whose dilemma Krauze loosely based his narrative. The film stimulated prolonged, impassioned polemics in the media, with some expressing sympathy for the two men, both sentenced in 1997 to twenty-five years of imprisonment for the 1994 murders. In late 2005, President Aleksander Kwaśniewski pardoned Sikora, and five years later his successor, Bronisław Komorski, followed suit in regard to Bryliński. Political expediency likely played a part in both pardons, given their timing. In any event, items in the newspapers frequently failed to distinguish between the real-life murderers and their analogues on screen, as evident from the title of a piece in *Rzeczpospolita* on December 19, 2008: "Hero of *Debt* closer to pardon."[22]

The Debt earned accolades from critics and audiences alike. Lech Kurpiewski in the publication *Film* succinctly summed up the film's strengths:

> *The Debt* has all the characteristics of a good thriller: there is a mystery, fast-paced subsequent events, there are of course plot twists and growing tension. It also possesses the best features of a psychological film. It brilliantly shows how the main characters sense a growing threat, how their fear evolves and is amplified by a sense of complete and utter helplessness that eventually turns into desperation. Finally, *The Debt* is also a drama that accurately portrays the transforming reality of Poland, where everything is in motion, where everyone is trying to find their place, where a game is taking place, yet the rules are unclear.[23]

In addition to winning the Grand Prix for Best Film at Gdańsk, Wrocław, and Września, *Dług* garnered half a dozen other awards, including one for best director at the International Film Festival in Philadelphia (2001). The weekly newspaper *Polityka*'s Passport acknowledged the film's admirable verisimilitude with a Cultural Award for conveying "the complex reality of the 90s accurately."[24] For his sterling performance as the thug Gerard, Chyra received two awards—for best actor and best supporting actor, an unusual situation resulting from how one perceives his role in the film. He would go on to become one of the most sought-after Polish actors of the twenty-first century, and his deceptive combination of disarming smile and mobster tactics likely won him the role of a serial killer eighteen years later.

MURDER WITH A SMILE: *ACH ŚPIJ KOCHANIE* (THE LULLABY KILLER 2017), KRZYSZTOF LANG

One of three recent Polish films based on real serial killers under socialism, *Ach śpij kochanie* (literally, *Sleep, My Darling*) takes its title from a popular

Polish lullaby composed for the 1938 comedy *Paweł and Gaweł* by Henryk Wars (1902–1977), who wrote numerous scores for films in Poland and the United States. Before Poland definitively separated itself from the Soviet Union in 1989, authorities discouraged the treatment of crime in all cultural genres, for state propaganda denounced lawlessness as one of the manifold evils intrinsic solely to the capitalist West, hence alien to socialism. Hardly numerous in socialist Poland, killers existed and were known to the public, but rarely appeared on the screen, unlike in Western cinema starting with gangster films in 1930s' Hollywood. Classics of later Anglophone films about serial murderers include such cinematic milestones as Alfred Hitchcock's *Psycho* (1960), Martin Scorsese's *Taxi Driver* (1976), Jonathan Demme's *Silence of the Lambs* (1991), and Oliver Stone's *Natural Born Killers* (1994). Today the genre has become a staple of TV series in the United Kingdom, United States, and Scandinavia as well as one of the numerous offerings on Netflix. Real-life serial killers have inspired many of the most popular crime films, from Fritz Lang's iconic *M* (1931) to Richard Fleischer's *Compulsion* (1959), Richard Brooks's *In Cold Blood* (1967), Arthur Penn's *Bonnie and Clyde* (1967), and a welter of kindred, widely publicized movies. It is no exaggeration to say that crime movies typically are identified as quintessentially American, whereas for Poland such dark narratives are rare and, as forays into the genre indicate, remote from the norms and traditions of Polish cinema. As much may be deduced from the quality of all three flawed films about serial killers, which American, British, and Scandinavian directors could have turned into excellent screen fare.

Lang's (b. 1950) *Sleep, My Darling* transferred to the screen the career of Władysław Mazurkiewicz (1911–1957), a post–World War II resident of Kraków hanged for killing six victims, though unverified reports had him dispatching as many as thirty. Nicknamed "handsome Władek" (piękny Władek) and "a gentleman murderer" (as well as "Kraków's vampire"), he poisoned or shot, then robbed, not strangers, but wealthy acquaintances so as to maintain his luxurious, glamorous mode of life. Elegant, appealing, and reputedly seductive, he had collaborated with the Nazis for gain, engaging in illegal schemes, and led a lavish life during and after the war, frequenting expensive restaurants, stylish cafes, and prestigious social events. A psychiatrist doubtless could find considerable explanatory power in his mother's death when he was only three, his early poverty, and his marriage to a woman whose name coincided with his mother's. In any event, despite his uneven skill in committing multiple murders and hiding his tracks, his demeanor, style, and connections protected him from detection, substantiating humans' tendency to judge by surfaces.[25]

Lang bypasses Mazurkiewicz's (Andrzej Chyra) wartime exploits, focusing on his killings in Kraków during the 1950s, capturing him in chic restaurants and in the company of powerful individuals to establish his social standing. The film forgoes mystery by opening with one of Mazurkiewicz's murders of someone who trusts him, later followed by others, before showing his arrest and incarceration, where the visual influence of *The Silence of the Lambs* becomes unmistakable. In the very first murder we witness, Mazurkiewicz appears as an incompetent killer, shooting erratically and forced to complete the job by beating his victim to death with a rock. And the second near-victim, clearly a "friend" of Mazurkiewicz, identifies him as the man who failed to kill him with a shot to the head to the two policemen questioning him in the hospital (Tomasz Schuhardt as Adam Karski, Arkadiusz Jakubik as his investigative partner, Pajek). These two sequences set the stage for the 1955 investigation that follows, comprising much of the film, with Karski dogged in his pursuit of Mazurkiewicz and the pessimistic, hard-drinking Pajek equally intent on apprehending the murderer.

Unanimously lamenting the film's inability to realize its considerable potential in light of the historical murderer's colorful career, all Polish reviewers rightly consider Lang's decision to open with the revelation of Mazurkiewicz as the murderer a fatal error, for doing so eliminates the suspense intrinsic to the genre. As two of them point out, Lang prematurely "lays his cards on the table," ignoring Mazurkiewicz's advice to Karski that bluffing and delayed surprise are essential to winning at poker ("The most important thing in poker is to bluff well"/Najważniejsze w pokerze to dobrze belfować).[26] Writing in *Kino*, Bartosz Żurawiecki accurately observes that "suspense evaporates before it even has a chance to develop." Since the identity of the killer is known from the outset, the major revelation within the film (though hardly news to anyone familiar with Poland's history) is the moral corruption within socialist officialdom: the police, the legal system (especially the cigar-chomping public prosecutor, Waśko, played by Andrzej Grabowski), and the secret service—most of them enjoying the perquisites of their positions and reluctant to prosecute Mazurkiewicz, who habitually bribes his way out of situations. If at first the chief secret service representative, Colonel Olszowy (Bogusław Linda), who virtually brought up the orphaned Karski, appears as his guardian angel, the accelerated conclusion exposes him as the most cynically self-serving individual in an influential official position. We early witness him enjoying part of the state's system of privilege, whereby well-placed political figures have access to special stores stocked with Western goods.[27] When purchasing foreign cigarettes, cognac, ham, and candy for himself, he buys a leather jacket for his protégé, but, we subsequently learn, even as he fakes friendly goodwill he secretly withholds official files incriminating Mazurkiewicz in a past murder, kills Pajek, and arranges Karski's arrest for the crime. Żurawiecki accurately points out that Grabowski and Linda play their roles in their usual modes of, respectively, boor and cynical *intelligent* (*cham* and *cyniczny intelligent*), whose ties to Mazurkiewicz are all too obvious ("dziecinnie proste") from the start.

Flashbacks show that a decade earlier, while torturing Mazurkiewicz during interrogation, Olszowy began offering him protection in exchange for gold and raped Anna (Karolina Gruszka), the widow of a restaurateur whom Mazurkiewicz had killed. Moreover, he continues to harass her sexually and at every turn does his utmost to undermine Karski's investigation. Only when Olszowy drinks himself into a stupor in his office, enabling Karski to take his keys and remove the files documenting Mazurkiewicz's guilt in the earlier murder, does Karski realize Olszowy's long-term culpability. Accordingly, when he finds Olszowy again forcing himself on Anna in her apartment and brazenly admitting his actions, Karski has no qualms about shooting him and providing Anna with a passport that allows her to leave Kraków with her daughter—quite a feat in the context of his professional impotence for much of the film. In the last shot Karski stands alone on the railway platform, having said his farewells and established his solid standing as the investigator who brought Mazurkiewicz to justice. And the film does not flinch from showing either the serial killer's hanging[28] or the *volte-face* of the officials who earlier had regularly impeded Karski's investigation but now bask in the self-satisfied glow of having succeeded in punishing a murderer—one with whom they had socialized on many occasions.

The film's grim events, urban setting, overcast skies and drenching rain, claustrophobic framing devices, dismal palette of grays and olive greens, and frequent nocturnal shots doubtless account for the notion, articulated on the DVD of the film by the cameraman, Adam Sikora, that *Sleep, My Darling* strove for a *film noir* aesthetic—one influenced by German expressionism and flourishing in Hollywood's 1940s and 1950s.[29] As he astutely notes, however, the reality of Poland's 1950s inevitably resulted in a Socialist Realist *film noir* (*socrealistyczny czarny kryminal*)—something of an oxymoron.[30] Indeed, Lang's efforts to attain the stylistic effects of *noir* succeed only partly, though thematically he adheres to *noir*'s chief preoccupations of corruption, immorality, and greed. The socialist framework nakedly politicizes these issues, however, whereas *noir* addresses psychological aspects and social ramifications of individual human behavior. Problems with *Sleep, My Darling* arise above all in the scale of representation, the script, and the handling of characters. Quite simply, the small budget of *Sleep, My Darling* prevented the inclusion of many sequences demonstrating Mazurkiewicz's lavish mode of life and conveying the geographical range of his operations, resulting in a rather humdrum "domestication" of his criminal activities. As Jacek Szczerba demurred, the sense of period is rendered modestly (*skromnie*): "A single street is transformed into an old one [of the 1950s HG], along it drive two old cars, while three people dressed in old-fashioned clothes stand at a bus stop."[31] This synecdoche, whereby one street represents an entire city, cannot avoid the erroneous impression of a small-time, confined arena of activity.

Apart from dissipating the tension of *film noir*, where, together with the investigator, the viewer typically attempts to solve the mystery at the heart of the genre, the film, peculiarly, not only makes Olszowy's treachery obvious to the viewer much earlier than to Karski but also fails to focus sufficiently on Mazurkiewicz or to convey his famous charisma, dividing its attention between him and the colorless investigator, whom one critic calls inert ("postacią pozbawioną życia").[32] Quite simply, the serial killer remains a rather bland cypher, and Chyra's considerable talent as an actor cannot overcome the director's and the screenwriter's limitations. Though the film acknowledges officials' venality, the upbeat conclusion violates *film noir* conventions. Far from being fatally compromised, Karski's career now appears on a dramatic upswing.[33]

Perhaps most disappointing is Lang's misunderstanding of women in *film noir*. Initially, he seems to play an original variation on the inscrutable femme fatale who typically leads the male protagonist of *noir* astray: he cloaks the two major women in the film—Anna and Helena Mazurkiewicz (Katarzyna Warnke)—in mystery. Working as a waitress in the Astoria restaurant, Anna has a past that is revealed via flashback only toward the film's end: namely, she socialized with Mazurkiewicz and Olszowy during the forties, when her husband owned the restaurant; was violated by Olszowy after her husband was killed for financial reasons; and remains the unhappy object of his sexual overtures. After Olszowy's death, when she and Karski, who is instantly attracted to her, become intimate, she readily clarifies her circumstances, though it remains uncertain to what, if any, extent she had knowledge of Olszowy's collusion with Mazurkiewicz. Ultimately, she proves to be a decent, intimidated victim and caring mother—hardly the mystery woman of *noir*.

By contrast, Helena Mazurkiewicz, more in keeping with the *noir* female, remains an enigma to the end, but for the wrong reasons. A high-maintenance woman who dresses like a fashion plate, she divorces Mazurkiewicz but continues to live with him in opulent style, simultaneously enjoying a sexual relationship with a younger lover. At one point, when Mazurkiewicz arrives home with a large bouquet of flowers, only to find her in the midst of intercourse, he tactfully refrains from entering her bedroom. Reputedly a magnet for women, he self-assuredly advises Karski about female tastes but gives no indication of sexual interest in any woman and, moreover, appears wholly amenable to the presence of Helena's lover. Through these details Lang may wish to hint at his homosexuality or his impotence.[34] In any event, Helena's relations with her former husband are unexplained but intimate: in one "cozy" sequence, he manually brings her to a climax as she takes a bath; she twice visits him in prison; and she insists to Karski that Mazurkiewicz is a unique individual, presumably therefore deserving special consideration. Her valuable jewelry and chic clothes make it highly probable that she remains with him primarily because he can support her in the style that she favors. Yet she appears to harbor genuinely warm feelings for him and, unlike in *noir*, does not function as the instrument of the criminal's or the investigator's downfall. In other words, the chief female role in *noir* of the cold-blooded seductress who deploys her sexuality to incite the male to crime is absent. As so frequently in East European cinema, women play secondary roles in men's lives and in the plot development, lack both the primacy and the blatant immorality of femme fatales in *film noir*.

Use of Wars' famous lullaby for his title shows creativity on Lang's part, and at one juncture Mazurkiewicz hums the tune, which certainly would be familiar and therefore disconcerting for Polish audiences, who likely would associate it with two beloved singers in the comedy that popularized the song. Evoking the security Mazurkiewicz's victims trustingly but mistakenly feel in his presence and making for dark humor in the horrific discrepancy between a child-associated lullaby and vicious murder, the possibilities of that disjuncture remain unexplored by Lang. Żurawiecki justly notes that Lang here, as elsewhere, misses a rich opportunity for foregrounding a grisly irony.

Finally, whereas most films, perhaps especially in the United States and Russia, are inadequately edited, *Sleep, My Darling* is overedited, and would benefit from at least fifteen to twenty minutes of additional footage to clarify sections left unexplained. Parts of it, especially sequences dramatizing Mazurkiewicz's homicidal plans and executions, lack sufficient treatment, as does the interaction between the serial killer and the ex-wife with whom he lives. Helena seems enigmatic not because of her complexity but because she receives too little attention to establish any sense of character. Doubtless a modest budget accounts for the occasional abruptness between sequences that seem cut off prematurely, such as the murder of the two sisters later discovered underground in Mazurkiewicz's garage. At the same time, Lang's possible insecurity about his ability to deliver a bona fide *film noir* may account for the sense of jaggedness that occasions viewers' frustration rather than creating suspense.

CONVENIENT BUT DUBIOUS GUILT: *JESTEM MORDERCĄ* (I'M A KILLER 2016), MACIEJ PIEPRZYCA

Critics compared Lang's *Sleep, My Darling* unfavorably to *I'm a Killer* about Wiesław Kalicki, based on the real-life notorious "Zagłębie vampire" serial killer, Zdzisław Marchwicki (1927–1977). From 1964 to 1970, Marchwicki

purportedly murdered fourteen women, including the niece of Edward
Gierek, Upper Silesia's party leader. Arrested in 1973 and sentenced to death
in 1975, Marchwicki was executed two years later, and those members of
his family condemned for colluding with him received harsh sentences. Yet,
starting in the 1990s, doubts arose about his culpability in light of his passive demeanor during the prolonged trial and the blatant inauthenticity of his
self-incriminatory diary, cited during the proceedings. A recent, thoroughly
researched study documenting all aspects of the case impugns the legitimacy
of the evidence submitted by investigative forces eager to please Gierek, who
from 1970 was first secretary of the ruling Polish United Workers' Party
(PZPR) in the Polish People's Republic (PRL).[35] Intrigued by the unprec-
edentedly media-intensive case, which caused an uproar in the country,
Pieprzyca (b. 1964) in 1998 released a documentary about Marchwicki and
the inconclusiveness surrounding his responsibility for the murders.

Almost two decades later, he returned to the topic, but now in a feature
film centered on Captain Jerzy Gruba (1935–1991), the twenty-nine-year-
old policeman heading the investigation, on whom Pieprzyca's protagonist,
Janusz Jasiński (Mirosław Haniszewski), is loosely based. That shift in
focus raises moral issues, not about the man accused of murder, but the one
intent on ensuring his capture and punishment. Whereas the state places
Marchwicki on trial, the film subjects the socialist system that executed him
to moral judgment. As Michał Piepiórka phrased it, the accused in the film is
official power, which in the seventies rewarded conformism above all else,
for its centralized mechanisms were firmly in place.[36]

I'm a Murderer tracks measures taken by Jasiński to find the serial murderer from the day he learns, to his understandable surprise (given his inex-
perience), that he has been named chief investigator of the notorious case.
Originally presented as an earnest police officer and loving family man, under
the weighty pressure of Chief Officer Olek Stępski (Piotr Adamczyk) and
his own ambitions, he gradually devolves into a dishonest opportunist eager
to receive the material rewards for capturing anyone who seems potentially
guilty of the crimes that have created a national uproar. In the process of
bringing Kalicki (Arkadiusz Jakubik) to trial, he favors arbitrary name-selec-
tion in the huge catalogue of possible suspects; fakes sympathy for Kalicki
and tries to bond with him over sports, food, and a deprived background;
suppresses counterevidence about a possible other killer, Ulicki; blackmails
into silence a voluntary potential witness, Górecka, willing to swear that
the accused was with her during one of the murders; and orchestrates a sex
scenario to blackmail the chief judge in the case. By film's end Jasiński is
a major in the police force, with a new apartment and color TV, though his
disgusted wife, Teresa (Magdalena Popławska), has left him; his longtime,
close friend in the force, Marek (Michał Żurawski), has separated himself

from him; and his junior colleague Romek has requested a transfer to another police station, refusing a promotion for his role in the fraudulent "successful indictment" of the executed Vampire.

Pieprzyca conveys Jasiński's moral erosion step by step: he begins drinking to excess; slides into a sexual relationship with Anka the hairdresser, who likely initiates intercourse with him to obtain the passport that he eventually arranges for her; slaps his wife when she accurately accuses him of cowardice; and ultimately is prepared "to do whatever it takes" to ensure Kalicki's sentence. Acquisition of a new apartment, a color TV, and a promotion apparently suffices to quiet his conscience, which makes all the more amazing the director's claim that he sees himself in Jasiński ("W jakimś sensie Janusz Jasiński to ja") and that everyone faces the man's dilemma of compromising his beliefs.[37] Yet Jasiński's series of compromises result in the death of what the film shows to be an innocent man, and the refusal of the investigator's wife and colleagues to tolerate or collude in his stratagems indicates that how one deals with the temptation to violate one's sense of ethics depends on one's moral fiber, the willingness to forgo material gain so as to maintain one's personal integrity. Kalicki's vulgar, promiscuous wife, Lidia (Agata Kulesza, excellent in a role unusual for her), is Jasiński's female counterpart in yielding to pragmatic self-interest, though less successfully. Tempted by the announced one million złoty for information about the murderer, she not only appears as a witness for the prosecution (indeed, we never see any defense) but coaches the two children to whom she is a notoriously bad mother to testify that they saw their (genuinely loving) father wash his footwear, presumably of blood.

At the Gdynia Film Festival in 2016, *I'm a Murderer* won not only the Silver Lions (second prize for best film) but also the award for best script.[38] Yet these are hardly the strengths of the film, which provides a startlingly inaccurate picture of the immense scope of the real-life investigation: 3,000 policemen participated in the search for the killer and male suspects numbered 23,000—the latter statistics mentioned in the film, then almost immediately forgotten.[39] To give Pieprzyca credit, he includes the accurate information that Gruba/Jasiński takes the unprecedented step of contacting Western specialists in serial killers, but overall the film, not unlike *Sleep, My Darling*, fails to convey the dimensions of the murderer's activities and the country's corresponding panic. Tension flags, editing is somewhat erratic, and Pieprzyca's habit of repeatedly shifting to a close-up of Haniszewski's/ Jasiński's face reveals bad skin rather than the subtleties of psychological conflict for which both director and leading actor strive. The film's chief assets, as one critic acknowledged, are the performances of the veteran actors in secondary roles: Jakubik as the uncomprehending, naïve victim of the system (a role he earlier shouldered in Wojciech Smarzowski's bleak *Dom zły* [Dark/Evil House 2009]) and Kulesza as his impressively crude spouse.[40] What *I'm a Murderer* shows, in fact, is just how foreign the quintessentially American genre of violent crime was (and remains) to Polish cinema apart from the clichéd action crowd-pleasers by Władysław Pasikowski and Patryk Vega.

CAUGHT IN A WEB OF HIS OWN MAKING: *CZERWONY PAJĄK* (THE RED SPIDER 2015), MARCIN KOSZAŁKA

Famous for his TV camerawork, documentaries, and cinematography in many successful films, including *Reverse* (see chapter 6), *The Lovers from Marona* and *Torpor* (see chapter 8), Koszałka (b. 1970) in his eagerly awaited first full-length feature offered an original perspective on the (here, imaginatively intertwined) careers of two serial killers, one genuine (Karol Kot), the other a product of urban legend (Lucjan Staniak, the "Red Spider"). Although the latter never existed except as myth and threat in the populace's credulous fears, his phantom and Kot operated in Kraków during the mid-1960s. Kot acquired renown largely because he was a teenage serial murderer, and a remarkably inept one, managing to kill only two of the fourteen people whom he attacked: an older woman and a little boy. Sentenced to death and hanged in 1968, he inspired a poem and various paintings, for his lack of remorse and eagerness to share details of his murders, as well as his youth and the unusualness of the case, brought him the fame that he strenuously sought. He declared: "I wanted to be people's executioner, and I was. My work delighted me. I don't regret anything. If I could, I'd continue murdering."[41]

For his title Koszałka adopted the nickname conferred upon the mythical Staniak (Adam Woronowicz),[42] and combined his activities with those of Kot (here, Karol Kremer, acted by Filip Pławiak) into what one critic called "a serial killer double act."[43] To put it mildly, however, the plot could hardly be more surprising for a cinematic narrative about serial killers, for its focus bypasses the genre's conventions. In grimly inhospitable socialist Kraków during the winter of 1967, after his successful participation in a competition, the nineteen-year-old military champion diver Kremer visits an amusement park, where he is mesmerized by a reckless motorcycle act. Going outdoors to urinate, he unexpectedly notices the body of a dead boy on the ground and a man with a beret walking away from the scene. Rather than call the police, he follows the perpetrator, learns that he is a veterinarian, and poisons his own dog so as to obtain an appointment with him. As a vet Staniak proves mild-mannered, helpful, and responsive to Kremer, whom he unwittingly fascinates. Very quickly Kremer, an obedient son, attached to his mother

(Małgorzata Foremniak), and Staniak, a childless husband, recognize the killer in each other, and when Kremer wishes to murder his photojournalist girlfriend, Danka (Julia Kijowska), but cannot bring himself to do it, Staniak, by then an object of Kremer's consuming adulation, fulfills the task for him. Yearning for fame, Kremer confesses to the crimes that are terrorizing the city, is arrested and executed, though toward the end he begins doubting his priorities. A decade later, Staniak, who never arouses anyone else's suspicions, visits the Modern Art Gallery to view a portrait of Kremer.[44]

We never witness Kremer committing murder, though Koszałka does show Staniak's savage assault of Danka with a hammer—a choice that demonstrates the director's independence from the sources that inspired him. What the film dwells on is the symbiosis between the two men and, more briefly, their domestic lives, which reveal that the father plays a vestigial role in the Kremer family and that Staniak's relationship with his wife lacks intimacy. Yet, what motivates Staniak's homicides remains a puzzle, and the same may be said of Kremer's pursuits, apart from his overweening desire to attain fame. Neither exhibits violent tendencies in his observable everyday life. On the contrary, Kremer has a pleasant, attractive demeanor, is the epitome of politeness, seems eager to please his mother by appearing punctually for dinner, and in his relations with Danka manifests passivity rather than aggression. Superficially, he seems the ideal high-school student who can charm parents and peers. His sole peculiarity is his fascination with death, manifested early when he watches the death-defying, blindfolded motorcyclist racing around an indoor wall-track, and, of course, when he discovers the boy's corpse and becomes obsessed with Staniak's murders. Perhaps Staniak's rebuke to his wife for mentioning to Kremer that they do not have children (when he invites the youth to dinner) may hint at childlessness or impotence as a partial explanation for his repeated murders.[45] Certainly nothing else revealed in the film elucidates the enigma of his startling double life. Apparently, Koszałka's research yielded the information that the postmortem on Kot revealed a brain tumor, which, the director maintained, explained the teenager's confession, his deification of Hitler and hatred of people, as well as his drinking blood in a slaughterhouse.[46] These facets of Kot's personality or even a hint of the physiological foundation for Kremer's actions never appears in the film. More directly relevant is Koszałka's expressed amazement at the link between art and crime, inasmuch as serial murderers, according to the criminologist who served as Koszałka's specialist adviser, consider their actions art[47]—an equation that illuminates Staniak's visit to the museum at film's conclusion.

During his many interviews with Polish and Anglophone critics, Koszałka has iterated that instead of creating a crime film guided by generic conventions he wished to approach his topic psychologically: "I didn't want to make a genre film, I'd rather make a psychological one, where emotions, ambience and storytelling by image are most important. I was searching my own way, to avoid the American classic story of a serial killer. [. . .] The most important thing in this film was not to give clear causes as to the characters' behavior. It would be too clichéd."[48] Indeed, the film offers virtually no clues to the psychology of the two men, forcing viewers to speculate in something resembling a vacuum. One Anglophone reviewer characterized the film as an engagement in "hypothetical speculation" in "the 'pure cinema' tradition, where strong visual scenes are allowed to unfold without the crutch of explanatory dialogue or helpful audio clues."[49] Another deemed it "a series of reflections on such themes as man courting death, whether by causing it or submitting to it, youthful angst and a desire to dare and do something extraordinary, even if it's through a third person."[50] For speculation to be fruitful, the film needed to provide more information, if only implicitly, about both men's lives. Does Kremer's fascination with death stem from his problematic relations with his parents? Though distant from his father and obedient to maternal expectations, he displays nothing suggesting difficulties sufficiently profound to maim his psyche. Even more opaque are reasons for Staniak's homicides. And there are many "extraordinary" things one can dare without snuffing out others' lives.

In his interview with Tadeusz Sobolewski, Koszałka cited his criminologist-adviser's diagnosis of dreadful isolation as part of serial murderers' lot. Their inability to socialize with other people, he asserted, renders their association with fellow murderers the equivalent of an orgasm, for in the presence of everyone else they need to be inconspicuous, subscribing to the given society's notion of normalcy. Staniak's woolen beret functions as part of that camouflage.[51] Clearly, Koszałka relied heavily on the information and analyses provided by Gierowski, a professor of criminology. Those unfamiliar with the latter's work and the director's interview with Sobolewski will find it difficult to decipher both the relationship between Kremer and Staniak and the reasons behind certain directorial decisions regarding what to reveal in the film.

THE PAST WITH ITS HORRORS NEVER DIES: *ZAĆMA* (BLINDNESS 2016), RYSZARD BUGAJSKI

While his ambitious younger colleagues[52] struggled with the Western subgenre of serial murder, Bugajski (1943–2019), the maverick director from an older generation who had created a sensation with his bold, consequence-laden *Przesłuchanie* (Interrogation 1981/2),[53] in his subsequent films continued to tackle the question of political ethics, consolidating his skill in investigating crimes against humanity. In recent years, his coherent, implacable screen narratives, usually featuring Poland's best-known established actors, such as Janosz Gajos and Olgierd Łukaszewicz, form a unified oeuvre that invariably dwells on immorality among the country's past and present powerful political elite.

Not unlike his trilogy, launched by *Interrogation, Blindness* casts a glance at the opprobrious past of Julia Brystygier, née Preiss (Maria Mamona, Bugajski's wife), a woman of Jewish origins who under Stalin colluded with the Soviets as a colonel in the interrogation section of their post–World War II security services. Her sadistic torture of prisoners who were her fellow countrymen earned her the nickname of Bloody Luna (Krwawa Luna).[54] While flashbacks provide access to the devastating cruelty of her professional past, the present dramatizes her attempt to find peace with herself by consulting no one less than the Polish Primate, Cardinal Stefan Wyszyński (Marek Kalita), whom she formerly condemned to imprisonment but who now visits the church-run organization for the blind (Zakład dla Niewidomych w Laskach) where she arrives at the film's opening, in hopes of some form of expiation.[55]

Awaiting her perpetually delayed meeting with the Primate and finding the tires of her car deflated, at the local bar at which she tries to contact a garage she encounters two sleazy police officers who harass and humiliate her, as well as a drunken Pole commemorating a funeral who insists that she drink vodka with him. And on the grounds of the organization in Łaski (a village west of Warsaw), she confronts a member of the secret service posing as a gardener who presumably is spying on her; the nun Sister Benedicta (Małgorzata Zajączkowska), with whom she visits the Jewish cemetery but whom she fails to recognize from her past until well into the film; and the blind Father Cieciorka (Janusz Gajos), who rebuffs her with cold politeness. Highly educated, eloquent, well-dressed, and accustomed to authority, Brystygier suffers from alienated solitude and the indifference or enmity of those around her—some of which trigger memories and hallucinations, presumably prompted by guilt. Mamona's bravura performance manages to combine abrasiveness with a desperation that renders her character fully credible yet not particularly sympathetic.

While her past and present experiences guide the narrative, they create a sense of her character without providing a full understanding of her former heinous actions. Insistence on her idealistic communist convictions in her youth can hardly justify the abandonment of her son, husband, and all notions of decency so as to vent her psycho-sexual neuroses on fellow Poles. At one point in her many hallucinations in the present, the young former Armia Krajowa soldier[56] whom she whipped in a blind frenzy when he guessed that she wanted him to undress diagnoses her problem as deep-rooted hatred for everyone and above all herself. Not only self-hatred but also lust, and not only for power, seem crucial to her. As Richard von Kraft-Ebing (1840–1902) in *Psychopathia sexualis* (1886) and Sigmund Freud in *Three Essays on the Theory of Sexuality* (1905) both averred, the sadist derives sensual pleasure from cruel acts of mastery intended to dominate, and Brystygier's whipping session, after which she applies powder and lipstick, eloquently illustrates such a dynamic.[57] A contemporary psychologist argues that the sadist "may also harbour an unconscious desire to punish the object of sexual attraction for having aroused his desire and thereby subjugated him."[58] Though traditionally binary concepts of gender have attributed sadism primarily to men and masochism to women, Brystygier here fulfills the traditionally masculine role of official interrogator, and given the link between sadism and masochism, one may well wonder whether her putting a metal celice belt used for self-mortification by members of the church around her thigh as she drives away from the institute for the blind signals a transition to masochism that has little to do with penance.

Not only Brystygier, but all primary characters have a painful past linked to their present situation: Sister Benedicta, who helps Brystygier arrange an appointment with Wyszyński, was a poet and Jewess (therefore the object of anti-Semitism) before her conversion; Wyszyński, a prisoner of the Soviets, left his tormentor (Brystygier) a copy of the Gospel according to Matthew; Father Cieciorka (Janusz Gajos) was tortured and blinded by the Soviets during World War II. Yet, as the sole individual to have colluded with the Soviet system, only Brystygier cannot cope with guilt for years of having cost people their lives. And, apart from the secret service that seems to be shadowing her decades later, no one is holding her accountable for her abhorrent deeds. The film suggests that her desire to be forgiven is genuine, but her self-presentation leaves the question of her remorse ambiguous. Wyszyński and Cieciorka both ask her what she expects from them—a pointed question that likewise leaves uncertain whether she wishes to be pardoned by them as her former victims or as representatives of the church. The film's conclusion, in which we see her stop as she is driving back to Warsaw so as to fasten around her thigh the metal celice belt confiscated during her days as an interrogator, hints at her readiness to do penance through mortification of the flesh, but, as noted above, it could as easily convey her masochism.

On first glance, pitting the Catholic Church so insistently and explicitly against communism as Bugajski does seems simplistic. Yet there are sound reasons for doing so. The former focuses on the spiritual realm, whereas the latter follows a materialist philosophy indebted not only to Marx and his notion that religion is "the opium of the people," but also to the utilitarianism of Jeremy Bentham (1748–1842), who in his *Introduction to the Principles of Morals and Legislation* (1789) enshrined the goal of "the greatest happiness for the greatest number."[59] And, of course, in Poland the Catholic Church explicitly opposed the communist regime installed in countries of the Eastern Bloc by the Soviet Union, just as throughout the nineteenth century it had provided a sanctuary for Polish culture under the three partitioning powers. Bystygier participated in the communist initiative to demolish the impact of the Catholic Church—what one critic has called its "war against religion,"[60] which it correctly targeted as an institution of resistance. Though Bugajski perhaps excessively underscores the diametrically contrasting positions of the two "philosophies," he also mitigates that categorical polarization by having Bystygier comment on Wyszyński's "interrogation" of her. And, of course, the power relations between confessor and confessee to an extent parallel, if in muted form, those between interrogator and prisoner. Other analogies between the two "faith systems" include the notion of original sin, holy texts, and "infallible truths."[61] While Bugajski does not articulate these convergences, he manages to stage their clashes in a mode that leaves the viewer free to perceive their similarities.

Blindness, the film's title, is key as both literal condition and overarching trope, characterizing Father Cieciorka and Bystygier, respectively, or, as one critic puts it, pitting external versus internal blindness.[62] The priest's blindness, caused by torturers who burned his eyes, serves as his version of stigmata and does not prevent him from identifying Bystygier by her perfume (Chanel No. 5). By contrast, her blindness has been self-imposed (she concedes, "Byłam zaślepiona"), and though she purportedly seeks redemption and is ready for penance, it prevents her from acknowledging the full horror of her past actions and from understanding the revulsion that Cieciorka feels toward her. There is no question that the film conceives of her blindness as the more fundamental handicap *sub specie aeternitatis*. Cigarettes similarly carry a double valency, as appetite—Bystygier chain-smokes throughout the film—but also as a means of torture: Cieciorka's vision is destroyed by his tormentors' lit cigarettes, and Bystygier stubs out her burning cigarettes in the flesh of the young Armia Krajowa (Home Army resistance) prisoner who simply identifies himself as Jesus Christ. In one of her hallucinations, desire on her part has them sharing a light as they smoke cigarettes together, the fantasized moment of intimacy ruined by his frank diagnosis of her psychological problem as comprehensive hatred. As the self-nominated Jesus Christ, he sees "inside her," and the film unambiguously associates religion with profound insight, and communism with disabling myopia. The religious aspects of the film doubtless account for a reviewer's reference to the film as "a moral parable with messianic imagery."[63]

One critic rightly noted that the film leaves "some questions unanswered"—an irresoluteness that could be considered one of its strengths: "is a conversion from Communism to Catholicism really possible? Did she

[Bystygier] really believe in her new faith?"[64] Given the unpredictability and irrationality of human nature, the first question is easier to answer in the affirmative than the second one, which remains open. Bystygier's avowals to the contrary, both Wyszyński and especially Cieciorka mistrust her purported readiness to embrace Christian values and, more specifically, their Catholic exegeses; and a skeptical viewer likely would share their doubts. Comparing Bystygier to the cinema version of Bloody Luna in Paweł Pawlikowski's *Ida*, another critic found Bugajski's colonel wanting, faulting her as an artificial construction lacking "blood and bones" (*nie jest postacią z krwi i kości*) and less interesting than the ex-communist aunt in Paweł Pawlikowski's film.[65] Fascinatingly, another Polish reviewer called Bystygier precisely a "person of blood and bones," successfully embodied by Mamona, one of Poland's most renowned theater actresses.[66] At the same time, anyone who finds *Blindness* little more than a *film à thèse* is unlikely to appreciate the subtleties of Mamona's portrayal, which projects a persona in crisis but one genuinely enamored of communist ideology in the past and totally devoted to its cause—an authoritarian prosecutor demoted to a despised defendant whose past criminality faces judgment beyond a human court.

JURIDICAL MACHISMO AND THE SYSTEM: *UKŁAD ZAMKNIĘTY* (CLOSED CIRCUIT 2013), RYSZARD BUGAJSKI

Like numerous films depicting crime in post-socialist Poland, Bugajski's *Closed Circuit* drew on real events, which the director acknowledged in interviews and in the film itself as it opens. While pondering how to approach his materials, Bugajski decided to base its plot on several cases from the first decade of the new millennium, when capitalist ventures were risky and official corruption thrived.[67] That decision stemmed from his desire to universalize the central issue and "analyze the roots of evil in a normal human being."[68] Critics, however, tended to narrow the ethical dimension of the film, assessing it largely in terms of politics—a "political thriller"[69]—an exposé, not unlike the director's internationally renowned *Interrogation*. As Bugajski stated in an interview, his academic background in philosophy accounted at least in part for his preoccupation with ethics: "Certainly philosophy—and especially ethics—influenced my films. Ethics and morality are much more important to me than physics, chemistry and astronomy. I think that the moral choices that people make are way more significant than some laws of science."[70] As much is clear from his entire oeuvre, though, as he somewhat ruefully remarked, "I have come to be perceived as a specialist in issues dealing with the Secret Service and Security Service"—an observation attested by reviews of the film.[71] In fact, a critic for the major magazine *Kino* somewhat reductively maintained that *Closed Circuit* begs to be read as a *film à clef*,[72] whereas the narrative dramatizes the destructive potential of official power, the temptations of rapid enrichment, and the noxious consequences of envy.[73]

Apart from a few brief flashbacks, the plot of *Closed Circuit* is chronological and straightforward. In 2003, Gdańsk, three young entrepreneurs—Piotr Maj (Robert Olech), Marek Stawski (Przemysław Sadowski), and Grzegorz Rybarczyk (Jarosław Kopaczewski)—organize a lavish fête to commemorate the earlier opening of Navar, their high-tech electronics company. With sophisticated equipment from Denmark, the business has proved inordinately successful, a fact registered by the district prosecutor, Andrzej Kostrzewa (Janusz Gajos), in attendance and intent on usurping the thriving enterprise. With the head of the Tax Office/Inland Revenue (Urząd Skarbowy), Mirosław Kamiński (Kazimierz Kaczor), and a young prosecutor, Kamil Słodowski (Wojciech Żołądkowicz), he schemes to take over the company by arresting the trio for purported money laundering and then appropriating their shares.[74] Once the men are incarcerated and at the mercy of real criminals, Kostrzewa wrests their shares from their female partners and family members. Only the efforts of a dedicated young journalist, Robert Warzecha (Krzysztof Ogłoza), aided by Joanna Rybarczyk (Beata Ścibakówna), unmask the corrupt nature of the official conspiracy. Yet, in this instance, punishment hardly fits the crime: Kostrzewa retains his position, Słodowski is promoted, and Kamiński simply retires, while seven years later, the three partners are awarded a paltry 10,000 złoty (approximately 2,400 euros) in compensation for their ordeal.

Surprisingly, all critics and reviewers failed to mention how the film's opening sequence skillfully foreshadows what follows. Even before we see the six-month-delayed celebration of Navar's success, which belatedly doubles as its official launch, we first hear, then see Piotr Maj's sister, Dorota (Magdalena Kumorek), sing Cio-Cio San's famous aria from the second act of Giacomo Puccini's opera *Madama Butterfly* (1907). Betrayed by the American sailor Pinkerton, his Japanese "wife" and the mother of his son sings "Un bel di, vedremo" (One fine day we'll see), expressing the misguided conviction that "one fine day" Pinkerton will return and remain with her.[75] As a forlorn hope demolished by subsequent events, the aria captures the optimism of the three young entrepreneurs who have adopted the Western paradigm of capitalism, only to find their expectations destroyed and their lives ruined (as is Cio-Cio San's, who commits hara-kiri/honor suicide). Similarly, Marek Stawski's smiling remark that their enterprise is a "promised land" (ziemia obiecana) references Andrzej Wajda's award-winning 1975 film by that title, which likewise ends badly for all three of the friends/business partners in fin-de-siècle Łódź.[76] Bugajski replaces Poland's burgeoning textile industry with Western-linked technology, and insiders' efforts to undermine the nineteenth-century business with the greed of twenty-first-century officials, who succeed in destroying Navar and irreparably damaging its computer wizard, Piotr Maj, who is beaten up, jailed, and raped by two bribed fellow inmates. Subsequently, he attempts suicide and, after recovering, withdraws into himself in uncommunicative silence—a mere shadow of his former ebullient self. Whether his two partners, freed after seven months in prison, accept the Danish Bjorn Gustaffson's offer of co-work and shares in his company actually join its management remains an open question, but that invitation signals their chance for financial recovery.

Bugajski's perspective is historical only insofar as the narrative contrasts the dishonest habits of "old Poland," represented by Kostrzewa, Kamiński, and the minister (Krzysztof Gordon) who abets their scheme, with the optimistic and transparent business operations of the post-socialist generation (the Narva trio and the journalist). Yet, the seductive nature of lucrative corruption emerges persuasively in the evolution of the young prosecutor/lawyer, Słodowski. Though initially hesitant to collude with Kostrzewa, like Jasiński in *I'm a Murderer*, he ultimately compromises his moral convictions, succumbing to the lure of professional advancement and monetary gain, even trying to blackmail the wily Kostrzewa and his two coconspirators when arguing toward film's end for a percentage of the ill-gotten profits.

Writing for *Kino*, Robert Birkholc somewhat artificially separated out four plot lines in the film,[77] and accurately, if predictably, concluded that of the personae involved in each, the villains—Kostrzewa and Kamiński—are the most interesting and fully delineated. Of the two, Kostrzewa indisputably deserves the greater attention, on account of not only Gajos's role as the catalyst and his superb portrayal, which prompted a nomination for the best actor award,[78] but also the various contexts in which the film places him to convey the multifaceted complexity of his nefarious character.

Kamiński and Słodowski's visit to Kostrzewa's rich country house reveals the seemingly hospitable public prosecutor as a smug tyrant and killer. Here, as elsewhere, he overrides his guests' refusal of vodka, and presses them to eat the game he has killed—the only meat, he declares, that he is willing to consume. His proud display of hunting trophies—animals he has shot and stuffed or placed on the dinner table—links his role of literal killer with that of metaphorical destroyer. The blinkered insistence with which he urges his reluctant guests to eat the slain boar indicates his unhealthy pleasure in "swallowing up" his victims and his unawareness of others' disgust at that process. His "killer instinct" also manifests itself in his philosophy of social Darwinism, whereby he advocates the survival of the strong and the essential elimination of the weak—a philosophy that Kamiński, his friend of many years, questions, and to which he ultimately falls victim.

Furthermore, Kostrzewa's homelife underscores especially his pregnant daughter Emilia's (Urszula Grabowska) dislike of his overbearing control but also, quite simply, him. She resists his habit of forcing people to eat his "kill," and has no qualms about expressing her revulsion at his tactics. Though he seems a committed family man, when her contractions necessitate her checking into the hospital she adamantly and rudely rejects his presumptive offer of driving her, and after the delivery, we learn, she tells her mother that she does not want him to visit her—presumably to avoid moral contamination of her newborn. It is difficult to determine his wife's (Maria Mamona)[79] feelings for Kostrzewa, but she confesses to Joanna Rybarczyk and her daughter that she never had any interest in her husband's work. A ballet teacher, she enjoys a privileged mode of life and therefore has found it convenient to ask no questions and to turn a blind eye to his activities, presumably including his having a mistress, the "lawyer" Mecenas Wanda Budwiłł-Sarnecka (Beata Buczek-Żarnecka), who attempts to squeeze money out of Joanna.

As in *Blindness*, Bugajski reaches into the past to illuminate the present, but in this case not to clarify reasons for the protagonist's unassuaged sense of guilt (he has none), but to adduce betrayal as a starting point for other, later forms of abhorrent violations of morality that occasion no pangs of guilt whatsoever. During his student days under Soviet socialism, Kostrzewa's careless, inaccurate words about Professor Ryszard Maj, a specialist in law and the father of Piotr Maj, in 1968 caused the academic's dismissal from his job at the university.[80] When the professor dies at the age of eighty-two, Kostrzewa's fear that the old academic's reminiscences will reveal his youthful decisive role in the drama of the professor's political repression prompts the public prosecutor's extreme measures to prevent such a revelation. Whereas Birkholc unaccountably found these brief flashbacks superfluous, they indicate how from his youth Kostrzewa has advanced by stepping on the bones of his victims, and neither remorse nor regret impinges on his self-assured habit of contravening human and professional standards of morality. His clout as a public prosecutor merely renders his machinations easier than in the past.

Though Bugajski originally had difficulty financing the film—unsurprisingly, the Polish government refused to fund it—a consortium of businesses underwrote its production.[81] Well received by critics and popular with Polish audiences, *Closed Circuit* became one of the year's highest-grossing offerings, though, foreseeably, it was censured by the country's politicians.[82] Western reviewers found the film "compelling," "strongly performed,"[83] with "carefully written, [. . .] often engrossing dialogues," "fine acting and tightly-paced action."[84] A Polish critic deemed it probably Bugajski's best film since his epoch-defining *Interrogation*,[85] and it won the Polish Employers Organization's Wektor 2013 Award "for courage in presenting the truth about problems that Polish entrepreneurs face on a daily basis daring in pursuit of truth"; the Society Humanitarian Award at the Polish Film Festival in Chicago; the Audience Award at the Toronto Polish Film Festival; and the Golden Ticket Award from the Polish Cinemas Association.[86]

Audiences and organizations seemed impressed above all by Bugajski's daring rather than by any other aspect of the film. They were startled or shocked at the director's dark portrayal of post-socialist entrepreneurship in an East/Central European country that had served as a model of successful transition to a capitalist system. An advertising tagline for the film in England reportedly stated, "After this film you'll understand why you're living in Great Britain."[87] Whether such a line would carry any weight during today's prolonged Brexit disaster is debatable, but *Closed Circuit* indisputably numbers among the films that uncompromisingly confronts the disturbing problem of crime among those in power in Poland.

CONCLUSION

Polish film has never manifested strength in screen examinations of nonpolitical crime, and it is unsurprising that some of the most effective post-socialist screen explorations of criminal behavior have contained a healthy dose of politics, as illustrated above all by Bugajski. In contrast, Polish efforts at the genre of *film noir* have proved provocative but ultimately weak, especially as regards the generic paradigm codified by Hollywood. Tellingly, Roman Polanski's superb revision of that paradigm in *Chinatown* (1974) benefited from his experience in the West and had no direct connection to his Polish past.

One of the most successful series of Polish films about crime has been Juliusz Machulski's heist comedy *Vabank* (Go for Broke 1981), followed by the standard sequel, *Vabank 2* (1984), and plans for *Vabank 3*, thwarted by the death of Jan Machulski (1928–2008), the director's father in the lead role of Kwinto, a famous safecracker during the 1930s. Machulski's comic *Kiler* (*The Hitman* 1997) and *Kilerów 2-óch* (Two Kilers 1999), based on a linguistic misunderstanding, similarly attracted large audiences in Poland but hardly contributed anything significant to Polish cinema in the long term. But the same may be said of Patryk Vega's Polonized imitations of Western celluloid crime, such as his *Pitbull* movies, based on a TV series, the *Mafia Women* trilogy, and *Botox*, which reportedly was the UK's third highest-grossing foreign-language film of 2017.[88] Though Agnieszka Holland's *Pokot* (*Spoor* 2017), based on a novel by the Nobel Prize–winning Olga Tokarczuk, marginally qualifies as a dramatization of crime—sooner against animals than the wretched humans who hunt them, it leaves no doubt that violent crime is not her cinematic forte. Marek Kępa's 2017 article, "Trend Watch: Polish Crime Cinema on the Rise," should not mislead readers into assuming that a tidal wave of Polish films about criminals suddenly has washed onto the nation's shores, for "the rise" is noticeable only because formerly the genre virtually bypassed Polish cinema.[89] It likely will take at least another decade before directors intent on tackling crime on screen—if such eventuate—will find an original voice that compares to Krzysztof Kieślowski's in *Krótki film o zabijaniu* (A Short Film about Killing 1988) or Krauze's *The Debt*. More likely, crime (other than in Vega's formulaic "cheap thrills" variant targeting unthinking audiences)[90] will not become one of the industry's favored genres, though various Polish crime series recently have premiered on Netflix.

HG

NOTES

1. *Merriam-Webster Dictionary*, https://www.merriam-webster.com/dictionary/crime. Accessed August 19, 2018.

2. What is striking about the nomenclature that the Polish media conferred on serial killers is the repeated association of the murderers with vampires. Perhaps this connection originated in the old anti-Semitic notion of Jews as "economic bloodsuckers," and it is not impossible that the Beilis case reinforced such prejudices, dramatized in Bernard Malamud's award-winning *Fixer* (1967) and its cinematic transformation by John Frankenheimer the following year.

3. For information about Marchwicki and his family, see "Zdzisław Marchwicki A.K.A.: 'The Silesian Vampire'—'The Zagłębie Vampire,' " Murderpedia, https://murderpedia.org/male.M/m/marchwicki-zdzislaw.htm. Accessed October 4, 2018.

4. The film relies on voiceover by the main investigator and on many arbitrary close-ups, in a conventional narrative with occasional excellent atmospheric shots. The poor quality of the visuals suggests a modest budget. "Anna" in the title references the first victim's name, adopted for the group of policemen investigating the murders. Since the viewer sees the killer dispatching his first victim, there is little mystery other than whether the police will identify him as the guilty party. Janusz Majewski's *Sprawa Gorgonowej* (The Case of Gorgonowa 1977) dealt with the murder of a seventeen-year-old woman, reputedly by Rita Gorgonowa, who was sentenced to eight years in prison, though the question of her having committed the crime remains open. See Marek Haltof, *Polish Cinema: A History* (New York: Berghahan Books, 2002), 246.

5. "Trzęśli Warszawą, dziś znów są na wolności. Co robią teraz dawni bossowie Pruszkowa?" WarszawaNaszeMiasto, June 29, 2019, http://warszawa.naszemiasto.pl/artykul/trzesli-warszawa-dzis-znow-sa-na-wolnosci-co-robia-teraz,3924728,artgal,t,id,tm.html. Accessed January 15, 2020. Giving state evidence proved lucrative for the pseudonymous Masa, who receives monthly sums from the government and has

made a lucrative career giving interviews to Artur Górski, author of best-selling books about the Polish mafia, including "Masa o kobietach polskiej mafii" (2014) on which Patryk Vega's endless, derivative, laughably ludicrous film, *Kobiety mafii* 2018, is based.

6. "Global Study on Homicide." United Nations Office on Drugs and Crime, 2013, https://www.un-ilibrary.org/drugs-crime-and-terrorism/global-study-on-homicide-2013_c1241a80-en. Accessed January 15, 2020.

7. "Poland 2019 Crime & Safety Report," March 8, 2019, https://www.osac .gov/Content/Report/3a89580c-512f-404b-9f9a-15f4aeb14091. Accessed January 15, 2020.

8. "Poland Corruption Report," GAN—Business Anti-Corruption Portal, January 2018, https://www.ganintegrity.com/portal/country-profiles/poland/. Accessed January 15, 2020.

9. Tomasz Konopka, "The Anti-Bribery and Anti-Corruption Review—Edition 7," December 2018, https://thelawreviews.co.uk/edition/the-anti-bribery-and-anti -corruption-review-edition-7/1177236/poland. For more on the case, see kuba, "Stanisław Kogut: Wybory parlamentarne 2019. Senator Kogut znów wystartuje w wyborach," wyborcza.pl, August 21, 2019, http://krakow.wyborcza.pl/krakow /7,44425,25108492,wybory-parlamentarne-2019-senator-kogut-znow-wystartuje-w -wyborach.html. Both accessed February 2, 2020.

10. "Poland Corruption Rank," *Trading Economics*, 2019, https://tradingeconom ics.com/poland/corruption-rank. Accessed February 2, 2020.

11. Biegański's protégé, Waszyński was the assistant director on *Vampiry Warszawy*, which found favor with audiences, though less so among critics. For more on the film and its reception, see Juliette Bretan, "Lost & Destroyed: In Search of Classic Polish Films," culture.pl, August 22, 2018, https://culture.pl/en/article/lost -destroyed-classic-polish-films?utm_source=getresponse&utm_medium=email&utm _campaign=30082019en&utm_content=art4_title. Accessed February 1, 2020. For information on Biegański and Waszyński, see Charles Ford and Robert Hammond, *Polish Film: A Twentieth Century History.* (Jefferson, NC: McFarland & Co., Inc., 2005), 36–40 and 84–86, respectively. On Waszyński see also Stanisław Janicki, "Michał Waszyński—Artysta czy wyrobnik?" *Kino* 5 (2018): 27–31 and Joanna Ostrowska, "Książę i Dybuk," *Kino* no. 5 (2018): 70–71.

12. For a discussion of these offerings, see Marek Haltof, *Polish Cinema: A History*, 2nd edition (New York: Berghahn, 2019) and Ewa Mazierska, *Polish Postcommunist Cinema: From Pavement Level*, NSEC: New Studies in European Cinema (Bern: Peter Lang, 2007).

13. See Katarzyna Grynienko, "PRODUCTION: Władysław Pasikowski Shoots Dogs 3 Starring Bogusław Linda," FILMNEWEUROPE.COM, July 16, 2019, https:// www.filmneweurope.com/news/poland-news/item/118437-production-wladyslaw -pasikowski-shoots-dogs-3-starring-boguslaw-linda. Accessed November 23, 2019.

14. As one reviewer pointed out, Gerard decides on $1,000 as the daily interest rate for the nonexistent loan—a sum that "in 1995 [. . .] took an average Pole about four months to earn." "Film/The Debt 1999," https://tvtropes.org/pmwiki/pmwiki.php /Film/TheDebt1999. Accessed March 9, 2019.

15. Jarosław Kuisz, "Between Pigs and Debt," EUROZINE, May 6, 2009, https://www.eurozine.com/between-pigs-and-debt/. Accessed March 9, 2019.

16. During PRL, Poland's relationship to capital punishment fluctuated over the years, though it was officially adopted for the most part. In 1997 it was eliminated, despite Lech Kaczyński's push to reinstate it.

17. Michael Stevenson, "A Bitter Failure on the Road to Polish Capitalism: Krzysztof Krauze's *The Debt* (Dług), KinoKultura, 2005, http://www.kinokultura.com/specials/2/dlug.shtml. Accessed March 7, 2019.

18. Ewa Mazierska in her short, intelligent commentary on the film, erroneously refers to Adam and Stefan's visit to the police, whereas Stefan only learns of Adam's request for help there considerably later in the film. Mazierska 155.

19. Numerous Russian films of the 1990s and early 2000s reflected the proliferation of criminals and the mafia, as well as the New Russian oligarchs—categories often indistinguishable, particularly during the nineties. See Alelksei Balabanov's *Brother* (Brat 1997*) and Brother 2* (Brat 2 2000), Valery Todorovsky's *Land of the Deaf* (Strana glukhikh 1998), Stanislav Govorukhin's *Voroshilov Sharpshooter* (Voroshilovskii strelok), Pavel Lungin's *Tycoon* (Oligarch 2002), Petr Buslov's *Bumer* (2003), and many others.

20. Tadeusz Sobolewski, *Gazeta Wyborcza*, no. 2 (1999): 10. Review cited in Culture.pl, trans. Zuzanna Wiśniewska, https://culture.p.l/en/work/the-debt-krzysztof-krauze. Accessed March 7, 2019.

21. In a marvelously ironic sequence, given Gerard's treatment of humans, he gently rebukes Kasia for potentially hurting a squirrel.

22. Kuisz, "Between Pigs and Debt."

23. Cited in Culture.pl, trans. by Zuzanna Wiśniewska, originally published in *Film* 2 (1999): 10. Accessed March 7, 2019.

24. Culture.pl, translation adjusted for the sake of fluency.

25. For more information about Mazurkiewicz listen to the Polish podcast "Mordercy," describing his life and modus operandi, as well as those of other Polish murderers. "Władysław Mazurkiewicz—Elegancki morderca," Podcast #5, https://www.kryminatorium.pl/wladyslaw-mazurkiewicz-elegancki-morderca/. Accessed April 12, 2019.

26. Bartosz Żurawiecki, "Ach śpij kochanie," October 21, 2017, *Kino* no. 11 (2017), http://kino.org.pl//index.php?option=com_content&task=view&id=2840&Itemid=1944; Tomasz Zacharczuk, "Chyra jak Lecter, a reszta jest milczeniem. Recenzja filmu 'Ach śpij kochanie,'" *tojmiasto.pl*, October 22, 2017, https://kino.trojmiasto.pl/Chyra-jak-Lecter-a-reszta-jest-milczeniem-Recenzja-filmu-Ach-spij-kochanie-n117694.html. Both accessed April 12, 2019.

27. Like the USSR, countries in the Eastern Bloc made available to personnel safeguarding the existent sociopolitical structure special privileges and goods that regular citizens could only dream about. Though nominally socialist, the state starkly distinguished between the haves—the apparatchiks or the elite—and have-nots through this widely known but unacknowledged system of benefits. Such a system encouraged political conformity. See Bronislaw Misztal, ed. *Poland After Solidarity: Social Movements Versus the State* (Piscataway, NJ: Transaction Pubs., 1985).

28. Krzysztof Kieślowski's *Krótki film o zabijaniu* (Short Film about a Killing 1988) had prepared the way for on-screen hanging.

29. The huge scholarship on *film noir* was pioneered by Raymond Durgnat and Paul Schrader, who assert that *noir* is not a genre but a visual style. More recent scholarship has been divided on that issue. For an assessment of the numerous studies on the topic, see Pam Cook and Mieke Bernink, eds., *The Cinema Book*, 2nd edition (London: bfi Publishing 1999), 184–191. Raymond Durgnat, "Paint It Black: The Family Tree of the *Film Noir*," *Cinema* (August 1970): 48–56, reprinted in *Film Comment* 10, no. 6 (November/December 1974): 6–7 (half of the issue was devoted to *film noir*); Paul Schrader, "Notes on *film noir*," *Film Comment*, 8, no. 1 (Spring 1972): 8–13.

30. *Ach śpij kochanie*, dir. Krzysztof Lang, Studio Produkcyjne Orka, Monolith Films, Krakowskie Biuro Festiwalowe. Warsaw: Monolith Films, 2017: insert, 18.

31. Jacek Szczerba, " 'Ach śpij kochanie': rewelacyjny criminal. Andrzej Chyra jak polski Hannibal Lecter," Wyborcza.pl, October 18, 2017, http://wyborcza.pl /7,101707,22529498,ach-spij-kochanie-filmowa-rewelacja-made-in-poland-andrzej .html. Accessed April 5, 2019.

32. Bartosz Staszczyszyn, " 'Ach śpij kochanie,' reż. Krzysztof Lang, Culture.p l, https://culture.pl/pl/dzielo/ach-spij-kochanie-rez-krzysztof-lang. Accessed April 5, 2019.

33. Bartosz Staszczyszyn opens his review by attributing the problem to Lang's misguided effort to link the crime genre with romance and psychological drama, which resulted in a film lacking tension, darkness, and an aura of mystery. Yet Roman Polanski's superb *Chinatown* (1974) contains both psychological drama and romance, but is unanimously hailed as a classic of *film noir* because Polanski never loses sight of the genre's constitutive features. Though he transforms them, he subordinates all other elements to these traits. See John G. Cawelti, "*Chinatown* and Generic Transformation in Recent American Films," in *Film Genre Reader II,* ed. Barry Keith Grant (Texas: University of Texas Press, 1995), 227–245.

34. His fastidious preoccupation with both male and female sartorial style, his rather soft manner, and his relationship with Helena suggest that his pursuit of wealth substitutes for sexual desire or compensates for sexual dysfunction. And Lang's attempt to show women's attraction to him by two brief, utterly inept scenes with one of the sisters he murders (Izabela Kuna) and Ruda (a grotesquely vulgar, overblown Katarzyna Figura) utterly fails to convince. On this sorry aspect of the film see Zacharczuk.

35. "Zdzisław Marchwicki," in *Murderpedia*, http://www.murderpedia.org/male .M/m/marchwicki-zdzislaw.htm. For the recent study of the Marchwicki case by a reputable journalist, see Przemysław Semczuk, *Wampir z Zagłębia*, (Warsaw: Znak, 2016), and an impressively informative review of the book by Sebastian Chosiński, "Powiedzmy to sobie wprost—Marchwicki nie był 'Wampirem!'" April 18, 2016, at https://esensja.pl/ksiazka/recenzje/tekst.html?id=22619. Both accessed August 21, 2019.

36. Michał Piepiórka, "Jestem mordercą," *Kino*, no. 11 (2016): 77, http://kino.org .pl//index.php?option=com_content&task=view&id=2599&Itemid=1746. Accessed August 19, 2019.

37. Bartosz Wróblewski, " 'Jestem mordercą'—czy Zdzisław Marchwicki naprawdę był 'wampirem z Zagłębia?' " Wyborcza.pl, October 27, 2017, http://wyborcza.pl/7,90535,22272389,jestem-morderca-czy-zdzislaw-marchwicki-naprawde-byl.html. Accessed August 21, 2019.

38. Bartosz Staszczyszyn, "I'm a Killer—Maciej Pieprzyca," Culture.pl, October 2016, at https://culture.pl/en/work/im-a-killer-maciej-pieprzyca. Accessed August 21, 2019.

39. Chosiński, "Powiedzmy to sobie wprost."

40. Staszczyszyn, "I'm a Killer."

41. Chciałem i byłem katem ludzi. Cieszyła mnie moja robota. Niczego nie żałuję. Gdybym mógł, mordowałbym dalej. Cited in " 'Czerwony pająk.' 'Chciałem być katem ludzi.' Przerażająca historia 'Wampira z Krakowa,'" wPolityce.pl, October 27, 2015, https://wpolityce.pl/kultura/269832-czerwony-pajak-chcialem-byc-katem-ludzi-przerazajaca-historia-wampira-z-krakowa-zwiastun. Accessed September 1, 2019.

42. The nickname of Red Spider supposedly derived from the murderer's habit of sending letters "written in his own blood after each strike." Peter Debruge, "Film Review: 'The Red Spider,' " *Variety*, July 8, 2015, https://variety.com/2015/film/festivals/the-red-spider-film-review-1201535830/. Accessed September 1, 2019.

43. Stephen Dalton, "The Red Spider (Czerwony pajak): Karlovy Vary Review," *Hollywood Reporter*, July 13, 2015, https://variety.com/2015/film/festivals/the-red-spider-film-review-1201535830/. Accessed August 19, 2019.

44. Reportedly, the Kraków-based poet Marcin Świetlicki composed the poem, and various painters and visual artists found inspiration in Kot's deeds. See "Play Poland 2016 Film Festival," http://www.playpoland.org.uk/index.php5?name=newsy&old=737. Accessed August 17, 2019.

45. Koszałka revealed that at the annual film festival in Hajfa, some detected homosexual relations between the two men. Tadeusz Sobolewski, "Film 'Czerwony pająk': Morderstwo, czylie dzieło sztuki—rozmowa z reżyserem," Wyborcza.pl, November 27, 2015, http://wyborcza.pl/1,75410,19253228,film-czerwony-pajak-morderstwo-czyli-dzielo-sztuki-rozmowa.html. Accessed August 20, 2019.

46. Ibid.

47. Ibid.

48. Laurence Boyce, "Marcin Koszałka, 'The Red Spider,' " *Screen Daily*, July 3, 2015, https://www.screendaily.com/karlovy-vary/marcin-koszalka-the-red-spider/5090085.article. Accessed August 20, 2019.

49. Debruge, "Film Review: 'The Red Spider.' "

50. Dan Fainaru, "The Red Spider," *Screen Daily*, July 7, 2015, https://www.screendaily.com/reviews/the-red-spider-review/5090163.article. Accessed August 18, 2019.

51. Sobolewski, "Film 'Czerwony pająk.' "

52. Lang was born in 1950, Pieprzyca in 1964, and Koszałka in 1970.

53. Censored and prohibited from being shown in Poland, the film resulted in the closure of the X Film Unit helmed by Andrzej Wajda, and ultimately led to Bugajski's emigration in 1985 to Canada, from where ten years later he returned to

Warsaw. Premiered in 1989 and in 1990 voted the best Polish film of that year by the magazine *Film*, *Przesłuchanie* (Interrogation) made an instant star of Krystyna Janda in the lead role, as well as alerting audiences to the formidable talent of Janusz Gajos, Poland's premier actor today. Upon its release, the film garnered multiple awards.

54. For brief comments on his trilogy, see Konrad J. Zarębski, "General Nil—Ryszard Bugajski," culture.pl, March 2009, https://culture.pl/en/work/general-nil-ryszard-bugajski. Accessed July 22, 2019. Brystygier's biography parallels that of Anna's aunt in Paweł Pawlikowski's *Ida* (2013).

55. In the film the place is called Górki.

56. The major resistant movement in Poland, Armia Krajowa (Home Army) appeared in 1942 and disbanded in 1945. It opposed both Nazis and Soviets, supporting the Polish government in exile.

57. For more on the topic of sadism, see Thomson Gale, "Sadism," in *Encyclopedia of Sex and Gender: Culture Society History*, 2007, https://www.encyclopedia.com/social-sciences/encyclopedias-almanacs-transcripts-and-maps/sadism. Accessed July 24, 2019.

58. Neel Burton, "Hide and Seek: The Psychology of Sadomasochism," psychologytoday, August 17, 2014, https://www.psychologytoday.com/us/blog/hide-and-seek/201408/the-psychology-sadomasochism. Accessed July 24, 2019.

59. An ardent opponent of communism, Stanisław Lem satirized Bentham's utopianism in his hilarious *Kongres futurologiczny* (The Futurological Congress 1971).

60. Stephen Dalton, " 'Blindness' ('Zacma'): Film Review," *Hollywood Reporter*, September 15, 2016, https://www.hollywoodreporter.com/review/blindness-zacma-review-929161. Accessed July 24, 2019.

61. Ibid.

62. Robert Birkholc, "Zaćma," *Kino*, no. 10 (2016): 66–67, http://kino.org.pl//index.php?option=com_content&task=view&id=2623&Itemid=1767. Accessed July 23, 2019.

63. Dalto " 'Blindness' ('Zacma')."

64. Yola Czaderska-Hayek, "Blindness (Zacma) (Poland), Golden Globe Awards, November 18, 2017, https://www.goldenglobes.com/articles/blindness-zacma-poland. Accessed July 25, 2019.

65. Birkholc, "Zaćma."

66. Agnieszka Woch, "Zaćma," Histmag.org, December 28, 2016, https://histmag.org/Zacma-rez.-Ryszard-Bugajski-recenzja-filmu-14512. Accessed July 22, 2019.

67. Among genuine experiences on which Bugajski relied was that of the Kraków businessmen Lech Jerzorny and Paweł Rey. See Bijan Tehrani, "Ryszard Bugajski, The Closed Circuit, participating at Polish Film Festival," Cinema Without Borders, September 24, 2013, https://cinemawithoutborders.com/3491-ryszard-bugajsk-the-closed-circuit-polishfilmla/. Accessed June 30, 2019. Owing to lack of evidence in the real-life case, the arrested innocent businessmen were released and compensated with 10,000 złoty (approximately 2,400 euros) each. See Bartosz Statyszczyn, "Closed Circuit—Ryszard Bugajski," Culture.pl, March 25, 2013, https://culture.pl/en/work/closed-circuit-ryszard-bugajski. Accessed July 13, 2019.

68. Ibid. At the same time, the director stated that "the film is about a concrete situation in Poland." See Paulina Duda, "Ryszard Bugajski on his Career," eefb/East European Film Bulletin, 68 (October 2016), https://eefb.org/interviews/ryszard-buga-jski-on-his-career/. Accessed July 7, 2019.

69. See Alissa Simon, "A Compelling, Strongly Performed Political Thriller Set in Contemporary Poland," *Variety*, June 18, 2013, https://variety.com/2013/film/reviews/film-review-the-closed-circuit-1200496827/. Accessed July 12, 2019. Birkholc and Tehrani likewise pigeonholed the film as a political thriller.

70. Duda, "Ryszard Bugajski on His Career."

71. Statyszczyn, "Closed Circuit."

72. Robert Birkholc, "Układ zamknięty," *Kino*, no. 4 (2013): 82.

73. For an eloquent portrayal of the last, see the 1927 Russian novel *Envy* (Zavist') by Iurii Olesha.

74. The brutality with which the armed and masked anti-terrorist police treat the three and their partners recalls the persecution of the criminal's victims in *Dług*, but here the vicious persecution is executed by official forces.

75. Sung by a vocally undistinguished Agnieszka Tomaszewska, the aria, which she picks up halfway through, fails to convey its full emotional power, as when performed by outstanding singers, such as the unrivaled Maria Callas, whose thrilling rendition may be accessed at https://www.youtube.com/watch?v=c-r2vu4t9-g. Accessed October 18, 2018.

76. Wajda's adaptation of Nobel Prize–winner Władysław Reymont's 1899 novel with the same title remains one of Poland's most successful and popular films and was nominated for the Academy Award as Best Foreign Language Film.

77. A weak aspect of the film, according to Birkholc, is the line following the fates of the successful Navar trio, their violent persecution and clichéd, horrific experiences in prison. The second line traces the efforts of their "sisters, daughters, and wives," who attempt to cope with the trauma of their men's fates and help them. And the third line concerns the investigation and the persistent, idealistic journalist determined to uncover the truth. Yet it is impossible to separate these "lines," which converge as soon as Kostrzewa sets his insidious plot in motion.

78. Writing for *Variety*, Simon commented that "although short and rather ordinary-looking, Gajos can be terrifying." Simon, "A compelling, strongly performed political thriller."

79. Bugajski's wife and the female protagonist-criminal in *Zaćma*.

80. The carelessness was a calculated act of revenge, for the professor had just told the young Kostrzewa that he had not passed his exams, which would mean the loss of financial support. Even then, Kostrzewa maintained a false exterior of righteousness and politeness, as he does decades later in his dealings with Dorota Maj, oozing courtesy and concern even as he robs her of her Navar shares.

81. See Birkholc, Simon, Statyszczyn, and others.

82. Simon, Julie Hersh, "The Closed Circuit/Układ zamknięty," POPKULT, August 9, 2016, https://popkult.org/closed-circuit/. Accessed January 5, 2019.

83. Simon, "A compelling, strongly performed political thriller."

84. Patryk Czekaj, "Review: The Closed Circuit Depicts a Tragically True Story of Corruption," ScreenAnarchy, October 31, 2013, https://screenanarchy.com/2013/10/review-the-closed-circuit-depicts-a-tragically-true-story-of-corruption.html. Accessed January 4, 2019.

85. Birkholc. "Układ zamknięty."

86. See Polish Film Institute, New Polish Films 2014, http://en.pisf.pl/files/dokumenty/fpg/npf_2014.pdf. Accessed December 28, 2018.

87. Ibid.

88. Ryan Gilbey, "Why Polish Gangster Films 'On Steroids' Are Making It Big at the British Box Office," *The Guardian*, December 3, 2018, https://www.theguardian.com/film/2018/may/03/why-polish-gangster-films-on-steroids-are-making-it-big-at-the-british-box-office. Accessed January 5, 2019.

89. Marek Kępa, "Trend Watch: Polish Crime Cinema on the Rise," culture.pl, January 17, 2017, https://culture.pl/en/article/trend-watch-polish-crime-cinema-on-the-risen. Accessed April 17, 2019.

90. For an attempt to treat Vega's work seriously, see Grzegorz Stępniak, "Majami, padrini i falliczne węże," *Kino*, no. 2 (2019): 28–31. It is worth noting that some of Poland's best actresses, such as Agata Kulesza, Joanna Kulig, Maja Ostaszewska, and Grażyna Szapołowska, have appeared in Vega's movies, just as Janusz Gajos joined the cast of actors in Władysław Pasikowski's action "thrillers," such as *Psy* (Pigs), and in Vega's *Pitbull*.

Chapter 6

Cold War Retakes in the Twenty-first Century

SOCIOPOLITICAL HISTORY: THE COLD WAR IN EASTERN EUROPE

The Cold War that arose immediately after World War II and in consequence of its victors' frayed alliance has passed beyond living memory for most of the world's population.[1] Films that memorably imprinted or successfully recycled the Cold War experience for Western Europeans and North Americans (the camp of the West) tended to screen tales of espionage as derring-do with the latest gadgetry (the Bond franchise, *The Hunt for Red October*); spy-versus-spy dramas featuring jaded protagonists and baring the immorality of the game, regardless of player allegiance (*The Spy Who Came in from the Cold*, *Tinker Tailor Soldier Spy*, *Bridge of Spies*); and thrillers or black comedies about the dire consequences of nuclear warfare (*On the Beach*, *Seven Days in May*, *Dr. Strangelove or: How I Learned to Stop Worrying and Love the Bomb*).[2] When the United States, a new postwar superpower, flexed its policing might in the Korean and Vietnam Wars, powerful films critical of American imperialism and supportive of countercultural protests against America's military-industrial complex helped articulate the worldview of the boomer generation coming of age in the late 1960s and early 1970s (*M.A.S.H.*, *The Manchurian Candidate*, *Apocalypse Now*, *Easy Rider*, *Woodstock*).

Yet, up to the end of the Cold War in 1989, few in the West knew anything about their supposed enemies in Eastern Europe—how they lived, loved, suffered, and protested in a very different material world. The European countries in the Soviet bloc—East Germany, Poland, Czechoslovakia, Hungary, Romania, Bulgaria, Albania—underwent far greater postwar sociopolitical trauma than the West in their subordination to the world's other superpower, the USSR.[3] Emulating the rule of successive Soviet dictators, the Soviet bloc's postwar governments carried out mass arrests and incarcerations of alleged bourgeois reactionary "terrorists" during the period of high Stalinism (1949–1956) and, over the next four decades, entrenched a powerful secret police force and recruited a vast network of secret informants (both voluntary and involuntary) in all circles of society.

The resulting police states governed primarily by meting out punishments and bribes, responding either to political and economic pressure from Moscow or varying levels of national discontent manifested in public protests, riots, worker strikes (usually about high food prices and low wages), or, in Hungary's case, a widespread armed revolt in 1956. In order of severity, punishments encompassed execution, internment, professional demotion or unemployment, and denial of university education, residency permits in big cities, and passports necessary for travel abroad. Bribes included bestowing the privileges that punishments rescinded—better education and jobs, higher wages, more exclusive housing, opportunities for overseas travel, and access to special stores called Pewex in Poland, in which items ranging from household appliances and furniture to liquor and cigarettes could be purchased with US dollars and other hard currencies. A Pewex shopper could avoid the long wait for coveted items available to other Poles only through a nationwide rationing system.[4] In the later socialist period, some Soviet bloc nations attempted to quell worker unrest by mass producing such "prestige" commodities as televisions and automobiles. In short, citizens in the Soviet bloc, if not the Soviet Union itself, worried far less about the possibility of nuclear holocaust than their counterparts in the West. They were steeped in the ethos created by their governments: on the one hand, fearful of and implicated in state-wide surveillance that determined their socioeconomic welfare, and, on the other hand, avid for the consumer goods, fashions, and entertainment (popular music, movies, television) that they assumed were readily available in the West.[5]

Countercultural movements in the West also appealed to East European boomer generations, though their necessarily more modest protests targeted the concentric circles of Soviet bloc oppression radiating west from Moscow. Many Eastern Europeans were inspired by the 1968 Prague Spring, during which Czechs and Slovaks proposed greater democratization, economic decentralization, and lessened political censorship in their country—a program they dubbed "socialism with a human face." Soviet leader Leonid Brezhnev quickly declared this program to be a threat to the Soviet bloc, yet even as tanks and troops from the USSR, Bulgaria, Hungary, and Poland rolled into Czechoslovakia to crush the reforms, protests against the invasion arose in "Moscow, Kiev, Warsaw, and Budapest."[6] Approximately a decade later, reformers across Eastern Europe were buoyed up by the rise and 1980 legalization of *Solidarność* [Solidarity], the first independent (non-nationalized) trade union in Poland and the Soviet bloc, the product of close collaboration between workers and intellectuals. The inevitable repression of Solidarity, however, was carried out "domestically" by the Polish military, led by General Wojciech Jaruzelski. Imposing martial law on his country from 1981 to 1983, Jaruzelski claimed to be saving it from a far more devastating invasion by a coalition of Warsaw Pact forces, including Soviet troops and weaponry.[7] In any event, the physical, legal, and professional consequences for those protesting such repressions were much harsher in the East than in the West.

ARTISTIC LEGACY: THE "GOLDEN AGE" OF POLISH FILM MADE DURING THE COLD WAR

Poland, of the seven Soviet satellites, "stood at the center of conflicts arising from the Soviet takeover of Eastern Europe in the late 1940s and played an outsized role in the eventual collapse of the Soviet bloc," in the formulation of historian Philip Pajakowski.[8] Polish literature, theater, and, especially, film, the most powerful and accessible form of postwar media, fortified Poland's outsized role both within and beyond the Soviet bloc. Cold War-era Polish directors took advantage of political "thaws," facilitated by the ascent of less doctrinaire Soviet and/or national leaders, to project coded criticism of the system that oppressed them all. The Polish Film School established in Łódź in 1948 came to function as a laboratory for educating specialists in all aspects of film production as well as an oasis of relatively free political and artistic exchange between established and emerging talents. During the 1950s, the Polish School launched the careers of such famous oppositionist filmmakers as Andrzej Wajda, Andrzej Munk, and Kazimierz Kutz. Film critic Elżbieta Ostrowska argues that the first major works of this trio can be construed as "post-traumatic cinema in a double sense": "They address the trauma of the war experience [World War II—BH] as well as the trauma of the Stalinist mutilation of national memory from which a certain part of the World War II experience had been erased."[9] Following hard upon the thaw of 1956, after Nikita Khrushchev became the first secretary of the Communist Party in the USSR, and Władysław Gomułka assumed leadership of the Polish government, films such as Wajda's 1958 adaptation of Jerzy Andrzejewski's 1948 novel *Popiół i diament* [*Ashes and Diamonds*] and Andrzej Munk's 1960 *Zezowate szczęście* [Bad Luck] treated Polish moviegoers to representations of, respectively, Poland's Soviet "liberation" in 1945 as a joyless, morally murky passage and the postwar Communist Party's unabashed encouragement of amoral sycophancy.

After a decade disrupted by student protests against political and cultural repression and workers' strikes against government exploitation (1968, 1970, 1976), Polish filmmakers at last felt free in the late 1970s to probe "the legacy of Stalinism"—to wit, the relatively few years of high Stalinism.[10] Marek Haltof identifies Wajda's 1977 *Człowiek z marmuru* [Man of Marble] as the trailblazer of these celluloid exposés and Ryszard Bugajski's 1981 *Przesłuchanie* [Interrogation] as "arguably the strongest work dealing with the Stalinist past made in Central Europe."[11] *Man of Marble*, the first and best film in Wajda's trilogy about the emergence of the independent Polish worker and Solidarity, explicitly demonstrates the power of filmmakers in unmasking Stalinist propaganda and projecting the experienced truth in a communist state.[12] Its heroine, Agnieszka (Krystyna Janda), is an ambitious, fearless film student producing her final project on the fate of a fallen Stalinist-era star, the shockworker Mateusz Birkut. She gains special permission to pore over authentic and cleverly reconstructed black-and-white newsreels of the late 1940s/early 1950s—access the film shares with the viewer to underscore their visual and rhetorical strategies of falsification.[13] *Man of Marble* contrasts this black/white footage with Agnieszka's subsequent filmed interviews with, among others, Birkut's wife, closest friend, and promoter, and the realistic flashbacks (in color) that their testimonies evoke. Wajda conditions us to accept these flashbacks as the filmic breakthrough from newsreel lie to unmediated, omniscient truth. In the censored world of *Man of Marble*, however, Agnieszka can complete her project only by producing corporeal proof of Birkut's backstory. She does so by finding his son and lookalike (father and son roles both played by Jerzy Radziwiłowicz) and ushering him into the studio as his parent's political heir, the incarnation of a new worker-activist.

Whereas Wajda dared to address the experience of Polish Stalinism in *Man of Marble*, his film focuses as much, if not more, on the revolutionary potential of post-Stalinist youth. Actress Krystyna Janda, whose performance as Agnieszka vaulted her to stardom and cemented a lifelong friendship with the director, reflected decades later that "Andrzej [Wajda] knew that he was making one of the most important films in the history of our cinema to raise the consciousness of a new generation that had no idea of Stalinism."[14] The job of consciousness-raising rested almost entirely on the shoulders of Janda's Agnieszka, for her performance had to manifest the potential of the Solidarity generation onscreen: "[Wajda] told me that my role should announce to the world: 'Watch out, here comes a generation that will not only open doors that were closed for so long, but force them off their hinges.' "[15]

In comparison with Wajda's programmatic, upbeat trailblazer, Bugajski's *Interrogation* emerged, miraculously, as a faster-paced, riveting theatrical work of art, despite the fact that it dives deep into the horrors of Stalinist interrogation and imprisonment. Produced by Wajda and filmed during the eighteen months when political censorship was abolished (1980–1981), *Interrogation* demanded intense, nonstop investment from its entire crew. The resulting energy and high emotion infuse almost every one of its scenes, as do the creative talents of its actors. Bugajski ceded his players control over their characterizations, allowing them to complicate or add eccentricities to their parts, be they cogs or victims in the Stalinist system of terror. Janda, cast as Antonina (Tonia) Dziwisz, an apolitical, spontaneous, extroverted entertainer, appreciated the political importance of her leading role, yet insisted that "Tonia was staged by me . . . Tonia was me the actress creating the role."[16] The great Janusz Gajos, playing the sadistic interrogator Major Zawada, renders his villain a sometimes comical narcissist plagued by obsessive-compulsive disorder, a man whose elaborate torture schemes often misfire and who strives for elegant composure at his "work," even when he must juggle a cigarette with the nozzle of a high-pressure hose and wear a full-length apron over his pinstriped suit. Other talented actors blur the line between villain and martyr through their well-individuated character interpretations—Adam Ferency as Lieutenant Morawski, the ardent communist interrogator whose sense of decency and strong emotions undermine his belief in the party; Bożena Dykiel as the robust, voluble peasant axe murderess; and future director Agnieszka Holland, who plays the loyal communist prisoner as an owl-eyed girl scout.

Moreover, cast, director, and cinematographer (Jacek Patrycki) underscore the theatricality of most scenes—either the duels enacted between the interrogators and Tonia or the ensemble play in the crowded women's prison cell. The film benefits enormously from Tonia's sensibility as a comic, uninhibited actress who quickly shifts from snorting laughter to stubborn resistance, shameless impudence to expletive-spewing anger. Effective interrogation depends on effective acting, and Tonia easily recognizes missed cues. Despite or perhaps because of its subject, *Interrogation* mainly dwells on how its talented actresses swap stories (the camera panning from close-up to close-up of each storyteller's animated face); whisper advice or weep together to cope with their trauma (intimate two-shots), or deftly manage the outbursts and medical emergencies of individual cellmates (usually through medium shots that zoom in to or out from the perspective of the troubled party). Bugajski's film extends to and beyond the day of Stalin's death, the signal to most that political liberalization may follow, but its goal is to showcase the flawed, fine, horrific, comic, and impossibly complicated human responses (e.g., an infant conceived by interrogator and prisoner) to a repression that all its characters are doomed to endure.

POST-COMMUNIST POLISH FILM
ABOUT THE COLD WAR

The postwar Polish film industry suffered most in productivity and reputation from 1989 to 2005, as it struggled through the transition from government subsidies to capitalist funding. The masterpieces that filmmakers such as Wajda, Zanussi, Kieślowski, and others managed to create despite communist-era censorship remained for most Polish moviegoers the products of a golden age. Martin Scorsese was by no means alone in this perception. Indeed, the fact that superior movies about Cold War Poland had been made *in* Cold War Poland raised the question among critics about a possible synergy between political oppression and artistic quality, and left viewers with little appetite for new films about a grim past from which they had just emerged.[17]

With the underlying obstacle to financing innovative, ambitious new movies largely removed by the Polish Film Institute's establishment in 2005, a new generation of film artists and filmgoers were ready to review twentieth-century Polish history from various vantage points. As Thomas Anessi remarked in 2012, Poland's reentry into Europe, formally marked by membership in NATO and the European Union, shook "Polish culture from a 'post-traumatic' fixation with history as a realm reserved for martyrdom and mythological heroism, in which competing narratives were seen as violating sacred territory. In the wake of this 'return to history' late in the first decade of the 21st century, Polish cinema witnessed a flourishing of dramas with [a] historical setting, themes and backdrops rooted in the previous century."[18] Of the notable twenty-first-century historical films that Anessi lists in his review, this chapter analyzes four remarkable pictures that explore Poles' Cold War experience through very different stories and styles: Andrzej Wajda's *Katyń* (2007), Wojciech Smarzowski's *Dom zły* [Dark House] (2009), Jan Kidawa-Błoński's *Różyczka* [Little Rose] (2010), and Borys Lankosz's *Rewers* [Reverse] (2009). The fifth and final movie in this sequence, released a decade after this trend began, is Paweł Pawlikowski's *Zimna wojna* [Cold War] (2018), which identifies its subject by name as both historical and character-driven.

Katyń and *The Dark House* bookend the beginning and end of the Cold War, even though the events of Wajda's film take place during World War II. Once the August 1939 Molotov-Ribbentropp Pact between the USSR and Nazi Germany was signed, splitting Poland's territory between the two powers, Stalin started planning the roundup and execution of 22,000 Polish military and civil leaders by the Soviet secret police in spring of 1940. This atrocity, designed to purge Poland of the likeliest resisters to Soviet rule once it would be permanently annexed to the USSR, truly initiated the Cold War between the two countries, exposing the Soviet Union as a Polish enemy nearly equal to Nazi Germany.[19] Britain and the United States, Poland's main Western allies, chose to overlook what became known as the Katyń Massacre once the Soviet army switched sides to push back the invading Germans. Churchill and Roosevelt ultimately sacrificed a sovereign postwar Poland to the Soviet bloc to appease Stalin's imperial appetite.

Smarzowski's *The Dark House* depicts the events leading to a triple homicide in southeastern Poland in the late 1970s and a reopened investigation into that crime conducted during martial law in the early 1980s. It thus melds together two grim periods of Cold War Polish history, passing over Solidarity's sudden triumph as a fleeting delusion. While *Katyń* aims to expose a covert massacre and the subsequent lie about its commission (the Soviet government blamed the atrocity on the Nazis, a version upheld until the end of the Cold War), *The Dark House* sheds murky light on the dizzying proliferation of lies in a Poland where the secret police incessantly interfered with regular police business to political ends.

Little Rose, *The Reverse*, and *Cold War* might all be categorized as love stories gone wrong in postwar Poland, a premise enabling directors to gauge the psychological toll of a police state on the most intimate human relationship. Two of these films are loosely based on historical pairings: *Little Rose* on the unwitting marriage of a dissident Polish writer to a secret police informant assigned to him, *Cold War* on certain aspects of the turbulent marriage of director Pawlikowski's parents. Each film explores another important aspect of the Cold War in Eastern Europe—the odd mésalliances formed between a supposedly privileged working class under communism and members of a too-often mythologized intelligentsia, romances that lead to redemption, crime, or cross-class misunderstanding.

Framing the System: *Katyń* as Eulogy and Experience

I searched for how to tell the story and project it onscreen so that the topic of Katyń came to life. The viewer must decide if we succeeded.

—Andrzej Wajda

Reviewers typically point out that *Katyń* is a film that Wajda was compelled to make for personal reasons and professional obligations. Wajda's father, Jakub, was one of the 22,000 Polish citizens murdered by the Soviet secret police in the 1940 massacre. A teenaged Wajda, living with his mother in Kraków during the war, watched his parent "wither away" once she learned that her husband was not coming home.[20] *Katyń* pays careful tribute to several women agonizing over the fate of their missing husbands, fathers, brothers, and sons. It also dares to imagine, in its final twenty minutes, one sequence of the execution in which men like Wajda's father were killed and plowed under in a mass grave. *Katyń* completes a family history that Wajda had committed himself to film almost forty years prior: "Our generation is a generation of sons who must tell the story of their fathers because the dead can no longer speak."[21]

Wajda likewise had made it his artistic mission to reconstruct nineteenth- and twentieth-century Polish history in cinema, be it through adaptations of certain Polish literary works or feature films scrutinizing Poland's experi- ence of World War II, the high Stalinist era, and the decades of the Polish People's Republic. As *Polityka* reviewer Zdzisław Pietrasik remarks, *Katyń* fulfilled a lifelong professional and patriotic mission: "[Wajda] felt this obligation as an artist and chronicler of Poland's fate; that narrative would be incomplete without commemorating the Katyń massacre."[22] William Howard Guynn quotes the master's somewhat grander hope "that *Katyń* would constitute the last film of the 'Polish school,' a sort of farewell, the last movie of his type."[23]

Given *Katyń*'s unambiguous exposé of Soviet guilt for the massacre, this film could only have been made after the Cold War in a Poland at last free of Soviet domination. This meant that over sixty years—the span of several generations—had elapsed between the commission of the crime and the film that Wajda finally produced to evoke a collective mourning of its victims. Yet Wajda and his team seemed well aware of what their youngest audience of Poles would not know or feel. *Katyń*'s producers opted to launch the film as an important history lesson, a work implicitly more informative than artful, premiering it separately from any competitive categories at Poland's impor- tant Gdynia Film Festival in 2007 and distributing *Katyń*-related teaching materials to Polish schools.[24] The film's impressive box office success (an estimated 4 million Polish viewers by 2014) was boosted by extensive school screenings.[25]

While the Polish production team clearly did not want to leave the film's "lesson" open to misinterpretation by a generation of Polish students, *Katyń*'s screenings mainly impressed but sometimes confused moviegoers outside Poland. Magdalena Saryusz-Wolska reports that "the producers had huge difficulties finding a distributor abroad. When they finally succeeded, two years after the premiere in Warsaw, primarily Polish emigrants watched the film."[26] Indeed, an American reviewer, who admitted he could not sort out *Katyń*'s extensive cast of largely non-individuated characters, chose instead to gauge the film's "powerful shock of recognition" and "profoundly personal" message on the "predominantly Polish American audience" with whom he viewed it: "when the film concluded and the theatre lights went on, I saw tears streaming down many of the audience members' faces."[27] While British reviewer Michael Brooke maintained that the movie was "not a his- tory lesson," he recognized how burdened it was with exposition unfamiliar to a non-Polish viewer: "The abiding impression is of a much longer miniseries truncated to two hours."[28]

Brooke's "abiding impression" succinctly points out two of the film's key flaws: its overpacked plot and highly schematic characterization. *Katyń* is based on Andrzej Mularczyk's *Post mortem*, but, as Pietrasik dryly points out, the screenplay that Wajda cowrote with Przemysław Nowakowski and Władysław Pasikowski "is not the strongest part of the film. . . . We have perhaps one pair of fully developed heroes here, but most of the characters are barely sketched and psychologically thin."[29] It may be that in writing "the last film of 'the Polish school,' " this trio too dutifully added what they deemed to be important subplots referring to instances of Polish rebellion and Wajda's early biography. Unfortunately, these subplots disperse narrative focus and are tossed out like bromides—inspiring examples of male and female rebels—before the film opens wide the doors of despair, the final segment recreating the experience of the massacre.

Katyń begins with two sets of refugees colliding on a bridge, one group fleeing the Nazi invasion on September 1, 1939, the other fleeing the Soviet invasion launched sixteen days later, and each insisting that the greater danger lies behind them. This mise-en-scène decants four of the future female mourners onto Soviet-occupied turf: the earnest wife Anna (Maja Ostaszewska) and daughter Nika (Wiktoria Gaszewska) of the captured Polish Major Andrzej (Artur Żmijewski), and the imperious wife Róża (Danuta Stenka) and daughter Ewa (Agnieszka Kawiorska) of the captured Polish General Mieczysław Smorawiński (Jan Englert). Here Anna, who has devised an escape by bicycle for her family, at last locates her husband and pleads with him to run away. Andrzej stoutly resists, refusing to betray his oath as a Polish officer and unable to conceive of Soviet perfidy. The stage is set for inexorable tragedy. Wife and daughter watch in anguish as a Soviet transport train, rendered ominous by its black engine, bleak whistle, and the grinding bass notes of Krzysztof Penderecki's score, bears the captured Polish officers away. The visual and aural motifs of the train recur to signal the men's predetermined journey to mass execution.

The setting then shifts to the city of Kraków, to the comfortable bourgeois home of Major Andrzej's parents, where the officer's mother (Maja Komorowska) is helping her husband, Jan (Władysław Kowalski), a professor at Kraków's prestigious Jagiellonian University, prepare for an emergency faculty meeting with the new Nazi authorities—specifically, Obersturmbannführer Brunon Müller, an official they mistake for a "real" doctor of philosophy. The screenplay begins its pedagogical embellishments here, adding to the Katyń plot the tragic roundup of university rector and professors for execution and deportation to Nazi concentration camps. Andrzej's mother qualifies as the film's first official widow, a fact confirmed by her receipt of relics, a small box of the professor's effects with an attached tele-gram explaining that Jan "died of a heart attack" in Sachsenhausen.

Thereafter, *Katyń*'s plot alternates five times between the large group of Polish military officers and some civilian leaders now interned in the abandoned Optina Pustyn Monastery in Kozelsk, USSR, and several sites in Kraków—Andrzej's parents' home, where Anna and Nika take refuge after a narrow escape from Soviet-held territory; the well-appointed apartment of the general's family; and the main square of the city's Old Town, used by the Nazis for public announcements and later appropriated by the Soviets for projecting black-and-white newsreels. This last location works effectively for the film's propagandistic representations of the Katyń massacre. Though each scene shift is titled with date and location, it is important to bear in mind that the Kraków scenes leap forward by years, whereas the prisoners' scenes in Kozelsk move much more slowly in accord with the six months they spend there. The latter episodes deliver a livelier representation of how the men respond to their incarceration—their constant guessing about where they are being sent; arguments among those who insist on escaping, inferring Soviet betrayal, and those who believe that the Nazis' advance will release them into combat; and the prisoners' celebration of Wigilia (Christmas Eve), during which the General delivers a moving speech to his presumably all-Catholic officers and reminds those civilian leaders among them that they will be responsible for creating a "free Poland." Andrzej is established as diarist and stalwart optimist of the camp, whereas his lieutenant, Jerzy (Andrzej Chyra), emerges as the most fully, if predictably, drawn protagonist in the film, a sensitive pessimist who retains his suspicions about the Soviet authorities' plans, yet resists deflating his compatriots' morale.

The temporary internment camp at Kozelsk disappears once viewers are shuttled forward to Kraków on April 3, 1943—that is, three years after the Katyń massacre took place. In 1943, Kraków the Nazis are using the main square to broadcast the names of all those whose bodies the German army had exhumed and managed to identify at Katyń. Anna and her mother-in-law are relieved that Andrzej's name is missing from this list (an absence we later learn is a mistake). The general's family is doubly damned by news of his murder and the Nazi authorities' demand that his wife sign a public statement attesting to his death as a Soviet war atrocity. When Róża refuses, she—and we—are forced to watch footage from the movie's first authentic newsreel of the Katyń exhumation, a black-and-white Nazi-made horror show degrading the victims as their exhumed skeletons in disintegrating uniforms are hauled up from mass trenches and presented to the camera as forensic evidence of "Soviet-style" slaughter: their hands bound behind their backs, the single pistol shot to the back of their skulls. The otherwise stalwart military widow collapses once she exits the auditorium.

The next segment, date stamped January 18, 1945, in Kraków, portrays the Soviet liberation of Poland, mainly by emphasizing that victory's perversion of the truth about Katyń. Only the visit of Róża's former maid, now the wife of a newly minted Communist Party official, demonstrates any revolutionary change in the Polish class order. Both the camera and the actors continue to ally viewer sympathy with the general's mourning widow. The film focuses on the interventions of Andrzej's former lieutenant, Jerzy, promoted to major in the Polish branch of the Soviet-aligned People's Army. He functions as the precarious bridge between Poland and the USSR: a Pole who hates the Soviet secret police as executioners yet is grateful to the Soviet army for his salvation. Jerzy feels compelled to tell Anna that Andrzej's body was mistaken for his because he had lent her husband a sweater tagged with his name during their Kozelsk internment. He suffers the scorn of a former professor, now working for the Polish commission archiving German-compiled evidence of Katyń's victims, so that Anna might receive her husband's relics. Jerzy's last intervention occurs on Kraków's main square, where the Soviet authorities are screening their newsreel about rediscovering the mass graves at Katyń and "proving" that its displayed corpses are the victims of typical Gestapo methods of assassination (figure 6.1). Jerzy prevents Róża's arrest as she pounds on the door of a Soviet truck and demands that they halt projecting this lie. Jerzy and Róża's subsequent quarrel, in which he counsels pragmatism and she condemns him as a liar, causes his collapse. In short order, he gets drunk, confronts other soldiers in the bar with the truth about Katyń, and kills himself (a pistol shot to the side of his head) as he stalks away.

Jerzy's convenient erasure from the film removes the lone ambiguous figure in *Katyń*, which, as Polish and non-Polish reviewers note, generally displays nationalist and Christian symbolism and, by implication, Wajda's strangely complacent acceptance of prewar Polish nationalism.[30] When Wajda last projected Poland's Soviet liberation in his 1958 masterpiece, *Popiół i diament* [Ashes and Diamonds], albeit under the communist government's censorship, he ceded dignity and good intentions to the incoming Communist Party leader (a Pole), ridiculed the self-serving right-wing officers who were ordering partisan groups of the Polish Home Army to begin harassing Soviet instead of Nazi forces, and subjected his charismatic Home Army partisan Maciej to feelings of hope and guilt. A half-century later, Wajda projects the Polish army as patriotic Christian martyrs, ignoring the dominant presence of right-wing National Democrats in its officer corps and never distinguishing the Polish Jews who also served in the army or were interned as civilian leaders.[31] Diversity and dissonance yield to sentimental homogeneity in this group portrait. In one of the film's most moving scenes, a sea of uniformed men join in singing a stirring Polish Christmas carol as

Paweł Edelman's camera rises up to match the music's spiritual splendor with a long shot of the monastery's vaulted ceiling.

The pedagogical plotlines inserted after Jerzy's suicide reinforce this hagiographic orientation. One introduces Tadeusz (Antoni Pawlicki), a nineteen-year-old boy whose father died at Katyń. Fresh from fighting in the Home Army, Tadeusz is now eager to be admitted to Kraków's Academy of Fine Art (Wajda's own initial career path), though he refuses to expunge the facts of his father's murder from his application. The boy's rash act of tearing down a Soviet propaganda poster leads to his death just a few hours later. A more extended story stars Agnieszka (Magdalena Cielecka), a pristine blonde who fought in the failed 1944 Warsaw Uprising (like Maciej in *Ashes and Diamonds*) and has returned to Kraków to erect a memorial to her brother, Piotr, another Katyń victim, in the family plot. Agnieszka sells her beautiful hair to pay for the headstone, on which the year 1940 is inscribed as the date of Piotr's death, marking Soviet culpability. On the way to the cemetery, Agnieszka argues with her more pragmatic, cynical sister about this deliberate provocation; after the headstone is put in place, she is immediately picked up by the secret police for interrogation and internment. The screenplay thus preemptively interjects consoling examples of two hotheaded young Polish rebels in the first days of the Cold War, two determined preservers of the truth about Katyń, suggesting that this resistance will continue.

While the long film preceding the scene of the massacre might be categorized euphemistically as a eulogy in which both victims and mourners are consistently portrayed as virtuous and heroic, most reviewers agree that the conclusion of *Katyń* is its most important, powerful, unconventional segment. Prompted by Anna's receipt of her husband's effects (courtesy of Jerzy), which include Andrzej's diary, its pages blank after April 10, 1940, and its edges stained by blood or damp, the mise-en-scène shifts backward in time to Andrzej scribbling in the cramped space of a Soviet prison train, speculating about their destination. When the train halts, and the camera moves outside to frame the black engine with its red Soviet star, the black marias (prison trucks) lined up to transport prisoners, and the station labeled Gniezdovo, the film's mode of representation and our relationship to that representation fundamentally change. Wajda has saved the screening of the massacre as the film's jarring coda, an event projected to be ever present. Some Polish critics have savaged this strategy as "pornographic," for cinematographer Edelman and his team dispassionately shoot the assembly-line murders of at least a score of men by the Soviet secret police—the trussing of the prisoner around the throat and the hands, the single shot fired into the back of the head, the shoving of each man's body into a trench already plowed by the bulldozer that ominously waits to cover all the dead with dirt.[32]

Reflecting on the critique of Wajda's "pornography," Ostrowska does not agree outright but notes that this segment is akin to pornography in affecting the viewer physiologically, fusing the past of what is shown with the viewer's present visceral experience.[33] Guynn's reading interestingly furthers Ostrowska's, describing the coda as "an unmediated experience," unfiltered by character voiceover or identifiable character point of view, and thereby forcing viewers into the "uncomfortable position of observers, all too close to the action." He speculates that Wajda himself "needed to place the murder of his father before his own consciousness in the most direct and brutal manner possible."[34] Neither critic mentions, however, the outrage and sorrow that Penderecki's oratorio unleashes as soon as the movie ends, functioning as a musical catharsis.

One other reading should be considered. *Katyń*'s otherwise flawed screenplay most effectively creates the scaffolding for this brutal, disturbing, imperative end. Just as Wajda's optimistic *Man of Marble* progresses from authentic Stalinist-era propaganda films to the colorful "truth" marked as omniscient and uncovered by Agnieszka's dogged research, so *Katyń* first screens two historic propaganda films (Nazi and Soviet) that demote the lives of thousands of men to forensic evidence of enemy evil. This genuine footage repels viewers in its disrespectful display of the dead victims and heavy-handed political exploitation of their massacre. In comparison, Wajda's concluding representation of the massacre *in process*—conveyed as omniscient, "unmediated," and uncensored—at once restores the humanity and in-the-moment response of the betrayed victims (the general suddenly struggling with his captors when he recognizes the trap, Major Andrzej and others intoning sections of the Christian "Lord's Prayer" as they are being bound), and dehumanizes the perpetrators as the disconnected arms and hands of a death-dealing machine. Like Agnieszka the film student, but to a much grimmer end, the filmmaker must produce the cinematic equivalent of corporeal evidence to the viewer. Wajda gambled heavily on the fact that the truth of Katyń as it happened—how its mass murders were carried out and by whom, the terror that its living subjects were forced to suffer, and the ways they met their fate—had to be *seen* by the world to be believed.

FRAMING THE SYSTEM: *THE DARK HOUSE* AS HORROR FILM OF THE ABSURD

It seems you don't belong anywhere anymore.

—Zięba to Lieutenant Mróz

Truth? There is no such thing.

—Zięba to Lieutenant Mróz
Lieutenant Mróz to Środoń

Smarzowski's *Dom zły*, cited here as *The Dark House* to comply with
its translation in English-language references, is better rendered from the
Polish as *The Evil House*, given what takes place on its site. Though this
film, like Wajda's *Katyń*, damns the lies and violence generated by Soviet-
modeled communism on Poland and Poles, it contrasts almost completely
with its predecessor in its sensibility, plotlines, and fleshed out, yet oddly
broken, characters. In its focus on late communist Poland—the last years of
Gierek's consumer-oriented rule and the first year of martial law and strict
rationing under Jaruzelski—*The Dark House* sometimes echoes the work
of Stanisław Bareja, a director little known in the West because his comic
films spotlight the Poles' own experience of the crass, everyday absurdity
of Polish life in the 1970s and (to a lesser extent) 1980s. This absurdity
encompasses the hypocrisy and contradictions of Partyspeak; the kitsch of
material and media culture; and the ubiquitous illegal businesses and con
schemes pursued to achieve "the good life." Smarzowski has stated that his
"view of the PRL is a little different from what we know, for example, from
Bareja's films," yet *The Dark House* draws from Bareja's pool of period
characters who are both slippery and pathetic, unctuous and venal, and very
often falling-down drunk.[35] Smarzowski's film cannot help but interject the
humor involving illegally obtained or pitifully substandard and rationed
goods of those decades, including bobble-head dogs, plastic bags filled with
rationed cigarettes, matches that fail to light, and television sets switching
between poor-quality variety shows and static. Yet Smarzowski's direction
and his screenplay, coauthored with Łukasz Komicki, meticulously build a
horror film of the absurd.

Film critic Joanna Raflesz warns future viewers of *The Dark House* that
Smarzowski "demands that they step into the detectives' role, guess certain
facts or tease out important, but barely noticeable, details leading them to the
truth."[36] The film intertwines two plotlines, one unfolding largely within the
dark house in 1978, the other circling around the gutted house and its site in
February 1982, both of which end in murder. These plotlines are augmented
by (1) omniscient digressive scenes that contradict whitewashed character
narration, and (2) scenes flashing evidence in the minds of the two protagonists that they suddenly realize will be used against them. The alternating
plotlines are also sporadically interrupted by the black-and-white footage of
a Super 8 handheld camera, used by various policemen to record—or, rather,
coerce—the 1982 suspect's testimony.

This intricately composed film, with its incessant temporal shifts, rewards second, third, and fourth viewings, but a concise description of what takes place in both plots provides a useful tool, regardless of a viewer's familiarity with Smarzowski's work. *The Dark House* lays out the recurring misadventures of Edward Środoń (an uninhibited performance by Arkadiusz Jakubik), an ordinary oafish young man with a juvenile record as an arsonist, a technical degree in agronomy, lowbrow tastes, little sensitivity toward women, and some success in running con schemes and marketing moonshine. His pretty wife, Grażyna (Katarzyna Cynke), briefly appears as his contented sidekick. Środoń's happy life shatters when Grażyna dies of a cerebral hemorrhage as she serves his dinner. The scene of her death—her body stretched out the length of the small kitchen, the bright red borscht spilled like blood at her side—turns into tragicomedy as Środoń and the elderly neighbor he recruits for help remain clueless about what to do, more frustrated than devastated.

Środoń nearly drowns himself in vodka before he decides to begin a new life working on a state farm in southeast Poland, close to the Bieszczady Mountains. A malfunctioning bus forces him to walk the last leg of his trip; a violent thunderstorm convinces him to seek safety at a lonely farmhouse on the way. Weather, setting, and circumstance conspire to set the stage for a horror film. The occupants of the house, a gruff farmer and his much younger wife, Zdzisław and Bożena Dziabas (the magnificent Marian Dziędziel and Kinga Preis), give Środoń shelter, food, far too much alcohol, and local gossip about a disappeared agronomist named Jan Stec, whom Środoń is replacing at his new job. The thoroughly soused Środoń and Dziabas seal a deal to produce moonshine for a local base of Soviet soldiers, and a little while later the sullen, abused Bożena slips into Środoń's bed, mainly for the chance to complain of her miserable lot with Dziabas and his parasitic adult son, Janek (the product of her husband's first marriage). By daybreak the storm has lifted, but three people are dead—Dziabas, Bożena, and Janek. Horrified and traumatized, Środoń flees the dark house, carrying a shabby suitcase packed with his few possessions along with the considerable savings of the Dziabas family.

In the second plotline, policemen from the city of Rzeszów gather at the site of the dark house to investigate and reenact the Dziabas murders on a bright February day four years later. The crunching snow and the year 1982 remind most Polish viewers that the military, with help from the police, had recently imposed martial law and delegalized Solidarity. Criminologist Lieutenant Mróz (a fine, restrained performance by Bartłomiej Topa) is the de facto leader of this investigation. Though Prosecutor Tomala (Robert Więckiewicz) outranks Mróz, Tomala is rarely sober and invariably corrupt. Mróz does not drink (we later learn that he overcame his alcoholism by having the drug esperal implanted in his buttocks) and, as he reiterates, he "is not interested in politics." We know little of his backstory apart from observing that he tries to do his job honestly, protects those under his command from political punishments and denunciations, and is likely the lover of the pregnant policewoman Lisowska (also played by Katarzyna Cynke), whose abusive husband, Lieutenant Lisowski, serves in his squad.

The investigation intended to determine whether Środoń is guilty of murder utterly defies Western genre notions of a "police procedural."[37] The police "team" is disorganized, no spaces are set up to conduct proper interrogation or to preserve material evidence, and the action is anything but straightforward, with the cast meandering between the gutted house, the shells of its outbuildings, and the two police cars and van. Indeed, the van is used as a makeshift drunk tank. To make matters worse, Mróz is called away by the arrival of Zięba, the local secret police chief, who uses the back seat of his chauffeured black sedan as his office. The semi-close-up two shot used to film Zięba's menacing interaction with Mróz, a supposedly independent police officer, but de facto subordinate, positions the camera in the sedan's front seat looking back and conveys Mróz's maximal discomfort, as he is literally wedged into a tight space with no room to pivot and no ground for authority. Here Zięba orders Mróz to compromise his police inquiry for the needs of the Communist Party: he is to arrest Środoń for the murders and then release him in the West so that the Polish government can smear self-exiled Solidarity activists through their association with fugitive criminals. At the same time, Zięba warns Mróz whom he must denounce for what in his squad and what circulating information—in this case, news about embezzlements at the state farm—he must silence. In return, the chief bribes the lieutenant with an early promotion to captain and perhaps a *Polonez*, a new Polish-made car.

Incensed by Zięba's orders and bribes, Mróz escapes the "sedan seat" of political power to utilize the relative autonomy of the regular police car. He drives away from the chaotic inquiry in the dark house in order to dig up information about the very crimes that the chief insisted he suppress, interviewing locals at a grocery store about funny business at the state farm and its missing agronomist. It bears noting that Mróz uses the plastic bag of cigarettes to coax responses from a public with no love for the police; this bribe evidently does not suffice, since the car's windshield has been shattered by the time he drives away. The locals' raucous testimony leads him to a priest who had befriended Jan Stec and offers Mróz the young man's files, since Stec had been killed in a suspicious auto accident likely orchestrated by the secret police. Once again, the party conducts its dastardly business on the road, dispensing with a whistleblower in his private car.

Equipped with evidence, Mróz returns to the dark house feeling momentarily empowered, ready to fight back as a criminologist "not interested in politics," a protective team leader, and even a lover. There he discovers that an inebriated Lisowski had punched his wife in the face for presumed infidelity. Mróz packs Lisowska off to the hospital, since her (their?) baby's birth is imminent, and summarily beats up Lisowski when the latter finally emerges from the police van, having slept off his binge. Thereafter, Mróz studies the thick folder of materials that Stec has compiled, and finds documentation of Zięba and his brother's misuse of funds at the state farm as well as Prosecutor Tomala's signature of approval on a letter whitewashing their crime.

When Zięba's sedan reappears, Mróz is ready for a showdown with the villain within, presuming that he must eradicate just one. Yet Zięba preempts his attack by revealing that all of the colleagues whom Mróz has protected in the past have already denounced him, sometimes more than once, and been rewarded for their compliance. One of those amply compensated is Lisowski (and, by implication, his wife). Visibly stunned, Mróz rallies and presents his criminal case against Zięba, along with a particularly damning document. But when the secret police chief suggests that they make a deal, Mróz abruptly realizes his mistake and exits the car. What Mróz knows, and the viewers do not, is that all of his men are in Zięba's pocket, and, now that he has confronted the chief with a serious threat, he is in mortal danger. Back at the house, he entrusts Stec's file to a civilian, an old woman from whom he also buys vodka. He asks Środoń to remove the esperal ampule, entrusting him with the knife that was one of the weapons used in the Dziabas case. Suddenly, his suspect has become both ally and fellow victim. Mróz then proceeds to drink himself into a stupor as he waits for certain death.

By the chaotic conclusion of *The Dark House*, all of Mróz's men have been implicated in his fatal stabbing. Some show qualms of conscience by warning Środoń to escape (they know he will be framed for the lieutenant's murder). One policeman even knocks down another who is intent on shooting Środoń, as the prisoner, thoroughly bewildered, kneels by the lieutenant's body. Lisowska, who had returned to the site due to an unstaffed hospital, is the only one who displays open anguish over Mróz's murder, shoving and shouting at her husband until she is seized by contractions. She gives birth in the dark house, an event that symbolizes the perpetuation of a deeply flawed society rather than any rebirth. The crane shot used in the final scene surveys how the evil connected with the farmhouse has spilled out onto the surrounding snow, with Tomala dispensing promised favors, Mróz's body lying unattended, Środoń presumably running away in the distance, and one of the drunken policemen hurling an empty vodka bottle close to the camera. As Raflesz observes, the tiny figures scattered or racing in circles below look like "puppets in the hands of the communist system"[38] (figure 6.2).

These plot summaries map out the two phases of Środoń's misadventures and underscore the desultory action of the 1982 police "investigation." The film's highly affective construction emerges once viewers know what these

1978 and 1982 storylines entail and can better track how *The Dark House* shifts between them, at first regularly and then at a confusingly accelerated pace by the film's end. In effect, Smarzowski and Komicki have enmeshed their own updated version of an acclaimed Polish tragedy with a typically misdirected, but increasingly ominous, day of shoddy work carried out by inebriated policemen that abruptly ends in a murder that will surely be covered up. To a great extent, the riveting 1970s-era tragedy powers the film to the end, when we, if not the police characters, discover what role Środoń played in the violent death of a family. Resembling Karol Hubert Rostworowski's 1929 play, *Niespodzianka* [The Surprise], in which a poor peasant couple murder their son, whom they have mistaken for a well-dressed, wealthy stranger from America, Smarzowski and Komicki's rewrite delivers a primeval drama played by a superb, well-matched ensemble. Like Bugajski in *Interrogation*, Smarzowski in *The Dark House* relies on great actors to embody fluid, shrewd, ruthless, and complex characters: Dziędziel as the wiley peasant who loves his hooligan son blindly and treats his second wife as a whore; Preis as the coarse schemer with her eye on the next main chance (a peasant version of Phyllis Dietrichson in Billy Wilder's 1944 *Double Indemnity*); and Jakubik shifting convincingly between quaking fear and a kind of animal resourcefulness.

Just as well-acted drama in *Interrogation* enlivens bleak life in a Stalinist prison, so this trio's play infuses *The Dark House* with energy and emotional punch ranging from the comic and absurd to the horrific. We watch the drunken antics of Środoń and Dziabas as the former, following the farmer's instructions, bangs on the roof of a hen house while the latter strives and fails to catch a fleeing fox. Cinematographer Krzysztof Patak conveys the infectious excitement of the two men's moonshine-making plans by seeming to patch together the best outtakes of their exchange: their happy swap of information about where to purloin materials and cash in on secrets in order to build a new still, their realization of the boatload of money they will make and consequent display of their secret savings to each other, and their final bear hug and crazy growls of pleasure (figure 6.3). Dziabas and Bożena, in contrast, team up for the film's most chilling scenes of horror. Husband and wife discover that they have murdered an unexpectedly returned Janek, not Środoń, after they had crept into Janek's room and wildly stabbed the body in the bed. When the two subsequently hunt for Środoń outside, Bożena, covered in mud, competes with the thunderstorm itself as she shouts out her revised plan for killing and robbing their visitor; a dead Środoń can be framed as Janek's murderer. Ultimately, Środoń witnesses their gruesome death scenes as he exits the dark house at dawn. Bożena's body lies face down in the mud, her head bashed in by her husband, while Dziabas himself hangs dead from a leafless tree.

As the tragedy climaxes with this hyperreal carnage, the viewers lose track of what is happening in the 1982 plotline—the zigzagging police investigation that seems ever less concerned about the screened vivid murders and suicide that interrupt and overwhelm shots of their bumbling inaction. Smarzowski has ensured our confusion (and heightened our frustration) not only by fixing our attention on the Dziabas family horror show but also by relegating the planning and execution of Mróz's murder to the unmiked peripheries and backgrounds of the shots in the 1982 story. As Marcin Adamczak points out: "[In *The Dark House*] everything happens beyond the frame of the shot or in the distance, to the side or on the margins; the business that is key for what will be presented plays out beside what seems to be the main thrust of the action."[39] Only bursts of nondiegetic dissonant jazz (squealing saxophone, a scraping of strings) signal moments of alarm or distress, though without attribution to a specific character. The anti-theatricality of this plotline, muffled further by incessant vodka consumption, blots out any evidence of its actors' clear thinking, sense of morality, or feelings of affection or grief.

In contrast to the Soviet secret police's robotic massacre of Polish officers at the end of Wajda's *Katyń*, Smarzowski's *The Dark House* gauges the dehumanizing, unhinging effects of the Soviet system on the Poles themselves after more than three decades of control. Smarzowski's group portrait shows at length how the Polish police neither expect nor bother to maintain law and order. Instead, a squad of officers are persuaded to kill the one honest man among them at the party's behest. They do so because they must survive within the party's web of punishments, bribes, and mutual surveillance. Not one of the officers dares to mourn or seek justice elsewhere. The only man uninvolved in Mróz's expedient assassination is the prisoner whom the police force had been tasked to prosecute. The unremarkable Edward Środoń is a sometime arsonist and sometime thief, but, as we can conclude twice, not a murderer. When we last see him, he is still capable of feeling horror and shock at what he witnesses within and outside the dark house. But we do not know if he survives.

LOVE STORIES: THE WORKER AND INTELLIGENTSIA MÉSALLIANCE

Love is whatever you can still betray. Betrayal can only happen if you love.

—John Le Carré

Kidawa Błonski's *Little Rose* (2010), Lankosz's *The Reverse* (2009), and Pawlikowski's *Cold War* (2018) present heterosexual love stories, or facsimiles thereof, but none fits into the highly profitable genre of romantic comedy. As Goscilo elaborates in chapter 8, *Little Rose* features Kamila Sakowicz, a beautiful young woman who, in the puritanical context of Polish cinema, is exceptionally eager and well-equipped to experience the pleasures of sex with the man whom she initially loves and the man to whom she has been assigned as an intimate informant for the security services. The heroine of *The Reverse*, tall, gawky Sabina Jankowska, dreams of a romantic love that also promises to be gratifyingly sexual, though her grotesque notions of the mechanics of sex mislead her, and her male partner's practicum is brutal and brief. As regards *Cold War*, the director Pawlikowski best summarizes the relationship between Zuzanna (Zula) Lichoń and Wiktor Warski—the film's protagonists and lovers—as a romance of mutual destruction, with "two strong characters . . . fatally drawn to each other, but totally mismatched—condemned to a kind of war without end."[40]

All three films locate their love stories in different periods of the Cold War. The action of *The Reverse*, authenticated by the interspersion of newsreel footage, plays out in a black-and-white palette matching the grim days of high Stalinism in Warsaw, as the construction of the Stalinist baroque Palace of Culture and Science is underway, and the secret police are busy arresting high-ranking cultural figures as reactionary terrorists round the clock. The historical coverage of *Cold War* is most expansive chronologically and geographically, if not in detail, extending from 1949, the tipping point from wartime recovery into high Stalinism to 1964 in a more culturally liberal, but economically stagnant PRL. Tracking the meetings of its lovers, the film delivers snapshots of different cities in a divided Europe—Warsaw, Berlin, Split, Paris—as well as a starkly provincial Poland. *Little Rose*, the film that most explicitly functions as a period melodrama, attempts to cover the many protests and repressive actions that rocked Poland in 1967–1968. These include the government's banning of Kazimierz Dejmek's 1968 production of *Dziady* [Forefathers' Eve, 1832], a potent, classic play about Polish martyrdom by the Russians (in tsarist times) written by the nation's bard, Adam Mickiewicz (1798–1855); the March 1968 university student rallies and strikes against government corruption exacerbated by Gomułka's deployment of secret police riot squads to beat up the protesters; and the waging of General Mieczysław Moczar's infamous anti-Zionist campaign in 1967–1968 following the 1967 Arab-Israeli War, a bloodless purge that automatically denounced Polish Jews remaining in Poland after the Holocaust as "Zionists," that is, "pro-Israel" supporters, and resulted in the deportation of 25,000 Polish Jews.[41]

What links and importantly illuminates these three "love stories" is their exploration of a new kind of Cold War mésalliance between working-class protagonists, the class most overtly championed by the Communist Party, and protagonists belonging to an amorphous intelligentsia—self-identified by higher education, worldly orientation, involvement in uncensored cultural work, progressive-to-Marxist-Leninist political views, and their family's materially privileged background before the wars. Cross-class love affairs have been a staple of modern Polish literature and drama since the latter half of the nineteenth century. For decades a mésalliance portrayed between an aristocrat and a member of the lesser gentry, professional classes, or peasantry frequently misfired and exposed the former as representative of an intolerant, solipsistic, inbred upper class.[42] Yet in the post-communist era, a late twentieth-century mythology of the intelligentsia—the closest approximation of a former aristocracy—has simplistically ennobled them as persecuted liberal opponents of a despised regime, and this reverent attitude has tended to tip the romantic scales in their favor in literature and film.

LITTLE ROSE AND THE REVERSE: THE CHARMS AND CRIMES OF THE INTELLIGENTSIA

Little Rose and *The Reverse* invite comparison on the basis of their complementary plots. Both films imagine the romance of a member of the intelligentsia with the most suspect workers of the Communist era's vaunted dictatorship of the proletariat—secret policemen and their network of paid informants. *Little Rose* pursues a more conventional plot—a disappointing, if legally prudent, decision, given its echoes of the real-life affair and marriage between Paweł Jasienica (Leon Lech Beynar, [1909–1970]), a prominent historian, journalist, and dissident activist, and Nena Zofia Darowska O'Bretenny, a secret police informant who had been reporting on his activities since 1966.[43] According to historian Lawrence D. Orton, Jasienica helped spearhead the protest by the Polish Writers' Union against the banning of the 1968 *Forefathers' Eve* production and expressly accused Gomułka's government of fomenting anti-Semitism by distributing anti-Jewish leaflets among student protesters.[44] The government's backlash forced the writer out of the Writers' Union, and Gomułka slandered him falsely as a participant in a rightwing partisan group that murdered Belorussian peasants during World War II. Devastated by this censure, Jasienica leaned on O'Bretenny for emotional support, married her in December 1969, and died of lung cancer eight months later. He never suspected that the "Nena" in his bed was informing on him. She, in turn, continued to submit reports on Jasienica's dissident friends at his funeral and later anniversaries of his death.[45]

The parallel between Jasienica/O'Bretenny and two of the film's protagonists—noted older writer Adam Warczewski (Andrzej Seweryn) and the aforenamed Kamila Sakowicz (the stunning Magdalena Boczarska)—prompted

Jasienica's daughter to request that the public not confuse the film with her father's biography.[46] Perhaps she need not have worried. The screenplay of *Little Rose*, written by Kidawa-Błoński and Maciej Karpiński, opted to foreground the twofold education of its beautiful heroine rather than Warczewski's foolish mistake, for Kamila is scripted to study with two very different mentors. Instead of casting Kamila as a career secret police informant, the film initially pairs her romantically with the wholly fictional Roman Różek (Robert Więckiewicz), a secret policeman intent on upward mobility. Convincing Kamila to seduce and then inform on Warczewski for "their" better future, Roman exploits her love for him and saves her from the onus of choosing such a repugnant career on her own. As it happens, Roman's self-serving recruitment of Kamila, who soon delivers excellent intelligence on her new lover's associates, impresses his superiors and insulates him further from the discovery of his Jewish identity, a facet of the plot that, as reviewer Łukasz Maciejewski convincingly argues, is poorly integrated into the film.[47]

At the outset Kamila and Roman match each other well in youth, sexual appetite, and working-class notions of the high life. Kamila works as a lowly secretary at the university and, despite her beauty, lacks self-confidence. As XXX astutely remarks in XXX portrait of the heroine, Kamila never dazzles viewers with intelligence, yet incrementally attracts their sympathy by answering kindness with kindness. Tender, loving care was missing in her childhood: Kamila was raised in an orphanage where, she intimates, she was sexually abused. Roman's possessiveness and apparent professional success attract and reassure her. When he at last reveals his profession, admits her into his apartment (located in a special gated compound), and shows off his boxing trophies and, at her request, his gun, Kamila is genuinely impressed and he is genuinely proud. The scene reveals something of his private motivation to join the force, where his zeal, physical strength, and loyalty have already reaped him considerable material rewards. Yet at no point does Roman reveal his Jewishness to Kamila or discuss how that identity may have determined his career. On the contrary, in his "Party talks" with Kamila, he expresses his hatred for the intellectual "Jews" who betray Poland, and fingers Warczewski as one such traitor who must be outed and expelled.

Once Kamila consents to inform under Roman's supervision, their work together at first gives them a sexual rush. The code name she chooses, "Little Rose," is Roman's term of endearment for her. He greets her with roses at their rendezvous. Serving as an informant actually constitutes a step forward in Kamila's very limited education. Just as Roman is an athlete become officer, so Kamila is a secretary become "writer," a young woman who eagerly types up reports late into the night. Close-up shots of a bespectacled excited "Little Rose" at her typewriter intimate how empowering and addictive such a secret job would be for this character, a young woman either ignorant of or indifferent to politics and culture and thrilled to win praise at last for her detailed accounts. These scenes provide brief insight into Kamila's character; as several reviewers rightly note, *Little Rose* spotlights its heroine as the motivational figure, but does not articulate her aspirations, fears, or doubts as she acclimates to two such different worlds.[48]

In lieu of developing this intriguing immoral partnership between two secret police employees, *Little Rose* saves and purifies its limited, straying heroine by accentuating Roman's brutality and fleshing out Warczewski as a charismatic, generous intellectual. Roman grows jealous of and sexually aggressive toward Kamila once she succeeds in bedding Warczewski. He eventually vents his fury on the writer as well, revealing Kamila's informant status to him in a vain attempt to tear this odd couple apart. Warczewski, played by Andrzej Seweryn (b. 1946), a stage and screen actor renowned for his wide-ranging talent and enduring good looks, at first treats Kamila with the kind condescension that an established professor would show an unlikely student.[49] He never slips from his high dissident pedestal, even when he falls for this young woman half his age, flattered by *her* sexual attention. Warczewski introduces Kamila to high culture—fine wine she initially dislikes and forbidden twentieth-century Polish literary classics she never knew existed. Indeed, Warczewski's spacious, book-lined home, gracious mother (Izabella Olszewska) and precocious young daughter (Julia Kornacka) enhance his appeal for Kamila, because his lifestyle strikes her as materially luxurious and his family embraces her with a warmth and respect that she has never known. The orphan secretary turned informant is overwhelmed by the obvious charms of the intelligentsia. Even Kamila's lovemaking scenes with Warczewski, carefully lit, seem more tender and satisfying than her rough sex with the macho Roman.

Kamila's almost complete conversion takes place when the fictional Warczewski most overlaps with the historic Jasienica. (According to Zdzisław Pietrasik, Seweryn combines the features of three dissident writers—Jasienica, Jerzy Andrzejewski, and Stefan Kisielewski—in his exemplary impersonation of "a defiant Polish intellectual from those times."[50]) Warczewski takes Kamila's breath away when he speaks out in support of the young democratic forces at work in Poland during the now famous February 29, 1968, meeting at the Polish Writers' Union. His impassioned speech decides Kamila to quit her job as informant—ironically, only *after* she has delivered her final, highly detailed report. Though Kamila at first refuses Warczewski's marriage proposal later that year, she changes her mind when the writer, fully apprised of her role in his downfall, appears at her door, tells her he has forgiven her, and repeats his offer. The two marry with eyes opened, unlike the actual Jasienica and his wife, and Kamila writes no more.

Nevertheless, the vice-to-virtue melodramatic course of Kamila's education, shifting from the sex work and denunciation that she undertook to
unmask a "traitor" to the duties of a cultured dissident's wife and a loving
stepmother, requires a final sacrifice. Given her malleability, it seems fitting
that she does not die, as is the usual fate for the melodramatic heroine, but
is left to her own meager devices, deprived of her mentors. Roman takes his
revenge by murdering her husband, symbolically humiliating him by throwing him from his balcony to the pavement below. Roman himself is deported
along with thousands of other "Zionists" out of Poland from Warsaw's
Gdańsk railway station. Kamila is drawn to watch his departure from afar.
But the film and her expression do not divulge her motivation. Perhaps
Kamila wants to be sure that she and her adopted family are at last safe from
her persecutor, or ponder what Roman meant to her and who he really is. Or
perhaps Kamila simply serves as a convenient witness to a major tragedy in
Polish history that the filmmaker endeavored to squeeze into his final scene.

In contrast to *Little Rose*, *The Reverse* adroitly turns the tables on conventional good and evil in plot, casting, genre-mixing, and aesthetic style, and
consequently netted ten awards at the 2009 Gdynia Film Festival, including
its Golden Lion (Grand Prix).[51] A number of reviewers singled out the film's
welcome switch from recycling Polish national martyrology about high
Stalinism to approaching the subject with an oddball tale of ironic reversals,
leavened with humor and spiked with homegrown horror.[52] Instead of delivering a period revenge fantasy, like Quentin Tarantino's 2009 *Inglourious
Basterds* and 2012 *Django Unchained*, director Borys Lankosz and screenwriter Andrzej Bart seemed to be following in the footsteps of Andrzej Munk,
the early Polish School director who dared to underscore the ironic, absurd,
and mock-heroic in his films about Poland in World War II.[53]
   In *The Reverse*, Sabina Jankowska (Agata Buzek), a thirty-year-old virgin
who works as a poetry editor in the publishing house Nowina, is the wannabe
heroine nearly caught in the secret police's elaborate trap. The film's opening
scene focuses on Sabina's rapt reaction shots to a Stalinist-era propaganda
film showing scantily clad young men doing calisthenics. Such period newsreels featuring athletic bodies most nearly approximated pornography in 1952
Warsaw. Sabina feels an even more intense sexual thrill when she dresses up
as an ice skater, joining other publishing house employees uniformed as ath-
letes for a political parade. Flattered by her flirtatious boss, Sabina later takes
stock of her equipment at home, touching her breasts and raising her short
skating skirt above her crotch as she gazes in the mirror.[54]
   In tandem with her sexual fantasies, Sabina mourns her missed turn as a
Polish romantic heroine. She did not fight (in her words, "shoot") in the 1944
Warsaw Uprising against the Germans that left the city in ruins. The young

editor reveres a poet who survived in those ruins and would rather starve than publish a censored album of his work. Sabina's pathetic version of such heroism involves her daily swallowing and excreting a foreign coin that the state forbids private citizens to keep. In lieu of any bold public act, she defies the government with the base hiding place of her digestive tract, though she sometimes dramatizes her "internal dissidence" when she swallows the coin by playing Cio-Cio-san's "Tu, tu, piccolo iddio," from Giacomo Puccini's opera, *Madame Butterfly*, the aria the heroine sings before she commits hara-kiri, nobly removing herself from the lives of her faithless American husband and their child. In one such scene, the camera grants Sabina the diva's spotlight, poking fun at her solemn self-aware movements through high-angle shots.

In the meantime, the strong-willed women in Sabina's family—her unflappable grandmother (the excellent Anna Polony) and hyperactive mother, Irena (Krystyna Janda, who clearly relishes this juicy character role)—wheel a comical marriage plot into place, hoping to ensure Sabina's happy apolitical future with a good match. Grandmother and mother are always prepared for the worst and intent on achieving the possible. The mother tempts suitors to their home with her cooking, baking of enormous cakes, and distilled liqueurs. Irena is a dab hand in the kitchen since she ran the family's drugstore before the war; her cabinets are as well-stocked as a witch's pantry. The lone family member who ensures their political safety is Sabina's brother, Arkadiusz (Łukasz Konopka), an artist who paints flattering portraits of high-ranking party officials in his attic studio.

Dissatisfied with her unheroic life and appalled by the marriage prospects invited home, Sabina is the perfect mark for the secret police's con, which unfolds in a cleverly constructed *film noir* version of Stalinist Warsaw. In anticipation of Sabina's "romantic" encounter, cinematographer Marcin Koszalka and Lankosz's production crew transform the socialist capital into an early 1950s American film set, with *noir*'s characteristic urban nightscapes, sharp contrasts between light and shadow, claustrophobic framing of characters in doorways and windows, and looming threat of citizen-on-citizen (or, star-on-extra) violence. Sabina, walking quickly along a deserted street, is set upon by two crooks (not the usual secret police waiting by their sedan, but secret police cast as crooks). At this moment, very much as if he is being directed or playing director, Bronisław (Bronek) Falski (Marcin Dorociński) emerges from the shadows like a younger, taller Humphrey Bogart, smartly dressed in a Sam Spade trenchcoat, and saves the damsel in distress.[55] This mysterious stranger is handsome, sexy, and smooth, tailor-made for Sabina's romantic dreams. In an ingenious gambit, *Reverse* hooks a female *inteligentka*, a lover of poetry and valor, with a working-class secret policeman groomed to be her *homme fatal* (figure 6.4).

Like Roman in *Little Rose*, Bronek plans to recruit Sabina as an informant; her targets will be work colleagues. His initial effort, however, entails a sustained performance to keep up the façade that Sabina fervently believes is real—feigning intense desire for her, treating her to afternoon tea, sweeping her off her feet with kisses in the rain or the elevator, and posing as a working-class war veteran who aspires to better himself. Sabina worships him as her Hollywood-handsome lover and working-class project. She will cultivate Bronek and smooth his rough edges. She does not notice that Bronek delivers all his lines as if they were excerpts memorized by rote from different scripts.

Dorociński gives a virtuoso performance in his final meeting with Sabina, when all three Jankowski women believe he will pop the question. Speeding up his courtship out of revulsion or ignorance, Bronek makes crude advances on Sabina and finally takes her on the dining room table; in this instance, Sabina herself substitutes for Irena's enormous cake. As he closes in on his prey, Bronek's façade finally cracks. He owns up to his provincial background, sucks inelegantly on his teeth, and veers between mawkish and brusque in his patter. A still compliant Sabina listens to his ramblings until he pops a very different question about "helping him with his work," at which point she recognizes him as the enemy. Unveiled, Bronek threatens her with all the goods he has on her and her family, including her peculiar method of coin hoarding, and Sabina faces her greatest moral challenge.

This challenge galvanizes the timid, intellectual, family-oriented daughter to become Kamila's opposite: Sabina chooses homicide over collaboration. Taking advantage of her mother's pharmacological inventory, she poisons Bronek and is prevented from shooting herself only by her mother's fortuitous return. The picture's sudden morphing into a thriller/horror film focuses on how three respectable women succeed in dissolving the corpse of a secret policeman and disposing of his effects and bones. As Romańska notes, *The Reverse* recalls here the 1944 film *Arsenic and Old Lace*, though the earlier American comedy did not dwell on the awful effects of the elderly women's poisonings or their mad brother's labor in burying all the victims in the cellar.[56] Sabina and Irena, with advice from the grandmother, "liquidate" Bronek with scary efficiency. Irena uses her potions on the agent's flesh, covering his rapidly decaying body with her son's party portraits—a nice baroque juxtaposition. In desperation and perhaps deference, Sabina buries what remains of her agent-seducer (bones in a violin case) in the foundation of the Palace of Science and Culture. On this fictional page of Stalinist history, a modest matriarchal intelligentsia "disappears" a member of the secret police.

Yet, as Wróblewski points out, this film reveals a "second layer," conveying that "totalitarianism is inscribed in our genes, and the virus of communism circulates in our blood."[57] Lankosz and Bart represent this literally: in raping Sabina the virgin, Bronek has impregnated her.[58] Over Sabina's objections, mother and grandmother persuade her to keep the child, already imagining an improved biography for its dead father. "Perhaps he fought against Hitler," Irena speculates. Once the film has established that Sabina's baby is born on the happy day of Stalin's death, it leaps forward a half-century to the son's reunion with his aged mother on All Saints Day. The final scenes, filmed in color, explain the previously interspersed color flash forward. *The Reverse* thus conjures up the most chilling triumph of the intelligentsia over an entirely unsatisfactory specimen of a worker. Sabina and Bronek's son, also played by Dorociński, inherits his father's good looks but has been raised to be Bronek's opposite in terms of sophistication, sensibility, sexuality, and class. An affluent gay architect who lives in the United States, he cherishes his mother, and brings his lover to pay his respects to his largely deceased Polish family.

The final scene of *The Reverse* shows a hunchbacked Sabina commemorating Bronek's approximate grave, unbeknownst to her son. She places a candle strategically beside a statue of a strapping young man at the palace, reinforcing the film's link of Stalinist athleticism with the sexual excitement Bronek once promised. The thriller delivers a highly ambiguous verdict on the dissident intelligentsia as an aerial shot tracks Sabina's slow progress from the palace to her brother's waiting car, accompanied by Nina Simone's brooding rendition of the 1964 pop song, "Don't Let Me Be Misunderstood." The Jankowski women not only murdered, dismembered, and effectively erased one "inferior" worker serving the enemy, but also used his seed as raw material to fabricate their own version of an admirable member of the intelligentsia, a gay Pole, moreover, who chooses to live abroad. It is not clear whether these protagonists should be punished or commended, yet Simone's somber, yet defiant "songover" articulates a classy final plea in Sabina's defense.

COLD WAR: THE WORKING-CLASS
STAR STEALS THE SHOW

I'll be with you everywhere until the end of the world.

—Zula to Wiktor

As in *Little Rose*, two of the protagonists in Pawlikowski's *Cold War* are drawn in part from historical models—the director's parents, whose first names Wiktor and Zula (a nickname for Zuzanna) the characters bear.[59] While Pawlikowski resists drawing absolute correspondences between his closest family members (he was an only child) and fictional creations (he cowrote the screenplay with playwright Janusz Głowacki [1938–2017] and

the collaboration of Piotr Borkowski), some of his interviews reveal significant similarities.[60] His father, a doctor, and his mother, initially a ballerina
and later an English literature professor at the University of Warsaw, met
in 1948 and carried on a torturous romantic relationship, interrupted with
lengthy separations, for the rest of their lives. As Pawlikowski tells interviewer Elaina Patton in *The New Yorker*:

> [My father] was this tall, mysterious, very good-looking guy. . . . He kind of
> looked like Gregory Peck. [My mother] was blond [*sic*] and hotheaded. Full of
> energy. . . . Kind of like mood swings. He was a terrible womanizer. So when
> they got together, he kind of assumed a man can do it. And she immediately
> retaliated in kind.[61]

His parents' fights and different fates resulted in Pawlikowski's expatriation
from Poland. His father, whose Jewish mother perished in Auschwitz, was
deported from Poland in 1968 as a result of the Moczar-led purge. His mother,
then divorced, married a British man and moved with him and her fourteen-
year-old son to England in 1971. Yet, ultimately, Pawlikowski's parents
reunited in Munich, Germany (neither was allowed to return to Poland) when
they were both old, in bad health, and, according to their son, suddenly transformed into "the most tender, touching couple."[62] As Pawlikowski divulged
to Tim Adams in *The Guardian*, his parents ended their lives together in a
suicide pact in 1989, before the Berlin Wall came down: "they just took leave
in a peaceful way."[63]

The similarities between parental history and feature film breakthrough
in Pawlikowski's choice of actor Tomasz Kot to play his father, presumably
the best Polish approximation to Gregory Peck in his tall, lanky physique
and projection of quiet command, and the stark, but sanguine, conclusion of
their romance at the film's end. Pawlikowski's repeated observation that his
parents' relationship both spanned the Cold War and played out as interper-
sonal warfare underscore the double meaning of his film's title. Reviewers
have been quick to point out how Wiktor and Zula's peripatetic romance
demonstrates the harsh impact of a divided Europe on two such passionate,
willful lovers, what Ann Hornaday describes in *The Washington Post* as "a
chronic sense of dislocation that isn't just geographical or political, but also
existential."[64]

But others have claimed that both types of cold war receive insufficient
attention in this trim 89-minute film. On the one hand, Pawlikowski eschews
didacticism and overt historical exposition in his films. Of the five European
sites featured in *Cold War*—provincial Poland, Warsaw, East Berlin, Split
(Yugoslavia) in the East and Paris in the West—the camera only tracks
Wiktor and Zula on the streets in Paris, likely the most familiar city to a

global (though not necessarily Polish) audience. The footage devoted to their Seine cruise seems intended to reflect the awed point of view of two Poles at last free to share this iconic sight; in a movie inundated with musical productions the only sound here is the motor of the cruise boat. *Cold War* does not tip us off to the fact that no Wall had yet been built when Wiktor simply walks from East to West Berlin. Nor does it spell out the reasons for the less punitive attitudes of Yugoslav secret policemen toward a defector in Split, delivering him to a Zagreb, rather than Warsaw, bound train. We must infer a great deal about the local atmosphere and politics.

On the other hand, Pawlikowski resorts to the sort of plot development he first discovered in *Ida*—that is, "tell[ing] a complicated story kind of simply, through ellipsis."[65] This means that the cold war being waged between the cinematic Zula and Wiktor, already whittled down twenty-five years from the complicated relationship evolving between their real-life "inspirations," is further condensed to what the lovers say and how they act/react during the six meetings that actually transpire. (In Split, the two only glimpse each other across the footlights of the theater as Zula is performing.) In lieu of voiceovers in which either Wiktor or Zula reads the other's correspondence or scenes in which they show how they live their daily lives while somehow carrying a torch for their distant love, Pawlikowski projects blackouts, like a curtain between acts. The vast majority of viewers (that is, other than Poles of a certain age) have no inkling how difficult it was for intimates separated by the Iron Curtain to keep in touch. Reviewers complain or, more often, lament the fact that Pawlikowski's minimalist approach begrudges us character backstories and sociopsychological portraits. Marcin Kempista, one of the film's harshest critics, claims that Pawlikowski's obsession with the plot's tight structure and perfectly planned shots prevent the plausible development of the protagonists' "Great Love." He dismisses the progress of their relationship as "an unbearable rehash from films of the 1950s and 1960s."[66] Admitting that *Cold War* "could seem insufficient" to its viewers, Grzegorz Brzozowski nonetheless justifies the love story's elliptical presentation because it is only during their meetings, presumably, that the protagonists "have the impression that they are shaping their fates."[67]

Why, then, did *Cold War* attract record ticket sales in Poland (an estimated one million) and win a pile of awards ranging from six out of seven major prizes at the European Film Awards to the prize for best directing at Cannes? I contend that Pawlikowski and his cowriters' decision to refocus "the matrix" of his parents' story on popular musical performance not only enriched the film's sensual, accessible appeal but also transformed the love story into a de facto star vehicle for Joanna Kulig, who steals the show in her role as Zula. As Jonathan Murray smartly observes in his film review, Zula/ Kulig is most often filmed performing center stage, whether she is dressed in a standard folk costume and meant to blend in as yet another figure repeating the steps of an all-ensemble folk dance or if she is debuting as a singer in a Parisian jazz club and the camera tracks 360 degrees around her extraordinary solo performance: "Zula/Kulig is clearly privileged as the center point around which all other on-screen elements are compelled to pivot, a fact made even more powerful by the film's evocative black-and-white cinematography."[68]

What hooks the viewer from the beginning to the end in *Cold War* are the masterly filmed segments of different sorts of musical performances. This begins with the ethnomusicologists venturing out in 1949 to collect authentic folk music from the Polish and Lemko peasants who still sing and play these tunes. Here the performances are amateur, without costumes or sets. But the music they produce is hauntingly plaintive in sound and theme, and Łukasz Żal's cinematography renders each "recording" into a stunning motion picture masterpiece of hard-living subjects and authentic folk art. Żal's black-and-white camera work achieves the same magic with every aesthetic style, be it naturalist, kitschy, or overexposed "cool jazz," creating visuals that resonate with the finest black-and-white photography of the period and place. Just as cinematography poeticizes what we see in *Cold War*, so contemporary composers improve on or refresh the music we hear, an effect most distinct in Marcin Masecki's new arrangements of Tadeuz Sygietyński's music for Mazowsze (the real-life prototype for the Mazurek ensemble). Reviewer Janusz Wróblewski best conveys the enormously affective hybrid composition of the film's sight and sound:

> The black-white frames boxed into a 4:3 ratio on screen might have delivered the same effect [as in *Ida*]. But here there is more stylization anchored in different aesthetic forms—from silent film through the early filmmaking of [Wojciech] Has and Wajda to the photography of Jean Barthet and the vision of [Andrej] Tarkovsky. . . . Here prayer [as in *Ida*] is displaced by a phenomenal sound track expressing the emotions and tragic fate of the protagonists . . . the mix of Mazowsze's old repertoire incredibly rearranged by Marcin Masecki, which encompasses not only the work of the original composer, Tadeusz Sygietyński, but also George Gershwin, bebop and jazz as performed by Krzysztof Komeda and in the early performances of Zbigniew Namysłowski.[69]

Just as important, the screenplay's orientation toward popular musical performance realigns the power relations between the lovers. In her role as Zula, Joanna Kulig flourishes in *Cold War*'s "phenomenal sound track" because she is a superb, versatile singer. As producers in Hollywood's studio system quickly learned, the success of the musical film absolutely depends on the performing prowess of its stars.[70] Pawlikowski knew Kulig's musical talent very well when he chose her for the film's female lead; she had been featured as a pop chanteuse in *Ida.* Kot's Wiktor is a musician as well, but he first appears as rehearsal accompanist and orchestra director—the facilitator rather than the main event. His work as a jazz pianist in Paris entails no direct personal engagement with a live audience, nor is it clear that Kot himself is at the keyboard; he never exercises the power over the audience that Kulig's Zula so vividly commands. The film also highlights how the protagonists' class backgrounds differently shape their ambitions, priorities, survival strategies, and attitude toward "true love." Here, too, Zula's working-class pedigree underscores her heroism, for she must be more realistic, self-sacrificing, and emotionally invested in order to pursue Wiktor across Iron Curtain boundaries.

Wiktor Warski (played by Kot as a confident artist whose easygoing façade masks his demanding character) clearly belongs to the intelligentsia, a gifted composer and pianist with a conservatory degree and a keen, if closeted, interest in new Western popular music banned in communist Poland. Initially, he is a careerist who does not hesitate to betray his colleague, Irena Bielecka (Agata Kulesza), the cofounder of Mazurek, when she objects to the blatant politicization of the ensemble's repertoire. Once Wiktor decides to defect to the West in order to compose and play the bebop and jazz he admires, he pressures Zula to come with him, declaring that he does not want to live without her. Sure of himself, he cannot grasp the depth of her insecurity. When Zula does not appear on time at the appointed rendezvous, he walks into West Berlin alone.

From the film's outset until Zula leaves him a second time in Paris, Wiktor's grand passion for "the love of his life" stems in large part from artistic ambition. He responds to Zula's enormous sex appeal when he first meets her, but he makes sure that she can duplicate jazz intervals easily when he auditions her in private before he makes the next move in their relationship. Wiktor the composer desires Zula the performer as the artist who will best incarnate his more daring future work. Indeed, his sexual desire for her peaks after he (along with the tracking camera) bears witness to her command, charisma, and musicianship onstage in Mazurek's Warsaw premiere. Once Zula records the songs he has written for her and according to his specifications in Paris, he significantly declares the album, titled *Zula* and featuring her photograph, "our first child," despite the fact that he has overseen almost every aspect of its creation.

Early in *Cold War*, Zula, a diminutive girl with a long blonde braid, arrives with peasant lads and lasses to audition for Mazurek, though she is a cuckoo among the smaller field birds, a savvy working-class girl from town. Among the crowd of applicants sitting in the hallways and on the stairs, Zula quickly distinguishes herself by asking questions, sizing up the competition, and choosing a partner so that they can impress the judges with an effective duet. She excites the male judge (Wiktor) with her sensuality and audacity. When asked to sing a song of her own, she chooses a love song from a Soviet film that flaunts her comparatively greater sophistication among her peasant competitors. Because Wiktor prefers to live in the bubble of his professional milieu and artistic dreams, it is Bielecka, his shrewder colleague, who tries to dampen his ardor by telling him that Zula has a criminal record for murdering her father. As the two watch the candidates outside at play, Bielecka quickly notes Zula's modus operandi: "She's up to something."[71] Nonetheless, the talented felon soon qualifies as a member of Mazurek. During her private practice time with Wiktor, their first time alone together, Zula responds to his question about her criminal record with sauciness and assurance: "[My father] mistook me for my mother, so I showed him the difference with my knife. He survived, so don't be scared."

These early scenes are valuable in establishing Zula's complex, alternately calculating and freewheeling character. While other reviewers enthuse about Zula's "elemental," "volatile" nature, her embodiment of Slavic character, her blend of "wounded bird and tough dame," and her more "typically Polish" anxiety about being able to "be someone" in exile, no one points out that this character best exemplifies what it takes to survive as an ambitious working-class girl in Cold War Poland.[72] When Wiktor and Zula are lying in a meadow between rehearsals (he on his back with eyes closed, she on her side and characteristically studying his face), she launches what will become a confession with a sweeping child-like vow: "I'll be with you everywhere until the end of the world" (figure 6.5). Then Zula trusts him with the ugly truth of her existence—that she must inform on him regularly to their political overseer/manager, Kaczmarek (played with touching naïveté by Borys Szyc), and puts up with Kaczmarek's incessant passes. Wiktor was capable of selling out his colleague Bielecka without compunction, but he is shocked and enraged by Zula's news and unmoved by her justification that she, as a convicted felon, is "on probation" and therefore obliged to cooperate with the authorities. Wiktor stalks off as Zula curses him for obtuseness and class privilege, but then is obliged to save her when she jumps in the river nearby, floating away and singing the Soviet song with which she first attracted his interest.

What Wiktor prefers not to know, but we must presume, is that Zula pays a steep price for any special privilege she wins, encompassing her inclusion in Mazurek as the group travels abroad, her defection to Paris, and her rescue of Wiktor from a fifteen-year sentence to hard labor once he crosses the Polish border illegally to be with her. That price is intimated in East Berlin when Kaczmarek discovers her alone in the dressing room, mirror-gazing as she musters the courage to join Wiktor in his escape. The manager instead pushes her to join the post-show banquet and socialize with their East German comrades. Zula's subsequent scene dancing listlessly with a German partner to the Soviet wartime standard, "Katiusha," belongs in a gallery depicting the purgatory of the Cold War. Once Zula arrives "for good" in Paris, she tells Wiktor in a rush that she wed a Sicilian in order to be with him and that this "marriage does not count" because it involved no church wedding. What she does not add is that such a liaison surely cost her plenty—in Western currency and/or sexual favors. When Wiktor is at last reunited with Zula in 1964 Poland, Zula's payment is woefully clear: she has underwritten his release by marrying Kaczmarek, bearing her one-time manager a son she does not want, and earning money singing in a two-bit provincial summer theater—all to work her husband's political connections toward shortening Wiktor's camp sentence.

A similar sort of sacrifice seems required in the West. When Wiktor urges Zula "to be kind" to Michel, his record producer in Paris, she immediately assumes that his request includes sleeping with the Frenchman and playing nicely with the snooty Parisian company her lover keeps. At a party with Wiktor's new friends, a dismayed Zula stares at herself in a bathroom mirror, a contrasting variation on her mirror scene in Berlin, and orders herself to buck up: "You dope. Well, I love him, and that's that."[73] Yet Zula draws the line with Wiktor when he implies that she prostitute herself artistically. Whereas the composer believes he knows just how she should deliver his French-language songs, Zula the performer does not trust the material, the translations (produced by his former French lover), Wiktor's directions on intonation and phrasing, or the "wild" Eastern bloc performing persona he has fabricated for her in order to satisfy French consumers. After Wiktor identifies "their" work as their first child, Zula snarls that it is "a bastard" and tosses the album in the trash. In the heat of the ensuing argument, Zula deliberately praises Michel's sexual stamina over Wiktor's performance in bed, declaring that the French are more manly than some Polish artist in exile. Stunned by her admission and malice, Wiktor slaps Zula hard, no longer the easygoing gentleman. Zula retorts that this sort of abuse is something she understands, implicitly equating Wiktor with her violent father. She may have embellished on the ugly truth, but Wiktor at this point has no excuse for not knowing it.

The next morning Zula is already in the wind, on her way back to Poland, and Wiktor is desperate to follow her. Though his sudden transformation from an ambitious, self-involved artist into the utterly devastated lover is neither well-motivated in the screenplay nor convincingly acted by Kot, the fact that Wiktor finally pays for his love in a different Cold War currency— years in a labor camp and a pianist's hands ruined by quarry work—facilitates a level-playing field and mutual understanding between the lovers. Just as Zula schemed and sacrificed herself for years to come to him, so Wiktor at last schemes and sacrifices himself to come to her, and they finally meet as exhausted equals who want neither West nor East, but only a peaceful endgame. Wiktor has been stripped of his former arrogance and control, and Zula has embraced an uncompromising fatalism. In the final scenes, Zula at last directs the show, leading a completely docile Wiktor to a beautiful ruined church that had appeared early in *Cold War* (figure 6.6). There she lays out the pills that they will swallow, reads her marriage vow, and prompts Wiktor to read his, for this church wedding, she maintains, will "count." As the two wait for death on a bus stop bench in the fields, they hold hands like "the most tender, touching couple," until Zula bids them "to move to the other side, where the view is better." The cold war of their relationship concluded with Wiktor's return, and the Cold War of their context has become irrelevant. Zula, the working-class star, has emerged as the flawed, magnetic heroine in this film, for this gifted singer and unabashed schemer has sacrificed her integrity, body, and any chance for a successful career or a happy family in order to keep their fairytale love alive "until the end of the world."

CONCLUSION

In the free Poland of the twenty-first century, Wajda at last was able to make a film about Katyń, the Soviet Union's original sin against his homeland, a massacre of 22,000 important Polish officers and citizens that the Stalinist authorities falsely blamed on the Nazis. Soviet insistence on that lie prompted the Western powers to abandon Poland, an "inconvenient ally," thus placating Stalin and his powerful Red Army and stumbling into the Cold War. Wajda was so concerned about convincing the world of this "empire-paving" atrocity and proving the identity of its perpetrators that his film in large part sacrifices his art for his cause. In *Katyń*, he effectively jettisoned any psychological or ideological complexity from the fiction film preceding its horrific coda. He reiterated through main and branching plotlines that the only characters who counted were the Polish (Christian) men martyred, the Polish women who mourned their dead, and those who risked their lives to reveal the Soviet lie. Even the sympathetic figure of Jerzy, who chooses service in the Soviet People's Army over death in the Soviet gulag, is forced to kill himself upon his homecoming after he encounters the women who mourn. The final segment of *Katyń* draws on as many filmic strategies as possible to create the illusion that viewers are bearing witness to history in the making. Wajda assumes that after audiences have seen his movie, they, unlike Churchill and Roosevelt, will not be able to unsee the premeditated, massive, terrifying Soviet decapitation of a free postwar Poland.

The eponymous dark house in Smarzowski's 2009 film serves in part as a synecdoche for the last two decades of Poland's Cold War. The 1978 drama that takes place under its tin roof both ridicules and bares the dark versions of what many Polish citizens had become under Gierek's materialistic leadership—unabashed hedonists, petty black marketeers, and potential killers if too much money, sex, and alcohol have been part of an evening's fare. The hapless traveler Edward Środoń discovers, just in time, that his otherwise hospitable peasant hosts have decided to kill him so that they can steal his savings and buy, among other things, a new Polish auto for their adult son. The murderer Zdzisław Dziabas discovers, too late, that he has killed that son by mistake, and his overwhelming anger and grief led him to bludgeon his wife (his bedmate and accomplice) and hang himself. Środoń murders no one, but his fear does not prevent him from stealing the family nest egg that Dziabas showed him the night before.

In the 1982 plot, however, the dark house no longer functions as the scene of multiple apolitical crimes, the site where the Polish police have gathered supposedly to determine the victims and perpetrators by examining material evidence and interrogating the one surviving witness. Instead, the house serves as a stage on which the police "discover" and videotape false narratives about the crimes and carry out punishments devised by the secret policeman in the back seat of his black sedan outside. In and around the house, the regular police drink vodka nonstop to anesthetize their conscience; the one honest detective who uncovers the secret police's crimes of embezzlement and homicide is assassinated by his squad; and Środoń, the chief culprit in the 1978 crimes he did not commit, is framed for the detective's murder. In these two interwoven tales of the late Cold War, the Polish secret police—long schooled in the Soviet system's methods of using lies, bribes, and punishments to manage the population—not only replace an external Soviet enemy but also easily recruit the regular police (and the Polish military) to reinforce their venal, lawless rule.

Little Rose, *The Reverse*, and *Cold War* likewise underscore the power that Poland's secret police wielded over ordinary citizens through surveillance and informing. In comparison with the foreign espionage thrillers made in the West (and further east, in the USSR), these films demonstrate how Cold War-era love stories easily double as homegrown spy stories, with seduction leading to incriminating pillow talk. In *Little Rose*, the lovely limited Kamila agrees to seduce and spy on a writer in order to appease her lover in the secret police. She proves to be most successful at her new, but short-lived, job. The tall, dark, handsome secret policeman in *The Reverse* dispenses with his romantic façade when he proposes a second partnership to Sabina—working for him as an informant—and thus cuts his career short. In *Cold War*, a teenaged Zula with a criminal record falls hard for the older, urbane Wiktor before she realizes how the party will extort her service for consorting with an intellectual. She hopes, in a child-like way, that Wiktor will forgive and

continue to trust her once she confesses what she must do. She does not realize how long he will prefer to remain ignorant of how she must live.

At the same time, each one of these liaisons joins together a working stiff
and a member of the intelligentsia, a group that had only enhanced its moral
and political luster over the Cold War decades. Indeed, it is intriguing that
none of these films tarnishes the intelligentsia lover with the repugnant task
of informing on their partner, as if such cases never occurred. In two of the
three films, the protagonists from the intelligentsia do not stoop to selling
out their colleagues. Warczewski remains astonishingly unaware of Kamila's
"writing" until after his noble example moves her to quit. In *The Reverse*,
Sabina, despite her timidity, descends from two generations of eccentric,
strong-willed women who have instilled in her the capacity to vanquish the
enemy under the most unexpected circumstances. In contrast to Warczewski,
Sabina cannot convert an ambitious secret police recruit from the provinces.
Rather, she automatically chooses to destroy Bronek before he can weapon-
ize her to destroy many others. Sabina's like-thinking family closes ranks
with her to ensure Bronek's complete erasure and to raise his son to believe
romantic narratives of his father that reverse the truth.

Cold War, however, switches the customary privileging of intelligentsia
over working-class informants in its elliptical devotion to valiant love. In
the case of Zula and Wiktor, the male lover from the intelligentsia initially
demonstrates neither political courage nor loving solidarity with his much
younger, far less worldly "discovery." Wiktor's response to high Stalinism
leapfrogs from expedient collaboration with the new regime to an easy
defection for the sake of his artistic career. It is curious that the action of
Cold War defects west with Wiktor as well, leaving Zula to cope with the
political fallout back in Cold War Poland offscreen. We can only infer her
compromises and injuries from scattered comments and scenes. When they
first meet briefly in Paris, Zula insists that she "is worse, worse in general"
than Wiktor but subsequently mutters that she would never have defected
without him. During Zula's appearance with Mazurek in Split, as the camera
alternates between shots from her onstage point of view to centered shots of
her performing, we share her sighting of Szyc, her political manager, as he
keeps watch on her from an upstairs loge of the theater; see her suddenly anxious face and fumbling dance steps when she spies Wiktor in the audience;
and then note her devastated expression once Wiktor has disappeared. Unlike
her naïve lover, a politically experienced Zula senses that Szyc and the secret
police have set a trap for him and fears the worst.

After their attempt to make a life together in the West, Zula, Wiktor's
chosen artist and Parisian "discovery," turns on the man who presumes to be
her creator, informs him just how much she has boosted his career in another
man's bed, and chooses the likely purgatory of Poland over what has become

for her the faux paradise of Paris. Given Wiktor's past choices, we might expect that he will remain where ambition has lured him. Yet, the plot makes a sudden about-face, and we witness how Wiktor, the artist and *inteligent*, is unhinged by his working-class star's rejection of him as composer and man. To the surprise of everyone, including the Polish consul, Wiktor risks everything to be with Zula again. His return to Poland does not represent his choice of East over West, communism over capitalism, patriotism over artistic freedom, but a quest that at last perfectly matches Zula's—the pursuit of true love. The film follows him back to Cold War Poland, where both lovers do hard time—one in a labor camp and the other in a hapless marriage, unwanted motherhood, and demeaning gigs. When the pair finally reunite, lying in a heap on the floor of a public restroom, Zula, who alone has borne the moral and physical costs of their love, begs her partner "to get me out of here for good." An utterly devoted Wiktor complies. At the end of *Cold War*, the working-class heroine (and sometime informant) and her humbled, thoroughly reoriented intelligentsia lover finally marry themselves and redefine their happily ever after as union in death.

BH

NOTES

1. Carole Fink, "Teaching the History of Cold War Europe," in *Understanding and Teaching the Cold War*, ed. Mathew Masur (Madison, WS: University of Wisconsin Press, 2017): 13–14.

2. Eric J. Morgan indicates the rich cinematic mother lode of film adaptations of John Le Carré's cynical, riveting portrayal of British espionage: "Through their dark and antiheroic depictions of the Western intelligence community, these films provide alternative visions to the often patriotic fare of Hollywood, and *Tinker Tailor Soldier Spy* in particular offers an opportunity to look back and reflect upon the Cold War from the perspective of today, where the contested morality, secrecy, and accountability of espionage and intelligence within democratic societies remains as controversial as ever." "Whores and Angels of Our Striving Selves: The Cold War Films of John Le Carré, Then and Now," *Historical Journal of Film, Radio and Television* 36, no. 1 (2016): 88. From the 1965 release of *The Spy Who Came in from the Cold* (Martin Ritt, dir.) to the present day, Le Carré's espionage fiction and its transposition to the screen has informed virtually every serious Cold War spy drama produced in Western film and television.

3. For an excellent study of how the Cold War was "re-viewed" in both Russian and American film from 1990–2005, see Helena Goscilo and Margaret B. Goscilo's *Fade from Red: The Cold War Ex-Enemy in Russian and American Film, 1990–2005* (Washington, DC: New Academia Publishing, 2014).

4. See Paul Lewis, "The Lure of a Dollar in Poland," *New York Times*, October 9, 1981, https://www.nytimes.com/1981/10/09/business/the-lure-of-a-dollar-in-poland.html. Accessed February 12, 2020.

5. For more on consumer desire and its manipulation in postwar Eastern Europe, see, among many fine studies, Paulina Bren's *The Greengrocer and His TV: The Culture of Communism after the 1968 Prague Spring* (Ithaca, NY: Cornell University Press, 2010); Patrick Hyder Patterson's *Bought and Sold: Living and Losing the Good Life in Socialist Yugoslavia* (Ithaca, NY: Cornell University Press, 2012); *Communism Unwrapped: Consumption in Cold War Eastern Europe*, ed. Paulina Bren and Mary Neuberger (Oxford: Oxford University Press, 2012); and Krisztina Fehérváry's *Politics in Color and Concrete: Socialist Materialities and the Middle Class in Hungary* (Bloomington, IN: Indiana UP, 2013).

6. Carole Fink, "Teaching the History of Cold War Europe . . .," 20. For in-depth coverage on the Prague Spring see, among other studies, Gordon H. Skilling's *Czechoslovakia's Interrupted Revolution* (Princeton, NJ: Princeton UP, 1976).

7. For in-depth coverage on Solidarity and martial law in Poland, see Andrzej Paczkowski and Christina Manetti's *Revolution and Counterrevolution in Poland, 1980–1989: Solidarity, Martial Law, and the End of Communism in Eastern Europe* (Rochester, NY: University of Rochester Press, 2015).

8. Philip Pajakowski, "Viewing Poland's Cold War through Literature and Film," in *Understanding and Teaching the Cold War*, ed. Matthew Masur, 205.

9. Elżbieta Ostrowska, "Andrzej Wajda: How to Be Loved and Serve One's Country?" *Studies in Eastern European Cinema* 8, no. 1 (2017): 78–91, https://www.tandfonline.com/doi/abs/10.1080/2040350X.2017.1262122?scroll=top&needAccess=true&journalCode=reec20. Accessed February 20, 2020.

10. Marek Haltof, "The Representation of Stalinism in Polish Cinema," *Canadian Slavonic Papers/Revue canadienne des Slavistes* xlii, nos. 1–2 (March–June 2000): 48–52.

11. Ibid., 49, 53.

12. The other films in Wajda's trilogy are the 1981 *Człowiek z żelaza* [Man of Iron] and the much later 2013 *Lech Wałęsa: Człowiek nadziei* [Lech Wałęsa: Man of Hope].

13. Haltof, 2000, 50–51.

14. Michael Szporer, "Woman of Marble: An Interview with Krystyna Janda," *Cinéaste* xviii, no. 3 (1991), https://krystynajanda.pl/dorobek/an-interview-with-krystyna-janda/. Accessed February 13, 2020.

15. Ibid., 12.

16. Ibid., 14.

17. Marcin Adamczak, "Polish Cinema after 1989: A Quest for Visibility and a Voice in the Market," *Illuminace* 24, no. 4 (88) (2012): 49–55.

18. Thomas Anessi, "Moving Ahead into the Past: Historical Contexts in Recent Polish Cinema," *Images* XI, no. 20 (Poznań, 2012): 10.

19. Ostrowska notes in "Andrzej Wajda: How to be Loved and Serve One's Country?" that "for many Poles, the 'Katyń lie' has been perceived as a kind of 'foundational lie' for postwar Poland and it served as a symbol of Soviet oppression."

In his *Unspeakable Histories: Film and the Experience of Catastrophe* (New York: Columbia University Press, 2016), William Howard Guynn offers a similar observation: "The Soviet murder of the Polish officer corps was the act that dismantled Poland's future; it was an event that eventually culminated in the Soviet domination of Polish society for forty-five years following the end of World War II (66–67).

20. William Howard Guynn, *Unspeakable Histories* . . ., 61–62.

21. Ostrowska, "Andrzej Wajda: How to Be Loved and Serve One's Country?" (op. cit.)

22. Zdzisław Pietrasik, "Zostaną tylko guziki," *Polityka*, September 15, 2007, https://www.polityka.pl/tygodnikpolityka/kultura/228539,1,zostana-tylko-guziki .read. Accessed February 12, 2020.

23. Guynn, *Unspeakable Histories* . . .,58.

24. "*Katyń*," Culture.pl, https://culture.pl/pl/dzielo/katyn. Accessed April 4, 2020.

25. Ostrowska, "Andrzej Wajda: How to Be Loved and Serve One's Country?" The estimated number of viewers is listed by Magdalena Saryusz-Wolska in "The Theory of National Memory in Polish Post-War Cinema," *Studia Universitatis Cibiniensis*, series historic XI, supp. (2014): 210.

26. Ibid.

27. Leonard Quart, "Wajda's *Katyń*," *Slavic and East European Performance* 29, no. 1 (Winter 2009): 79.

28. Michael Brooke, "*Katyń*," *Sight and Sound*, London 19, no. 4 (April 2009): 66.

29. Pietrasik, "Zostaną tylko guziki,". . .

30. See, for example, Marek Bonarski's conflicted review, "Katyń—spóźniona recenzja," *Naszemiasto*, June 15, 2008, https://naszemiasto.pl/katyn-spozniona -recenzja/ar/c13-4425356. Accessed April 3, 2020. Bonarski admits he watched the film twice—first to yield to his emotional response, a second time to analyze it as a work of art. His analysis not only complains of the unengaging characters, but also "its obtrusive symbolism" of primarily Christian elements: a statue of Christ hidden under a soldier's coat, the General's hands bound with barbed wire (a circle of thorns) before he is shot. Leonard Quart observes that "one of the film's flaws is that almost all the Polish characters are given little dimension beyond heroic idealism and forbearance. And Wajda's portrait of Polish daily life during the occupation and right after the war is oddly sanitized—the women are all handsome and well-dressed, as if squalor and hunger were not the lot of Poles during that period" (2009, 80). In his comparative analysis of *Saving Private Ryan* and *Katyń*, Garbowski is uncritically descriptive of the film's blending of national and Catholic symbolisms: "*Katyń* has been aptly called a national mass for the dead. Indeed it demonstrates to what extent transcendent religion compliments [*sic*] civil religion at key junctures, since the religious symbolism, in this case appropriated from Catholicism, is rather close to the surface at times, and plays a prominent role" *Cinematic Echoes of Covenants Past and Present: National Identity in the Historical Films of Steven Spielberg and Andrzej Wajda* (Berlin: Peter Lang, 2018): 194.

31. Garbowski responds to Milija Gluhovic's similar criticism of the erased Jews in this and other scenes of the Polish POWs by characterizing the Jews among them as "highly assimilated, which would make it difficult for Wajda to

convincingly dramatize their Jewish identities," Garbowski's *Cinematic Echoes*
. . .: 185. Gluhovic's comments can be found in *Performing European Memories: Trauma, Ethics, and Politics* (Houndmills, UK: Palgrave, 2013): 154–55.

32. See, for the most vehement articulation of this point of view, Artur Żmijewski, "*Katyń*, Karole, Świadectwo, czyli praca ideologii," in *Kino polskie, 1989–2009. Historia krytyczna*, ed. A. Wiśniewska, P. Marecki (Warsaw: Wydawnictwo Krytyki Politycznej, 2010): 206–210.

33. In "Katyń Andrzeja Wajdy: melodramatyczny afekt i historia," *Pleograf. Kwartalnik Akademii Polskiego Filmu*, nr. 1, 2016, Elżbieta Ostrowska remarks that judgments such as Żmijewski's (see footnote 31) claim that evoking "lower emotions, such as agitation, fear, or empathy" interfere with a film's attempt at serious historical analysis. Located at https://akademiapolskiegofilmu.pl/pl/historia-polskiego-filmu/pleograf/andrzej-wajda/1/katyn-andrzeja-wajdy-melodramatyczny-afekt-i-historia/536. Accessed April 6, 2020.

34. Guynn, *Unspeakable Histories* . . .,89, 91.

35. Konrad J. Zarębski, "Wojciech Smarzowski," October 2009, https://culture.pl/pl/tworca/wojciech-smarzowski. Accessed March 7, 2020.

36. Joanna Raflesz, "Porąbane łóżko. Analiza *Domu złego* Wojciecha Smarzowskiego," *Film.org.pl*, October 4, 2016, https://film.org.pl/a/analiza/pora-bane-lozko-analiza-domu-zlego-wojciecha-smarzowskiego-32762/. Accessed March 13, 2020.

37. Reviewing the film for *Variety*, Alissa Simon is nominally correct in describing *The Dark House* as "a gritty masterpiece of genre cinema that blends period crime with political procedural," but the latter genre has nothing to do with the kind of police work conducted in Poland during martial law. "*The Dark House*," *Variety*, April 5, 2010, https://variety.com/2010/film/reviews/the-dark-house-1117942542/. Accessed March 10, 2020.

38. Joanna Raflesz, "Porąbane łóżko. Analiza *Domu złego* Wojciecha Smarzowskiego."

39. Marcin Adamczak, "Za garść papierosów, kilka paszportów lub mieszkanie," *Odra* 2 (2010): 114, cited in Joanna Raflesz, "Porąbane łóżko. Analiza *Domu złego* Wojciecha Smarzowskiego."

40. Jonathan Murray, "The Music of Freedom: An Interview with Paweł Pawlikowski," *Cinéaste* 44, no. 1 (Winter 2018): 4.

41. For more information on these events, see Andrea Genest, "From Oblivion to Memory. Poland, the Democratic Opposition, and 1968," *Cuadernos de Historia Contemporánea* 31 (2009): 89–106; Dariusz Stola, "Fighting against the Shadows: The *Anti-Zionist* Campaign in 1968," in *Antisemitism and Its Opponents in Modern Poland*, ed. Robert Blobaum (Ithaca, NY: Cornell University Press, 2005): 284–300; and David Engel, "Poland Since 1939," in *YIVO Encyclopedia of Jews in Eastern Europe* (online) https://yivoencyclopedia.org/article.aspx/Poland/Poland_since_1939. Accessed April 18, 2020.

42. On the use of mésalliance plots that undermine the aristocracy in late nineteenth-century and early twentieth-century Polish literature, see Beth Holmgren, *Rewriting Capitalism: Literature and the Market in Late Tsarist Russia and the Kingdom of*

Poland (Pittsburgh: University of Pittsburgh Press, 1998); and Holmgren's essay, "The Importance of Being Unhappy, or Why She Died," in *Imitations of Life: Two Centuries of Melodrama in Russia*, eds. Louise McReynolds and Joan Neuberger (Durham, NC: Duke University Press, 2002), 79–98.

43. For the fascinating story of this odd couple, see Cezary Łazarewicz, "Podwójne życie żony Jasienicy: Nesia wszystko doniesie," (The double life of Jasienica's wife: Nesia will report it all.) *Polityka.pl*, March 12, 2010, https://www.polityka.pl/tygodnikpolityka/kraj/1504026,1,podwojne-zycie-zony-jasienicy.read. Accessed April 18, 2020.

44. Lawrence D. Orton, "Paweł Jasienica—A Rectification and Appreciation," *The Polish Review* 29, no. 1–2 (1984): 15–29.

45. Cezary Łazarewicz, "Podwójne życie żony Jasienicy . . ."

46. Jasienica's daughter, Ewa Beynar Czeczott, has since published her own version of her father's life, *Mój ojciec Paweł Jasienica* (Warsaw: MG, 2018).

47. Łukasz Maciejewski, "'Różyczka': Znakomita, oparta na faktach historia," *Kultura.onet.pl* March 17, 2010, https://kultura.onet.pl/film/recenzje/rozyczka-znakomita-oparta-na-faktach-historia/tmp2bnk. Accessed April 19, 2020.

48. Łukasz Maciejewski, "'Różyczka': Znakomita, oparta na faktach historia,"; Iwona Kurz, "'Różyczka,' reż. Jan Kidawa-Błoński," *dwutygodnik.com*, March 2010, https://www.dwutygodnik.com/artykul/972-rozyczkarez-jan-kidawa-blonski.html. Accessed April 19, 2020.

49. It bears noting here that Seweryn was a coorganizer of the student protests against the banning of *Forefathers' Eve* in 1968. See "Andrzej Seweryn," https://culture.pl/pl/tworca/andrzej-seweryn. Accessed April 15, 2020.

50. Zdzisław Pietrasik, "'Różyczka,' czyli historia pewnego pisarza," *Polityka*, March 12, 2010, https://www.polityka.pl/tygodnikpolityka/kultura/1504012,1,rozyczka-czyli-historia-pewnego-pisarza.read. Accessed April 19, 2020.

51. Dagmara Romańska, " 'Rewers': polskie kino w najlepszym amerykańskim stylu," *Onet.pl*, October 13, 2009, https://kultura.onet.pl/film/recenzje/rewers-polskie-kino-w-najlepszym-amerykanskim-stylu/jj7cgxb. Accessed April 23, 2020.

52. Janusz Wróblewski, " 'Rewers': szydercza gra z narodową pamięcią," *Polityka*, November 14, 2009, https://www.polityka.pl/tygodnikpolityka/kultura/1500603,1,rewers-szydercza-gra-z-narodowa-pamiecia.read. Accessed April 23, 2020; Łukasz Maciejewski, "'Rewers'—największa filmowa niespodzianka roku," *Dziennik.pl*, November 12, 2009, https://film.dziennik.pl/artykuly/101727,rewers-najwieksza-filmowa-niespodzianka-roku.html. Accessed April 24, 2020; and Przemysław Piotr Damski, " 'Rewers'—reż. Borys Lankosz—recenzja i ocena filma," *Histmag.org*, June 14, 2010, https://histmag.org/Rewers-rez.-Borys-Lankosz-recenzja-filmu-4331. Accessed April 24, 2020.

53. Two reviewers link *The Reverse* with Munk's legacy: Wróblewski in *Polityka* and Bożena Janicka, "Rewers," *Kino* 43 (November 2009), 509: 71–72.

54. Damski praises *The Reverse* for its "brave representation of a young woman's sexual awareness." *Histmag.org*, June 14, 2010.

55. Romańska, Maciejewski, and Damski all remark on this *noir* effect, and Damski traces the influence of Raymond Chandler novels.

56. Romańska on *The Reverse* . . .

57. Wróblewski on *The Reverse* . . .

58. Any pun intended here is Andrzej Bart's work.

59. Tim Adams, "Paweł Pawlikowski: 'My Parents' Story Was the Matrix of All My Stories," *The Guardian*, February 8, 2019, https://www.theguardian.com/film /2019/feb/09/pawel-pawlikowski-poland-cold-war-ida. Accessed May 2, 2020.

60. In Pawlikowski's interview with Jonathan Murray, "The Music of Freedom: An Interview with Paweł Pawlikowski" . . ., for example, the director categorizes his parents' story as "a really good one," but maintains that the life-spanning romance depicted in *Cold War* is "not about [my] parents" (4).

61. Elaina Patton, "In *Cold War*, Paweł Pawlikowski Tells His Parents' Love Story," *The New Yorker*, December 22, 2018, https://www.newyorker.com/culture/ culture-desk/in-cold-war-pawel-pawlikowski-tells-his-parents-love-story. Accessed May 2, 2020.

62. Ibid.

63. Tim Adams, "Paweł Pawlikowski: 'My Parents' Story Was the Matrix of All My Stories."

64. Ann Hornaday, " 'Cold War' Is Already Getting Oscar Buzz, Because It's a Near-Perfect Movie," *Washington Post*, January 16, 2019, https://www.washington-post.com/goingoutguide/movies/cold-war-is-already-getting-oscar-buzz-because-its -a-near-perfect-movie/2019/01/16/7b154b94-1454-11e9-803c-4ef28312c8b9_story .html. Accessed May 2, 2020.

65. "The Music of Freedom: An Interview with Paweł Pawlikowski," *Cinéaste* . . ., 4.

66. Marcin Kempista, " 'Zimna wojna'—Recenzja," *Filmawka.pl*, May 25, 2018, https://www.filmawka.pl/zimna-wojna-recenzja/. Accessed May 3, 2020.

67. Grzegorz Brzozowski, "Spustoszona historia. Recenzja fimu 'Zimna wojna' Pawła Pawlikowskiego," *Kultura liberalna*, June 26, 2018, https://kulturaliberalna.pl /2018/06/26/grzegorz-brzozowski-spustoszona-historia-recenzja-zimna-wojna-pawel -pawlikowski/. Accessed May 3, 2020.

68. Jonathan Murray, *"Cold War,"* *Cinéaste* 44, no. 1 (Winter 2018): 44–46.

69. Janusz Wróblewski, " 'Zimna wojna,' reż. Paweł Pawlikowski. Polskość dla każdego," *Polityka*, June 5, 2018, https://www.polityka.pl/tygodnikpolityka/kultura/ film/1750864,1,recenzja-filmu-zimna-wojna-rez-pawel-pawlikowski.read. Accessed May 5, 2020.

70. As Thomas Schatz argues in *Hollywood Genres: Formulas, Filmmaking, and the Studio System* (Philadelphia: Temple University Press, 1981), that "the musical tends to be bound to the star system more closely than any other genre." "The principal reason for the enhanced significance of [the stars'] personalities has to do, of course, with the range of dramatic and performance demands that are placed upon the musical star," p. 191.

71. In the original, "Ona coś kombinuje."

72. Emily Yoshida, *"Cold War* Is a Stunning Love Story," *Vulture*, December 8, 2018, https://www.vulture.com/2018/12/cold-war-review.html. Accessed May 5, 2020; Joanna Szaszewska, " 'Zimna wojna' to film doskonały. Wywołuje

najprawdziwsze ciarki," *gazeta.pl*, June 7, 2018, https://kultura.gazeta.pl/kultura
/7,114628,23473033,zimna-wojna-to-film-doskonaly-wywoluje-najprawdziwsze
-ciarki.html. Accessed May 5, 2020; Anna Tatarska, " 'Zimna wojna' Pawła
Pawlikowskiego. Dramaturgia przez duże D," *wyborcza.pl*, June 4, 2018, https://
wyborcza.pl/7,101707,23491300,zimna-wojna-recenzja.html. Accessed May 5,
2020; Brzozowski on Cold War (op. cit.)

73. In the original, "Palant! No kocham go i już."

Chapter 7

Female Sexuality with and without Apologies

WOMEN'S BODIES UNDER SOCIALISM

In issues of sexuality, citizens of the Polish People's Republic—which lasted from 1947 to 1989—were caught between the prohibitions of the conservative Polish Catholic Church and the state's progressive agenda, spurred by the drive to modernization, which, however, was partly colored by official Soviet puritanism. At the same time, as a number of scholars addressing gender issues in Poland have emphasized, the myth of the Polish Mother (Matka Polka), established by such venerated romantic writers as Adam Mickiewicz (1798–1855), proved remarkably hardy throughout modern Polish history, abetted by the Catholic Church's glorification of the Mater Dolorosa (mourning mother). Marina Warner's excellent study of the European cult of the Virgin Mary traces the evolution, persistence, and ramifications of that cult, to conclude that the value-freighted mythical figure "is the instrument of a dynamic argument from the Catholic Church about the structure of society, presented as a God-given code. The argument changes, according to contingencies."[1] In Poland that situation obtains *a fortiori*.

Adducing copious cultural evidence, Joanna Szwajcowska persuasively contends that for at least two centuries Poland conflated Matka Polka with the Virgin Mary (Matka Boska). Both incarnate martyrdom/suffering, the paradox of virginity yet maternity, self-sacrifice for the sake of the son (in fervently Christological Poland, the Christlike nation), and the role of a mediatrix between conflicting entities that take precedence over a woman's own self.[2] Accordingly, this ideal of sexless yet maternal nurturing and subordination to a "higher cause" traditionally has inf(l)ected social and political dialogues in Poland, with official resolutions dependent on the fluctuating priorities of both church and state. That these two pillars of authority and power insist on controlling women's bodies under the merciless influence of this arbitrary icon may be deduced from the country's dearth of genuine sex education, problematic access to contraception, and inconsistent, often draconian laws regulating abortion.

Throughout much of the twentieth century, the assumption that sexual activity should be confined to married heterosexual couples, whether for the purpose of procreation so as to increase the ranks of God's grateful (church dogma) or to monitor the size of the population (governmental consider-ations), guided laws regulating sexual behavior and the related phenomena of abortion and contraception. The average Pole's ignorance of sexuality in the mid-twentieth century defies credulity. According to Patrycja Pustkowiak, in the 1950s rural males were complaining about their uterus [*sic*], while in the late 1970s most Polish women had no idea what an orgasm entailed.[3] Pleasure in sexual intercourse was a non-topic and non-expectation—especially for women. After all, church doctrine indicted Eve as the Virgin Mary's antipode in inflicting all manner of woes on humankind for the sinful choice of active, disobedient pleasure-seeking. Some Poles, doubtless, equated ignorance with virtue in a country where many misidentified sexual information as pornogra-phy, which was illegal and anathematized by the Catholic Church.

As in the Soviet Union and the rest of the Eastern Bloc, traditional notions of gender laid the responsibility for preventing pregnancies at women's door, and paucity of contraceptives resulted in abortion as the chief means of birth control, though prayers [*sic*], the rhythm method, and *coitus interruptus* also constituted strategies that were common but, unsurprisingly, ineffectual. After the harsh pronatalist policies of the Stalinist era and sustained debates during 1955 and early 1956,[4] the high maternal mortality rates caused by unsafe terminations led Poland in 1956 to legalize abortion.[5] While the church and the party were at ideological loggerheads, several talented, stub-born sexologists strove to enlighten the remarkably nescient public, listen-ing to it attentively so as to improve the sexual relations and the emotional/psychological circumstances of a populace at the mercy of two conflicting and unappealable authorities intent on legislating the nation's sexual praxis.

POLISH SEXOLOGY

As noted by Agnieszka Kościańska, one of the most informed Polish eth-nologists/cultural anthropologists writing today on matters of sex, Polish sexology peaked during the 1970s and 1980s, owing to the pioneering work of Kazimierz Imieliński (1929–2010), Michalina Wisłocka (1921–2005), and Zbigniew Lew-Starowicz (b. 1943).[6] All three operated differently from their Western counterparts' "highly medicalized and market-bound" mode by soliciting lively dialogues with their patients and correspondents, whose perspectives and narratives informed the sexologists' interdisciplinary publications: Imieliński's *Zarys seksualogii i seksiatrii* (An Outline of Sexology and Sexiatry 1982); Wisłocka's famous bestseller, *Sztuka kochania* (The Art of Loving, 1978),[7] and its follow-up in 1988, *Sztuka kochania dwadzieścia lat później* (The Art of Loving Twenty Years Later);[8] Lew-Starowicz's *Seks partnerski* (Sex on Equal Terms 1983) and many others.[9] These sexologists developed their theories on the basis of their practice as therapists, and their holistic approach, forcefully advocated by Imieliński, left the door open to "the development of feminist and queer sexology" today.[10] Focused on "the sexual relationships between heterosexual married couples" and elaborating a "culture of sexuality," combined with a commitment to "conscious motherhood" grounded in social and economic factors,[11] these sexologists furnished information about the human body, sexuality, contraception, and abortion while counseling patients and readers about the (largely unheard-of) pleasures of sexual activity—a revolutionary concept for the majority of the female population. By contrast, the state showed indifference to the availability of contraceptives, while the church vehemently opposed their usage; neither institution was invested in educating the populace in matters of sex, being concerned primarily with the issue of abortion, which in Poland and throughout the Eastern Bloc and the USSR was considered a mode of "contraception."

POST-SOCIALIST IGNOMINIES: LIBERTY TO REGRESS

As two American male academics have noted, "The issue of legal abortion, because it involves the core values of religion, sexuality, gender roles, and the value of life itself, has been a vexing one in both Europe and North America."[12] Yet, perhaps unexpectedly, they discovered that in the 1990s "Polish Catholics [. . . were] considerably less opposed to abortion than their American counterparts," despite "elaborate multivariate controls."[13] Easily accessible abortion during the country's socialist period doubtless played a role in Poles' attitudes. Events following Poland's liberation from the USSR's repressive "supervision" support the academics' conclusion, while simultaneously indicating post-socialist problems within the sovereign institutions of church and government as regards the politics of gender.[14] In other words, the population and the nation's institutionalized centers of power were and continue to be at odds.

Retrograde as the socialist experience may have seemed to most Poles, ironically, in 1989, soon after shedding the Soviet yoke, the new "democratic" Polish government sought a comprehensive ban on abortion. During the early 1990s a new, politically charged discourse on abortion started to dominate discussions: "mother" replaced the term "pregnant woman," "unborn baby" or "life" replaced "fetus."[15] This freighted terminology invaded official documents and law, with predictable consequences. Widely viewed as a reward to the Catholic Church for its strong role in opposing the Soviet regime, the government's harsh proposal, which became law in 1993, equated the moment of conception with life and decreed that abortion be permissible only if the mother's life is threatened, the fetus shows abnormality, or the pregnancy results from rape or incest.[16] Efforts to liberalize the law succeeded in the passage of an amendment in 1996 that, however, was overturned the following year.

With its victory in the 2015 elections, the Law and Justice Party (PiS) subsequently attempted to institute an even more stringent law that would sweepingly ban all abortions. Grateful for the church's support of his candidacy, its head, Jarosław Kaczyński, approved the campaign, which culminated in a draft bill submitted to the Polish parliament (Sejm) and endorsed by the episcopate.[17] The Polish population's reaction, reported throughout the world, demonstrated the effectiveness of public activism. Though feminism, as Jill Bystydzienski observed, has been slow to develop in Poland and has a weak presence,[18] thousands of feminists, women, and men across the country mobilized in massive protests in 2016 that came to be known as Black Protests, culminating on October 3 in Black Monday.[19] Inspired by the female protesters, who wore black clothes, the label evoked the traditionally feminized role and robe of mourners in imitation of the Marian cult (Mater Dolorosa).[20] A symbol of loss and suffering, mourning attire was "a stable attribute of the Polish Mothers in nineteenth-century representations," appearing in numerous poems, novels, and paintings.[21] And two centuries later, this concerted upsurge of historically evocative civic demonstrations quashed the bill.

This success notwithstanding, circumstances for Polish women intent on avoiding pregnancy yet not committed to a life without sexual intercourse remain dire,[22] largely because of two extraordinarily restrictive legal clauses involving the medical profession. While contraceptives are available, they not only are expensive—prohibitively so for some Poles—but also require doctors' prescriptions. Furthermore, the abortion law's "conscience clause" sanctions doctors' refusal to perform abortions on the grounds of religious faith, even if bringing the pregnancy to term endangers a woman's life or results in a severely handicapped child.[23] Given their dearth of options, women seeking abortions frequently travel abroad, especially to the United Kingdom, Germany, and Slovakia, where the laws are more enlightened. That costly solution, however, is possible only for those able to afford it. As one commentator phrased it, "the combined forces of right-wing Catholic ideology and neoliberal economic reforms have resulted in reproductive and social injustice,"[24] codified by an ultra-conservative government. Psychological and financial assistance is available not from Poland but from the Berlin-based activist group Ciocia Basia (Aunt Barbara). Founded in 2014 by the German filmmaker Sarah Diehl, director of a 2008 documentary about abortion rights, it consists of approximately twenty regular volunteers who facilitate Polish women's safe abortions in the city.[25] Though today abortion may well qualify as women's single most troubling concern in Poland (where classes on "Preparation for Family Life," taught by schools' religious instructors, substitute for sex education[26]), as a topic it is stigmatized and tabooed.[27] With PiS still in power after the 2019 elections, options for women remain lamentably scant. And in 2020 Polish women, supported by many men, took to the streets again to demonstrate against a new law that in principle would virtually eliminate abortion altogether.[28]

Perhaps the official insistence on erasing thorny issues related to sexuality from public discourse partially explains why Polish films avoid dissecting abortion as a personal, social, or political dilemma, yet focus on sex both within and outside of marriage in their portrayal of women who pursue a variety of goals, relying on the appeal of their bodies and men's seemingly infinite susceptibility to them. The images of womanhood in the films analyzed below starkly counter traditional gender stereotypes of sexuality and could not be more remote from Matka Polka. They advocate agency, subversion, and the power of "sisterhood"—the call of early American feminism that failed to take deep root but that today seems to be emerging, if intermittently and only in limited spheres.[29]

SEX AS POLITICAL STRATEGY/ ENTRAPMENT: *RÓŻYCZKA* (LITTLE ROSE 2010), JAN KIDAWA-BŁOŃSKI

Sexual espionage has a long and cinematically rich history, as illustrated perhaps above all by one of the world's most famous spies, Mata Hari. A Dutch exotic dancer who collaborated with the Germans during World War I as an ideological weapon against the French and Russians, she inevitably became incarnated on screen in an improbable Greta Garbo vehicle (1931) directed by George Fitzmaurice, more memorable for extravagant costumes than for international political intrigue. Even one of the most famous Cold War James Bond films, *From Russia with Love* (1963), contained a higher dose of realism, with both Bond (Sean Connery) and his Soviet counterpart, Tania Romanova (Daniela Bianchi), deploying sex on behalf of their respective countries. Other, lesser Bond spy films followed, such as *The Spy Who Loved Me* (1977), with Roger Moore as Bond, and the franchise and its fantasies seem deathless, especially given the popularity of Daniel Craig in the key role of the British sophisticate who beds beauties for Britain. Yet, in some ways, the Polish *Little Rose* presents the most implausible example of all sexually fueled espionage stories, though it draws on real-life events transpiring in Poland under socialism (for a view of the film as a depiction of Cold War activities, see chapter 6).

Winner of multiple awards at home and abroad,[30] Kiwada-Błoński's (b. 1953) *Little Rose* forthrightly dramatizes the state's co-optation of women's bodies in the case of Kamila Sakowicz (Magdalena Boczarska), a naïve young typist at the University of Warsaw endowed with boundless, unapologetic sexual energy and enthusiasm. During 1967–1968, under pressure from her boozy SB (Służba Bezpieczeństwa/Security Service) lover, Colonel Roman Rożek (Robert Więckiewicz), she reluctantly consents to seduce a considerably older distinguished academic clandestinely writing inflammatory anti-Soviet articles for Radio Free Europe under the name of Adam Warczewski (Andrzej Seweryn). Her mission entails trapping him in the state's paranoid nets by reporting on his activities so as to discredit him on the groundless accusation that he is a Zionist agent (his real surname is Weiner). Unexpectedly, she comes to care for him and accepts his offer of marriage, but continues her espionage activity, while her former lover succumbs to alcohol-fueled spasms of furious jealousy. All members of the fraught triangle end up suffering incalculable losses.

Even if Kidawa-Błoński had not acknowledged his debt to *The Lives of Others* (2005)—Florian Henckel von Donnersmarck's Oscar-winning drama about the Nazis' comprehensive surveillance—attentive viewers instantly would recognize parallels between the two films on the level of plot. Polish history additionally inspired the director, such as the biography of Paweł Jasienica (real name Leon Beynar, 1909–1970), a respected historian cum journalist persecuted by the Communist Party as a dissident owing to his outspoken criticism of the state's censorship. The persona of Kamila evokes Zofia Darowska O'Bretenny, who in 1969 became Jasienica's second wife, subsequently widowed. Reputed to be a man of impeccable integrity, Jasienica never suspected that she was an informant planted by the Secret Service, to whom, astonishingly, she reported about her husband's daily life throughout their relationship, until his death.[31] According to at least one Polish reviewer, Jasienica's case was not unique and other, kindred cases may have influenced the film's trajectory.[32]

Like most biopics, *Little Rose* departs from history, primarily in the interests of intensifying the dramatic impact of events that were already extraordinary. For instance, though Jasienica died from cancer, the film has Rożek kill Warczewski (offscreen) out of jealous rage. Similarly, the interaction between Rożek and Kamila is often violent and full of obscenities on his part, though there is no verifiable evidence that such a relationship even existed. These and kindred aspects, however, do not compromise the film, which benefits from the excellent evocation of the period, convincing dialogue, a solid structure, eloquent mise-en-scènes, and fine performances. As one Anglophone reviewer wrote, "This is a vivid, sharp and compelling film that is well-structured and rooted in a sincere bid to wrestle with uncomfortable truths. [. . . The director] deserves applause for handling these thorny subjects in a lucid, measured yet engrossing fashion."[33] Various reviews commended the film as "gripping," "a fascinating intimate drama,"[34] "with a strong sense of time and place,"[35] "moving" (poruszający).[36] One can only wonder at a couple of Polish reviews that faulted the film precisely where its strengths lie. For instance, Łukasz Maciejewski, while lauding the film, unaccountably considers the first half of the film personal and intimate, at odds with the second half, which showcases history and is allegedly tacked on.[37]

Yet the very theme of surveillance as the explicit goal of the Security Service' anti-Semitic campaign is introduced early in the film through Rożek and his superior, Colonel Wasiak (Jan Frycz), not to mention the nameless SB agent (Jacek Braciak) photographing a funeral at a cemetery as the credits roll. Indeed, the film deftly weds its historical drama and individual fates from the start, with the epigraph from Mickiewicz's play *Dziady* (Forefathers' Eve 1822) that introduces the film: "Gentlemen, why don't you wish to write about this?" (Czemu to o tym pisać nie chcecie Panowie?),[38] which points to the film's readiness to address a national phenomenon that others eschew (on the issue of the play and its role during the Cold War, see chapter 6). Ever since its appearance, *Forefathers' Eve* has functioned as the first and ultimate declaration of Polish resistance to oppression, specifically by Russia. Accordingly, the introductory citation proleptically embeds the significance of boldly speaking out against tyranny and injustice that the subsequently shown historic 1968 performance of *Forefathers' Eve*—traditionally equated with a call to freedom at all costs—will emphasize as a summons to the student protests that the film documents, with the help of archival documentary. Historical and personal are inseparable in the film, inasmuch as Weiner invites Kamila to Kazimierz Dejmek's consequence-loaded staging of *Forefathers' Eve* at the National Theater in Warsaw, defends the performance at the subsequent literary meeting, and as a result becomes *persona non grata*,[39] along with the thousands of Jews who identified as Poles but were forced out of the country with no option to return—the devastating expulsion with which the film ends.

The specific occasion that accelerates Warczewski's persecution is the June 1967 Six-Day War, in which Israel defeated the combined Arab forces of Egypt, Jordan, and Syria. As the Arabs' ally, the Soviet Union launched an anti-Semitic campaign that fabricated a Zionist plot on the part of Jews in Poland and elsewhere in the Eastern Bloc. In other words, the film's plot on the level of personal tragedy is driven by historical forces. And in a final irony, personal and historical merge when the Secret Service, along with the audience, learns that Rożek, not Warczewski, is Jewish and therefore, under Gomulka's programmatic anti-Semitic initiative, is forced to leave along with the approximately 15,000 Polish Jews who board the train at film's end. Not Warczewski, whose Austrian forebears explain his original surname of Weiner, but Rożek has hidden his Jewish roots, exposed in his real name of Rosen—ironically, the German for roses.[40]

From the film's establishing shot, offering a high-angle view of Warsaw followed by a seemingly neutral sequence of unidentified people gathered at a funeral, we deduce that the person being interred worked in some capacity at the city's famous university, since both Warczewski and Kamila attend the event. And only in retrospect do we realize that the man photographing those present during the opening sequence at the cemetery is not a fellow mourner intent on preserving the occasion for sentimental reasons, but a Secret Service agent tasked with identifying those suspected of Zionism or other political wrongdoing. It is he who witnesses and records Rożek's vengeful revelation of Kamila's dishonesty to Warczewski and exposes Rożek's long-concealed Jewishness. As the humiliated Rożek leaves Poland forever at the Gdańsk train station in Warsaw, the information in the concluding sequence brings us to the beginning: the writing superimposed on the screen notes that the departing thousands comprise members of the intelligentsia, literati, artists, students, and politicians. Rożek is but one among thousands, and were Warczewski still alive, he likely would have been another.

While the historical and the individual remain indivisible throughout, as the film's title makes explicit, the plot turns on Kamila and her role of sexualized informant—a role insisted upon by her politically compromised lover, who has no doubts that her physical endowments and prowess in bed will entice Warczewski to reveal incriminatory secrets. Her lack of intelligence and integrity leads her to comply, and, commendably, the film refuses to white-wash her limitations and dishonesty. Yet, she gradually learns to appreciate the older man to the detriment of his rival: Warczewski's tender lovemaking, so unlike Rożek's violent bouts of sexual desire; his extensive knowledge and liberal outlook; his polite, cultured interaction with everyone; and his affectionate relations with his mother (Izabella Olszewska) and daughter, Dorotka (Julia Kornacka), all introduce the parochial Kamila to a new world of human decency that the film unambiguously upholds.[41] While retaining her vigorous enjoyment of sexual intercourse, Kamila abandons her cheap, suggestive outfits for more discreet, stylish clothing, bonds with Dorotka, reads the émigré Polish literature with which Warczewski acquaints her, and starts to fit into his educated, civilized world—the intelligentsia opposing precisely the regime that employs her. Quite simply, she is neither overly bright nor honorable, but sufficiently attractive and receptive to accomplish her task of sexual seduction. If she is a "slut" (*kurwa*)—a public slur by a man attempting to pick her up (unsuccessfully) at a bar-restaurant when Rożek briefly leaves her alone at the table—then to a large extent under Warczewski's influence she manages to overcome her sluttishness and assume the genuine role of a loving partner and stepmother to Dorotka, of whom she takes care after Warczewski's death (for a contrasting view of Kamila, see chapter 6).

It speaks eloquently of Kamila's womanly appeal that she can be genuinely loved by two such dissimilar men as Rożek and Warczewski. And the film refuses to simplify here also: his boorishness notwithstanding, Rożek loves her in his own, brutal way (he actually sheds tears upon witnessing her wedding), and the code name of Różyczka that she chooses stems from his affectionate name for her and the red roses he brings her the first time we see them together at a rendezvous. That flower changes valency, becoming an ominous calling card when she finds it on the stairs leading to Warczewski's apartment after Rożek has murdered the academic. Paradoxically, whereas the coarse Rożek brings her romantic roses, the refined Warczewski offers her an expensive engagement ring, and Kamila's distress at receiving it at the otherwise festive familial Christmas Eve at Warczewski's apartment nicely points to her pangs of conscience. And, despite Kamila's systematic deceit, once Warczewski overcomes his shock at her duplicity, he does wed her. Whatever her betrayals, both men continue to love and desire her.

Though the film advantageously embraces complexity and paradox in its representation of the three major personae, it does contain a startling and inexplicable sequence that seems ill-judged. After learning that Warczewski knows of her betrayal, Kamila returns the engagement ring and miserably retreats to her modest apartment. When Rożek, with whom she has broken off relations, visits, however, she removes her clothes and backs invitingly toward the bed in a clear invitation to sexual intercourse. That unexpected twist is unconvincing, contrary to the change in Kamila that the director has been at pains to underscore, and suffers from the overly accelerated pace of the film's last twenty minutes. It remains inexplicable in the film's rush to a conclusion. Purposely or unwittingly, it also leaves open a question posed by the film's ending. About to leave Poland forever, at the train station Rożek looks up and notices Kamila at an elevated walkway, standing still as she observes the teeming deportees. What he cannot see before and after boarding the train is that she is heavily pregnant, and the identity of her unborn child's father remains unknown to the viewer and possibly Kamila herself (as Freud memorably phrased it, "pater incertus est"). Is the child Warczewski's or Rożek's? While the rich implications of the uncertainty could hardly be more welcome for the viewer (will Kamila's child be the issue of a disgraced Polish

Jewish secret police agent or of the intellectual Pole inaccurately accused
of such an identity? Will the unknowability of the child's ethnic/religious
origins become a key factor if the events of 1967–1968 are replayed?), the
sexual episode in her apartment shows poor judgment on the director's part.

Yet, apart from its many other assets, the film is memorable for portraying a highly sexed woman[42] in largely positive, often beguiling terms—not
a common aspect of cinema in either PRL or post-socialist Poland. That
portrayal seems to have been a key factor in the largely negative review of
the film by Iwona Kurz, director of the Institute for Polish Culture at the
University of Warsaw. Fulminating against the absence of motivation on
Kamila's part (sex and love, apparently, cannot qualify as motivations), Kurz
views the film and its posters as exploiting women's bodies. Her myopia, in
tandem with startling inaccuracies (identifying Warczewski as Jewish[43] and
confusing chronology), betrays discomfort with the notion of a woman's
body as not only a political weapon but also a source of personal pleasure.
She apparently believes that a film should presuppose an audience that needs
everything spelled out. In any event, hers is one of the few dissenting reviews
puzzlingly troubled by the film.

One could argue that the maternal aspect of Kamila's transformation—her
commitment to Dorotka and her pregnancy—colludes with the Matka Polka
imperative that exercises such a stranglehold on Poland's notions of gender.
Both developments, however, are an unforeseen consequence of her genuine
and uninhibitedly sexualized love for Warczewski, as well as Rożek, and
she not only bonds with Dorotka early on but also becomes her official stepmother upon marrying Warczewski. Ultimately, the mere fact that she can so
wholeheartedly and generously enjoy carnal relations with both men renders
her a rare instance of the Polish woman as an unabashedly, exuberantly
sexual being candidly pursuing her own pleasure with men she loves, even
while simultaneously "serving the state."

THE TRIALS OF SEXOLOGY: *SZTUKA KOCHANIA* (THE ART OF LOVING 2016/2017), MARIA SADOWSKA[44]

Boczarska's univocally lauded acting as the "sexy" political informant in
Różyczka doubtless prompted Sadowska (b. 1976) to cast her as Wisłocka
(1921–2005) in the colorful, well-received biopic of the sexologist, for which
Boczarska energetically agitated. The film, which proved the most popular
box office hit of 2017 in Poland,[45] appropriated the title of the sexologist-
gynecologist's milestone study (*The Art of Loving*), adding the subtitle *The
History of Michalina Wisłocka* (Historia Michaliny Wisłockiej) and constructed the screen narrative primarily around her repeatedly thwarted efforts

to publish her book. Yet, Sadowska casts a broader temporal net—from the 1940s through the 1970s—showing how Wisłocka's personal life prior to and apart from *The Art of Loving* (1976) is not without interest, indeed, is inextricable from her determination to bring "sexual enlightenment" to her fellow country(wo)men.

By any standards Wisłocka was an idiosyncratic personality. The only notable female sexologist during PRL, she dressed tackily; adopted as her life's goal the initiation of Poles, and especially women, into the pleasures of sex; favored a combatively and tactlessly forthright manner that ignored social etiquette; and led a personal life that violated all established conventions. Somewhat indiscriminately, she tended to call women "skarbie" and "kochanie" (honey, sweetheart). Née Michalina Braun, she married the biologist Stanisław/Stach Wisłocki (Piotr Adamczyk), with whom she proved sexually incompatible, and arranged a ménage à trois[46] with her closest school friend, Wanda (Justyna Wasilewska), who bore Wisłocki a son, while Wisłocka had his daughter. The "love of her life," with whom she conducted a passionate affair over several years, was Jurek (Eryk Lubos)—a married sailor intent on freeing her from all inhibitions who persuaded her to write *The Art of Loving*. Long delayed, the pioneering guidebook finally came out in 1978, preceded by numerous pirated versions hawked at markets, and became a sensational bestseller, eventually selling seven million copies. Just how dramatically independence from the Soviet Union altered Polish officialdom may be inferred from the fact that for services rendered to the country, in 1997 Aleksander Kwaśniewski, then Poland's president, awarded her the Knight's Cross of the Order of Polonia Restituta.

The key facts of Wisłocka's life were conveyed in a condensed 21-minute documentary of 2001 by Konrad Szołajski, *Sztuka kochania według Wisłockiej* (The Art of Loving according to Wisłocka), with which Sadowska's film converges.[47] Like the male sexologists who were her contemporaries, Wisłocka was liberal in matters of sex but conservative as regards gender, which is why some might demur as regards her pronouncement that she "is the revolution" in the sphere of sex. While writing uninhibitedly about the body and its normally euphemized parts, she assumes conjugal heteronormativity and essentially adheres to traditional gender roles. Adamant about the profound difference between men and women, she cautions the latter to forget emancipation when at home and never to initiate sex, for such "aggression" by women, who are passive by nature, could trigger various complexes and ruin marital relations.[48] In her view, as in Lew-Starowicz's, sexual fulfillment relies on women's maintenance of their femininity; men, whose "natural" domain constitutes activity and public life, complement and respond to the passive-domestic in women.[49] Tellingly, one of the many sources she cites in her volume is the British Victorian poet Coventry Patmore, remembered best for his concept of woman as "The Angel in the House" (1854), which limns a saccharine, highly influential icon of the ideal woman as men's servile appendage ("Man must be pleased; but him to please/Is woman's pleasure . . .").[50]

At the same time, she informs her readers about "petting" and "necking," advises teens on contraceptive methods, has no qualms about discussing various positions to maximize pleasure during intercourse, and provides detailed drawings of the penis and "head on" illustrations of the vagina that recall Gustave Courbet's *L'origine du monde* (1866) but in greater close-up.[51] Additionally, she quotes from the *Kamasutra*, Laclos's *Les liaisons dangereuses* (1782), and the poetry of the "scandalous" Polish writer-translator Tadeusz Boy Żeleński (1874–1941), a fellow gynecologist cum pediatrician renowned for his anti-clerical, pro-abortion feminism and overall progressive views.[52] Little wonder that the Catholic Church and Communist Party bureaucrats determinedly blocked the book's publication for so long.

Relying on her subject's works,[53] Sadowska and her screenwriter, Krzysztof Rak, capture these contradictions and convey a vivid sense of the singular personality behind Poland's first *vade mecum* on sex as an activity to be enjoyed. Sexuality, in fact, tethers the various eras portrayed in the film to Wisłocka's lifelong preoccupation with sexual issues, starting with the incident that leads to her marriage: in 1939, she and her closest friend, Wanda, observe Wisłocki, a biology professor reputedly attractive to female students, bathing naked in a river. When he discovers his duo of voyeurs, he laughingly rebukes Michalina for staring at his physical endowments instead of his face. A rapid cut transfers us to 1941, when the imprisoned married couple is saved by Wanda, who simulates noisy intercourse with a homosexual Nazi to save his reputation with his fellow officers, thereby winning her friends' freedom. Soon afterward, finding Wisłocki's athletic, insatiable sexual demands painful and unwanted, Michalina arranges for Wanda to join them as the third in the apartment for the purposes of sex, convinced, however, that she alone is the one whom Jurek loves. Both women become pregnant, and Wanda's son (Krzyś) and Michalina's daughter (Krysia) are passed off as the married couple's offspring.

While Wanda incarnates sexuality, Michalina observes and records its manifestations. Unsurprisingly, Wanda eventually tires of her role. Soon after she leaves with her son, Michalina and Stach also part ways, with recriminations on both sides. In 1958, Michalina travels to a spa in the provinces (Lubniewice), where she meets the gynophilic Jurek and falls in sexual love with him.[54] A man who actually sews a skirt for her and affirms her womanly beauty as well as her brain, he provides her first orgasm and persuades her to write the book that eventually will make her famous. Sexuality becomes personally experienced delight instead of a phenomenon to be witnessed and documented. On one of her subsequent trips to Lubniewice, however, her meeting with his friendly, unsuspecting wife, Ela, and his baby daughter prompts her to leave, never to return. When in 1970 she accidently runs into Ela in Warsaw; upon learning that Jurek has died of a heart attack, she faints in the street, then proceeds to go home as if in a daze and starts writing her guidebook. The film closes with her sitting at her typewriter, smiling as she types in the title of the work.

Flashbacks to decisive moments in her life, as well as those showing her efforts to further women's cause through medical research in an inflexibly patriarchal system, alternate with the "now" of the 1970s, focused on revealing aspects of her gynecological practice and her struggles to see her *Art of Loving* into print. Humor and zestful earthiness infuse some of these scenes in equal measure, as, for example, when she illustrates to a colleague how to examine women's "private parts" or tells a male functionary that he came "from the vagina." Women visit her in droves, seeking advice and solutions to sundry problems. And some of her recommendations are, to say the least, unorthodox: for instance, when Karolina Siwicka (Karolina Gruszka), the attractive wife of a high-placed functionary, confides that her husband is physically incapable of fathering a child yet yearns for a son, Wisłocka advises her to sign into a spa where she can enjoy a romance with a fellow visitor there who will impregnate her. Karolina follows this bold advice, becomes pregnant with a son, and as her unsuspecting spouse expresses delight at this happy development, she seizes the moment to urge him to facilitate the publication of Wisłocka's guide. Similarly, when a general's wife (Danuta Stenka) complains that her husband is a sadist, Wisłocka points out that, as the victim, she is the more powerful one and should take control of the situation.

It is not difficult to imagine how the Catholic Church would respond to such counsel,[55] and the Central Committee official Eugeniusz (Arkadiusz Jakubik), who speaks of her in demeaning terms, is no better, dismissing her book as cheap pornography. Prudery and hypocrisy prompt both church and party, respectively, to accuse the other of being the insuperable obstacles to her endeavors. Fired by the conviction that her work will ease women's lot, however, she tirelessly pursues her pedagogical plans: as one laudatory critic put it, "[ona] uczy pacientki masturbacij, rozdaje preserwatywy i radzi, jak urozmaicić życie łóżkowe"/she teaches a patient masturbation, distributes condoms, and advises how to vary activities in bed.[56] Unquestionably, her daily consultations and her research are gynocentric, and only women come to her aid when she combats men "in high places" to get her handbook into print.

Although *The Art of Loving* is only Sadowska's second film, it reveals a strong talent for narrative and control of atmosphere, as well as some subtle touches.[57] A sterling instance of the last is both evocative and insightful. During the argument among Michalina, Stach, and Wanda directly preceding their breakup, Michalina voices her earlier deluded conviction that she was the only one whom Stach loved, though he bedded at least a score of women apart from Wanda. In an eloquent echo, at a dinner with Jurek and Ela during Michalina's later visit to Lubniewice, Ela self-assuredly confides to Michalina that her husband loves only her. Boczarska's face marvelously reflects her awareness of how the words repeat her own misguided conviction. That awakening inspires the conclusion that lies at the core of her book: namely, that genuine or meaningful love, which she calls "terribly difficult work" (miłość jest okropnie ciężka praca), depends on the union of body and emotions or sex and affection—an insight provided by the sexual awakening that comes relatively late to her in life.

Unusually in the Polish context, the film illustrates the rewards of female solidarity, for ultimately, it is the women whom Wisłocka has helped (married to influential party officials) who gratefully reciprocate by ensuring the publication of her handbook.[58] Moreover, Tereska (Jaśmina Polak), the young editor at Iskra, unlike her wavering male boss, Krystian (Boris Szyc), remains committed to Wisłocka's volume from start to finish. Women indisputably are at the center not only of Wisłocka's concerns but also of director Sadowska, an avowed feminist who finds the problems confronted by the sexologist just as relevant in today's Poland.[59] Inasmuch as under PiS, Poland seems to have regressed to the 1970s in its refusal to ensure women's sexual freedom and health, availability of contraception, and guarantee of safe abortion, despite what one critic called Wisłocka's "old fashioned" views, the film evidently struck Polish audiences as most timely, for they flocked to the biopic.[60]

SEX AS THE OLDEST AND ODDEST PROFESSION: *SPONSORING (ELLES* 2011), MAŁGORZATA SZUMOWSKA

Young women directors' unprecedented focus on the female body accounts for Szumowska's (b. 1973) examination of prostitution or "sex work," according to the preferred linguistic usage of many prostitutes and the sociologists recently writing about them in the West.[61] One of Szumowska's least successful films,[62] *Elles* tackles what formerly was a largely gendered profession spoken of in hushed tones but today is far from startling, often adopted by males, and increasingly exploits children. Attitudes toward the phenomenon span a broad spectrum, from those condemning prostitution as a crime against women to those who wish to legalize and oversee it as just another form of labor.[63] With an estimated 40–42 million prostitutes in the world accounting for the approximately $180 billion sex trade, Poland figures marginally in the statistics, with 19,000 prostitutes by comparison with one million in America and 400,000 in Germany and 58,000 in the United Kingdom.[64]

To a large extent those statistics account for the discrepancy in the number of Polish and American films that address the topic. More than a hundred films about prostitution have appeared in the United States, from grim documentaries to the "comic" Xaviera Hollander biopic (1975), based on her bestselling memoir, *The Happy Hooker* (1971), followed by two sequels. At the ludicrous end of the spectrum, one finds such risibly candied fare as *Pretty Woman* (1990), labeled a "romantic comedy." Billy Wilder's smart, bitter-sweet comedy *Irma La Douce* (1963) set the pattern for a humorous view of prostitution, with less talented directors imitating his typically ironic perspective on a socio-sexual issue, as was the case with his earlier classic, *Some Like It Hot* (1959). A rare exception to this dominant trend was Louis Malle's *Pretty Baby* (1978), which managed to treat women's brothels and child prostitution without being tawdry and lachrymose or taking refuge in comedy.[65] A mere glance at the Wikipedia inventory of American movies about prostitutes suffices to convince even the most skeptical observer that cinema in the United States has not flinched from visualizing the lives of women employed in "the oldest profession," though the preference for a comic treatment indicates an avoidance of profound social problems for the sake of greater box office receipts.[66]

Poland, however, has no such repository of titles, and in the national context *Elles*—a Polish/French/German production—might appear revolutionary.[67] Tellingly, to cast the protagonist of her film Szumowska turned to France (in the popular imagination, the stronghold of sex and romance[68]) and one of its best-known actresses, Juliette Binoche, who to considerable acclaim earlier had starred as a devastated widow in Krzysztof Kieślowski's *Blue* (1993).[69] Her name certainly helped to sell Szumowska's film, which garnered considerable critical attention, though it failed to recoup its costs.[70] Paradoxically, perhaps the most fascinating aspect of *Elles* is neither its topic nor its treatment, but the gender divide in responses to the film abroad: Anglophone male reviewers virtually dismissed it in reviews riddled with factual errors (Holden,[71] Honeycutt,[72] Pulver[73]) that suggest either inattentive viewing or a viscerally negative, subjective reaction disguised as professional critique. After all, males could hardly come off worse in the film, shown as terminally self-involved, violent, or pathetic, given to instrumentalizing women. Anglophone female critics, by contrast, either praised *Elles* or opted to interview its director, seeking clarification instead of parading condemnation (Barlow,[74] De Castro,[75] Johnson). And only a Frenchman attuned to Szumowka's intentions authored an insightful, unqualifiedly positive assessment of the film (Lemercier). Polish critics similarly proved attuned to the film's reliance on prostitution as a means of commenting on society at large (Tambor).

Though the plot is uncommonly simple, chronology and the status of certain sequences are difficult to pinpoint and also complicate the film. As its Polish title, *Sponsoring*, indicates, Binoche's character, Anne, an upper-middle-class journalist writing a piece for the magazine *Elle*, interviews not street prostitutes but Parisian female students who ply their trade indoors.[76] Their affluent clients "sponsor" them. The largesse of that sponsorship enables the French Charlotte (Anaïs Demoustier) to live fairly comfortably and the Polish Alicja (Joanna Kulig) to rent a chic apartment where she clearly lacks for nothing. Both young women readily answer most of Anne's questions and volunteer information that demolishes all her preconceptions about paid sex. To her incredulity, the two sooner consider their "clients" as companions and themselves, not as victims, but as independent and powerful, choosing whom to "service," and when and where to do so. That service covers a wide range of activities: conventional intercourse, fellatio, "golden showers" (Alicja), anal penetration (Charlotte in her professional role as Lola), mutual onanism, but also singing together (Alicja) and genuinely enjoying each other's company. At one meeting with an older man who ejaculates just by caressing her, then weeps, Charlotte/Lola kindly reassures him in a maternal manner. Matter-of-factness characterizes the women's approach to their "work," which they deem normal: "I'd do the same thing with my boyfriend," "the only difference is that they're all old enough to be my father," "I thought I would get screwed for hours, but they tell me about their lives" (Charlotte); "my clients are bored husbands," "they could never do this with their wives" (Alicja).[77] Charlotte dislikes the smell of cleaners in the grocery store where she works part time, not the smell of sex, which she also enjoys with her boyfriend and a young client approximately her own age. Intimacy is a part of her job, inasmuch as many of the men like to talk a great deal, telling her about themselves. As she learns, they also revel in "dirty talk."

The openness of the two women gradually creates a closeness between them and Anne—a bonding of sorts that she lacks with members of her family and that manifests itself in farewell hugs with Charlotte and a drunken session over pasta with Alicja as the two of them dance, culminating in Anne's kiss on Alicja's mouth. Just as importantly, the two students may be said to effect a "consciousness raising," for in listening to their stories, Anne gains increasing awareness of how barren her domestic life is, with the antiseptic white-and-grey tones of her richly appointed apartment suggesting the lack of communication, let alone warmth, among those living in it.[78] Her younger son, Stéphane (Pablo Beugnet), is obliviously indentured to computer games, the older, Florent (François Civil), cuts school, smokes pot, watches porn on his computer, and ridicules his parents. Above all, her successful husband,

Patrick (Louis-Do de Lencquesaing), likewise consumes porn, criticizes her, and shows no interest in her or their boys.

In a country where Simone de Beauvoir's milestone feminist text (*The Second Sex/La deuxième sexe* 1949) appeared seventy years ago, the chic, employed Anne still labors under what scholars in Soviet culture have called a double burden: though a professional, she assumes responsibility for all household tasks and the children's well-being, which renders Patrick's warning that she should desist from voicing her feminist views during that evening's dinner ludicrous. Nothing remotely feminist attaches to the convention-bound Anne, who cooks the dinner for her husband's colleagues, obliges her hospitalized father's (Jean-Marie Binoche) request to massage his feet, tries to cope alone with their sons' unresponsiveness to her efforts, and above all tolerates her husband's undisguised indifference. Being employed outside the home as well as performing all household tasks hardly qualifies as feminism. Tellingly, she resorts to masturbation and when she readies to pleasure her husband by fellatio, he spurns her angrily, confirming Alicja's contention that husbands are unwilling to engage in "unorthodox" sexual acts with their wives, saving those for prostitutes. In short, Anne and Patrick lack intimacy in all spheres of their nominally shared lives.

Those reviewers who complained that the film offers insufficient informa- tion about Charlotte and Alicja assume that the film focuses on them, whereas it actually spotlights Anne, as only a couple of critics and Szumowska herself have noted.[79] Anne's synecdochic role as a representative of the upper-middle class, the echelon traditionally equated with social stability, explains why the film begins and ends with her. What we witness in *Elles* is the breakdown of the family as the long-proclaimed cornerstone of society. In that sense the film echoes Tolstoy's *Anna Karenina* (1877), which dramatizes precisely the same degeneration, with the aristocratic demi-monde as the socially accepted parallel to prostitution. Fatherhood is nonexistent in *Elles*, while motherhood seems perfunctory, for generations embrace utterly disparate goals, as evident in Anne and Patrick's case, but also in that of the two student prostitutes. Charlotte's mother has no idea of her daughter's lucrative profession, and Alicja's mother (Krystyna Janda) stares in bewilderment at her dildo/vibra- tor and remains likewise clueless about the source of Alicja's finances. The closing sequence leaves no doubt that nothing will change, for when the four family members assemble at the breakfast table the morning after the dinner for Patrick's boss, they carry on as usual.

In one of her numerous interviews, Szumowska has tried—unconvinc- ingly—to compare Anne's status with that of the student prostitutes in an illogical either/or choice: "Is what the girls are doing bad, or is it worse to be in Anne and [. . .] Patrick's position, to not have any sexual contact?"[80] An answer of sorts to this faulty question is provided by a violent experience shockingly undergone by Charlotte. One of her clients (Andrzej Chyra), who initially exudes friendliness and smiles, all of a sudden anally rapes her with a bottle of wine from which he had been drinking. As the director herself says about the incident, it shows that "shit happens for [*sic*] the girls. [. . .] The beginning of the scene, I think, is quite exciting [. . .] and suddenly, it turns into this extremely violent and brutal, asexual thing."[81] Such a sadistic violation is inconceivable in Anne's world, however arid it may seem. A categorical difference exists between being violated by a bottle and not having sexual relations with one's husband—a difference that Szumowska unquestionably realizes, whatever her thoughtless analogy.

One of the innovative, effective aspects of the film is the relationship Szumowska establishes between events, which operate on three levels, and their depiction on screen. The simplest of the three visual-narrative categories of the film comprises the various tasks Anne accomplishes during the day: she listens to tapes of her interviews, types, smokes as she stares pensively into space, visits her father, shops for dinner, talks briefly with her sons, prepares dinner, joins the group at the dinner table, then walks out, and subsequently tries to interest Patrick in some form of sexual activity. These episodes are rendered directly in the "now," but they unobtrusively coalesce with Anne's recollections of her meetings with Alicja and Charlotte, which, obviously, belong to the past but do not differ stylistically from Anne's present. Nor do they differ from the third visual-narrative mode, which, at a further remove, entails Anne's visualization of the encounters between the two prostitutes with their clients as described by them, which, of course, she could not have witnessed. This unusual device of having Anne as the mediator who both recalls and visually imagines the film's key exchanges firmly anchors the narrative focus in her persona. Szumowska visually treats the three narrative categories as one until late in the film, when she unexpectedly opts for a startling change that conveys the two students' influence on Anne's psychology. When the dinner guests assemble, under the influence of what she has learned from her interviewees, Anne suddenly imagines all of them as the men who have paid for the duo's sexual services, and Szumowska briefly substitutes the actors who have played those roles for Patrick's invitees. The moment conveys Anne's alienation and recalls her earlier question to her husband, whether (in men's eyes) all women are prostitutes. And it certainly emphasizes the director's notion that men tend to objectify and abuse women.

Fascinatingly, the French magazine *Elle* (Anne's employer) reviewed the film positively, and adduced five reasons for watching it: "Juliette Binoche's acting, Polish actress Joanna Kulig, the aesthetics of certain scenes, [. . .] the research into the subject done by (documentary filmmaker) Hélène de Crécy, and to participate in the discussion the film could cause."[82] Grammar aside, these are legitimate reasons for viewing *Elles*, which, however, fails to find a balance between Anne's domestic and professional life, on the one hand, and, on the other, her interviews with the two students, overly dwelling on the latter. Szumowska's reliance on *mise-en-scène* is skillful if simple—the lack of color in the décor of the apartment, the refrigerator door that refuses to close, the family members' escape into their discrete spaces, and so forth. But more attention to Anne's relationship with Patrick would have benefited the film, for the scarcity of scenes that communicate their complete estrangement chiefly accounts for Anglophone critics' belief that prostitution, to which Szumowska allots an inordinate amount of time, is the main subject of *Elles*.

SEX AS SIBLING INCEST: *BEZ WSTYDU* (SHAMELESS 2012), FILIP MARCZEWSKI

Whereas prostitution *mutatis mutandis* has been acknowledged worldwide as a fact of life, incest remains tabooed in the modern Western world for reasons both moral and medical, though paternal rape of daughters as a significant, perennial problem is reported by the media and dramatized on TV. Greek mythology abounds in incestuous siblings, from Cronus and Rhea, their offspring Zeus and Hera, Zeus and Demeter, to Phorcys and Cato, Nyx and Erebus, plus many others, as is also common in other early national myths. Probably the best-known incestuous siblings are Richard Wagner's twins, Sieglinde and Siegmund, in his opera *Die Walküre* (The Valkyrie 1870) and the novella by Thomas Mann that it inspired, *Wälsungenblut* (The Blood of the Walsungs, wr. 1905, pd. 1921), adapted into a 1965 film with the same title by Rolf Thiele. Anglophone cinema has tackled sibling incest quite frequently but for the most part superficially (preponderately in the genres of fantasy and horror),[83] and TV programs such as the British *Midsomer Murders* and the Australian *Miss Fisher's Murder Mysteries*[84] have devoted thoughtful episodes to brother-sister unions. Among the welter of screen explorations of such relationships figure the Greek Yargos Lanthimos's bizarre *Dogtooth* (2010), the Italian Bernardo Bertolucci's 2004 film *The Dreamers*, Albertina Carri's Spanish *Geminis* (2005), Vilgot Sjöman's Swedish *Syskonbädd* 1782 (My Sister, My Love 1966), Leos Carax's French *Pola X* (2000), and in the United Kingdom, Stephen Poliakoff's *Close My Eyes* (1991), Andrew Birkin's *The Cement Garden* (1993), and Philip Haas's *Angels and Insects* (1995), plus a host of lesser offerings. While the topic carries appeal for sexploitation, it simultaneously affords a serious glance at unorthodox familial relations that in some cases beg for Freudian analysis. Whereas *Angels and Insects* adopts an unambiguously critical moral stance, *Close My Eyes* concludes irresolutely after the sister's husband (Alan Rickman, in an impressive performance) realizes the nature of the siblings' (Saskia Reeves and Clive Owen) relationship.[85]

Until *Shameless*, incest constituted a nonsubject in Polish cinema. Perhaps it is unsurprising that the sole director to have explored the ticklish dilemma of sibling incest is Filip Marczewski (b. 1974), whose director-father's name (Wojciech Marczewski) is synonymous with investigating the rebarbative sides of Polish history influencing the young generation that many other directors tend to sidestep: *Zmory* (Nightmares 1978), *Dreszcze* (Shivers 1981), *Ucieczka z kina "Wolność"* (Escape from the "Liberty" Theater 1990), and *Weiser* (2001). Following in his father's footsteps, Filip Marczewski enrolled in the renowned Łódź Film School and while still there directed his award-winning 19-minute short *Melodramat* (Melodrama 2005)[86]—a condensed rehearsal for *Shameless*, which premiered seven years later at the Karlovy Vary International Film Festival.

Interestingly, reviewers criticized not the topic of incest but the film's misguided effort to combine that plotline with the issues of ethnic prejudice and neo-Nazism—a justified criticism, for Marczewski fails to intertwine firmly the three narrative strands. At the heart of the film is young Tadek's (Mateusz Kościuokiewicz) unplatonic love for his older half-sister, Anka (Agnieszka Grochowska), whom he visits, unannounced, in a provincial town that is also home to a Romany community. While the feisty, fearless gypsy Irmina (Anna Próchniak) seems smitten with Tadek and makes several overtures to him, he has eyes only for his sister, who is involved with Andrzej (Maciej Marczewski),[87] an aspiring politician and married leader of a neo-Nazi gang persecuting the gypsies. When Tadek discovers Andrzej engaged in sex with another woman in Anka's apartment, he exposes him to his sister, who throws Andrzej out. Increasingly drawn to Tadek and full of guilt for having palmed him off on their aunt after their mother's death, Anka visits his improvised "bedroom," where the two engage in sexual intercourse. Yet when Andrzej returns, Anka reconciles with him and only when he proposes that she go to a hotel room with the minister whom he wishes to impress does she break definitively with him. Largely ignored by the unresponsive Tadek, Irmina unhappily marries the man of her family's choice, the neo-Nazis set fire to the raucous wedding party, and during the same evening Anka weeps over yet another failed romance. Clearly uncomfortable with their incestuous union, the following morning she insists that Tadek leave, but when he silently prepares to do so, she holds him back. The final sequence ends inconclusively as regards their future relationship, not unlike that of the siblings in *Close My Eyes*.[88]

In an interview in 2013, the director expressed pride that Andrzej Wajda had served as the film's artistic supervisor and also the belief that what he calls "the main story" (of incest) is aided by "the others"—presumably, the subplots of the gypsies and the neo-Nazis.[89] Critics, however, almost unanimously maintained that in tackling the three tabooed subjects the 80-minute film could not do justice to them or integrate them satisfactorily. As a couple of commentators pointed out, the subplots emerged belatedly, after filming in Wałbrzych in southwestern Poland already had started.[90] Mark Adams objects that "the Irmina and neo-Nazi subplots [. . .] get in the way of the core story at times and feel too contrived and poorly developed to convince."[91] Another critic concurs, stating that "where the film falters is in its attempts to expand the story beyond the central tryst."[92] A third reviewer, however, believes precisely the opposite, contending that "the film would have benefitted from spending less time on the splashy, logline-grabbing [*sic*] brother/sister romance, and a little more on the supporting cast and subplots that actually turn out to be a great deal more intriguing."[93] The most astute commentary came from a critic writing in *Variety*: Marczewski "added the subplots involving Irmina and the neo-Nazi attacks [. . .]. Even though these threads aren't as well integrated into the pic's brief running time as they could be [. . .], they nonetheless complement the central tale of the incestuous half-siblings, making the entire film an argument for tolerance."[94] To strengthen that argument, Marczewski and his coauthor Grzegorz Łoszewski made Tadek and Irmina appealing and sympathetic, by contrast to the Neanderthal, violent neo-Nazis and especially Andrzej, whose role as the group's leader, like his treatment of Anka, is repellent. In an interview, the director spoke of the film as "a portrayal of the pain of growing up and standing up against societal taboos and finally about the freedom to follow one's own path in life."[95] Only Irmina and Tadek combat those taboos, she by wishing to become a doctor and falling in love with a man outside the Romany world; he by frankly declaring his love, both emotional and sexual, for his older half-sister, and by fighting one of the neo-Nazis (a former friend) after the group has attacked the gypsies. Whereas Irmina is perceptive, strong, and self-confident, Tadek is vulnerable and blinded by his obsession with Anka, so that by the time he suggests to Irmina that they run away together not only has she married a fellow gypsy, but her love for Tadek has turned into hatred.

If *Elles* dwells too long on multiple scenes of sexual activity, *Bez wstydu* opts for tasteful discretion. As one reviewer observed, "The sexuality is handled thoughtfully and shot in a non-exploitative way, despite [. . .] a good deal of intense sensuality between the pair [of siblings]."[96]

Another commended Marczewski's treatment as "perhaps the cinema's most natural depiction of incest since Louis Malle's *Murmur of the Heart*." Other reviewers, however, found the director's restraint a flaw. Artur Zaborski grudgingly praised him for not courting controversy, thereby avoiding the trap into which Szumowska fell by trying "to transgress a taboo where there was none" (przekroczyć tabu tam, gdzie go nie było). Anxiety about the sensationalism of the topic, however, supposedly led Marczewski to limit himself to "signaling" "the forbidden" (zakazane jest [. . .] tylko zasygnalizowane), which leaves an impression of insufficiency (wrażenie niedosytu).[97] While

Zaborski's review merely implies that a comparison with Marczewski's short *Melodrama* can only benefit the earlier film, Sebastiano Pucciarelli's in *Nisi Magazine* explicitly complains, "Compared to *Melodramat*, in *Shameless* the forbidden passion and its emotional consequences are kind of cleaned up."[98] Both seem to miss the point that *Melodrama* favors a naturalistic style and approach to the issue of incest. Shot in drab colors, it focuses on a fourteen-year-old who sniffs his sister's underwear, masturbates, and exhibits thuggish tendencies. By contrast, *Shameless* proceeds by sophistication and understatement, is "stylishly made," "attractively shot," and testifies to the director's skill in narrative and cinematic "grammar."[99] Its protagonist is a sensitive eighteen-year-old university student appreciably more mature than his onanistic predecessor. Cavils notwithstanding, the film leaves no doubts about Tadek's carnal desire for his sister, demonstrated by his many, escalating attempts to ignite a sexual response in her, including awkwardly getting into the bathtub where she is relaxing amid bubbles. One can only applaud the use of shadow and a reticent camera in the sequence of their intercourse, for such discretion accords with the overall stylistics of the film. Furthermore, Marczewski's judiciousness is a welcome change from countless directors' inability to resist extended shots of naked bodies engaged in sexual frolics, even when such scenes are utterly gratuitous.

What reviews did not address, somewhat surprisingly, was the character of Anka, apart from registering her instability and lack of judgment in her choice of men. A comment by Tadek makes clear that Andrzej is merely the last in a dispiriting series of men in her life. Additionally, the film conveys her irresponsibility when she buys clothes instead of paying the electric bill, which leads to a blackout in the apartment. And at one juncture she cries and confesses to a sense of guilt for not having taken care of her younger half-brother after their mother died. On the basis of such incidents, viewers know that she habitually makes poor choices. Her feelings for Tadek, however, remain unclear, and her behavior with him inconsistent, to say the least. Does she reciprocate his sexual desire or is she simply a careless tease or a sadist? When she undresses at one point, she leaves the door to her room ajar, then admonishes him for watching her, though he is the one who then closes the door. She makes no objection when he comes into the bathroom, bringing her the pistachio ice cream that he bought for her ("your favorite"), and proceeds to feed her. Her visit to him at night as he lies asleep is what leads to their intercourse. Finally, when he readies to leave the apartment, she uses the ice cream to hold him back, and the final shot shows them sharing the ice cream at the kitchen table. If the ice cream tropes sexual pleasures, then the incestuous inclinations are fully shared. At other times, however, she ignores him, tells him to leave, and points out the illicitness of his love for her. Ultimately, it is difficult to determine whether her neurotic personality and fear of violating sacrosanct taboos explain such contradictions or whether they spring from the director's indecisiveness regarding the nature of her feelings as a sister.

CONCLUSION

The twenty-first century has opened the door to previously prohibited terrain in Polish film, and what is particularly striking is new directors' readiness to examine various facets of sexuality in bold and original ways. Perhaps most unexpected and welcome is the emergence of female directors in their forties who treat controversial topics related to sex with self-assurance and complete lack of prudery, not hesitating to portray women with healthy sexual appetites indifferent to church strictures: Sadowska, Szumowska, Agnieszka Smoczyńska, Magdalena Piekorz—all of them recipients of sundry awards. Above all, it is Szumowska, also a prolific documentarian, whose feature films have investigated various forms of sexuality and the importance of the body as a legitimate source of pleasure, self-expression, and identity. Not unlike Agnieszka Holland, she has forged cont(r)acts with entities abroad without relying solely on funds from Polish sources, notably PISF (Polski Instytut Sztuki Filmowej/The Polish Film Institute). Moreover, she regularly premieres her films at foreign festivals, such as Cannes, Berlin, Toronto, and Sundance, easily finds distributors, and has released both the French-language *Elles* and an Anglophone movie, *The Other Lamb* (2019), in English. In the meantime, Smoczyńska enjoys the unique distinction of having her first film, *Córki dancingu* (The Lure 2015) chosen for the elite Criterion Collection, alongside several long-established classics by Andrzej Wajda and Krzysztof Kieślowski and Roman Polanski's *Nóż w wodzie* (Knife in the Water 1962)—the only other recent Polish entry being Paweł Pawlikowski's *Zimna wojna* (The Cold War 2018). Though, historically, Poland, unlike Australia, has hardly teemed with women behind the camera, that situation is changing rapidly, as confirmed by even a casual perusal of recent Polish directors listed on Wikipedia—hardly an authoritative site but important for its universal accessibility.[100]

Along with the rise of new female directors, Poland has witnessed the sudden popularity of new actresses, such as Boczarska (b. 1978), Grochowska (b. 1979), Gruszka (b. 1980), Kulig (b. 1982), and Próchniak (b. 1988).[101] And Europe has noticed and snapped up these talents. All have appeared in non-Polish films, and Próchniak, in addition to roles in several European offerings (including Anne Fontaine's *The Innocents* 2016), currently has a part in the BBC hit series *Baptiste*. If the trend continues, the future looks bright for women in Polish cinema and for further screen forays into sexuality from an open, nonjudgmental perspective.

HG

NOTES

1. Marina Warner, *Alone of All Her Sex: The Myth and the Cult of the Virgin Mary* (New York: Vintage Books, 1983), 338.

2. Joanna Szwajcowska, "The Myth of the Polish Mother," in *Women in Polish Cinema*, eds. Ewa Mazierska and Elżbieta Ostrowska (New York/Oxford: Berghahn Books, 2006), 15–33. Russian culture has tended in the same direction, as the medieval text of "The Virgin's Descent into Hell" and literature glorifying the all-forgiving, self-abnegating maternal icon (from Dostoevsky to Solzhenitsyn) attest. See Dmitry Grigorieff, "The Theotokos in the Orthodox Tradition and Russian Thought," https://www.theway.org.uk/back/s045Grigorieff.pdf, which presents the convictions of "the faithful." Accessed August 26, 2014.

3. Her comment reports observations made in an interview with the gynecologist Michalina Wisłocka. Patrycja Pustkowiak, "There the Most Common Method of Contraception Is Prayer," *Aspen Review*, 2 (2017), https://www.aspenreview.com/article/2017/where-the-most-common-method-of-contraception-is-prayer/. Accessed April 2, 2018.

4. Natalia Jarska, "Modern Marriage and the Culture of Sexuality: Experts between the State and the Church in Poland, 1956-1970," *European History Quarterly* 49, no. 3 (2019): 467–90, 467.

5. Alexandra Sifferlin, "It's Almost Impossible to Get an Abortion in Poland. These Women Crossed the Border to Germany for Help," *Time*, January 31, 2018, https://time.com/poland-abortion-laws-protest/. Accessed March 27, 2018.

6. Agnieszka Kościańska, "Sex on Equal Terms? Polish Sexology on Women's Emancipation and 'Good Sex' from the 1970s to the Present," *Sexualities* 19, no. 1/2 (2016): 238.

7. It was translated into English in 1987—quite unaccountably, as *A Practical Guide to Marital Bliss*. Though an obvious polonization of Ovid's ingenious *Ars amatoria* (2 BC), the title derives, no doubt, from Erich Fromm's international bestseller, *The Art of Loving* (1956).

8. The volume, in fact, appeared ten years later, and the discrepancy between the title of her second monograph and the publication of her first book occurred because of the prolonged delay in permission to publish the latter owing to official censorship.

9. As Kościańska notes, two progressive magazines during this period were the student weekly *itd* (1965–1990) and the magazine issued by the socialist League of Polish Women, *Zwierciadło* (The Mirror 1957–2012). Kościańska, "Sex on Equal Terms?," 240, 238.

10. Ibid., 242.

11. Jarska, "Modern Marriage," 468–69, 473, 480.

12. Ted G. Jelen and Clyde Wilcox, "Attitudes toward Abortion in Poland and the United States," *Social Science Quarterly* 78, no. 4 (December 1997): 907–921, 907.

13. Ibid., 915.

14. Jelen and Wilcox found that in responses to their polls, "approximately 70 percent of the Polish sample regards the Catholic Church as 'too powerful.' " Ibid., 917.

15. Agata Chełstowska, "Stigmatisation and Commercialisation of Abortion Services in Poland: Turning Sin into Gold," *Reproductive Health Matters* 19, no. 37 (2011): 102.

16. Madeline Roache, "Poland Is Trying to Make Abortion Dangerous, Illegal, and Impossible," *Foreign Policy*, January 8, 2019, at https://foreignpolicy.com /2019/01/08/poland-is-trying-to-make-abortion-dangerous-illegal-and-impossible/. Accessed January 29, 2019.

17. Edyta Pietrzak and Anna Fligel, "'Black Protest': Abortion Law in Poland in the Context of Division into Private and Public Sphere," in *Mothers in Public and Political Life*, eds. Simone Bohn, Pinar Melisa Yesali Parmaksiz (Bradford, Canada: Demeter Press, 2017), 293–294.

18. For an astute answer to the question posed by the title, see Jill Bystydzienski, "The Feminist Movement in Poland: Why So Slow?" *Women's Studies International Forum* 24, no. 5 (2001): 501–511.

19. Additionally, though then prime minister Beata Szydło favored the law completely banning abortion, three former "first ladies"—Anna Komorowska, Jolanta Kwaśniewska, and Danuta Wałęsa—wrote an open letter against the radical new law. Edyta Pietrzak and Anna Fligel, "Black Protest," 296, 298.

20. The gendering of mourners has been ubiquitous in everyday life, art, and film. On the phenomenon in Russia, see Helena Goscilo, "Playing Dead: The Operatics of Celebrity Funerals," in *Imitations of Life: Two Centuries of Melodrama in Russia,* eds. Louise McReynolds and Joan Neuberger (Durham and London: Duke University Press, 2002), 283–319 and Helena Goscilo, "Widowhood as Genre and Profession à la Russe: Nation, Shadow, Curator, and Publicity Agent," in *Gender and National Identity in Twentieth-Century Culture*, eds. Helena Goscilo and Andrea Lanoux (DeKalb IL: Northern Illinois University Press, 2006), 55–74; Annette Michelson, "The Kinetic Icon and the Work of Mourning: Prolegomena in the Analysis of a Textual System," in *The Red Screen: Politics, Society, Art in Soviet Cinema*, ed. Anna Lawton (London: Routledge, 1992), 125–26; and Iurii Sokolov, *Russian Folklore* (Hatboro, PA: Folklore Associates, 1966), 225–34.

21. Szwajcowska, "The Myth of the Polish Mother," 26.

22. Indeed, in late October 2020 Poland's highest court decreed abortions owing to fetal defects unconstitutional, a decision that entails "a near-total ban on terminations." Rob Picheta, "Polish court rules against abortion due to fetal defects," CNN, October 22, 2020, https://www.cnn.com/2020/10/22/europe/poland-abortion-fetal -defect-ruling-intl/index.html. Accessed October 23, 2020.

23. Roache, "Poland Is Trying."

24. Chełstowska, "Stigmatization," 104.

25. Sukhada Tatke, "Meet the 'abortion aunts' of Berlin who help Polish women terminate unwanted pregnancies," *GlobalPost*, August 8, 2019, https://www.pri.org /stories/2019-08-08/meet-abortion-aunts-berlin-who-help-polish-women-terminate -unwanted-pregnancies. Accessed August 8, 2019.

26. Roache, "Poland Is Trying."

27. See Chełstowska, *passim.*

28. Tomek Rolski, "Poland's new abortion law triggers broader discontent as women lead protests," ABCNews, October 27, 2020. https://abcnews.go.com/International/polands-abortion-law-triggers-broader-discontent-women-lead/story?id=73853693. Accessed October 30, 2020.

29. Amazingly, much of current feminist activity is located in Hollywood, where actresses, directors, and screenwriters are agitating for more equitable salaries, the removal of obstacles for women in what traditionally has been a male-dominated business, and for legal measures to be taken against the sexual harassment, including alleged rape, by powerful men such as Harvey Weinstein, who earlier felt free to take advantage of women with impunity. See the Geena Davis Institute (at https://seejane.org/), the copious items on Twitter and publications about the #MeToo movement, as well as media coverage of battles with financial inequities in all spheres of filmmaking. Accessed throughout 2019–2020.

30. In addition to snagging several awards in Poland, it won in Moscow and California for the best director, and in California also for best film and best actress. For awards in Poland and elsewhere, see http://www.filmpolski.pl/fp/index.php?film=1223331. For foreign awards, see Nick Hodge, "Review: Little Rose (Różyczka)," *The Krakow Post*, July 7, 2010, at http://www.krakowpost.com/2210/2010/07; Nigel M. Smith, " 'Little Rose' Wins Big at Tiburion International Film Festival," IndieWire, April 18, 2011, https://www.indiewire.com/2011/04/little-rose-wins-big-at-tiburion-international-film-festival-242907/. All accessed July 28, 2018.

31. Encomia for Jasienica's publications and his courageous stance vis-à-vis the repressive regime under the Soviets have come from Adam Michnik as well as the British historian Norman Davies. See Adam Michnik, "Michnik o Jasienicy: pisarz w obcęgach," *Gazeta Wyborcza* (August 19, 2005); Davies, Norman, *God's Playground: The Origins to 1795* (New York: Columbia University Press, 2005), 14.

32. See Ks. Andrzej Luter, "Różyczka," *Kino*, no. 3 (2010): 64–65, http://kino.org.pl//index.php?option=com_content&task=view&id=679&Itemid=434. Accessed July 15, 2018.

33. Nick Hodge, "Review: Little Rose."

34. Robin Menken, "Little Rose," cinemawithoutborders, January 7, 2011, https://cinemawithoutborders.com/2423-little-rose/. Accessed July 23, 2018.

35. Hodge, "Review: Little Rose."

36. Beata Cielecka, " 'Różyczka': Miłość i inwigilacja," telemagazyn, May 3, 2018, https://www.telemagazyn.pl/artykuly/rozyczka-milosc-i-inwigilacja-recenzja-47847.html. Accessed July 22, 2018.

37. Łukasz Maciejewski, " 'Różyczka': Znakomita, oparta na faktach historia," Kultura.onet.pl, March 17, 2010, https://kultura.onet.pl/film/recenzje/rozyczka-znakomita-oparta-na-faktach-historia/tmp2bnk." Accessed July 24, 2018.

38. The line belongs to a young woman implicitly rebuking a writer in *Dziady*, Part III, Act 1, Scene 7, which takes place in a Warsaw salon. See *Dziady* in Adam Mickiewicz, *Wybór pism* (Warsaw: Książka i Wiedza, 1951), 296.

39. In predictably cowardly fashion, his academic superior (Aleksander Bednarz) and his publisher, Ms. Roma (an appropriately cold, ironic Grażyna Szapołowska), abandon him.

40. For an incisive treatment of the 1967–1968 events, see Dariusz Stola, "Fighting against the Shadows: The *Anti-Zionist* Campaign of 1968," in *Antisemitism and its Opponents in Modern Poland*, ed. Robert Blobaum (Ithaca: Cornell University Press, 2005), 284–300.

41. Although the film does not belabor Kamila's lack of family, her solitude may account for her poor judgment and inability to recognize Rożek's unappealing traits as fundamental flaws in character.

42. During an episode in public, Kamila uses her foot under the table to caress Rożek's upper thigh so as to arouse him, whereas he peremptorily orders her to desist, for his primary concern is political advancement, while hers is physical and emotional intimacy with her lover.

43. "I co, wreszcie, miałoby wynikać z tej edukacji, w efekcie której Polka z sierocińca swoje wychowanie i swój stan posiadania, wszystko, co ma, i wszystko, co traci, zawdzięcza dwóm polskim Żydom?" Iwona Kurz, "Rożyczka," dwutygodnik .com, March 2010, at https://www.dwutygodnik.com/artykul/972-rozyczkarez-jan -kidawa-blonski.html. Accessed July 22, 2018.

44. The film should not be confused with Jacek Bromski's 1989 frivolous comedy with the same title, likewise dealing with sexology. See footnote 8.

45. Ola Salwa, "Polish Film: The Art of Loving Tops Local 2017 Box Office," Cineuropa, March 21, 2017, https://cineuropa.org/en/newsdetail/325822. Of the almost $9 million grossed worldwide, all but $100,000 or so were earned at the Polish box office ($8,765,783), which in Central Europe and Russia translates to a significant hit. See Box Office Mojo, at https://www.boxofficemojo.com/title/tt5370828/?ref_ =bo_gr_ti. Both accessed August 1, 2018.

46. Strictly speaking, the relationship instanced polyamory, since Stach is the only member of the trio to have sex with both women.

47. For a review of the documentary, see http://www.filmpolski.pl/fp/index.php ?film=4213754. Accessed August 1, 2018.

48. Michalina Wisłocka, *Sztuka Kochania* (Warsaw: Agora, 2016), 97–98.

49. On this aspect of the sexologists' preconceptions see Kościańska, "Sex on Equal Terms?," especially 243–50.

50. Wisłocka, *Sztuka Kochania*, 283. Precisely the ascription of such attributes to women is what French feminist theorists such as Hélène Cixous, Luce Irigaray, and Monique Wittig combated and Western feminism continues to deplore today.

51. Ibid., 66–67, 206–12, 159, 200.

52. He criticized the Romantics for what he identified as their conservative views, which relegated women to the manifestly subordinate and dehumanized position of inspiration and helpmate, endowed with all the traits incarnated in Matka Polka. Citations from Boy-Żeleński also populate the pages of Wisłocka's later, related monograph, *Kultura miłości* (The Culture of Loving 1980), which references a cornucopia of literary texts (including Stanisław Lem's *Return from the Stars!*), films, and Masters and Johnson's *Human Sexual Inadequacy* (1970), which she read in French translation (60).

53. Regrettably, Wisłocka's autobiography (*Autobiografia*) covers her life only until 1937.

54. Notably, her love for her husband, as she phrased it, was spiritual. Jurek enables her to find sexual and professional fulfillment, for he stands apart from all the other males featured in the film—a sorry lot of misogynistic hypocrites intent on using women for their sexual enjoyment and denying them a voice in sociopolitical matters.

55. When she attempts to get the support of the local bishop (Krzysztof Dracz) for her book, he brushes her off with the Jesuitical advice to appeal to the Party, knowing full well that the official functionaries will block her efforts.

56. Robert Birkholc, "Sztuka kochania. Historia Michaliny Wisłockiej," *Kino*, no. 1 (2017): 78, http://kino.org.pl//index.php?option=com_content&task=view&id =2662&Itemid=1802. Accessed July 25, 2018.

57. A pop singer, actress, singer, and screenwriter, Sadowska (b. 1976) directed her full-length debut feature, ironically titled *Dzień kobiet* (Women's Day), in 2012, with a 2013 premiere. Dubbed "the Polish *Erin Brockovich*," it is also gynocentric, stars Eryk Lubos in the major male role, and garnered several awards.

58. As a Polish site formulates it, "dzięki interwencji pacjentek Wisłockiej oraz jej wytrwałości w dążeniu do celu, w końcu [poradnik] zostaje wydany w 1976 roku." See "Sztuka kochania," http://www.filmpolski.pl/fp/index.php?film=1239568. Accessed January 7, 2019.

59. "Jestem feministką. . ." See "Maria Sadowska: Fragment wywiadu z reżyserką," the interview with her in the booklet accompanying the DVD of *Sztuka Kochania: Historia Michaliny Wisłockiej* (Warsaw: Agora SA, 2017).

60. One female critic calls Wisłocka's views "old fashioned." See Iza Desperak, "Michalina Wisłocka: Revolutionary Sexologist or Modern Heroine of Pain?" March 2, 2017, Network 4 Debate, Poland, http://politicalcritique.org/cee/poland/2017/ wislocka-sex-feminism-polishfilm/. Though Desperak rightly criticizes commentators expecting a protagonist whose views would be deemed feminist by today's standards, she herself fails to historicize adequately the import of the sexologist's ideas. Accessed December 14, 2018.

61. See her *W imię* . . . (In the Name of . . .), *Ciało* (Body), and *Twarz* (Mug), in which the body supervenes as a site of identity and desire. For an example of the "new" perception of prostitution, see Annie McClintock, *Sex Workers and Sex Work* (Raleigh NC: Duke University Press, 1994), and *Social Text*, no. 37 (1973), a special issue edited by her.

62. Reviews were lukewarm at best and internationally the film made only $911,466 at the box office. See https://www.boxofficemojo.com/releasegroup/ gr655380997/. Accessed December 12, 2018.

63. On the range of perceptions and proposals for officially professionalizing prostitution, see Ronald Weitzer, "Prostitution: Facts and Fictions," *Contexts*, 6, no. 4 (Fall 2007): 28–33, https://journals.sagepub.com/doi/pdf/10.1525/ctx.2007.6.4.28. Accessed September 1, 2009.

64. "How Many Prostitutes Are in the United States and the Rest of the World?" ProCon.org, January 11, 2018, https://prostitution.procon.org/view.answers.php ?questionID=000095. Accessed March 3, 2019.

65. As Roger Ebert wrote, "Given the film's subject matter and its obligatory sex scenes, Malle shows taste and restraint" as well as "a good deal of compassion." Roger Ebert, "Pretty Baby," June 1, 1978, https://www.rogerebert.com/reviews/pretty-baby. Accessed May 1, 1998.

66. See https://en.wikipedia.org/wiki/Category:Films_about_prostitution_in_the_United_States. Accessed March 20, 2018.

67. Presumably on the assumption that Poles are incapable of understanding a basic French pronoun, the film's title in Poland was *Sponsoring*—hardly, one would think, a choice facilitating instant comprehension.

68. The estimated number of prostitutes in France, however, differs little from that in Poland, approximating 20,000. See https://prostitution.procon.org/view.answers.php?questionID=000095. Accessed March 3, 2019.

69. In an interview, Binoche confessed that perhaps nostalgia for her work with Kieślowski may have prompted her to accept the part of Anne in Szumowska's film: "I also think I had a sort of melancholic need to work with a Polish director again since Krzysztof Kieslowski," Julie Bloom, "Tribeca: Juliette Binoche on Acting from Insecurity," *New York Times*, April 25, 2012, https://artsbeat.blogs.nytimes.com/2012/04/25/tribeca-juliette-binoche-on-acting-from-insecurity/. Accessed March 1, 2019.

70. Costing slightly over $4 million, it failed to earn even a million dollars at the box office. See https://www.imdb.com/title/tt1549589/. Szumowska in an interview said, "This is the first time in my life that I've had a commercial success," Helen Barlow, "Elles: Malgoska Szumowska interview," SBS, February 29, 2012, https://www.sbs.com.au/movies/article/2012/02/29/elles-malgoska-szumowska-interview. While she succeeded in selling the film to several countries, it did not attract large audiences. Both accessed March 3, 2019.

71. Stephen Holden, "Who Loses and Who Profits When Sex Is a Commodity?" *New York Times*, April 26, 2012, https://www.nytimes.com/2012/04/27/movies/elles-with-juliette-binoche-about-prostitution.html. Accessed February 28, 2019.

72. Honeycutt condescendingly states, "you know you're watching actors playing roles dreamed up by people without much familiarity with the subject itself. In other words, *Whore's* [sic] *Glory* is real; *Elles* is complete fiction and should be judged as such." Kirk Honeycutt, "Elles: Toronto Review," *The Hollywood Reporter*, September 13, 2011, https://www.hollywoodreporter.com/review/elles-toronto-review-234669. These comments suffer from inaccuracy and illogic. As Szumowska noted, she and her French cowriter, Tine Byrckel, met student prostitutes in Paris, read copious articles on the topic, and only then wrote the script: "It Was Two Years of Work." Margaret Wheeler Johnson, "Małgorzata Szumowska, 'Elles' Director and Co-Writer, Talks Prostitution, Love," *HuffPost*, May 3 2012, https://www.huffpost.com/entry/malgorzata-szumowska-elles-juliette-binoche-joanna-kulig-anais-demoustier_n_1469094. And Binoche claimed that a friend of hers during their student days worked as a sponsored prostitute. See Bloom. Finally, to compare a feature film with a documentary as Honeycutt does is ridiculous, for the former is by definition "fiction," whereas a documentary is an interview-based genre striving to capture everyday reality. And *Elles* deals with two French student prostitutes in

Paris, whereas Michael Glawogger's *Whores' Glory* (2011) investigates brothels in Thailand, Bangladesh, and Mexico. Both accessed March 1, 2019.

73. Andrew Pulver, "Elles—Review," *The Guardian*, February 10, 2012, https://www.theguardian.com/film/2012/feb/10/elles-review. Accessed March 10, 2019.

74. Barlow, "Elles."

75. Colette de Castro, "Invisible Girls," *East European Film Bulletin*, 14 (February 2012) https://eefb.org/perspectives/malgorzata-szumowskas-elles-2011/, and "Interview," 14 (February 2012), https://eefb.org/interviews/joanna-kulig-and -malgorzata-szumowska-on-elles/. Both accessed March 5, 2019.

76. For the differences between these two categories, see Weitzer, "prostitution," *passim*.

77. On this facet of the prostitutes' self-perceptions, see Fabien Lemercier, "Elles," *Cineuropa*, January 24, 2012, https://cineuropa.org/en/newsdetail/215084/. Accessed March 2, 2019.

78. As Konrad Tambor concisely phrased it, "To wreszcie film o komunikacji między ludzmi. [. . .] Dlaczego tak daleko, skoro tak blisko? Tym pytaniem jest małżeństwo Anne: razem, a jednak osobno"/Ultimately the film is about communica- tion between people. [. . .] Why are they so distant if they're so close? That's the ques- tion in Anne's marriage: together, yet apart. Konrad Tambor, "Sponsoring," *Kino*, no. 2 (2012): 85, http://kino.org.pl/index.php?option=com_content&task=view&id =1328&Itemid=742. Accessed February 22, 2019.

79. See Johnson, "Małgorzata Szumowska." Offering no evidence for her unten- able notion that "Anne envies Charlotte and Alice [*sic*] while the two girls [*sic*] seek the security Anne appears to be taking for granted," Marta Jazowska reduces the psychological shadings of the film. Anne has financial security, but part of it stems from her own employment as a successful journalist. And her goal in the film is to understand the two young prostitutes, not to measure her life as middle-aged wife and mother against their youthful and ultimately questionable solution to their financial problems. Moreover, her peculiar idea is that the film is "an almost entirely feminine project"—an unfortunate phrasing possibly explained by an inadequate command of English. See Marta Jazowska, "Elles: Malgorzata Szumowska," culture.pl, n.d., https://culture.pl/en/work/elles-malgorzata-szumowska. Accessed February 27, 2019.

80. Johnson, "Małgorzata Szumowska."

81. Ibid.

82. Jazowska. "Elles."

83. For a long catalogue of these, see Wikipedia https://en.wikipedia.org/wiki/ Incest_in_film_and_television#Siblings. Accessed February 5, 2019.

84. See, for instance, the fifth episode in series three of the show, titled "Death and Hysteria" (2015).

85. Witold Stok provides the excellent camerawork.

86. The film is available on YouTube at https://www.youtube.com/watch?v =rWIZ6SfcXZY. Accessed February 1, 2019.

87. Maciej Marczewski is the director's older brother.

88. One reviewer called the ending "deceptively ambiguous," without clarifying what is deceptive about the ambiguity. Ben Nicholson, "Kinoteka 2013: 'Shameless'

review," March 13, 2013, https://cine-vue.com/2013/03/kinoteka-2013-shameless-review.html. Accessed December 4, 2018.

89. See "Filip Marczewski, Director: Interview," Cineuropa, March 14, 2013, https://cineuropa.org/en/video/234700/. Accessed March 1, 2019. Accessed May 28, 2019.

90. For instance, see Artur Zaborski, "Bez wstydu," *Kino*, no. 7–8 (2012): 98.

91. Mark Adams, "Shameless," ScreenDaily, July 8, 2012, https://www.screendaily.com/shameless/5044254.article. Accessed May 28, 2019.

92. Nicholson, " 'Shameless' review."

93. Jessica Kiang, "Shameless," IndieWire, July 15, 2012, https://www.indiewire.com/2012/07/karlovy-vary-film-fest-review-roundup-shameless-hay-road-nos-vemos-papa-108416/. Kiang's erroneous claims that Tadek's obsession with his sister "causes the breakdown of all of [*sic*] the other relationships within the film," however, makes one wonder whether she actually paid attention to what she was watching. Accessed April 11, 2019.

94. Alissa Simon, "Shameless," *Variety*, July 23, 2012, at https://variety.com/2012/film/reviews/shameless-2-1117947933/. Accessed April 30, 2019.

95. "Filip Marchewski," Cineuropa.

96. Adams, "Shameless."

97. Zaborski, "Bez wstydu."

98. Cited in Marta Jazowska, "Shameless—Filip Marczewski," culture.pl, n.d., https://culture.pl/en/work/shameless-filip-marczewski. Accessed April 27, 2019.

99. See Adams, Simon, Zaborski.

100. See https://en.wikipedia.org/wiki/Category: Polish_women_film_directors. Accessed November 22, 2018.

101. For information on how Próchniak's screen debut in *Bez wstydu* launched her career, see https://www.bustle.com/p/who-is-anna-prochniak-the-actor-playing-baptistes-natalie-has-been-in-some-big-european-films-15959320. Accessed January 12, 2020.

Chapter 8

Male Gays under a Female Gaze

MIXED MESSAGES: HOMOSEXUALITY IN POLAND

As a selective inventory of Western films about male homosexuality by the British publication *TimeOut. London* in mid-2018 confirmed, in addition to the familiar oeuvre of Pedro Almodóvar, Reiner Fassbinder, Paolo Pasolini, and Luchino Visconti, mainstream movies in the last few decades by Anglophone directors exceed thirty well-known titles, from *Philadelphia* (1993) and Ivory Merchant's adaptations of E.M. Forster's novels to the more recent *Brokeback Mountain* (2005) and Francis Lee's *God's Own Country* (2017).[1] Almodóvar's popularity with international audiences suggests that screen homosexuality and prostitution are perfectly acceptable to audiences if they animate an absorbing film with challenging themes wedded to an ironic or grotesque sense of humor. Indeed, it can launch a successful career, as in the case of Penélope Cruz[2] and especially Antonio Banderas, who at the time of his early films' release was unknown to cinema audiences. Banderas's rise to fame was indebted to Almodóvar, for after his first appearance in *Labyrinth of Passion* (1982), followed by *Matador* (1986), the subversive *Law of Desire* (1987), and a string of similarly idiosyncratic visual musings, Banderas caught the attention of Hollywood. His Almodóvar-certified role as the gay lover in Jonathan Demmes' generally well-received *Philadelphia* (1993) paved the way for his dramatic transformation into a macho megastar after the release of the vastly popular, money-making swashbuckler *Mask of Zorro* (1998).

Adulatory reviews of Luca Guadagnino's *Call Me by Your Name* (2017) index the West's openness to screen depictions of same-sex male love as precisely that, rather than as a lamentable anomaly or perversion between limp-wristed men whose amorous-sexual orientation necessitates psychological rationalization or apology. Given Central Europe's attitude toward LGBTQ rights,[3] it surprises no one that significant Polish films about homosexuality are extremely rare and, until recently, hardly insightful or sympathetic, despite the country's legalization of homosexuality in 1932 and of homosexual prostitution in 1969.[4] As one of Poland's most astute feminist commentators on Polish society and its attitude toward gender notes, public discourse anathematizes LGBTQ phenomena and blends with that of traditional anti-Semitism.[5]

An overwhelming majority of Poles consider same-sex love "unnatural" and oppose same-sex marriage and adoption of children.[6] They believe, however, that as long as such relationships remain private, they should be tolerated.[7] Needless to say, the current conservative government of the Law and Justice Party (Prawo i Sprawiedliwość—PiS), together with the Catholic Church, opposes all liberal tendencies, including abortion rights, receptivity to immigrants, and manifestations of LGBTQ identity. Campaigning for reelection and winning the vote in 2020, President Andrzej Duda, in a statement both ludicrous and ominous, called the struggle for LGBTQ rights "an ideology," "neo-Bolshevism," "even more destructive to the human being."[8] Jarosław Kaczyński, as leader of PiS "the most powerful politician in Poland," at the party's convention in March 2019 equated LGBTQ with "sexualization of children from the earliest childhood," and insisted, "We need to fight this. We need to defend the Polish family [. . .] it's a threat to civilization, not just for Poland, but for the [*sic*] entire Europe, for the entire civilization that is based on Christianity."[9] His speech responded to a declaration issued by Rafał Trzaskowski, the liberal mayor of Warsaw, urging tolerance—a declaration that prompted a well-known Catholic priest and educator to state that the plus in LGBTQ+ stood "for pedophiles, zoophiles, necrophiles," whose ultimate goal was "to make people into infertile erotomaniacs."[10] And Duda's victory over Trzaskowski in the 2020 presidential elections does not bode well for liberalism regarding sexual identity and praxis in Poland. Little wonder that, according to Artur Pawlak, owner of Warsaw gay bar Miami, the "big problem is still the Church. No matter what you say, this is still a Church state."[11]

Yet the country's historical tradition of tolerance,[12] though now beleaguered, has not vanished, and in the opinion of many, has been rekindled, if only partially, by the ubiquity of the internet, Poland's membership in the European Union since 2004, and decreased faith in the Catholic Church, especially among the younger generation. That church has had to weather a major scandal surrounding Poznań's Archbishop Juliusz Paetz's resignation in 2002, when accused of molesting young priests and seminarians (Hundley). On the one hand, numerous reported cases of abuse have merely corroborated the power of the church. As one journalist put it, "Although prosecutors have brought charges against dozens of Polish priests, securing sentences has been difficult. When imposed, these have mostly been light, suspended jail terms. Most convicted clergy are still serving in parishes, often working with children, while their victims face hostility and exclusion."[13] On the other hand, symptomatic of the population's changing attitude to the church are the huge audiences who flocked to Wojciech Smarzowski's hard-hitting film *Kler* (Clergy 2018)—an exposé of the Polish clergy's iniquities, which include greed, corruption, alcoholism, child abuse, and fornication. While outraged conservative politicians have slammed the film, its director calmly has declared that he wished to heighten people's awareness that priests "are not saints . . . . They just wear cassocks."[14]

Accordingly, though contemporary Polish citizens are generally homophobic (constitutional protection of gay rights notwithstanding), the country boasts a small but vital gay/lesbian culture, including LGBTQ cafes, clubs, publications, physical and virtual sites, and gay parades, particularly in the country's capital. Moreover, Gdańsk—the workers' northern city that incubated the Solidarity movement—despite the retrograde pronouncement on television of its celebrity leader, Lech Walesa, that gays should not play "a prominent role in Polish politics,"[15] also held a gay rights march in recent years. But the murder of Paweł Adamowicz, Gdańsk's liberal mayor, in January 2019 revealed what some Western journalists called "absolutely horrifying political polarization," attributing the homicide to the widespread "hatred and malice" under the ultraconservative PiS Party.[16] In a kindred vein, Białystok's first LGBTQ equality march took place on July 21, 2019, with approximately 1,000 participants, outnumbered by the 4,000 "nationalist football 'ultra' fans, far-right groups and others" who threw "flash bombs, rocks and glass bottles" at them.[17] Since the area is a stronghold of PiS-supporting conservatives, the local response hardly came as a surprise.

Liberalism persists, albeit espoused by a minority and severely challenged under an increasingly repressive government. The openly gay LGBTQ activist Robert Biedroń not only was elected to Parliament (Sejm) in 2011 but also won the mayoral elections in Słupsk three years later, becoming the first self-identified homosexual mayor in Poland's history. His most recent initiative, the launch of a new pro-EU party optimistically labeled Wiosna (Spring), intends to "bring fresh air to Polish politics," as he phrased it. Yet "Poland's post-communist political landscape is littered with the bones of new parties, particularly on the fragmented left."[18] As so often in Poland, signs of conflicting tendencies abound.[19] In fact, even under proclaimed communism, Poland issued two magazines devoted to homosexuality: *Biuletyn*, inaugurated in March 1983 and three years later renamed *Etap*, which ceased publication at the end of 1987; and *Filo*, a gay and lesbian publication that appeared in late 1986 and lasted until mid-1990.[20]

With the demise of communism, the LGBTQ monthly *Inaczej* (full title *Magazyn Kochających Inaczej* [Magazine of Those Loving Differently]), which ran from June 1990 to May 2002, included everything from soft-porn visuals and personal ads to useful in-group information and thoughtful if necessarily brief articles. As cautious popular gay publications frequently do, its August 1995 issue contained what easily could be read as an anxious, if superfluous, validation of homosexuality by a short item ruminating on the renowned authors of the famous Skamander group, who numbered among Poland's many gay or bisexual *Kulturarbeiter*.[21] In fact, many of the country's most renowned writers were homosexual, some not bothering to hide their sexual inclinations: Bolesław Leśmian, Jarosław Iwaszkiewicz, Jan Lechoń, Tadeusz Breza, Witold Gombrowicz, Jerzy Andrzejewski, and Miron Białoszewski, plus eminent composer Karol Szymanowski.[22] The implicit assumption in the brief article is that such individuals' invaluable input into Poland's international reputation—Iwaszkiewicz's prose received state recognition and prompted a wide range of screen adaptations—indicates that homosexuality occupies a high cultural ground and should be exempt from prejudice. More recent developments, however, have abandoned such an approach, with cinema contributing to a less defensive concept of homosexuality as, inter alia, an unexceptionable phenomenon, albeit potentially rendered problematic in a homophobic, fundamentally Catholic milieu.

GAYNESS ON THE RECENT POLISH SCREEN

Polish cinema's portrayal of homosexuals has undergone a sea change in several recent films. Given Ewa Mazierska's cogent analysis of earlier relevant screen offerings on the phenomenon—all by male directors—as mostly uncomprehending or clichéd, or both,[23] I bypass them to focus on a trio of films released in the new millennium finally countering that mothballed trend: Izabella Cywińska's (b. 1935) *Kochankowie z Marony* (The Lovers from Marona),[24] Magdalena Piekorz's (b. 1974) *Senność* (Drowsiness/Torpor),[25] and Małgorzata Szumowska's (b. 1973) *W imię . . .* (In the Name of . . .). Countless polls and studies have verified women's greater acceptance of homosexuality than men's, and the female directors of the three films, as well as the reception of them, indicate that Poland is no exception to that international rule.[26] All three award-laden films portray homosexuals as simply decent human beings profoundly attached to other men. Inasmuch as the more recent the film, the more explicit and detailed its engagement with gay love, it makes sense to discuss them in chronological order and, in conclusion, to compare them with a recent male-directed film about a homosexual relationship—Tomasz Wasilewski's *Płynące wieżowce* (Floating Skyscrapers).

KOCHANKOWIE Z MARONY (THE LOVERS FROM MARONA 2005), IZABELLA CYWIŃSKA

Like several other Polish films (especially by Wajda[27]), *The Lovers from Marona* adapts an autobiographical novella (1961) by Iwaszkiewicz while simultaneously drawing on his diaries, which are remarkably frank about his homosexuality.[28] The relatively uneventful film focuses on the triangle of a young female schoolteacher, Ola, her fatally ill lover, Janek, a resident of a local TB sanatorium, and his close friend, Arek. The exiguous plot is based on what Iwaszkiewicz called his "last, greatest love" at the age of sixty-two—for Jerzy Błeszczyński—curtailed by the latter's death from tuberculosis.[29] A blog review by Ewa Bieńczycka somewhat puzzlingly accuses Cywińska's adaptation (as well as Wajda's screen versions of Iwaszkiewicz's prose) of vulgarity—in Cywińska's case, for purportedly addressing homosexuality explicitly—something Iwaszkiewicz opted for in his diaries but left implicit in his fiction: "In Iwaszkiewicz's literary text of *The Lovers from Marona* there are many insinuations pointing to Janek's and Arek's homosexual traces (*tropy*), but they are purposely only insinuated."[30] By contrast, the blurb on the DVD of the film claims, "A refined homosexual play goes on between the men" (Między mężczyznami toczy się wyrafinowana homoseksualna gra).[31] These are two marginally dissimilar viewpoints worth examining, particularly in light of the circumspect treatment of Arek's love for Janek by Cywińska, Poland's former Minister of Culture and Art (1989–1991) under Tadeusz Mazowiecki.[32]

Bieńczycka's accusation is puzzling, for the film opts for subtlety throughout, never plunging into explicitness. Though it unproblematically shows Ola (Karolina Gruszka) and Janek (Krzysztof Zawadzki) in bed, the sexual pull between the two men is confined to hugs, touching, and Arek's inability to stay away from Janek. At one point, Janek casually tells Ola that Arek (Łukasz Simlat) always comes back to him, but such a remark hardly qualifies as vulgarity and lacks sexual suggestiveness, for friendship could explain such a bond. The opening crosscutting between Ola's and Arek's spheres instantly establishes them as potential rivals for the sick protagonist's affections. Her rapturous classroom tribute to Icarus as she dictates to her unseen students Iwaszkiewicz's words about the fate of the youth (indicative of her romanticism and a proleptic symbol of her future beloved and his demise) contrasts to Arek's noisy (and, we later learn, repeated) motorcycle trip to visit Janek in the sanatorium.[33] As the film subsequently reveals, Janek is the object of desire not only for Ola and Arek, but also for the nurse Eufrozynia and Janek's wife, Basia—the latter remaining irrelevant until she appears at the close of the film and the novella, immediately before Janek dies. And the magnet for all is Janek's beauty, which seems an irresistible attraction regardless of gender, legality, and propriety. Passive and fatally ill, he nonetheless constitutes the magic center on which everyone and everything pivot.

With this concentration of erotic energy, grounded in aesthetics and directed at the consumptive, Janek tropes the inseparability of love and death—the *Liebestod* at the heart of both the literary and the cinematic text. Neither Janek nor Arek is framed as inverted (i.e., effeminate) or perverted. Both men are physically attractive: Iwaszkiewicz describes Janek as "piękny" (beautiful/handsome), with vivid, sapphire-blue eyes, and endows Arek with physical strength, a beautiful voice, and administrative as well as practical skills. His loud motorcycle, the first sound we hear in the film, while the camera captures a stunning landscape of winter mist and trees bordering a seemingly endless country lane, is the auditory announcement of his presence and via skillful audio-synchronization alternates with Ola's impassioned classroom recitation about the death of Icarus. This visually and thematically rich sequence introduces premature death, linking the romantic Ola and the masculine Arek as Janek's would-be lovers even before Ola meets both men. In short, while Cywińska, like Iwaszkiewicz, shows Ola and her "illicit" love edged out at the film's conclusion by socially sanctioned conjugal ties, neither Ola's nor Basia's relationship to Janek belittles Arek's love for him. Indeed, Ola and Arek's shared feelings for the consumptive draw them close; she even believes that Arek loves her, and before and after Janek's death he proves to be invested in taking care of Janek's family as well as the man himself.

Cywińska has said of her film:

> This film is a sort of laboratory of love. It's a story about universal love, on which no sexual option has a monopoly, for it's a feeling directed not so much at a woman or a man, but at a human being. Love for them is the only salvation – also in their struggles with death. It's given them to feel eternal, absolute love, which constructs their world, lends sense to life, is capable of everything. In short, it's a laboratory of love and death.[34]

(quoted in Pawluśkiewicz 2006)

The connection between love and death, in fact, lies at the core of the film, rendering it extraordinarily romantic, in a long series of tales about lovers willing to die for their immoderate passion. Icarus, after all, served as a warning about the failure to tread the golden mean by (literally) overreaching, recognizing no bounds.

Liebestod or Eros +Thanatos

What the film ultimately conveys is not a clichéd conflict between heterosexual and homosexual love, but a hierarchy of emotional/erotic power, with
Janek at its apex: as a discerning reviewer observed, he is passive beauty,
allowing others to love him,[35] not unlike a divinity or a lofty principle located
above the common run of humanity. That psychological-physical ranking
recalls Pasolini's film *Teorema* (1968/1969), in which "The Visitor" (a divine
presence, enacted by Terence Stamp) has sexual intimacy with all members
of a bourgeois family, male and female, thereby changing their lives forever.
Though Janek is far from divine, his status as the supreme object of desire
and yearning is beyond question. Desire (largely thwarted) rules the lives of
the film's personae. Whereas in Iwaszkiewicz's text, Ola comes upon him as
he sits on the ground, the film spatially establishes their relationship, locat-
ing him on a lookout platform at an elevated vantage point, as she gazes
enraptured up at him, while he looks down upon her with interest but little
else. Next in the hierarchy of emotional/erotic power comes Ola, then Arek,
followed by Janek's wife and Eufrozynia, then the boy Józio, clearly in love
with Ola. At the bottom of this ladder is Józio's dog, Picuś, whom Józio
drowns after misunderstanding a careless comment by Ola. *Liebestod* as
an existential given eliminates both man and dog. Relative locations within
frames and the length of visual focus allotted characters emphasize their
placement in this hierarchy.

Pointedly, at one juncture Cywińska has Ola declare, "Love is as strong
as death," and Janek explicitly and irrationally expects her love for him to
perform a miraculous prophylactic function. Yet, though love may challenge death, it also may conduce to it: Picuś dies not only because of his
fidelity and trust in Józio but also because of the latter's love for Ola, while
Janek's final minutes are triggered by a fatal hemorrhage after the two lovers
enjoy sexual intimacy. Eros and Thanatos, as in Andrzej Wajda's *Brzezina*
(The Birchwood 1970), likewise adapted from a narrative by Iwaszkiewicz,
merge. Love in *The Lovers from Marona* ultimately proves impotent vis-à-
vis mortality—indeed, seems inseparable from it—and plays out in tragic
ways for all concerned in a film that celebrates love and refuses to degrade
its homosexual variant. There is no doubt that Arek, with his commitment to
Janek, will fulfill his promise to take care of the dead man's widow and son.
After all, the narrative gives us to understand that he has been embedded in
Janek's life for quite a while, and all his actions and statements confirm his
loyalty to the man he has loved. Tellingly, while Ola is barred from Janek's
deathbed, Arek attends his last moments as virtually a member of the family
and its future caretaker, according to Janek's instructions. Nothing scandalous or perverse attaches to Arek, who conveys stability and dependability

throughout the narrative and who will serve as the bulwark for Janek's family after his beloved's death. In a sense, Cywińska domesticates homosexual love, casting it as familial rather than as an "unnatural" threat to a heterosexually based family.

Never deviating from the central issue of *Liebestod*, Cywińska's film features not only several modes of love but also half a dozen deaths in sundry forms. Opening with the motif of death in Ola's recital of the fate of the mythical Icarus, whose unbridled aspirations occasioned his fatal downfall, it then shows a man at the TB sanatorium die, attended by Janek. Subsequently, a fish and the dog Picuś (whose offscreen death is reported) perish; vigorously proliferating mushrooms are annihilated by Józio, and, finally, Janek expires. In short, death is the thematic *ostinato* of the film, always in the background but brought to the fore at strategic narrative moments. While love propels the plot, death lies in wait throughout its development in a narrative focused on various instances of love. In that respect *The Lovers from Marona* recalls Andre Gide's *L'immoraliste* (1902) and Thomas Mann's "Der Tod in Venedig" (1912) and *Der Zauberberg* (1924), as well as Richard Wagner's opera *Tristan und Isolde* (1859/1865). All evoke the Romeo-and-Juliet scenario, which casts passionate love and death as indivisible.

TRIUMPH OF GAY LOVE: *SENNOŚĆ* (DROWSINESS/ TORPOR 2008), MAGDALENA PIEKORZ

Unlike *The Lovers from Marona*, with its echo of Shakespearian love-death, Piekorz's *Torpor*, which received enthusiastic audience responses but left critics less satisfied, interweaves three significantly more down-to-earth plotlines, linked by the protagonists' psychological lethargy, from which all of them eventually emerge. In a strikingly original move, the quasi-portmanteau film juxtaposes the homosexual narrative to two depictions of quietly vicious heterosexual marriages. One limns a faithless, pragmatic businessman (Michał Żebrowski) manipulating a vulnerable, affluent actress-wife, Róża (Małgorzata Kożuchowska), who genuinely loves him, while the other focuses on a hysterically dependent, incessantly nagging woman, Anna (Joanna Pierzak), whom the success-seeking writer Robert (Krzysztof Zawadzki) married for her father's social and political status. To emerge from their torpor the miserable wife, suffering from narcolepsy, needs to recollect the shock of discovering her deceitful spouse's infidelity and throw him out, while the frustrated husband needs to escape from his insufferable spouse and in-laws so as write the novel that he has been unable to produce under the stifling circumstances of his oppressive marriage. At dramatic variance with these two mirrored situations is the appreciably less conventional plot of the homosexual relationship.

This unusual narrative begins by establishing the stifling parental affection that suffocates Adam (Rafał Maćkowiak), a newly qualified young doctor, whose proud provincial parents have planned his future life, complete with the house they have arranged for him. Against all odds, he manages to jettison his familial burden under the influence of his gay neighbor and patient—an agile, good-natured hoodlum nicknamed Bystry (Smart), played by Bartosz Obuchowicz, who astutely called their onscreen love "a typical Romeo and Juliet story"—but with a happy conclusion. Indeed, the two men's amorous union equally appalls the Montague-like thuggish gang who replace family for Bystry, and Adam's father (Andrzej Grabowski) as the overbearing Capulet, though the mother (Dorota Pomykała) may be more tolerant, were she to know of her son's sexual orientation, which her husband withholds from her.

After Adam and Bystry become lovers, the latter publicly disavows their relationship, cognizant that the street toughs who are his regular companions will subject both to violent beatings, if not worse, in a neighborhood of Śląsk/Silesia that is crime-ridden, down-at-heel, and radically homophobic—working-class Poland. Yet ultimately the two overcome the odds, and end up together in the home of Adam's parents, presumably prepared to live in the house nearby that Adam earlier rejected.

Unlike Cywińska, Piekorz treats the gay relationship and prejudice against it in explicit terms. She does not hesitate to show Bystry naked when Adam's affectionate but insensitive father unexpectedly visits his son and has the shock of his limited life, nor to film the young couple in bed, with a sleeping Bystry embracing Adam once the latter joins him there. The camerawork makes it clear that the bond between the two is both sexual and emotional, as well as freely chosen in a bid for personal happiness. Close-ups of a tearful Bystry nestling against Adam's shoulder or trying to stem the blood from the gashes on Adam's face administered by his vicious sidekicks communicate the depth of the seemingly rough Bystry's feelings for the man who has surmounted the torpor in the film's title, to embrace his inconvenient but genuine sexual identity. As the director herself has observed, Adam "discovers his identity, his real self, and takes the first serious step towards being true to himself. And this is what the film is about—that it's worth being true to yourself in life. The sooner you start acting in accordance with your own conscience and morals, instead of acting against them, the easier it becomes to achieve genuine happiness."[36] Self-knowledge and the strength to act according to its demands trump adherence to the dictates of social conventions and the constraints of acceptability.

Responses to Piekorz's treatment of the gay relationship in this plotline of the film were largely laudatory. In a review devoid of moralistic bromides, Paulina Kwas rightly deemed the Adam-Bystry relationship the most convincing, expressive, and visually projected ("liryczny i subtelnie erotyczny") of the three narratives, contrasting to the heterosexual stories that intersect at several junctures.[37] Her positive view was shared by Paulina Luciak on another site.[38] Interestingly, unlike the homosexual relationship, the two heterosexual conjugal contracts in the film resolve in divorce in one case, and death in the other. The psychologically abused and deluded wife finally rids herself of her dastardly husband, and the writer manages not only to leave his egocentric wife and in-laws, but also finally to write a best-selling novel. Zawadzki, playing the disillusioned, henpecked husband here, yet again is effective as a man doomed to an early death, this time from cancer. One could argue that one of the film's few weaknesses somewhat unconvincingly has Róża, the formerly deluded wife, establish trusting relations with him before his death in an *amor ex machina*. More importantly, however, in *Torpor* homosexual ties surpass their heterosexual counterpart, chiefly because Adam and Bystry are joined by love, not by pragmatic considerations of the sort exposed in the two radically mismatched yet socially sanctioned marriages. A loving intimacy that defies social prejudice surpasses the stereotypical conjugal union, often sought for reasons other than sincere feelings.

Piekorz does not idealize the gay couple's relationship: Bystry originally betrays Adam by denying their bond and ignoring his lover. Moreover, to escape the hostile violence of Bystry's former buddies the two men have to flee town and find refuge in the countryside with Adam's parents—hardly an ideal arrangement. And the final sequence, in which Adam's father, in silent but unmistakable revulsion at the couple, abandons the table at which Adam and his parents have been eating, leaves no doubt that life for the two lovers will be far from easy. In short, what happiness the two may have attained has necessitated painful effort and seems likely to involve struggle in the future. Similarly, Robert dies soon after his professional success, and Róża is left alone. In other words, Piekorz wisely sidesteps the facile solutions that European filmmakers identify with the Hollywood happy ending.

Somewhat unexpectedly, she cleverly shoots the narrative of the two heterosexual relationships in standard color, but the contrastive gay affair in subdued hues that border on bluish-black and white, with a handheld camera. Such a choice allies the gay segment of the film with documentary, or, as one critic opined, "social realism,"[39] as if normalizing it and simultaneously implying its social status as commonplace or under the radar—something necessarily outside the instantly visible. Partly as a result, the gay relationship has struck viewers as more realistically portrayed or, as Kwas observes, visually projected.

THE SEEMING WOLF IN CATHOLIC SHEEP'S CLOTHING: *W IMIĘ* . . . (IN THE NAME OF . . . 2013), MAŁGORZATA SZUMOWSKA

While Piekorz surpasses Cywińska in explicitness, Szumowska ups the ante by choosing to portray a gay priest in a conservatively Catholic country at a time when charges of inappropriate behavior on the part of clergy at various rungs of the church hierarchy have received considerable media attention. A director avowedly centered on the body and its sexual praxis, Szumowska dramatizes the unavailing battle with his sexual desires of the significantly named Adam (Andrzej Chyra, who won the Gdynia Złote Lwy [Golden Lions] award for best actor).[40] Chyra excels as a priest with a strong social conscience devoted to his "parish" at the detention center in the provincial village within the Mazury region to which he has been transferred from Warsaw (for reasons disclosed quite late in the film).[41] From the outset, Szumowska shows him enjoying positive relations with his coworker, the teacher Michał (again, played by Simlat—Arek in Cywińska's film and the husband in *Fugue*), and the foul-mouthed, young male delinquents with whom he bonds through kindness, sport, and work, in the rural retreat intended for their rehabilitation. The impressively high frequency of *kurwa* (whore) and *pierdolić* (to fuck) in the film constitutes only one measure of that rehabilitation's desirability.[42]

Like his namesake's in *Torpor*, however, Adam's mode of life is tested by a local youth who participates in the center's activities, the reputed pyromaniac Łukasz Szczepan "Dynia"[43] (Mateusz Kościukiewicz). The latter's first, obliging response to Adam's request that someone help him with a girl in convulsions prepares the viewer for what subsequently develops: Łukasz comes to love Adam, defends his reputation, and in a remarkable scene prompts the priest to reveal his "animal side" as the two communicate through primal, simian mating calls "in nature"[44]—a cornfield so thick with greenery that it is impossible for Adam to locate Łukasz.

Adam sublimates his homosexual desires by running, tries to douse them by excessive drinking,[45] gently rejects the overtures of Michał's disappointed wife, the over-symbolically named Ewa (Maja Ostaszewska), and through Skype directly speaks to his sister in Toronto of the conflict between his calling and his homosexuality—an acknowledgment that she hastily dismisses. Once the enamored Łukasz pursues him at his new residence, however, he succumbs.

Before we see Adam finally cede to his sexual/amorous urges, Szumowska makes a concerted and largely successful effort to sacralize the love between him and Łukasz: in addition to borrowing the names of the heterosexual couple in the Garden of Eden, she adopts various religious symbols, such as Adam's position during sleep, which copies Mantegna's foreshortened painting of the dead Christ (*Lamentation of Christ* 1480);[46] Adam's embrace of Łukasz in a Pietà-like pose after he bathes the wounds inflicted by the latter's violent peers; and his swimming lesson at Łukasz's request, in which he "baptizes" the youth.[47] While such a diffusion of associations with Christ between the two may strike the viewer as inconsistent, it effectively joins them in the suffering of homosexuals in a hyperbolically macho environment comprising male teenagers who compete with one another in exhibitions of toxic masculinity.[48]

For much of the film the audience witnesses Adam's intense struggles with his sexuality, and his proper behavior vis-à-vis Ewa, Łukasz, and the unruly young thugs over whom he exerts an imperfect but steadying influence. He remains a passive and concerned respondent to Łukasz's silent overtures until the film's end, when the two men engage in sexual intimacy on Adam's mattress. Significantly, the camera focuses on their positions as face-to-face, in contrast to the anal intercourse Adam earlier witnesses between two of the delinquents. To underscore the contrast between the two "couples," soon after the latter episode the youth sodomized by the nasty newcomer, Adrian/Blondie (Tomasz Schuchardt), commits suicide, whereas "the morning after" reveals Adam and Łukasz smiling affectionately at each other as they lie on the mattress and the younger man caresses Adam's face. Neither betrays any hint of regret or guilt.

The last extended shot of the film leads viewers to understand that some time has lapsed, for it shows several seminarians in cassocks, among them Łukasz. Presumably, his love and admiration for Adam have led him to follow his choice of profession or possibly may suggest that Catholic priesthood is an ideal refuge for men hiding their homosexuality from the world. In other words, the conclusion, which has drawn criticism from various quarters, is ambiguous: on the one hand, we may come away thinking that homosexual love does not diminish a priest's effectiveness and may even swell the ranks of Catholic priesthood. Such an implication is anathema to Catholicism, but may strike some viewers as humane. On the other hand, *The Irish Times* review noted, "The closing sequence points toward a dark and vicious cycle,"[49] one, supposedly, in which hypocrisy thrives. Yet the camera through repeated POV shots, as well as Chyra's universally acclaimed performance, solicits audience identification with and sympathy for him. As *The Hollywood Reporter* declared, "The proximity of the sacred and the profane in his [Adam's] ministry makes him at once a magnetic authority figure with a real vocation and a fragile fellow much in need of a hug."[50] And an insightful reviewer stated:

What's implied by the final shot is that Polish society or simply the culture in this particular area might be so homophobic that the only avenue for a gay man who might not have the means of escaping on his own is to join the priesthood. The homophobia or uber-machismo is established early on with shots of the teen boys being so aggressive. For Adam and Lucasz [*sic*] the option in the end can't be expression. It's only suppression. It's why Szumowska's final shots are the most tragic and the most haunting.[51]

In one of her many interviews, Szumowska has claimed, "ironia i sarkazm—to klucz do moich filmów" (irony and sarcasm are the key to my films)[52] and precisely that approach to her materials is what leads me to think that *In the Name of*. . . mounts a strong critique of Polish Catholicism and machismo, while embracing homosexuality as one of humans' completely acceptable and understandable, albeit socially stigmatized, ways of loving. This is surely why the film seems simultaneously so extraordinary yet so "natural." Indeed, as in *Torpor*, heterosexual marriage—such as Michał and Ewa's—is exposed as so empty or insufficiently fulfilling for the woman that she seeks sexual satisfaction from a priest who is, moreover, her husband's colleague. Neither Adam nor Łukasz is shown attempting sexual congress with anyone else other than the one to whom each man's profound attraction is cast as a form of incipient and finally realized love. Szumowska's insistence that the film is about loneliness is borne out by the psychology and conduct of all the major characters, particularly Adam. Both he and Łukasz, who completely lacks connection with his rough family, overcome that loneliness through a singular, hard-won, and genuine love.

THE MALE VIEW: *PŁYNĄCE WIEŻOWCE* (FLOATING SKYSCRAPERS 2013), TOMASZ WASILEWSKI

To juxtapose these three films by female directors with the award-winning *Floating Skyscrapers* by Wasilewski (b. 1980), known for his *Zjednoczone Stany Miłości* (United States of Love 2016), is instructive. Touted as "the most interesting voice in the young Polish directing scene,"[53] Wasilewski arrogantly claimed in an interview, "I can't think of a Polish movie, which [*sic*] spoke of homosexuals seriously"—until his, of course.[54] Either ignorant of the films by Cywińska and Piekorz (*In the Name of*. . . was released the same year as his film) or wishing to seem more original than he is, Wasilewski not only proclaimed his film as the first to address gay issues but also apparently found sympathy with audiences, for at festivals he garnered a variety of awards for the film and his work as director. According to one Polish critic, Wasilewski "blazed a new trail. He showed homosexual characters as full-fledged dramatic heroes."[55] Yet female directors had pioneered that "trail" before him, and in terms devoid of the clichés that Wasilewski failed to circumvent.

In a wittily crushing review for *The Guardian*, Jack Cullen, having watched a BFI festival of short gay films in 2013, identified "the top 10 gay movie clichés": "artistic shots of trees; the ironing mother; scenes of gratuitous rage; the long and unexplained shower scene; beautiful eyes staring into the distance; the heartwrenching piano score; an introspective fag break [presumably, no pun intended HG]; the generic clubbing scene; a firm body filmed very slowly in close-up; complex acknowledgements."[56] *Floating Skyscrapers* subscribes to only half of these, but when juxtaposed with the three women-directed films analyzed above, it seems sufficiently clichéd for one to wonder why it earned any award or claims to originality.[57] As an American art critic put it, "For many years, gay characters in films were doomed to die a gruesome death. Whether they were brutally murdered or a tree fell on them, death was the only logical methodology for dealing with the existence of a living, breathing onscreen homosexual."[58] Regrettably, Wasilewski's belongs to that formulaic category.

By comparison with both *The Lovers from Marona* and *Torpor*, as well as Szumowska's film, *Floating Skyscrapers* is fragmented and unconvincing, its treatment of homosexuality following the well-trodden path of a male's gradual transition from a heterosexual bond to a gay one. Moreover, the symmetrical contrastive treatment of the two male protagonists—the gifted swimmer Kuba (Mateusz Banasiuk) and the student Michał (Bartosz Gelner)—is reductive: the morose, laconic, and unpleasant Kuba ("something of a lout as well as an emotional and intellectual cipher"[59]) lives with his compliant female lover, Sylwia (Marta Nieradkiewicz) and domineering mother (Ewa [Katarzyna Herman]) in the latter's house, while the agreeable, outgoing student, Michał, resides with his sympathetic mother (Iza Kuna) and remote father (Mirosław Zbrojewicz). Whereas Kuba "discovers" that he is gay, Michał not only accepts his romantic/sexual orientation from the outset but frankly informs his mother of his homosexuality, of which she already is fully aware. With gentle solicitude she merely asks her son whether he loves Kuba, whereas upon learning of the two men's involvement, Ewa bullies him into ending the relationship so as to marry Sylwia, who, it suddenly transpires, is pregnant. In short, the film embraces the all too familiar binarism of Jung's negative and positive maternal archetypes,[60] the black swan versus the white swan, the witch/bitch versus the Madonna, and so forth throughout the ages.

These superficial contrasts presumably are intended to substitute for genuine insight into human psychology. As a perceptive review of the film noted, "One of the weaknesses of the film is that while Kuba convincingly comes across as a closeted, self-loathing gay man, his sudden declaration of love for Michał at the one-hour mark seems out of character." More importantly, "their relationship is shown to revolve around physical desire; we never get to hear their conversations or find out what makes the not particularly likable

Kuba tick"[61]—surprising in a film that the director avowedly believes is about "the search for intimacy" between protagonists whom he describes as "complex personalities."[62] Silence and omission do not equate to complexity. Bewilderingly, Wasilewski announced that his film "portrays Kuba most of all as a human being. Okay, he's homosexual but that's not what's most important about him. Kuba is a son and a swimmer. He has his own dreams and he's got a girlfriend" (Heymont). This rather absurd and incoherent statement simply is not borne out by the film, for, as yet another commentator has noted: "our leads seem unknowable, unreachable even. Kuba and Mikal [*sic*] grow closer and closer, but what appears to be love is only captured through lust, the duo rarely exchanging any meaningful words."[63]

Skill in composition, excellent underwater shots, eloquent lighting and audio effects can compensate only so much for the lack of depth in the film's male characters and a stereotypical presentation of homosexuality as furtive anal intercourse in the dark between a crude macho athlete and an effeminate student, whose gullibility facilitates his death by three homophobic toughs. That abrupt savage turn in the plot is sufficiently arbitrary to have led a reviewer to believe, erroneously, that "Michal offers himself up like a sacrificial lamb to a group of local thugs who delight in bashing queers" (Heymont).

Ultimately, the film dwells too long on the self-obsessed, asocial Kuba (it is no accident that we hear him experiencing an orgasm, presumably via fellatio in the swimming pool's lockers, before he actually appears on screen) and too little on meaningful interaction with Michał. In fact, Wasilewski's sequences of Kuba and Sylwia's romps in bed convey a greater emotional tie than the single shot of Kuba's furtively sodomizing his male "beloved." Wasilewski's lauded minimalism and privileging of the image over the word do not serve him well in the film, at least as regards the depiction of homosexual love, for the two men's relations receive no revelatory attention and his images focus on the sexual rather than the emotionally affectionate that *Torpor* and *In the Name of...* portray so eloquently. In light of Wasilewski's choices, viewers would be forgiven if they interpreted homosexuality in the film in overwhelmingly or even exclusively physical terms. Panting, grunts, and a single declaration of love hardly persuade viewers that homosexuality transcends anal intercourse, male fellatio, and onanism, even if all these phenomena are orchestrated with technological skill.

Vive la différence?

Whereas the films by Piekorz and Szumowska spotlight a flawed society's acceptance and conventionalization of violent machismo as a definition of manhood against which homosexual love is portrayed as simply human and optimally capable of resisting or overcoming such destructive social constructs, Wasilewski's film follows cinematic stereotypes by dwelling on savage intolerance and the dark side of gay love, which inexorably ends in betrayal and death. His stereotyping differs from that in earlier films by male directors such as Treliński, which equate homosexuality with effeminate mannerisms and failed relationships, but it adheres to the cinematic clichés ironized by Cullen and identifies homosexuality as a dead end, both figuratively and literally.

All four films under discussion appeared in liberal post-socialist Poland before PiS came to power (2015), and a question worth asking is whether directors—male or female—now would risk undertaking projects that depict homosexuality sympathetically against the background of sexual discrimination in Poland. Of current directors, Smarzowski in such films as *Wesele* (The Wedding 2004), *Róża* (Rose 2011), *Wołyń* (Volhynia 2016), and *Kler* (Clergy 2018) has proved the boldest in exposing the underbelly of the country's vaunted myths, but it is unlikely that he will turn his merciless eye to the disquieting circumstances of Polish homosexuals.[64] And, of course, the topic poses a greater challenge and potential threat to male directors than to their female counterparts. Perhaps that explains why thus far Poland's female directors have demonstrated greater sensitivity to and empathy for gay males in their films, as well as developing absorbing plotlines and elaborating credible characters that ultimately encourage audiences' understanding of homosexuality as merely another mode of loving. A comparably enlightened film about gay love by a Polish male director has yet to appear.

American cinematic depictions of homosexuality have been numerous, some overlapping with the stereotypical efforts ironized by Jack Cullen. Perhaps two fairly recent films suggest the wide range of possible perspectives on male gayness as conceived by Hollywood in the twenty-first century. *Boy Erased* (2017) adopts a mixed if somewhat reductionist view of the phenomenon. Its young protagonist, Jared Eamons (Lucas Hedges), struggles to come to terms with his homosexuality and has the emotional if uninformed support of his loving but not overly bright mother, Nancy (Nicole Kidman). Though struggling to understand her son, she subordinates herself to her authoritarian, narrow-minded Baptist husband, Marshall (a fat and generally repellent Russell Crowe), who cannot countenance homosexuality, and certainly not his son's sexual orientation. Above all, the film (rather simplistically) exposes conversion therapy as a criminal endeavor but redeems its narrative through the final sequence of Jared's triumph in surviving his family's conservative prejudices, making a success of his life, confronting his father, and forging a life with his lover as a successful fledgling writer in New York. The film's conclusion comes saccharinely close to the Hollywood "happy ending" that Europeans deride, but enough questions remain open so that audiences can appreciate the uphill climb that homosexuality entails, especially in the southern, conservative, religious part of the United States.

By stark contrast, the unusual and beguiling romantic comedy by Mike Mills, *Beginners* (2010), tackles not only homosexuality, but its pleasures experienced by Hal, a man in his seventies (a superb Christopher Plummer), who for decades led a heterosexual life, sired a son, and only acknowledged his sexual orientation after his wife's death. His last years recalled by his shy, isolated designer son, Oliver (Ewan McGregor), and Hal's honesty about his love of men (especially his affectionate younger male lover) inspire his hesitant son to pursue his attraction to a female French actress, Anna (Mélanie Laurent). Avoiding vapid sentimentalism, the film privileges decency and integrity in familial and sexual bonds while showcasing the rich emotional possibilities of father-son relations. In fact, Plummer convincingly portrays emotional generosity and commitment as desiderata in "romantic" relationships no different from paternal-filial ties. One could argue that *Beginners* (a title relevant to both father and son) avoids all sorts of problematic issues— retirees' ill health, society's inimical attitude toward both homosexuality and older people's interest in (and capacity for!) sex, and sons' competition with fathers, but the film is more interested in examining precisely the neglected topics of older men's homosexuality and its role in father-son relations. Poland, obviously, will have to wait quite a while before films begin exploring such dynamics, for virtually any cultural genre dealing with aspects of homosexuality is too explosive during the current rule of PiS for directors to risk addressing it.

CATHOLICISM AND HOMOSEXUALITY—A DEVIL'S CONTRACT OR A SAFE HARBOR?

In the meantime, the publication of *Sodoma*, a self-consciously startling and highly controversial study by the French journalist Frédéric Martel, arraigns the Vatican and the Catholic Church in general as a hotbed of homosexuality. Translated into English as *In the Closet of the Vatican: Power, Homosexuality, Hypocrisy* (2019), and simultaneously released in Poland as *Sodoma. Hipokryzja i władza w Watykanie* (Agora Press),[65] the 500-plus-page series of tawdry "revelations" based on numerous alleged interviews (though containing no footnotes) discusses the regular reliance of the Vatican's alleged numerous homosexuals on prostitutes, their longstanding affairs with fellow ordained personnel (bishops and cardinals), and especially the conservative Polish Pope John Paul II's (1920–2005) so-called homophilia even as he excoriated abortion, the use of condoms, same-sex marriage, extra-marital affairs, and gay coupling. Martel's undifferentiated thesis, developed and iterated in granular detail, is that impassioned public denunciations of homosexuality by elite Catholic representatives almost automatically signal closet gayness.

Amazingly, the Polish leading daily *Gazeta Wyborcza*, acclaimed Martel's volume as "probably one of the best books by a journalist ever written," whereas detractors justifiably have deplored its self-indulgent length, turgid, gossipy prose, and lack of scholarly apparatus. Unencumbered by discipline and objectivity, Martel tirelessly iterates his thesis without refining it to take even basic human diversity into account.[66] Whatever its drawbacks, however, the pertinence of this questionable tome to Szumowska's *In the Name of . . .* is immediately apparent and made explicit by the author when he quotes the Spanish former priest José Manuel Vidal, one of his purported interviewees in Madrid. Vidal asserts that "for many young homosexuals [in Spain], the priesthood seemed like the only solution against persecution. Many became priests. That was the key, the rule, the model."[67]

A thoughtful critic of the book demurred, "Although Martel himself is openly gay, he sensationalizes gayness by devoting his inquiry to Catholic officials who have had sex with men, not ones who have had sex with women."[68] Establishing to what extent Pope John Paul II was secretly homophilic while he publicly elaborated draconian anti-gay proscriptions is a considerable challenge, but what is relevant to my discussion is how what Martel describes coincides with aspects of Szumowska's film. *In the Name of . . .* makes all too clear that Adam's transfer has been the Catholic Church's "solution" to allegations of sexual impropriety on priests' part, and the screen bishop's response to Michał's report about Adam's inappropriate behavior with Łukasz is to move him elsewhere yet again and to emphasize how effectively and committedly Adam works with parishioners. Łukasz, possibly one of many gay seminarians, will be able to flourish in the Catholic Church, even if his sexual activities will lead to a mode of life marked by professional peregrinations to avoid scandal. Though Szumowska, unlike Martel, hardly presents the Catholic Church as a beehive of homosexual promiscuity, her film's conclusion does imply that it may function as a sanctuary for gay priests unable or unwilling to settle for celibacy. Unlike Smarzowski in *Clergy*, she tackles not sexual abuse of altar boys but consensual intercourse between men committed to "the service of God." By comparison with *Clergy* and its emphases, her treatment of the topic is not only restrained but also profoundly sympathetic. The Polish Catholic Church nonetheless could hardly be expected to endorse either film, both of which in their different ways demonstrate the need to reexamine the laws and caveats imposed upon "God's servants" within Poland's historico-religious repository of the nation's traditional values.

HG

NOTES

1. "50 Best Gay Movies: The Best in LGBT + Filmmaking," https://www.time-out.com/london/film/the-50-best-gay-movies-the-best-in-lgbt-film-making. Accessed November 21, 2017.

2. On the relationship of the director and Cruz (touted as his muse), see https://www.theguardian.com/film/2009/aug/23/almodovar-cruz-film-interview. Accessed August 5, 2018.

3. Obviously, countries in the region do not have identical attitudes to LGBTQ issues, and urban centers such as Berlin and Budapest stand out for their liberal views, by contrast with Moscow and Kyiv, though since 2017 Ukraine has softened its rigid stance on homosexuality.

4. Indeed, under Communism, Poland published two gay magazines, for which the Soviet Union, which criminalized homosexuality, lacked counterparts. And though homosexuality became decriminalized after the implosion of the Soviet state, under the obsessively "macho" Putin, both official dicta and much of the population continue to express virulently homophobic attitudes. For an original and highly stimulating analysis of post-Soviet Russian cultural production about homosexuality, see Brian James Baer, *Other Russias: Homosexuality and the Crisis of Post-Soviet Identity* (New York: Palgrave/Macmillan, 2009). For a list of Polish LGBTQ films over several decades, see https://www.imdb.com/list/ls055150286/. Accessed August 3, 2018.

5. Among her many publications and television interviews, see Agnieszka Graff's sophisticated article titled "Looking at Pictures of Gay Men: Political Uses of Homophobia in Contemporary Poland," *Public Culture* 22, no. 3 (Fall 2010): 583–603.

6. On May 17, 2019, Taiwan became the twenty-eighth country to legalize same-sex marriage, and was the first Asian country to do so. Both Spain and Ireland, dominantly Catholic countries, approved such marriages in 2005 and 2015, respectively. Like Poland, Italy has not joined the international group.

7. A 2019 opinion poll found that 56 percent of Poles do not oppose civil partnerships between gays, albeit only 18 percent support adoption by gay couples. Marc Santora, "Poland's Populists Pick a New Top Enemy: Gay People," *New York Times*, April 7, 2019, https://www.nytimes.com/2019/04/07/world/europe/poland-gay-rights.html. Accessed July 31, 2019.

8. Vanessa Gera, "Polish President Calls LGBT 'Ideology' Worse Than Communism," June 13, 2020, https://apnews.com/72fab166f1cfd02794c9add62247960e. Accessed June 14, 2020.

9. Ibid. In May 2019 conservative supporters of PiS gathered in one of the major heavily trafficked centers in Warsaw, at the intersection of Aleji Jerozolimskie and Marszalkowska, with leaflets and microphones, loudly urging passersby to resist the "sexualization of children," that is, to condemn LGBT rights. (Personal observation during a research stay in Warsaw in late April and early May.) See also "Poland's Ruling Party Confronts the 'LGBT Dictatorship,' " *The Economist*, May 4–May 10, 2019, 23.

10. Ibid.

11. Cited by Tom Hundley, "Poland's Gays Awake to a New Era," reproduced by Richard Ammon, GLOBALGAYZ.COM, 2006, https://www.globalgayz.com/poland -s-gays-awake-gradually-to-a-new-era/251/. Accessed July 12, 2018.

12. From the thirteenth century, Poland was renowned as one of the most liberal countries in Europe, particularly regarding Jews, who found both religious tolerance and economic opportunity not afforded them elsewhere.

13. Jonathan Luxmoore, "Clerical Power Thwarts Victims in Poland," *National Catholic Reporter,* February 8, 2012, https://www.ncronline.org/news/accountability /clerical-power-thwarts-victims-poland. Accessed August 7, 2018.

14. Marcin Goclowski, "Movie about Corrupt Priests Outrages Politicians in Catholic Poland," Reuters, September 28, 2018, https://www.reuters.com/article/us -poland-religion-movie/movie-about-corrupt-priests-outrages-politicians-in-catholic -poland-idUSKCN1M82FR. Accessed June 7, 2019.

15. Soraya Sarhaddi Nelson, "For Poland's Gay Community, A Shift in Public Attitudes, if Not Laws," NPR, June 25, 2015, https://www.npr.org/sections/paral-lels/2015/06/25/417446107/for-polands-gay-community-a-shift-in-public-attitudes-if -not-laws. Accessed September 20, 2017.

16. Editorial Board, "In Poland, the Limits of Solidarity," *New York Times,* January 22, 2019, https://www.nytimes.com/2019/01/22/opinion/gdansk-mayor-mur-der.html?action=click&module= Opinion&pgtype=Homepage. Accessed January 24, 2019.

17. Tara John and Muhammad Darwish, "LGBTQ Pride Parade in Bialystok, Poland, Met by Far Right Attacks," CNN, July 21, 2019, https://www.cnn.com/2019 /07/21/europe/bialystok-polish-lgbtq-pride-intl/index.html. Accessed July 23, 2019.

18. Derek Scally, "Robert Biedron Is Latest Political Hope of Poland's Left," *The Irish Times*, February 4, 2019, https://www.irishtimes.com/news/world/europe/rob-ert-biedron-is-latest-political-hope-of-poland-s-left-1.3781863. Accessed April 25, 2019. A poll conducted in early May 2019 saw PiS maintaining 39 percent of support, liberal Warsaw Mayor Rafał Trzaskowski's Civic Platform party with 33 percent, and Wiosna attracting only 8 percent of voters. *The Economist*, May 4, 2019, 45.

19. For instance, the Polish Catholic publication *Więz* (Link) actually devoted one of its issues to homosexuality. See ft. 11.

20. For additional information see Lukasz Szulc, *Transnational Homosexualism in Communist Poland* (Cham, Switzerland: Palgrave Macmillan/Springer International Publishing, 2018). For information about these and other publications, see especially chapter 1 in the volume, 123–154.

21. *Magazyn Kochających Inaczej* 8, no. 62 (August 1995).

22. Richard Ammon, "A Brief History of Gay Poland," GLOBALGAYZ ahttps:// www.globalgayz.com/a-brief-history-of-gay-poland/ provides a wealth of informa-tion about past and current gay culture in Poland. It draws on John D. Stanley, *An Encyclopedia of Gay, Lesbian, Bisexual, Transgender, and Queer Culture–Poland.*

23. These include Andrzej Wajda's *Ziemia obiecana* (The Promised Land 1975), Andrzej Domalik's *Zygfryd* (Siegfried 1987), Filip Bajon's *Magnat* (1987), Mariusz Treliński's *Egoiści* (Egoists 2000), and Andrzej Barański's *Parę osób, mały czas*

(Several People, Little Time 2005). Ewa Mazierska, *Masculinities in Polish, Czech and Slovak Cinema* (New York, Oxford: Berghahn Books, 2008): 177–87, 192–212. A recent superficial chapter given to listing in an otherwise fine volume myopically fails to distinguish between earlier, conventional treatments of homosexuality, such as Treliński's, and post-socialist attempts to overcome such belittling portraits through a nuanced understanding, such as Cywińska's *Kochankowie z Marony* (The Lovers of Marona). See Anita Piotrkowska, "Is Poland a woman? Feminist and homosexual Themes in Polish film from 1989–2009," in *Polish Cinema Now! Focus on Contemporary Polish Cinema*, ed. Mateusz Werner (London and Warsaw: John Libbey Publishing-Adam Mickiewicz Institute, 2010), 104–128, specifically 124.

24. Nominated for two other awards, the film won the main actress, Karolina Gruszka, an award for best actress at the Polish Film Festival in Gdynia in 2005.

25. Existent translations include *Somnolence* and *Drowsiness*, but neither renders the crucial psychological inability or unwillingness to struggle out of a dead-end situation, which lies at the center of the film. Piekorz's debut film, *Pręgi* (Welts 2004), like her subsequent *Zbliżenia* (Close-ups/Close Relations 2014), offers a fearless, sensitive examination of relations between family generations and their psychological consequences.

26. Note, for instance, the preponderance of women in the struggle with prejudice against LGBT in Poland's major cities, such as the roles of psychologist Marta Kosinka and Marta Abramowicz in Gdansk, Marianna Szczygielska and Mirosława Makuchowska in Warsaw, which opened a homeless center for LGBT teens (Nelson). For men's greater homophobia in the West, see David A. Moskowitz, Gerulf Rieger, and Michael E. Roloff, "Heterosexual Attitudes towards Same-Sex Marriage," NCBI, October 14, 2016, https://www.ncbi.nlm.nih.gov/pmc/articles/PMC5065072/. Accessed December 11, 2017.

27. Three narratives by Iwaszkiewicz served as sources of Wajda's *Brzezina* (Birch Wood 1970), *Panny z Wilka* (Maidens of Wilko 1979), and *Tatarak* (Sweet Rush 2007). Jerzy Kawalerowicz also adapted an Iwaszkiewicz text for his *Matka Joanna od Aniołów* (Mother Joan of the Angels 1961).

28. Joanna Pawluśkiewicz, December 2006, https://culture.pl/pl/dzielo/kochankowie-z-marony. Accessed November 7, 2017. A screen version of the novella appeared in 1966, directed by Jerzy Zarzycki. Iwaszkiewicz is probably the one writer whose works most commonly have been adapted to the screen by various directors. In his memoirs Wajda declares his prose "fantastic material for film"/fantastyczny material na film, but difficult for a beginning director owing to its fluidity and its temporal distance. Andrzej Wajda, *Kino i reszte świata* (Cracow: Wydawnictwo Znak, 2000), 212.

29. Mikołaj Gliński, "The Other Life of Jarosław Iwaszkiewicz," February 28, 2014, https://culture.pl/en/article/the-other-life-of-jaroslaw-iwaszkiewicz. Accessed December 14, 2017.

30. Jest w tekście literackim *Kochanków z Marony* Iwaszkiewicza wiele niedopowiedzeń wskazujących na tropy homoseksualne Janka i Arka, ale celowo właśnie są niedopowiedziane." See http://bienczycka.com/blog/?p=1370. Accessed December 17, 2017.

31. A subtle homosexual play takes place between the men [in the film]. Izabella Cywińska, *Kochankowie z Marony* (2005), Agencja Media Plus/Agencja Produkcji Filmowej/Techfilm.

32. For a concise, informative sketch of Cywińska's career, see Monika Mokrzycka-Pokora, *Izabella Cywińska*, November 2004, updated November 2016, https://culture.pl/en/artist/izabella-cywinska. Accessed December 20, 2017.

33. Ola recites from memory a segment of Iwaszkiewicz's narrative, "Ikar" [Ikarus], which records his confrontation with the painting *Landscape with the Fall of Icarus* (1560s), long attributed to Pieter Breughel the Elder, but in 1996 exposed as a skillful copy. As depicted on the canvas, a death unnoticed by various strata of society yet mourned by those who loved him, will be Janek's fate. The myth of Icarus, which has inspired numerous poems and paintings worldwide, originated with Ovid.

34. Ten film to takie laboratorium miłości. Powstała historia o uniwersalnej miłości, na którą nie ma monopolu żadna opcja seksualna, bo jest to uczucie skierowane nie tyle do kobiety czy mężczyzny, co do człowieka. Miłość jest dla nich jedynym ratunkiem—także w ich zmaganiach ze śmiercią. Dane jest im dotknąć miłości wiecznej, bezwzględnej, która buduje ich świat, nadaje życiu sens, jest zdolna do wszystkiego. Jednym słowem—laboratorium miłości i śmierci.

35. Katarzyna Taras Źródło, "Kochankowie z Marony," June 23, 2006, https://kultura.onet.pl/film/recenzje/kochankowie-z-marony/zncte48. Źródło's review brims with sensitive insights and justly draws parallels between this film and Visconti's. Accessed December 11, 2017.

36. Quoted in Konrad J. Zarębski, "Feature Film Directed by Magdalena Piekorz, 2008," culture.pl, October 2008.https://culture.pl/en/work/drowsiness-magdalena-piekorz. Accessed December 11, 2017.

37. Barbara Kwas, "Ten film ma momenty," Gazeta.pl, January 1, 2013, http://kultura.gazeta.pl/kultura/1,114438,5823979,Sennosc___ten_film_ma_momenty.html. Accessed December 9, 2017.

38. http://coolturalni24.pl/2012/05/27/recenzja-filmu-magdaleny-piekorz-sennosc/. Accessed December 11, 2017.

39. Krzysztof Świrek, "Senność," *Kino*, no. 10 (2008): 80. Świrek believes that the narrative of the narcoleptic actress is cast in the tones of nightmare, and that of the nagging wife in those of the absurd—an intriguing idea, with which I disagree.

40. The Grand Prix Golden Lion (Złote Lwy), in existence since 1974, is awarded at the annual film festival in Gdynia, Poland, for excellence in film. Paweł Pawlikowski won the award for *Ida* (2013) and *Zimna wojna* (Cold War 2018) as those years' best pictures, while a special award went to Smarzowski's *Kler* (Clergy 2018) in 2018 for courage in exploring a topic of particular importance to the public.

41. Like other countries, Poland prefers to transfer its erring priests from one parish to another rather than to confront their inappropriate (in some cases, criminal) behavior. Smarzowski's "scandalous" film *Kler* (Clergy 2018) is the sole Polish film to confront directly Polish Catholic priests' immoral conduct.

42. Though *kurwa* literally means whore, in contemporary Poland when used in a rap-like way as a "filler" within sentences, it sooner may be rendered as "fuck [it]."

43. In Polish, *szczep* means "tribe" or "seedling," which provides an early clue to the final union of the young man and Adam, though the English subtitles bewilderingly give him the name Humpty.

44. The setting serves as a modern-day Garden of Eden, with Adam and Adam—the second Adam (Łukasz) substituting for Eve and seducing his loved one through primeval mating calls instead of actual flesh-knowledge.

45. The sole scene of Adam's becoming inebriated leads a Polish critic to assume that he is an alcoholic. See Piotr Śmiałowski, "W imię...," *Kino*, no. 9 (2013): 64–65. Accessed March 13, 2018.

46. Earlier used by Andrei Zviagintsev in his first feature film, *Vozvrashchenie* (The Return 2003), the painting offers a culturally evocative, economical, and naturalized symbol of combined love and suffering.

47. Intriguingly, Piekorz also uses Adam and Eve as a reference point, for Adam's apartment has Dürer's famous engraving of the Edenic couple on a bookshelf.

48. In a review in *Variety*, Alissa Simon virtually dismisses the film for purportedly "Treating loaded subject matter—homosexuality, priests who break their vows—in a way that feels far past its sell-by date in the West (after all, it's been nearly 20 years since Antonia Bird's *Priest*)," as though Bird's poorly reviewed film rendered any subsequent cinematic exploration of gay priests superfluous. Seeming ignorance of the significance of the Catholic Church in Poland led her to underestimate the impact of the film in Poland. Alissa Simon, "In the Name of," *Variety*, February 8, 2013, at https://variety.com/2013/film/markets-festivals/in-the-name-of-1117949193/. Unsurprisingly, a Polish journalist pointed out the discrepancy in significance of taking on the Catholic Church in the West and Poland. See Małgorzata Sadowska, "Małgośka Szumowska wraca z nowym filmem—'W imię'. Pan jest blisko," *Newsweek*, March 11, 2013, http://www.newsweek.pl/kultura/film/malgoska-szumowska-wraca-z-nowym-filmem---w-imie--pan-jest-blisko,101302,1,1.html. Both accessed March 12, 2018.

49. https://www.irishtimes.com/culture/film/in-the-name-of-w-imie-1.1665609. Accessed January 7, 2019.

50. https://culture.pl/en/work/in-the-name-of-malgorzata-szumowska. Accessed January 5, 2019.

51. Marlon Wallace, "The M Report," May 22, 2014, http://themreporter.blogspot.com/2014/05/dvd-review-in-name-of-w-imie.html. Accessed March 12, 2018.

52. "Ironia i sarkazm—to klucz do moich filmów," interview with Kuba Armata, *Kino*, no. 4 (2018): 24–27, esp. 27.

53. Bartosz Staszczyszyn, "Tomasz Wasilewski," culture.pl, September 26, 1980, https://culture.pl/en/artist/tomasz-wasilewski. Accessed February 18, 2019.

54. Ibid.

55. Ibid.

56. Jack Cullen, "The Top 10 Gay Movie Clichés," *The Guardian*, March 25, 2013, https://www.theguardian.com/books/2013/mar/25/top-10-gay-movie-cliches. Accessed July 28, 2015.

57. See the review by Peter Beech, "Floating Skyscrapers—Review," *The Guardian*, December 5, 2013, https://www.theguardian.com/film/2013/dec/05/floating-skyscrapers-review. Accessed February 18, 2019.

58. George Heymont, "The Hung and the Restless," *Huffington Post*, December 6, 2017, https://www.huffingtonpost.com/george-heymont/the-hung-and-the-restless_b_5811664.html. Accessed February 16, 2019.

59. Alissa Simon, "Polish Director Tomasz Wasilewski Delivers a Feel-bad Coming-out Drama in Artful, Sexually Provocative Fashion," *Variety*, July 3, 2013, https://variety.com/2013/more/global/film-review-floating-skyscrapers-1200567231/. Accessed February 18, 2019.

60. See lewislafontaine, "The Mother Archetype," Carl Jung Depth Psychology, March 13, 2018, https://carljungdepthpsychologysite.blog/2018/03/13/the-mother-archetype/#.W8OXy2hKiUk. Accessed February 16, 2019.

61. Simon, "Polish director Tomasz Wasilewski."

62. Cited in Staszczyszyn, "Tomasz Wasilewki."

63. Gabe Toro, "'Floating Skyscrapers' Never Dodges the Inevitability of the Modern Gay Indie Film Tragedy," IndieWire, April 19, 2013, https://www.indiewire.com/2013/04/tribeca-review-floating-skyscrapers-never-dodges-the-inevitability-of-the-modern-gay-indie-film-tragedy-99204/. Accessed July 28, 2015.

64. Now he reportedly is working on a new film titled *Jedwabne wesele* (Jedwabne Wedding/Silk Wedding), presumably treating the land-mined topic of Polish anti-Semitism.

65. For support of the book as accurate and well researched by Paweł Goźliński, chief editor of *Agora*, see https://www.youtube.com/watch?v=yFIDSxzea7Q. Accessed June 15, 2019.

66. In addition to snide comments and emotional outbursts, Martel cannot resist protracted descriptions of rings, furniture, perfume, and his interviewees' reactions to him ("he liked me," "he gave me his private number," etc.). Frédéric Martel, *In the Closet of the Vatican: Power, Homosexuality, Hypocrisy* (London: Bloomsbury, 2019), 367–68, and *passim*.

67. Ibid., 357. Repetitious, lugubrious, smug in tone, and peppered with innuendos, rickety surmises, overly rapid conclusions, and exclamation marks, the book makes for unexpectedly tedious and annoying reading, possibly because Martel is so clearly proud of himself and so condescending to everyone else. Ultimately, trusting his judgment is difficult, at times impossible.

68. Frank Bruni, "The Vatican's Gay Overlords," *New York Times*, February 15, 2019, https://www.nytimes.com/2019/02/15/opinion/vatican-gay-priests.html?fallback=0&recId=1HJVKJDZ5Fb8ac47GunDddeByKC&locked=0&geoContinent=NA&geoRegion=OH&recAlloc=als1&geoCountry=US&blockId=trending&imp_id=760337278&action=click&module=trending&pgtype=Article&region=Footer. Accessed February 18, 2019.

Chapter 9

Polish Film Tomorrow?

The year-end statistics for the Polish film industry in 2019 were astonishing, according to journalist Stjepan Hundic in *The Hollywood Reporter* and sundry other reports. Not only had the domestic box office topped $290 million, "with 60.9 million admissions, continuing a long run of record-breaking years," but also Polish art house films had made the cut for Oscar nominations two years in a row. After Pawlikowski's film *Ida* won Poland's first foreign-language film Oscar in 2015, the director's next feature, *Zimna wojna* (Cold War), was in the running for 2019, and Jan Komasa's excellent, low-budget film, *Boże Ciało* (Corpus Christi), about a youth with a criminal record who successfully impersonates a priest and inspires an entire community, was under consideration in 2020. Though neither won the statuette in Hollywood, both nominated films garnered other awards and performed exceedingly well at the box office. Produced with a budget of $4.8 million, *Cold War* grossed more than $20 million globally while *Corpus Christi* netted $8 million domestically and was "virtually sold out worldwide for New Europe Film Sales."[1] Currently, Małgorzata Szumowska and Michał Englert's *Śniegu już nigdy nie będzie* (Never Gonna Snow Again 2020), a Polish-German comedy-drama, already has become the 2021 contender for the International Feature Film Award at the Oscar ceremony.[2]

Moreover, homegrown feature films, not imported blockbusters, remain the driving force for domestic revenue growth. Given consistent critical acclaim and strong domestic and international box office figures, it seems clear that the Polish film industry in the twenty-first century has succeeded in cultivating the talent for production, networking, and marketing that Alexandra Sosnowski and director Barbara Sass (1936–2015) found so woefully inadequate two decades ago. Thus far, regardless of the left-leaning or hard-right-leaning governments in power in independent Poland, a new age of adventurous, high-quality cinema is thriving, perhaps best categorized as dazzlingly multicolored rather than a monolithic gold.

This cinema's innovative aesthetic approaches, progressive topics, and savvy outreach are reflected in a respectful changing of the artistic guard. Though the industry has lost a number of major figures, most of whose careers were made in "the golden era of the PRL"—directors Ryszard Bugajski (1943–2019), Krzysztof Krauze (1953–2014), and Wajda (1926–2016); cinematographers Piotr Sobociński (1958–2001) and his father, Witold Sobociński (1929–2018); composers Wojciech Kilar (1932–2013) and Krzysztof Penderecki (1933–2020)—new talents, many of them featured in this volume, have been busy establishing themselves. The directorial ranks at last include a sizable number of women, in addition to the enormously prolific Agnieszka Holland: among them, Kasia Adamik, Urszula Antoniak, Kinga Dębska, Anna Jadowska, Joanna Kos-Krauze, Magdalena Piekorz, Katarzyna Rosłaniec, Maria Sadowska, Agnieszka Smoczyńska, Jagoda Szelc, and Małgorzata Szumowska. For the first time in its existence, PISF awarded production grants mainly to female directors in its second competition for 2020: four of the five .46 million euro awards were given, respectively, to Adamik, Anna Kazejak (making her third feature film), established "auteur" Dorota Kędzierzawska, and debuting director Justyna Tafel.[3] Moreover, the newly elected rector of the historic Łódź Film School who replaced Mariusz Grzegorzek for the term 2020–2024 is a woman—Milenia Fielder (b. 1966), a film editor who worked with Wajda on several features, including *Katyń* (2007), and earlier received an award for her editing of Wojciech Marczewski's *Weiser* (2001).[4] Polish male directors now range from well-known "senior" artists (in their late fifties and early sixties) such as Dariusz Gajewski, Władysław Pasikowski, Paweł Pawlikowski, Maciej Pieprzyca, and Wojciech Smarzowski, to those in their mid- to late forties—Borys Lankosz, Małgorzata Szumowska, Marek and Tomasz Sekielski—to relative newcomers in their late thirties—Olga Chajdas, Piotr Domalewski, Jan Komasa, Jan P. Matuszyński, and Tomasz Wasilewski. Today all directors in Polish film identity as European filmmakers; possess extensive knowledge of film; and are fully cognizant of the market's pressures and opportunities. Michał Oleszczyk, a film scholar and the artistic director of Poland's respected film festival in Gdynia from 2013 to 2017, offers this perceptive assessment of contemporary Polish filmmakers:

This is a generation incredibly aware of film language in all its variety. They have absorbed large chunks of both arthouse and mainstream world cinema. No earlier generation of Polish filmmakers has had this wide an access to cinema, no other was so Westernized in its approach and communication skills, and no other had such complex and searching approaches to Polish history, identity and class tensions.[5]

Current film production combines continuity and change, partly owing to the welcome surge of educational options within cinema. In addition to the world-renowned National Higher School of Film, Television, and Theater in Łódź established in 1948 and the Faculty of Radio and Television at the University of Silesia in Katowice, dating from 1978, new entities such as the Andrzej Wajda Master School of Film Directing (2001–), the Kraków Screenplay School at the Film and Audio-Visual Communication School in Kraków (2009), which introduced the departments of production and directing.[6] Workshops, lectures by older, successful directors, some with experience abroad, such as Wojciech Marczewski, and the opportunity to make their own features or documentaries are available to those enrolled in these institutions, which also sustain a lively, creative atmosphere of collegiality and exchange with both old and young.

Likewise, the integration of established film actors with new talent has been relatively seamless. While actors and actresses who dominated the screen during the PRL era, such as Anna Dymna, Janusz Gajos, Krystyna Janda, Maja Komorowska, Daniel Olbrychski, Andrzej Seweryn, and Grażyna Szapołowska, still remain impressively active, a host of actors and actresses who debuted or were brought center stage relatively recently have become the new stars of varying ages, some of them cast in what seems an improbable number of groundbreaking films and, moreover, a staggering variety of roles: Magdalena Boczarska, Andrzej Chyra, Marcin Dorociński, Marian Dziędziel, Jakub Gierszal, Agnieszka Grochowska, Arkadiusz Jakubik, Julia Kijowska, Mateusz Kościukiewicz, Tomasz Kot, Agata Kulesza, Joanna Kulig, Gabriela Muskala, Marta Nieradkiewicz, Dawid Ogrodnik, Michalina Olszańska, Maja Ostaszewska, Cezary Pazura, Kinga Preis, Anna Próchniak, Maciej Stuhr, Bartołomej Topa, and Robert Więckiewicz. The films examined in our book showcase their talent for incarnating multiple, dissimilar personae on screen—an ability for more than half a century superlatively illustrated by the chameleon-like Gajos and to a slightly lesser degree by Seweryn.

Yet, the actors and actresses now achieving stardom perceive themselves as not merely East European but international players in a global market. During PRL a few Polish actors and actresses appeared on either the big or small screen in Western Europe or the United States. In general, even their names were barely recognized outside of Poland, with the exception of Olbrychski and Jerzy Skolimowski; the latter, better known as a director, worked in Italy, Britain, and the United States after emigrating in 1967. Ironically, in recent years both Olbrychski and Skolimowski have played Russians—moreover, convincingly—in Anglophone movies, notably

Phillip Noyce's *Salt* (2010) and David Cronenberg's *Eastern Promises* (2007) respectively—a casting inherited by Marcin Dorociński, who already had worked in Anglophone productions,[7] as a Russian chess champion in the recently touted seven-episode Netflix miniseries, *The Queen's Gambit* (2020), which has attracted enormous attention. Indeed, a measure of the dramatic changes that have occurred, especially in the 2010s, is the participation of Poles in series and films streamed on Netflix, some of them in English and all accessible to millions in the West. These ever-increasing series include Boczarska and Kulig in *Zbrodnia* (Crime 2014), Kulesza and Topa in *Ultraviolet* (2017), Grochowska in *Nielegalni* (Illegals 2018), Ogrodnik in *Rojst* (The Mire 2018–), Grochowska, Jakubik, and Pazura in *W głębi lasu* (The Woods 2020), Kościukiewicz and Olszanska in *1983* (2018, directed by a quartet of women—Holland, Adamik, Olga Chajdas and Smoczyńska). Furthermore, *Ślepnąć od świateł* (Blinded by the Light 2018–2020), *Pakt* (The Pact 2015–2020), and other Polish offerings are available on Amazon Prime, HBO, Hulu, and other services.

Expanded collaboration of Polish directors with Western colleagues has transformed them as well as their casts into international names not only in TV series but also in film, now available on various platforms. To cite just a few examples, Piotr Szkopiak directed the British-Polish film about Katyń, *The Last Witness* (2017), starring Więckiewicz amid an almost entirely British cast. Continuing her long-standing pattern of international collaboration and awards (for *W ciemności* [In Darkness 2011]), Holland recently released her latest coproductions, the Polish-Ukrainian-British *Obywatel Jones* (Mr. Jones 2019), winner of the Grand Prix Golden Lions at the 44th Gdynia Film Festival the year of its release, and the Czech-Irish-Polish-Slovak biopic, *Šarlatán* (Charlatan 2020), the Czech entry for the Best International Feature Film at the 93rd Academy Awards. Szumowska, the repeated recipient of prizes at the Berlin Film Festival (for W imię . . . [In the Name of . . . 2013], *Ciało* [Body 2015], and *Twarz* [Mug 2018]), whose *Sponsoring* (Elles 2011) was underwritten by Poland, France, and Germany, debuted as director of an Anglophone film, *The Other Lamb* (2019), produced by funds from the United Kingdom, Ireland, and Belgium, without a single Pole in the cast. Her latest feature, the Polish-German comedy-drama *Never Gonna Snow Again*, as Poland's submission to the 93rd Academy Awards' International Feature Film category, will compete with another Polish female director's entry—Holland's *Charlatan*. Furthermore, Smoczyńska's musical horror, *The Lure* (Córki dancingu 2015), now is part of the prestigious, highly selective Criterion Collection—the only entry by a comparatively young Polish woman director, alongside revered "classics" by Wajda, Polański, and Kieślowski.

The "production hegemony" of PISF has also expanded opportunities for international collaboration by pitching Polish locations and crews *in situ* as both top-notch and affordable. Since February 2019, the institute has been offering a 30 percent tax rebate for film and series production in Poland, and its current director, Radosław Śmigulski, has announced that they are negotiating for new production facilities.[8] As Ewa Puszczyńska, "one of Poland's top producers," attests in a June 2020 interview for *Deadline*, Polish locations "can offer practically anything, from the seas to the mountains, lakes, modern, old . . . hopefully it will make Poland a center of central Europe for everybody to come and make their films."[9] Another Polish producer praises the "below-the-line" talent on offer in his country: "I'll give you two major reasons why foreign producers should come to Poland with their projects: the 30 percent cash rebate, which was a definitive game changer for the Polish film industry, and fantastic talents, from DOPs, composers, production developers, VFX supervisors, whatever," says Lukasz Dzieciol, a producer at Opus Film (2015 Oscar-winner *Ida*). "The prices for Poland's skilled film crews are unbeatable in the region."[10] It bears noting that the Krzysztof Kieślowski Film School, associated with the University of Silesia in Katowice, just recently launched an initiative called Film Proxy, designed to "match-make" professionals in cinematography, editing, sound, animation, and special effects with "international and local professional audiovisual producers, production houses and directors."[11]

Evidence of not only the Polish film industry's but also other professionals' grasp on the financial aspects of filmmaking manifests in publications and redefined notions about the primacy of film locations. As a telling instance, in 2010, the journalist and film aficionado Marek Szymański published the singular, copiously illustrated book titled *Polska na filmowo: Gdzie kręcono znane filmy i seriale* (Poland on Film: Where Famous Films and Series Were Shot), detailing the regions that have served as key locations for Polish and foreign films as well as TV series. A reader unfamiliar with Polish geography learns that the crew of Rafał Wieczyński's *Popiełuszko: Wolność jest w nas* (discussed in chapter 1) physically retraced and shot the routes of the priest's habitual contemplation in the areas of the majestic Tatra Mountains.[12] Elsewhere, the author reveals an intriguing cinematic connection drawn by a director on the basis of a central square in Warsaw—the circular Plac Zbawiciela (Savior's Square): reportedly, Krzysztof Krauze laughingly remarked that he conceived the setting of his *Plac Zbawiciela* (2006) as a "female" continuation of his earlier film *Dług* (The Debt 1999, analyzed in chapter 5), which concludes with one of the murderer's telephone confession to the police in precisely the locale that determined the latter film's title and setting.[13] And, in an unexpected evocation of an iconic PRL TV production, the first sequences of Wajda's *Katyń* (which chapter 6 examines in detail) were shot in Poświętne na Pilicą—a richly wooded region associated above all with the cult black-and-white TV series *Czterej pancerni i pies* (Four Tankmen and a Dog 1966). That choice surely draws on older Polish viewers' memory about one of the sites for the resistance of the World War II tankmen and their redoubtable German shepherd, Szarik, against the Nazis.[14]

Additionally, such Hollywood productions as *Schindler's List* (1994), *The Aryan Couple* (2004), and *The Chronicles of Narnia* (2005), among others, have benefited from the variegated multitude of Poland's cities, villages, and remote localities, whereby preserved castles and ancient architectural structures can provide a wholly credible background for historical films, rural settlements can render persuasively a bucolic or stagnant backwater frozen in time, and thriving metropolises such as Kraków and Wrocław, as well as the capital, can instantiate the vibrant energy of urban contemporaneity. Directors seeking medieval geography could hardly improve on Gniew (northern Poland, in Pomerania), with its thirteen-century castle, evoking memorable associations with the ultimately defeated Teutonic Knights, while those wishing to dramatize past glories would find today's neglected streets of the once-bustling textile town of Łódź (portrayed in Wajda's award-winning *Zimia obiecana* [The Promised Land 1975]), ideal—once they leave the completely refurbished central section of the city, and particularly its stylish major thoroughfare, Piotrkowska Street.

A kindred volume containing similar information, though narrower in scope, appeared two years later: Grzegorz Soltysiak's *Filmowy przewodnik po Wawszawie* (A Film Guide to Warsaw 2012), which identifies the areas in the metropolis that have served as sites for numerous films. Enhanced with colorful photographs, posters, and fascinating commentaries by their designers such as the premier graphic artist Andrzej Pągowski, it offers stills from over a hundred screen features spanning more than five decades, starting with Leonard Buczkowski's *Zakazane piosenki* (Forbidden Songs 1947) and ending with Roman Polański's *Pianista* (2003).[15] And it is no accident that Soltysiak supplies the hours during which various museums, castles, and other venues operate, for his guide works in tandem with the contemporary Polish strategy of enticing readers to the cities in which the action of the relevant films takes place. Published by the Museum of the Warsaw Uprising, the guide is intended to attract visitors to Poland's capital by seducing them with a wide assortment of images that spotlight architecture, monuments, churches, parks, and other sites while deftly linking them to the visual genres of film and poster. The cumulative effect of these cleverly packaged and lavishly documented advertisements is to "sell" the city as a mecca to filmmakers and tourists.

These and similar publications anticipated and have overlapped with a phenomenon that Bartosz Statyszczyn calls "city placement," by analogy with the quintessentially American device of product placement on screen. Thus far, TV series have proved more successful in promoting regions through a single, repeatedly featured setting. For instance, the popularity of *Ojciec Mateusz* (Father Mathew 2008–), with the bicycling priest cum sleuth as protagonist, has made Sandomierz "one of Poland's best-known towns," increasing the numbers of tourists from 80,000 to 250,000 annually. In fact, Father Mathew has become a character in a popular board game.[16]

This phenomenon has worked hand in glove with local financial support for Polish film. While PISF operates energetically on the national level, regions have helped to underwrite a large percentage of productions that otherwise might have had to reduce costs. Patently, it is in the interests of a given administrative area to invest in films set in its jurisdiction, especially if they promote that setting through prolonged shots and prominently displayed attractive features. As Statyszczyn perceptively contends, regional film foundations "have become one of the most valued instruments of local and regional promotion," starting in Łódź in 2007, with Katowice, Kraków, Wrocław, Szczecin, Lublin, Gdynia, Poznań, Białystok, Warsaw, Olsztyn, and Rzeszów following suit. Each foundation invests in films whose action transpires in its region or relates to historical events that occurred there.[17] In addition to increasing domestic and possibly international tourism, city placement can improve the reputation of areas, such as that of the province in which *Father Mathew* is set, or Silesia, the location of Magdalena Piekorz's and Kazimierz Kutz's films, as well as the Netflix series *The Mire*. Ultimately, the cooperation between municipal authorities and producers of series benefits both, and a growing number of features receive funds from both PISF and regional film foundations, drawing on the opportunity to reward such investments with the lucrative benefits of a hit.[18] In short, after more than a decade's delay, the post-socialist Polish film industry has mastered the principles of a market economy, originally enabled by the foresight of the government that legislated the establishment of PISF, but subsequently taking the initiative itself to ensure its international reputation as one of Europe's outstanding national cinemas.

Recent developments give cause for optimism about the future of Polish film. Krzysztof Świrek, in his survey of filmic institutions in Poland, envisions two main approaches to that future:

> The first approach is to seek a balance between adaptation and tradition—this is the approach of traditional public schools [those in Łódź and Katowice HG].
> The second approach is to find a niche in the market and respond to current

needs—this is the approach of public schools, which have appeared in Polish education in the last several years.[19]

Having interviewed students and graduates of all such schools, he predicts that "the ethos of auteur films promoted in public schools will probably continue" and "likely will result in an artistic cinema bent [*sic*] towards social issues." Certainly, Smarzowski's films suggest such a continuation. The second model, according to Świrski, will attempt to forge a balance between artistry and popular entertainment.[20] Arguably, several of Szumowska's films qualify as examples of that golden mean, though the most likely candidate, *The Other Lamb* (2019), did not meet with popular enthusiasm.

Of course, the immediate obstacle confronting Polish film tomorrow is the coronavirus pandemic that has disrupted and set back film industries worldwide. For a country of 38 million, Poland's mortality rate thus far has been low in contrast to alarming spikes in the virus and consequently renewed shutdowns in the United States, Russia, Brazil, and India. Though the government began lifting restrictions in June, the upsurge of cases in parts of Poland during October has led to reversals. Polish producers and distributors recognize that their box office will take a tremendous hit in 2020, largely because their market depends mainly on local films. At least a dozen projects have yet to be completed, though the relentlessly prolific Szumowska already has released her newest film, *Śniegu już nigdy nie będzie* (Never Gonna Snow Again 2020), and Piotr Domalewski has followed his debut feature, *Cicha Noc* (Silent Night 2017) with *Jak najdalej stąd* (I Never Cry; literally, The Farthest Possible from Here), which appeared on Polish screens in late September 2020.[21] Additionally, Komasa's *Hejter* (The Hater 2020) became accessible on Netflix in the second half of the year. Given the country's relatively small population, Poland's film industry, clearly, cannot and does not entertain fantasies of competing with such behemoths as Hollywood or the current fastest-growing film industry—in China, which has just replaced North America as the world's largest market in box office revenue and audience numbers.[22] Yet, Jakub Duszyński, the head of acquisitions and creative director for Gutek Films, Poland's leading art house company, sounded sanguine during an interview in late June. Earlier that month, he had glimpsed hundreds of Poles lined up outside the Gutek-owned Muranów Cinema in Warsaw, eager to see the show. " 'You feel that you are doing things that are important to a lot of people,' says Duszyński. 'At the end of the day, you have audiences that are waiting for films.' "[23] And, if the spread of the pandemic can be curbed, the Polish film industry seems primed to regain the high-quality production, domestic revenue, and enhanced international renown of its cinema.

HG and BH

NOTES

1. Stjepan Hundic, "Why the Polish Film Industry Is Quietly on a Roll," *The Hollywood Reporter*, February 19, 2020, https://www.hollywoodreporter.com/news/why-polish-film-industry-is-quietly-a-roll-1279973. Accessed October 10, 2020.

2. For a survey of earlier triumphs since 1989, see Janusz Wróblewski, "Polish Cinema Success Stories," in *Polish Cinema Now! Focus on Contemporary Polish Cinema,* ed. Mateusz Werner (London and Warsaw: John Libbey Publishing-Adam Mickiewicz Institute, 2010), 170–192.

3. Ola Salwa, "The Polish Film Institute Announces Second Batch of Production Grants for 2020," *Cineuropa*, July 14, 2020, https://cineuropa.org/en/newsdetail/390154/. Accessed October 14, 2020.

4. See https://pisf.pl/en/. Accessed October 24, 2020.

5. Leo Barraclough, "New Generation of Filmmakers in Poland Are Grabbing Artistic Reins," *Variety,* February 9, 2017, https://variety.com/2017/film/spotlight/new-generation-of-filmmakers-in-poland-are-grabbing-artistic-reins-1201977157/. Accessed July 21, 2018.

6. Krzysztof Świrek, "Tradition and Diversity: An Outline of Polish Film Education," in *Polish Cinema Now! Focus on Contemporary Polish Cinema*, ed. Mateusz Werner (London and Warsaw: John Libbey Publishing-Adam Mickiewicz Institute, 2010), 239.

7. By then Dorociński had appeared in the British series *Spies of Warsaw* (2013), the films *Star Wars: The Force Awakens* (2015) and *Anthropoid* (2016), as well as other non-Polish screen offerings.

8. Stjepan Hundic, "Why the Poland Film Sector Is Quietly Thriving," *The Hollywood Reporter*, November 8, 2019, https://www.hollywoodreporter.com/news/why-poland-film-sector-is-quietly-thriving-1253258. Accessed July 14, 2020. For a comprehensive survey of the current infrastructure of the Polish film industry, see the excellent chapter by Jerzy Płażewski, "Polish Cinema—A Return to a Market Economy," in *Polish Cinema Now!* 150–169.

9. Tom Grater, "Polish Filmmakers Behind 'Corpus Christi,' 'Cold War,' and 'Kill It and Leave This Town' Discuss Country's Recent Successes and Future Prospects," *Deadline,* June 24, 2020, https://deadline.com/video/polish-film-recent-successes-future-prospects-video/. Accessed July 14, 2020.

10. Stjepan Hundic, "Why the Polish Film Industry."

11. FNE Staff, "Polish Film School Launches Talent Resource Agency," *FilmNewEurope.com,* June 29, 2020, http://filmneweurope.com/news/poland-news?start=26. Accessed October 11, 2020.

12. Marek Szymański, *Polska na filmowo; Gdzie kręcono znanw filmy i seriale* (Poznan: MJ Media Szymański i Glapiak, 2010), 26.

13. Ibid., 338–39.

14. Ibid., 224, 230–231.

15. See Grzegorz Soltysiak, *Filmowy przewodnik po Warszawie* (Warszawa: Muzeum Powstania Warszawskiego, 2012), *passim*. The book contains a helpful timeline of important filming events in Warsaw from the late nineteenth century until

the early twenty-first and gives a lightning-quick glance at early Polish cinema until World War II (9–13).

16. Bartosz Statyszczyn, "Polish City Placement: A New Kind of Travel Agency," culture.pl, August 31, 2020, https://culture.pl/en/article/polish-city-placement-a-new -kind-of-travel-agency. Accessed September 15, 2020.

17. For additional details about the economics of filmmaking in Poland today, see Płażewski, "Polish cinema now!"

18. Ibid.

19. Świrek, "Tradition and Diversity," 239.

20. Świrek, "Tradition and Diversity," 240.

21. The literal translation of the Polish title is *As Far Away from Here as Possible.*

22. See Patrick Brzeski, "It's Official: China Overtakes North America as World's Biggest Box Office in 2020," *The Hollywood Reporter,* October 18, 2020, https:// www.hollywoodreporter.com/news/its-official-china-overtakes-north-america-as -worlds-biggest-box-office-in-2020. Accessed October 18, 2020.

23. Christopher Vourlias, "Pandemic and Price Wars Put a Dent in the Polish Box Office," *Variety,* June 23, 2020, https://variety.com/2020/film/spotlight/cannes-polish -movies-hater-1234645699/. Accessed October 10, 2020.

Bibliography

"50 Best Gay Movies: The Best in LGBT + Filmmaking." https://www.timeout.com/london/film/the-50-best-gay-movies-the-best-in-lgbt-film-making.

Adamczak, Marcin. "Hard Power and Film Distribution: Transformation of Distribution Practices in Poland in the Era of the Digital Revolution." *Studies in Eastern European Cinema* 11, no. 3 (2020): 243–61.

———. "Instytucja festiwalu filmowego w ekonomii kina." *Panoptikum*, no. 16 (23) (2016): 20–37.

———. "Polish Cinema after 1989: A Quest for Visibility and a Voice in the Market." *Illuminace* 24, no. 4 (88) (2012): 45–59.

———. "Za garść papierosów, kilka paszportów lub mieszkanie." *Odra* 2 (2010): 114.

———. "Zderzenie z globalizacją." *Kino*, no. 6 (2019): 23–26.

Adamczak, Marcin, and Agnieszka Orankiewicz. "Film and Finance. An Attempt at a Statistical Comparison of the Attendance Results and Ratings of Polish Films in the Years 2012-2015." *Images. The International Journal of European Film, Performing Arts and Audiovisual Communication*, no. 32 (2018): 197–209.

Adamczak, Marcin, Marcin Malatyński, and Piotr Marecki. *Restart zespołów filmowych*. Cracow-Lodz: Korporacja Ha!art, 2012.

Adamkiewicz, Sebastian. "W ciemności, reż. Agnieszka Holland –recenzja." January 10, 2012. https://histmag.org/W-ciemnosci-rez.-Agnieszka-Holland-recenzja-filmu-6261.

Adams, Amy Singleton, and Vera Shevzov, eds. *Framing Mary: The Mother of God in Modern, Revolutionary, and Post-Soviet Russian Culture*. DeKalb, IL: Northern Illinois University Press, 2018.

Adams, Mark. "Shameless." July 8, 2012. https://www.screendaily.com/shameless/5044254.article.

Adams, Tim. "Paweł Pawlikowski: 'My Parents' Story Was the Matrix of All My Stories.'" *Guardian*, 11 February 2019. https://www.theguardian.com/film/2019/feb/09/pawel-pawlikowski-poland-cold-war-ida.

Adamski, Łukasz. "Cicha noc. Polska Sieranevada. Przenikliwe i mądre dzieło."
    September 21, 2017. https://wpolityce.pl/kultura/358868-adamski-z-festiwalu-w
    -gdyni-cicha-noc-polska-sieranevada-przenikliwe-i-madre-dzielo-recenzja.
————. "Obce niebo. Polska rodzina vs. 'szwecjalizm.' Czy naprawdę chcemy
    takiego autorytaryzmu w Polsce?" October 13, 2015. https://wpolityce.pl/kul-
    tura/268357-obce-niebo-polska-rodzina-vs-szwecjalizm-czy-naprawde-chcemy
    -takiego-autorytaryzmu-w-polsce-recenzja.
Aderets, Ofer. "Historian Who Shed Light on World War II Massacres Goes from
    Honoree to 'Pole Hater.'" March 1, 2016. https://www.haaretz.com/jewish/.pre-
    mium-the-pole-who-is-breaking-the-silence-1.5410809.
Akademii Polskiego Filmu, no. 1 (2016). https://akademiapolskiegofilmu.pl/pl/histo-
    ria-polskiego-filmu/pleograf/andrzej-wajda/1/katyn-andrzeja-wajdy-melodramaty-
    czny-afekt-i-historia/536.
Alexiou, Margaret. *The Ritual Lament in Greek Tradition*. Cambridge: Cambridge
    University Press, 1974.
Ammon, Richard. "A Brief History of Gay Poland." https://www.globalgayz.com/a
    -brief-history-of-gay-poland/.
Anderson, James B. "The Spanish Mystical Aesthetic." *Mystics Quarterly* 19, no. 3
    (September 1993): 115–22.
"Andrzej Seweryn." https://culture.pl/pl/tworca/andrzej-seweryn.
Anessi, Thomas. "Moving Ahead into the Past: Historical Contexts in Recent Polish
    Cinema." *Images* XI, no. 20 (2012): 5–22.
Archer, Greg. "A Town Called Brzostek Among the Compelling Documentaries at
    the 27th Polish Film Festival in America." December 6, 2017. https://www.huff-
    post.com/entry/a-town-called-brzostek-am_b_8535638.
Aristotle, *Poetics*. Translated by Malcolm Heath. London: Penguin Books, 1996.
Baer, Brian James. *Other Russias: Homosexuality and the Crisis of Post-Soviet
    Identity*. New York: Palgrave/Macmillan, 2009.
Barraclough, Leo. "New Generation of Filmmakers in Poland Are Grabbing Artistic
    Reins." *Variety*, February 9, 2017. https://variety.com/2017/film/spotlight/new
    -generation-of-filmmakers-in-poland-are-grabbing-artistic-reins-1201977157/.
Beardsworth, Sara. *Julia Kristeva: Psychoanalysis and Modernity*. New York: SUNY
    Press, 2004. https://www.sunypress.edu/pdf/61009.pdf.
Beech, Peter. "Floating Skyscrapers—Review." *Guardian*, December 5, 2013.
    https://www.theguardian.com/film/2013/dec/05/floating-skyscrapers-review.
Bennett, William. "Stronger Families, Stronger Societies." *New York Times*, April
    24, 2012. https://www.nytimes.com/roomfordebate/2012/04/24/are-family-values
    -outdated/stronger-families-stronger-societies.
Berendt, Joanna. "Catholic Church in Poland Releases Study on Sexual Abuse by
    Priests." *New York Times*, March 14, 2019. https://www.nytimes.com/2019/03/14/
    world/europe/catholic-church-abuse-poland.html.
Bertov, Omer. *The "Jew" in Cinema: From the Golem to Don't Touch My Holocaust*.
    Bloomington, IN: Indiana University Press, 2005.
Bieńczycka, Ewa. "Izabella Cywińska 'Kochankowie z Marony' (2005)." na druk
    jeszcze za wcześnie…, 12 June 2009. http://bienczycka.com/blog/?p=1370.

Bikont, Anna. *My z Jedwabnego* [We from Jedwabne]. Wołowiec, PL: Wydawnictwo Czarne, 2015.

———. *The Crime and the Silence: Confronting the Massacre of Jews in Wartime Jedwabne.* Translated by Alissa Valles. New York: Farrar, Straus and Giroux, 2016.

Birkholc, Robert. Birkholc, Robert. "Sztuka kochania. Historia Michaliny Wisłockiej." *Kino*, no. 1 (2017): 78. http://kino.org.pl//index.php?option=com_content&task=view&id=2662&Itemid=1802.

———. "Układ zamknięty." *Kino*, no. 4 (2013): 82.

———. "Zaćma." *Kino*, no. 10 (2016): 66–67. http://kino.org.pl//index.php?option=com_content&task=view&id=2623&Itemid=1767.

Bitel, Anton. "Fugue (Fuga 2018)." April 13, 2019. https://projectedfigures.com/2019/04/13/fugue-fuga-2018/.

Bittencourt, Ella. "Review: Aftermath." *Slant*, October 28, 2013. https://www.slant-magazine.com/film/aftermath/.

Bloom, Julie. "Tribeca: Juliette Binoche on Acting from Insecurity." *New York Times*, April 25, 2012. https://artsbeat.blogs.nytimes.com/2012/04/25/tribeca-juliette-binoche-on-acting-from-insecurity/.

Bonarski, Marek. "Katyń—spóźniona recenzja." June 15, 2008. https://naszemiasto.pl/katyn-spozniona-recenzja/ar/c13-4425356.

Bondanella, Peter. *The Cinema of Federico Fellini*. Princeton: Princeton University Press, 1992.

Booth, Robert. "Widow, 88, Faces Arrest Warrant over Death of Polish Hero." *Guardian*, November 20, 2007. https://www.theguardian.com/uk/2007/nov/21/secondworldwar.ukcrime.

Box Office Mojo. https://www.boxofficemojo.com/title/tt5370828/?ref_=bo_gr_ti.

———. https://www.boxofficemojo.com/releasegroup/gr655380997/.

Boyce, Laurence. "Marcin Koszałka, 'The Red Spider.'" July 3, 2015. https://www.screendaily.com/karlovy-vary/marcin-koszalka-the-red-spider/5090085.article.

Brady, Tara. "In the Name of…/W imie…." *Irish Times*, January 24, 2014. https://www.irishtimes.com/culture/film/in-the-name-of-w-imie-1.1665609.

Bren, Paulina. *The Greengrocer and His TV: The Culture of Communism after the 1968 Prague Spring*. Ithaca, NY: Cornell University Press, 2010.

Bren, Paulina, and Mary Neuberger, eds. *Communism Unwrapped: Consumption in Cold War Eastern Europe*. Oxford: Oxford University Press, 2012.

Bretan, Juliette. "Lost & Destroyed: In Search of Classic Polish Films." August 22, 2018. https://culture.pl/en/article/lost-destroyed-classic-polish-films?utm_source=getresponse&utm_medium=email&utm_campaign=30082019en&utm_content=art4_title.

Brody, Richard. "The Distasteful Vagueness of Ida." *New Yorker*, May 9, 2014. https://www.newyorker.com/culture/richard-brody/the-distasteful-vagueness-of-ida.

Brooke, Michael. "Katyń." *Sight and Sound* 19, no. 4 (April 2009): 66.

Bruni, Frank. "The Vatican's Gay Overlords," *New York Times*, February 15, 2019. https://www.nytimes.com/2019/02/15/opinion/vatican-gay-priests.html?

Brzeski, Patrick. "It's Official: China Overtakes North America as World's Biggest Box Office in 2020." *Hollywood Reporter*, October 18, 2020, https://www.hollywoodreporter.com/news/its-official-china-overtakes-north-america-as-worlds-biggest-box-office-in-2020.

Brzozowski, Grzegorz. "Spustoszona historia. Recenzja fimu 'Zimna wojna' Pawła Pawlikowskiego." June 26, 2018. https://kulturaliberalna.pl/2018/06/26/grzegorz-brzozowski-spustoszona-historia-recenzja-zimna-wojna-pawel-pawlikowski/.

Burton, Neel. "Hide and Seek: The Psychology of Sadomasochism." August 17, 2014. https://www.psychologytoday.com/us/blog/hide-and-seek/201408/the-psychology-sadomasochism.

Bystydzienski, Jill. "The Feminist Movement in Poland: Why so Slow?" *Women's Studies International Forum* 24, no. 5 (2001): 501–11.

Callenbach, Ernest "Mother Joan of the Angels by Jerzy Kawalerowicz." *Film Quarterly* 17, no. 2 (Winter 1963–1964): 28–31.

Cardullo, Bert, and André Bazin. "Cinema and Theology: The Case of Heaven Over the Marshes." *Journal of Religion & Film* 6, no. 2 (2016): Article 15. https://digitalcommons.unomaha.edu/jrf/vol6/iss2/15.

Carroll, Noël. *The Philosophy of Horror*. New York and London: Routledge, 1990.

Catholic World Report. https://www.catholicworldreport.com/2016/06/28/polands-history-is-a-story-of-resilient-catholic-faith/.

Cawelti, John G. "Chinatown and Generic Transformation in Recent American Films." *In Film Genre Reader II*, edited by Barry Keith Grant, 227–45. Austin TX: University of Texas Press, 1995.

Chełstowska, Agata. "Stigmatisation and Commercialisation of Abortion Services in Poland: Turning Sin into Gold." *Reproductive Health Matters* 19, no. 37 (2011): 98–106.

Chiger, Krystyna, and Daniel Paisner. *The Girl in the Green Sweater*. New York: St. Martin's Press, 2008.

Chosiński, Sebastian. "Powiedzmy to sobie wprost—Marchwicki nie był 'Wampirem!'" April 18, 2016. https://esensja.pl/ksiazka/recenzje/tekst.html?id=22619.

Chrostowski, Waldemar. "He Hold His Story in Film." In *Jerzy Kawalerowicz: malarz X muyzy/painter of the tenth muse*, 66–77. Lodz: Muzeum Kinematografii, 2012.

Cielecka, Beata. "'Różyczka': Miłość i inwigilacja." May 3, 2018. https://www.telemagazyn.pl/artykuly/rozyczka-milosc-i-inwigilacja-recenzja-47847.html.

Cmentarze żydowskie w Polsce [Jewish Cemeteries in Poland]. http://cmentarze-zydowskie.pl/kaluszynhistoria.htm.

Coates, Paul. *Cinema, Religion and the Romantic Legacy*. London: Routledge, 2003
———. *The Red and the White: The Cinema of People's Poland*. London and New York: Wallflower Press, 2005.

Cook, Pam, and Mieke Bernink, eds., *The Cinema Book*, 2nd edition. London: BFI Publishing, 1999.

Cullen, Jack. "The top 10 gay movie clichés." *Guardian*, March 25, 2013. https://www.theguardian.com/books/2013/mar/25/top-10-gay-movie-cliches.

Curb, Rosemary, and Nancy Manahan, eds. *Lesbian Nuns: Breaking Silence.* Tallahassee, FL: Naiad Press, 1985.

Cywińska, Izabella. *Kochankowie z Marony* (2005). Agencja Media Plus/Agencja Produkcji Filmowej/Techfilm.

Czaderska-Hayek, Yola. "Blindness (Zacma) (Poland), Golden Globe Awards." November 18, 2017. https://www.goldenglobes.com/articles/blindness-zacma -poland.

Czeczott, Ewa Beynar. *Mój ojciec Paweł Jasienica.* Warsaw: MG, 2018.

Czekaj, Patryk. "Review: The Closed Circuit Depicts a Tragically True Story of Corruption." October 31, 2013. https://screenanarchy.com/2013/10/review-the -closed-circuit-depicts-a-tragically-true-story-of-corruption.html.

Dalton, Stephen. "'Blindness' ('Zacma'): Film Review." *Hollywood Reporter*, September 15, 2016. https://www.hollywoodreporter.com/review/blindness-zacma -review-929161.

———. "The Red Spider (Czerwony pajak): Karlovy Vary review." *Hollywood Reporter*, July 13, 2015. https://variety.com/2015/film/festivals/the-red-spider-film -review-1201535830/.

Damski, Przemysław Piotr. "'Rewers'—reż. Borys Lankosz—recenzja i ocena filma." June 14, 2010. https://histmag.org/Rewers-rez.-Borys-Lankosz-recenzja-filmu-4331.

Danielsen, Shane. "A Dour Exploration of a Nun's Descent." SBS, October 8, 2012. https://www.sbs.com.au/movies/review/name-devil-review.

Davies, Christian. "Polish Film The Clergy Sparks Hundreds of Allegations of Abuse." *Guardian*, 17 October 2018. https://www.theguardian.com/world/2018/oct /15/polish-film-the-clergy-sparks-hundreds-of-allegations-of-abuse-kler-catholic.

Davies, Norman. *God's Playground: The origins to 1795.* New York: Columbia University Press, 2005.

———. *Heart of Europe: The Past in Poland's Present.* Oxford: Oxford University Press, 2001.

de Beauvoir, Simone. *The Second Sex.* Translated by H.M. Parshley. New York: Vintage Books, 1989.

de Castro, Colette. "Invisible Girls." *East European Film Bulletin*, 14 (February 2012). https://eefb.org/perspectives/malgorzata-szumowskas-elles-2011/.

Denby, David. "Ida: A Film Masterpiece." *New Yorker*, May 27, 2014, https://www .newyorker.com/culture/culture-desk/ida-a-film-masterpiece.

Derdowski, Krzysztof. "Byli eskek nakręcił film o ks. Jerzym Popiełusze." November 18, 2014. https://bydgoszcz24.pl/pl/11_wiadomosci/9374_byly_esbek _nakrecil_film_o_ks_jerzym_popieluszce.html.

Desperak, Iza. "Michalina Wisłocka: Revolutionary Sexologist or Modern Heroine of Pain?" March 2, 2017. *Network 4 Debate, Poland.* http://politicalcritique.org/cee/ poland/2017/wislocka-sex-feminism-polishfilm/.

Doane, M.A. *The Desire to Desire: The Woman's Film of the 1940s.* Bloomington, IN: Indiana University Press, 1987.

Dobrzyński, Przemysław. "Nasze wspaniałe polskie święta. Cicha noc recenzja." *Rozrywka blog*, November 24, 2017. https://www.spidersweb.pl/rozrywka/2017/11 /24/cicha-noc-recenzja-filmu/.

————. "O Polaku, co Niemcem chciał zostać. Pomiędzy słowami—recenzja." *Rozrywka.blog*, February 15, 2018. https://www.spidersweb.pl/rozrywka/2018/02 /15/pomiedzy-slowami-recenzja-filmu/.

Dry, Jude. "The Devils': Ken Russell's Banned 1971 Religious Horror Film Finally Gets Streaming Release." *IndieWire*, March 15, 2017. https://www .indiewire.com/2017/03/devils-ken-russell-banned-horror-streaming-shudder-x -rated-1201793838/.

Duda, Paulina. "Ryszard Bugajski on His Career." *East European Film Bulletin* 68, October 2016. https://eefb.org/interviews/ryszard-bugajski-on-his-career/.

Dudkiewicz, Jedrzej. "'W ciemności'—recenzj." January 9, 2012. https://maga-zynkontakt.pl/w-ciemnosci-recenzja/.

Durgnat, Raymond. "Paint it Black: The Family Tree of the Film Noir." *Cinema* (August 1970): 48–56.

Dzięciołowska, Karol. Interview by Weksler-Waszkiniel. May 2009, Lublin. https:// sprawiedliwi.org.pl/en/stories-of-rescue/your-stories/interview-pr-romuald-jakub -weksler-waszkinel.

Ebert, Roger. "Pretty Baby." June 1, 1978. https://www.rogerebert.com/reviews/ pretty-baby.

————. "To Kill a Priest." October 13, 1989. https://www.rogerebert.com/reviews/ to-kill-a-priest-1989.

Editorial Board. "In Poland, the Limits of Solidarity." *New York Times*, January 22, 2019. https://www.nytimes.com/2019/01/22/opinion/gdansk-mayor-murder.html ?action=click&module= Opinion&pgtype=Homepage.

"*Elles* (2011)." https://www.imdb.com/title/tt1549589/.

Engel, David. "Poland Since 1939." In *YIVO Encyclopedia of Jews in Eastern Europe* (online). https://yivoencyclopedia.org/article.aspx/Poland/Poland_since _1939.

Fabicki, Slawomir. Interview by Moritz Pfeifer. *East European Film Bulletin* 38, February 2014. https://eefb.org/interviews/slawomir-fabicki-on-loving/?pdf=2091.

————. "Sławomir Fabicki—Loving—Video Interview." https://culture.pl/en/video/ slawomir-fabicki-loving-video-interview.

Fainaru, Dan. "The Red Spider." July 7, 2015. https://www.screendaily.com/reviews /the-red-spider-review/5090163.article.

Fehérváry, Krisztina. *Politics in Color and Concrete: Socialist Materialities and the Middle Class in Hungary*. Bloomington, IN: Indiana University Press, 2013.

Felperin, Leslie. "The Last Family Review—Mesmerising Portrait of a Battling Brood." *Guardian*, December 3, 2018. https://www.theguardian.com/film/2016/ nov/03/the-last-family-review-jan-p-matuszynski-polish-film.

"Film/The Debt 1999." https://tvtropes.org/pmwiki/pmwiki.php/Film/TheDebt1999.

Fink, Carole. "Teaching the History of Cold War Europe." In *Understanding and Teaching the Cold War*, edited by Mathew Masur, 13–28. Madison: University of Wisconsin Press, 2017.

Fischer, Russ. "The Essentials: The 5 Best Andrzej Zulawski Films." *IndieWire*, February 19, 2016. https://www.indiewire.com/2016/02/the-essentials-the-5-best -andrzej-zulawski-films-268216/.

FNE Staff. "Polish Film School Launches Talent Resource Agency." June 29, 2020. http://filmneweurope.com/news/poland-news?start=26.

Ford, Charles, and Robert Hammond. *Polish Film: A Twentieth Century History.* Jefferson NC: McFarland & Co., Inc., 2005.

Fortuna, Grzegorz. "Obce niebo—Gdynia 2015). September 23, 2015. https://film.org.pl/r/recenzje/obce-niebo-gdynia-2015-68781/.

France, Louise. "Pedro Almadóvar and Penelope Cruz...the Mentor and the Muse." *Guardian*, 22 August 2009. https://www.theguardian.com/film/2009/aug/23/almodovar-cruz-film-interview.

"'Fuga,' reż. Agnieszka Smoczyńska." https://culture.pl/pl/dzielo/fuga-rez-agnieszka-smoczynska.

Fujiwara, Chris. "Convent Erotica." 22 December 2000. https://web.archive.org/web/20110719183028/http://www.hermenaut.com/a48.shtml.

Gale, Thomson. "Sadism." In *Encyclopedia of Sex and Gender: Culture Society History*, 2007. https://www.encyclopedia.com/social-sciences/encyclopedias-almanacs-transcripts-and-maps/sadism.

gazeta.pl, 5 March 2007. http://wiadomosci.gazeta.pl/wiadomosci/1,114873,3963488.html.

Gebert, Konstanty. "'We Need More Jews': Interview with Polish Jewish Activist Konstanty Gebert." Interview by Helena Gindi, Public Programs Director, YIVO Institute. YIVO Institute for Jewish Research, November 7, 2014. https://www.yivo.org/we-need-more-jews-interview-with-polish-jewish-activist-konstanty-gebert.

Genest, Andrea. "From Oblivion to Memory. Poland, the Democratic Opposition, and 1968." *Cuadernos de Historia Contemporánea* 31 (2009) 89–106.

Gera, Vanessa. "Poland Shaken by Documentary about Pedophile Priests." AP, May 13, 2019. https://www.ctvnews.ca/world/poland-shaken-by-documentary-about-pedophile-priests-1.4419673.

———. "Polish President calls LGBT 'Ideology' Worse than Communism." June 13, 2020. https://apnews.com/72fab166f1cfd02794c9add62247960e.

Gilbey, Ryan. "Why Polish Gangster Films 'On Steroids' Are Making It Big at the British Box Office." *Guardian*, December 3, 2018. https://www.theguardian.com/film/2018/may/03/why-polish-gangster-films-on-steroids-are-making-it-big-at-the-british-box-office.

Gliński, Mikołaj. "The Other Life of Jarosław Iwaszkiewicz." February 28, 2014. https://culture.pl/en/article/the-other-life-of-jaroslaw-iwaszkiewicz.

"Global Study on Homicide." United Nations Office on Drugs and Crime, 2013. https://www.un-ilibrary.org/drugs-crime-and-terrorism/global-study-on-homicide-2013_c1241a80-en.

Gluhovic, Milija. *Performing European Memories: Trauma, Ethics, and Politics.* Houndmills, UK: Palgrave, 2013.

Goclowski, Marcin. "Movie about Corrupt Priests Outrages Politicians in Catholic Poland." Reuters, September 28, 2018. https://www.reuters.com/article/us-poland-religion-movie/movie-about-corrupt-priests-outrages-politicians-in-catholic-poland-idUSKCN1M82FR.

Goddard, Michael. "Beyond Polish Moral Realism: The Subversive Cinema of Andrzej Żuławski." In *Polish Cinema in a Transnational Context*, edited by Ewa Mazierska and Michael Goddard, 236–57. Rochester: University of Rochester Press, 2014.

Gogler, Maggie. "Fugue." *View of the Arts*, May 16, 2018. https://viewofthearts.com /2018/05/16/71st-cannes-film-festival-fugue-review/.

Goscilo, Helena. "Playing Dead: The Operatics of Celebrity Funerals." In *Imitations of Life: Two Centuries of Melodrama in Russia,* edited by Louise McReynolds and Joan Neuberger, 283–319. Durham and London: Duke University Press, 2002.

———. "Widowhood as Genre and Profession à la Russe: Nation, Shadow, Curator, and Publicity Agent." In *Gender and National Identity in Twentieth-Century Culture,* edited by Helena Goscilo and Andrea Lanoux, 55–74. DeKalb IL: Northern Illinois University Press, 2006.

Goscilo, Helena, and Margaret B. Goscilo. *Fade from Red: The Cold War Ex-Enemy in Russian and American Film, 1990-2005.* Washington, DC: New Academia Publishing, 2014.

Goźliński, Paweł. Agora. https://www.youtube.com/watch?v=yFIDSxzea7Q.

Grabowski, Christopher. *Cinematic Echoes of Covenants Past and Present: National Identity in the Historical Films of Steven Spielberg and Andrzej Wajda.* Berlin: Peter Lang, 2018.

Graff, Agnieszka. "'Ida'—subtelność i polityka." November 1, 2013. https://krytyka-polityczna.pl/kultura/film/graff-ida-subtelnosc-i-polityka/.

———. "Looking at Pictures of Gay Men: Political Uses of Homophobia in Contemporary Poland." *Public Culture* 22, no. 3 (Fall 2010): 583–603.

Grater, Tom. "Polish Filmmakers Behind 'Corpus Christi,' 'Cold War,' and 'Kill It and Leave This Town' Discuss Country's Recent Successes and Future Prospects." June 24, 2020. https://deadline.com/video/polish-film-recent-successes-future -prospects-video/.

Grigorieff, Dmitry. "The Theotokos in the Orthodox Tradition and Russian Thought." https://www.theway.org.uk/back/s045Grigorieff.pdf.

Grollmus, Denise. "In the Polish Aftermath." *Tablet*, April 17, 2013. https://www .tabletmag.com/sections/arts-letters/articles/in-the-polish-aftermath.

Grynberg, Henryk. "Powodzenie 'Pokłosia' i 'Idy' w Nowym Jorku [Fragment 'Pamiętnika II']." *Kultura liberalna*, July 8, 2014. https://dzismis.com/2014/07/18 /powodzenie-poklosia-i-idy-w-nowym-jorku-fragment-pamietnika-ii/.

Grynienko, Katarzyna. "PRODUCTION: Władysław Pasikowski Shoots Dogs 3 Starring Bogusław Linda." July 16, 2019. https://www.filmneweurope.com/news /poland-news/item/118437-production-wladyslaw-pasikowski-shoots-dogs-3-star- ring-boguslaw-linda.

Guszkowski, Piotr. "Pomiędzy słowami: studium emigracji." 15 February 15, 2018. https://wyborcza.pl/7,101707,23028516,pomiedzy-slowami-studium-emigracji -recenzja.html.

Guynn, William Howard. *Unspeakable Histories: Film and the Experience of Catastrophe.* New York: Columbia University Press, 2016.

Guzik, Paulina. "Church in Poland Disturbed by Success of Anti-clerical Film." *CRUX*, October 6, 2018. https://cruxnow.com/church-in-europe/2018/10/06/church-in-poland-disturbed-by-success-of-anti-clerical-film/.

Halbiniak, Martyna. "Okruch lodu w sercu. 'Syn Królowej Śniegu'—recenzja filmu." January 31, 2018. https://ostatniatawerna.pl/okruch-lodu-w-sercu-syn-krolowej-sniegu-recenzja-filmu/.

Haltof, Marek. "A Fistful of Dollars: Polish Cinema after the 1989 Freedom Shock." *Film Quarterly* 48, no.3 (Spring 1995): 15–25.

———. *Polish Cinema: A History*. New York: Berghahn Books, 2002.

———. *Polish Cinema: A History*, 2nd edition. New York and Oxford: Berghahn Books, 2019.

———. *Polish Film and the Holocaust: Politics and Memory*. New York: Berghahn Books, 2012.

———. "The Representation of Stalinism in Polish Cinema." *Canadian Slavonic Papers/Revue canadienne des Slavistes*, xlii, nos. 1–2 (March-June 2000): 47–61.

Hanna, Aoife. "'Baptiste's Natalie Has a Background in Ballet & Appeared in This Anne Fontaine Film." February 17, 2019. https://www.bustle.com/p/who-is-anna-prochniak-the-actor-playing-baptistes-natalie-has-been-in-some-big-european-films-15959320.

Hanna, Beth. "Critics Get Behind Controversial Polish Drama 'Aftermath.'" *IndieWire*, November 15, 2013. https://www.indiewire.com/2013/11/critics-get-behind-controversial-polish-drama-aftermath-trailer-195063/.

Helman, Alicja. "Jerzy Kawalerowicz—wirtuoz kamery." In *Kino polskie w dziesięciu sekwencjach*, edited by Ewelina Nurczyńsk-Fidelska, 45–55. Lodz: Wydawnictwo Uniwersytetu Łódzkiego, 1996.

———. "Jerzy Kawalerowicz—wirtuoz kamery." In *Kino polskie w trzynastu sekwencjach*, edited by Ewelina Nurczyńsk-Fidelska, 79–91. Cracow: Rabid, 2005.

Heymont, George. "The Hung and the Restless." *Huffington Post*, December 6, 2017. https://www.huffingtonpost.com/george-heymont/the-hung-and-the-restless_b_5811664.html.

Hodge, Nick. "Helena Wolińska-Brus: 1919-2008." *Kraków Post*, December 31, 2008. http://www.krakowpost.com/pdf/Krakow_Post_issue_51.pdf. page 7.

———. "Review: Little Rose (Różyczka)." *Kraków Post*, July 7, 2010. http://www.krakowpost.com/2210/2010/07

Holden, Stephen. "Review: In *The Innocents*, Not Even Nuns Are Spared War Horrors." *New York Times*, June 30, 2016. https://www.nytimes.com/2016/07/01/movies/review-in-the-innocents-not-even-nuns-are-spared-war-horrors.html.

———. "Who Loses and Who Profits When Sex Is a Commodity?" *New York Times*, April 26, 2012. https://www.nytimes.com/2012/04/27/movies/elles-with-juliette-binoche-about-prostitution.html.

Hollender, Barbara. "'Pokłosie'—recenzja filmu." *Rzeczpospolita*, November 9, 2012. https://www.rp.pl/artykul/950085-Poklosie---recenzja-filmu.html.

Holmgren, Beth. "Holocaust History and Jewish Heritage Preservation: Scholars and Stewards Working in PiS-ruled Poland." *Shofar: An Interdisciplinary Journal of Jewish Studies* 37, no. 1 (2019): 96–107.

———. *Rewriting Capitalism: Literature and the Market in Late Tsarist Russia and the Kingdom of Poland.* Pittsburgh: University of Pittsburgh Press, 1998.

———. "The Importance of Being Unhappy, or Why She Died." In *Imitations of Life: Two Centuries of Melodrama in Russia,* edited by Louise McReynolds and Joan Neuberger, 79–98. Durham, NC: Duke University Press, 2002.

Honeycutt, Kirk. "Elles: Toronto Review." *Hollywood Reporter,* September 13, 2011, https://www.hollywoodreporter.com/review/elles-toronto-review-234669.

Hornaday, Ann. "'Cold War' Is Already Getting Oscar Buzz, Because It's a Near-perfect Movie." *Washington Post,* January 16, 2019. https://www.washingtonpost.com/goingoutguide/movies/cold-war-is-already-getting-oscar-buzz-because-its-a-near-perfect-movie/2019/01/16/7b154b94-1454-11e9-803c-4ef28312c8b9_story.html.

Horowitz, Jason and Elisabetta Povoledo. "The Most Talked about Non-Topic at the Vatican? Homosexuality." *New York Times,* February 23, 2019. https://www.nytimes.com/2019/02/23/world/europe/vatican-summit-gay-priests.html?action=click&module=News pgtype=Homepage.

Howard, Ed. "Diabel." *Only the Cinema,* January 19, 2011. http://seul-le-cinema.blogspot.com/2011/01/ diabel.html.

"How Many Prostitutes Are in the United States and the Rest of the World?" *ProCon.org,* January 11, 2018. https://prostitution.procon.org/view.answers.php?questionID=000095.

Hudson, Deal. "Ken Russell's The Devils Is Badly Misunderstood." 7 February 2019. https://catholicherald.co.uk/magazine/ken-russells-the-devils-is-badly-misunderstood/.

Huetlin, Josephine. "Here's Who Drives the Anti-LGBTQ Agenda in Poland Elections," July 13, 2020. https://www.thedailybeast.com/in-polands-elections-heres-who-drives-the-anti-lgbtq-agenda?fbclid=IwAR2tMHbERvTdH7izDbBPxM3wiK0ByV9L2sIzI4s6lxga7LPCig_woEhBsQ0.

Hundic, Stjepan. "Why the Polish Film Industry is Quietly on a Roll." *Hollywood Reporter,* February 19, 2020. https://www.hollywoodreporter.com/news/why-polish-film-industry-is-quietly-a-roll-1279973.

———. "Why the Poland Film Sector is Quietly Thriving." *Hollywood Reporter,* November 8, 2019. https://www.hollywoodreporter.com/news/why-poland-film-sector-is-quietly-thriving-1253258.

Hundley, Tom. "Poland's Gays Awake to a New Era." Reproduced by Richard Ammon, 2006. https://www.globalgayz.com/poland-s-gays-awake-gradually-to-a-new-era/251/.

"Ida." *RogerEbert.com,* May 2, 2014. https://www.rogerebert.com/reviews/ida-2014.

Insdorf, Annette. *Indelible Shadows: Film and the Holocaust.* 2nd Edition. Cambridge: Cambridge University Press, 2002.

Jacobson, Matthew Frye. *Whiteness of a Different Color: European Immigrants and the Alchemy of the Poor.* Cambridge, MA: Harvard University Press, 1998.

Jagiellonian University Institute. http://www.judaistyka.uj.edu.pl/instytut/historia.

Janicka, Bożena. "'Rewers.'" *Kino* 43, no. 11 (2009): 71–72.

Janicka, Elżbieta. "Corpus Christi, corpus delicti—nowy kontrakt narracyjny. 'Pokłosie' wobec kompromitacji kategorii polskiego świadka Zagłady." *Studia Litteraria et Historica*, no. 7 (2018): 1–93.

Janicka, Elżbieta, and Tomasz Żukowski, "Przemoc filosemicka [Philosemitic violence]." *Studia Litteraria et Historica*, 12, no. 1 (2012): 1–39.

Janicki, Stanisław. "Michał Waszyński—Artysta czy wyrobnik?" *Kino,* no. 5 (2018): 27–31.

Jarska, Natalia. "Modern Marriage and the Culture of Sexuality: Experts between the State and the Church in Poland, 1956-1970." *European History Quarterly* 49, no. 3 (2019): 467–90.

"Jasminum." Culture.pl. https://culture.pl/en/work/jasminum-jan-jakub-kolski.

Jazowska, Marta. "Elles: Malgorzata Szumowska." https://culture.pl/en/work/elles -malgorzata-szumowska.

———. "Loving—Sławomir Fabicki." https://culture.pl/en/work/loving-slawomir -fabicki.

———. "Martin Scorsese Presents 21 Masterpieces." October 14, 2013. https://culture.pl/en/article/martin-scorsese-presents-21-masterpieces.

———. "Shameless—Filip Marczewski." https://culture.pl/en/work/shameless-filip -marczewski.

Jelen, Ted G., and Clyde Wilcox. "Attitudes toward Abortion in Poland and the United States." *Social Science Quarterly* 78, no. 4 (December 1997): 907–21.

"Jewish Culture Festival in Kraków." https://www.jewishfestival.pl/en/.

Jewish Heritage Europe. https://jewish-heritage-europe.eu/.

John, Tara, and Muhammad Darwish. "LGBTQ Pride Parade in Bialystok, Poland, Met by Far Right Attacks." CNN, July 21, 2019. https://www.cnn.com/2019/07/21 /europe/bialystok-polish-lgbtq-pride-intl/index.html.

Johnson, Margaret Wheeler. "Małgorzata Szumowska, 'Elles' Director and Co-Writer, Talks Prostitution, Love." *HuffPost*, May 3 2012. https://www.huffpost.com/entry /malgorzata-szumowska-elles-juliette-binoche-joanna-kulig-anais-demoustier_n _1469094.

Kalan, Dariusz. "Poland's Ruling Party Pressures Cinemas to Stop Showing Blockbuster Film about Catholic Church abuse." *Telegraph*, 16 October 2018. https://www.telegraph.co.uk/news/2018/10/16/polands-ruling-party-pressures-cin emas-stop-showing-blockbuster/.

Karolak, Sylwia. "Utwory o matkach i córkach: kobiece narracje postmemorialne." *Politeja*, no. 35 (2015): 171–88.

"Katyń." Culture.pl. https://culture.pl/pl/dzielo/katyn.

Kawin, Bruce. "The Mummy's Pool." *In Film Theory and Criticism*, edited by Gerald Mast et al., 549–60. New York and Oxford: Oxford University Press, 1992.

Keinon, Herb. "Poland Changes Its Controversial Holocaust Law." *Jerusalem Post*, June 27, 2018. https://www.jpost.com/diaspora/poland-changes-its-controversial -holocaust-law-561025.

Kempista, Marcin. "Homo viator—recenzja filmu Pomiędzy słowami." *Pełna sala*, October 17, 2017. http://pelnasala.pl/pomiedzy-slowami/.

———. "'Zimna wojna'—Recenzja." *Filmawka.pl*, May 25, 2018. https://www.fil-mawka.pl/zimna-wojna-recenzja/.

Kerner, Aaron. *Film and the Holocaust: New Perspectives on Dramas, Documentaries, and Experimental Films*. London, New York: Continuum, 2011.

Kępa, Marek. "Trend Watch: Polish Crime Cinema on the Rise," January 17, 2017. https://culture.pl/en/article/trend-watch-polish-crime-cinema-on-the-rise.

Kiang, Jessica. "Shameless." *IndieWire*, July 15, 2012. https://www.indiewire.com /2012/07/karlovy-vary-film-fest-review-roundup-shameless-hay-road-nos-vemos -papa-108416/.

King, Danny. "In Poland's 'The Last Family,' an Artist's Clan Unravels Over Decades." *Village Voice*, January 26, 2018. https://www.villagevoice.com/2018/01 /26/in-polands-the-last-family-an-artists-clan-unravels-over-decades/.

Kipp, Jeremiah. "DVD Review: The Devil." *Slant*, October 4, 2007. https://www .slantmagazine.com/dvd/the-devil/.

Kobus, Justyna. "'Kler' wzbudzil dyskusję, zanim ktokolwiek go zobaczył. Smarzowski dotknął tabu." Tvn24, September 19, 2018. https://www.tvn24.pl/ kultura-styl,8/kler-smarzowskiego-zachwycil-i-oburzyl,869469.html.

Kołodyński, Andrzej. "Fuga." *Kino*, no. 6 (2019): 89.

Konopka, Tomasz. "The Anti-Bribery and Anti-Corruption Review—Edition 7, December 2018. https://thelawreviews.co.uk/edition/the-anti-bribery-and-anti-cor-ruption-review-edition-7/1177236/poland.

Kościańska, Agnieszka. "Sex on Equal Terms? Polish Sexology on Women's Emancipation and 'Good Sex' from the 1970s to the Present." *Sexualities* 19, no. 1 / 2 (2016): 236–56.

Kowalczyk, Maciej. "W potrzasku—recenzja filmu Dzikie róże." *Pełna sala*, January 9, 2018. http://pelnasala.pl/dzikie-roze/.

Kristeva, Julia. *Powers of Horror: An Essay on Abjection*. Translated by Leon S. Roudiez. New York: Columbia University Press, 1982.

———. "Stabat Mater." In *The Portable Kristeva*, edited by Toril Moi, 160–86. New York: Columbia University Press, 1986.

Kruk, Adam. "Ostatnia rodzina." *Kino*, no. 9 (2016): 69. http://kino.org.pl//index.php ?option=com_content&task=view&id=2567&Itemid=1729.

"Krzysztof Warlikowski Director 20/21 Artist." https://www.operadeparis.fr/en/art-ists/krzysztof-warlikowski.

Kuba. "Stanisław Kogut: Wybory parlamentarne 2019. Senator Kogut znów wystar-tuje w wyborach." August 21, 2019. http://krakow.wyborcza.pl/krakow/7,44425 ,25108492,wybory-parlamentarne-2019-senator-kogut-znow-wystartuje-w-wybo-rach.html.

Kuisz, Jarosław. "Between Pigs and Debt." Translated by Zuzanna Wiśniewska. *Film* no. 2 (1999): 10.

———. "Between Pigs and Debt." *Eurozine*, May 6, 2009. https://www.eurozine .com/between-pigs-and-debt/.

Kurtz, Glenn. *Three Minutes in Poland: Discovering a Lost World in a 1938 Family Film*. New York: Farrar, Straus, & Giroux, 2014.

Kurz, Iwona. "Różyczka." *dwutygodnik.com*, March 2010. https://www.dwutygodnik .com/artykul/972-rozyczkarez-jan-kidawa-blonski.html. Accessed July 22, 2018.

Kuśmierczyk, Seweryn. "The Form of an Image: *Mother Joan of the Angels* and *Pharaoh*." In *Jerzy Kawalerowicz, malarz X muzy*, 92–100. Lodz: Muzeum Kinomatografii, 2012.

Kwas, Barbara. "Ten film ma momenty." January 1, 2013. http://kultura.gazeta.pl/ kultura/1,114438,5823979,Sennosc___ten_film_ma_momenty.html.

Lang, Krzysztof. *Ach śpij kochanie.* Insert, 18. Studio Produkcyjne Orka, Monolith Films, Krakowskie Biuro Festiwalowe. Warsaw: Monolith Films, 2017.

Lebecka, Magdalena. "Prawie psychodrama." *Kino*, no. 9 (2008): 17. http://filmo-tekaszkolna.pl/dla-uczniow/materialy-filmoznawcze/prawie-psychodrama.'

Lehrer, Erica. *Jewish Poland Revisited: Heritage Tourism in Unquiet Spaces.* Bloomington, IN: Indiana University Press, 2013.

Lem, Stanisław. *The Futurological Congress.* Translated by Michael Kandel. San Diego and New York: Continuum Publishing, 1974.

Lemercier, Fabien. "Elles." Cineuropa, January 24, 2012. https://cineuropa.org/en/ newsdetail/215084/.

Lewis, Paul. "The Lure of a Dollar in Poland." *New York Times*, October 9, 1981. https://www.nytimes.com/1981/10/09/business/the-lure-of-a-dollar-in-poland.html.

lewisfontaine. "The Mother Archetype." *Carl Jung Depth Psychology*, March 13, 2018. https://carljungdepthpsychologysite.blog/2018/03/13/the-mother-arche-type/#.W8OXy2hKiUk.

Lodge, Guy. "Film Review: 'Fugue.'" *Variety*, May 16, 2018. https://variety.com /2018/film/reviews/fugue-review-1202812117/.

———. "San Sebastian Film Review: 'Beyond Words.'" *Variety*, September 27, 2017. https://variety.com/2017/film/reviews/beyond-words-review-1202574984/.

Loshitzky, Yosefa. *Screening Strangers: Migration and Diaspora in Contemporary European Cinema.* Bloomington and Indianapolis: Indiana University Press, 2010.

———. "Screening Strangers in Fortress Europe and Beyond." *Crossings: Journal of Migration and Culture* 5, no. 2/3 (2014): 187–99.

Lubińska, Dorota. "Polish Migrants in Sweden: An Overview." *Folia Scandinavica*, Poznań 15 (2013): 73–88.

Luciak, Paulina. "Recenzja filmu Magdaleny Piekorz 'Sienność.'" May 27, 2012. http://coolturalni24.pl/2012/05/27/recenzja-filmu-magdaleny-piekorz-sennosc/.

Luter, Ks. Andrzej. "Różyczka." *Kino*, no. 3 (2010): 64–65. http://kino.org.pl//index .php?option=com_content&task=view&id=679&Itemid=434.

Luxmoore, Jonathan. "Clerical Power Thwarts Victims in Poland." *National Catholic Reporter*, February 8, 2012. https://www.ncronline.org/news/accountability/cleri-cal-power-thwarts-victims-poland.

———. "Poland's Catholic Church Takes on Its Critics." *National Catholic Reporter*, February 16, 2018. https://www.ncronline.org/news/world/polands-catholic-church -takes-its-critics.

Luzar, Adrian. January 16, 2018. https://film.interia.pl/recenzje/news-syn-krolowej -sniegu-recenzja-zimno-coraz-zimniej,nId,250888.

Łazarewicz, Cezary. "Podwójne życie żony Jasienicy: Nesia wszystko doniesie." March 12, 2010. https://www.polityka.pl/tygodnikpolityka/kraj/1504026,1,podwojne-zycie-zony-jasienicy.read.

Maciejewski, Łukasz. "Dzikie róże: jedyny taki duet w polskim kinie." *Narodowe centrum kultury*, April 12, 2018. https://nck.pl/projekty-kulturalne/projekty/kultura-dostepna/aktualnosci/dzikie-roze-kultura-dostepna-w-kinach.

Maciejewski, Łukasz. "'Rewers'—największa filmowa niespodzianka roku." November 12, 2009. https://film.dziennik.pl/artykuly/101727,rewers-najwieksza-filmowa-niespodzianka-roku.html.

———. "'Różyczka': Znakomita, oparta na faktach historia." March 17, 2010. https://kultura.onet.pl/film/recenzje/rozyczka-znakomita-oparta-na-faktach-historia/tmp2bnk.

Macnab, Geoffrey. "Martin Scorsese Celebrates Masterpieces of Polish Cinema from Ashes and Diamonds to Black Cross." *Independent*, April 17, 2015.

Magazyn Kochających Inaczej 8, no. 62 (August 1995).

Małkowska, Monika. "Ostatnia rodzina. Mit wciśnięty w banal." *Rzeczpospolita*, September 27, 2016. https://www.rp.pl/Film/309279859-Ostatnia-rodzina-Mit-wcisniety-w-banal.html.

Marczewski, Filip. "Filip Marczewski, Director: Interview." *Cineuropa*, March 14, 2013. https://cineuropa.org/en/video/234700/.

Marinoe-pl. "Polish Movies with LGBTQ Motive." 16 August 2019. https://www.imdb.com/list/ls055150286/.

Marshall, Alex. "Movie about Church Sexual Abuse Is a Contentious Hit in Poland." *New York Times*, October 8, 2018. https://www.nytimes.com/2018/10/08/arts/poland-clergy-movie.html.

Marshall, Robert. *In the Sewers of Lwów: A Heroic Story of Survival from the Holocaust*. London and New York: Bloomsbury Press, 2013, reprint.

Martel, Frédéric. *In the Closet of the Vatican: Power, Homosexuality, Hypocrisy*. London: Bloomsbury Continuum, 2019.

"Martin Scorsese Explains His Fascination with Polish Cinema." January 30, 2014. https://culture.pl/en/article/martin-scorsese-explains-his-fascination-with-polish-cinema.

Masur, Matthew, ed. *Understanding and Teaching the Cold War*. Madison: University of Wisconsin Press, 2017.

Mazierska, Ewa. "Barbara Sass: The Author of Women's Films." In Ewa Mazierska and Elżbieta Ostrowska. *Women in Polish Cinema*, 166–84. New York and Oxford: Berghahn Books, 2006.

———. *Masculinities in Polish, Czech and Slovak Cinema*. New York and Oxford: Berghahn Books, 2008.

———. *Polish Postcommunist Cinema: From Pavement Level*. New Studies in European Cinema. Bern: Peter Lang. Volume 4, 2007.

McBride, Nuri. "The Odour of Sanctity: When the Dead Smell Divine." *The Order of the Good Death*. http://www.orderofthegooddeath.com/odour-sanctity-dead-smell-divine.

McCahill, Mike. "Counting the Sins of the Catholic Priesthood." *Guardian*, 11 October 2018. https://www.theguardian.com/film/2018/oct/11/kler-review -wojciech-smarzowski-robert-wieckiewicz.

McClintock, Annie. *Sex Workers and Sex Work*. Raleigh, NC: Duke University Press, 1994.

Menken, Robin. "Little Rose." January 7, 2011. https://cinemawithoutborders.com /2423-little-rose/.

Merriam-Webster Dictionary. https://www.merriam-webster.com/dictionary/crime.

Michelson, Annette. "The Kinetic Icon and the Work of Mourning: Prolegomena in the Analysis of a Textual System." In *The Red Screen: Politics, Society, Art in Soviet Cinema*, edited by Anna Lawton, 113–31. London: Routledge, 1992.

Michnik, Adam. "Michnik o Jasienicy: pisarz w obcęgach." *Gazeta Wyborcza*, 19 August 2005.

Mickiewicz, Adam. *Wybór pism*. Warsaw: Książka i Wiedza, 1951.

Mirowski, Mikołaj. "Bo to bardzo ważny, choć niewybitny film jest. Recenzja filmu 'Pokłosie.'" March 28, 2013. https://liberte.pl/bo-to-bardzo-wazny-choc-nie -wybitny-film-jest-recenzja-filmu-poklosie-wladyslawa-pasikowskiego/.

Misztal, Bronisław, ed. *Poland After Solidarity: Social Movements Versus the State*. Piscataway, NJ: Transaction Pubs., 1985.

Modleski, Tania. "Time and Desire in the Woman's Film." In *Film Theory and Criticism*, edited by Gerald Mast et al., 536–48. Oxford: Oxford University Press, 1992.

Mokrzycka-Pokora, Monika. "Izabella Cywińska." November 2016. https://culture.pl /en/artist/izabella-cywinska.

Morgan, Eric J. "Whores and Angels of Our Striving Selves: The Cold War Films of John Le Carré, Then and Now." *Historical Journal of Film, Radio and Television* 36, no. 1 (2016): 88–103.

Mortensen, Antonia. "Polish Priest Blames 'Devil' as He's Confronted by Alleged Victim Whose Life Was Ruined." CNN, May 26, 2019. https://www.cnn.com/2019 /05/26/europe/poland-catholic-church-abuse-intl/index.html.

Moskowitz, David A., Gerulf Rieger, and Michael E. Roloff, "Heterosexual Attitudes towards Same-Sex Marriage." NCBI, October 14, 2016. https://www.ncbi.nlm.nih .gov/pmc/articles/PMC5065072/.

Murray, Jonathan. "Cold War." *Cinéaste* 44, no. 1 (Winter 2018): 44–46.

———. "The Music of Freedom: An Interview with Paweł Pawlikowski." *Cinéaste* 44, no. 1 (Winter 2018): 2–7.

Nelson, Soraya Sarhaddi. "For Poland's Gay Community, A Shift in Public Attitudes, if Not Laws." NPR, June 25, 2015. https://www.npr.org/sections/parallels/2015/06 /25/417446107/for-polands-gay-community-a-shift-in-public-attitudes-if-not-laws.

"New Polish Films 2014." Polish Film Institute. http://en.pisf.pl/files/dokumenty/fpg /npf_2014.pdf.

Nicholson, Ben. "Kinoteka 2013: 'Shameless' Review." March 13, 2013. https://cine -vue.com/2013/03/kinoteka-2013-shameless-review.html.

Norsworthy, Cameron. "How Many Children Are Victims of Homicide Each Year? The U.S. Has High Numbers." August 23, 2016. https://www.romper.com/p/

how-many-children-are-victims-of-homicide-each-year-the-us-has-high-numbers
-17008.

Orton, Lawrence D. "Paweł Jasienica—A Rectification and Appreciation." *The Polish Review* 29, nos. 1–2 (1984): 15–29.

Ostrowska, Elżbieta. "Andrzej Wajda: How to be Loved and Serve One's Country?" *Studies in Eastern European Cinema* 8, no. 1 (2017): 78–91. https://www.tandfon-line.com/doi/abs/10.1080/2040350X.2017.1262122?scroll=top&needAccess=true&journalCode=reec20.

———. "Filmic Representations of the 'Polish Mother' in Post Second World War Polish Cinema." *The European Journal of Polish Studies* 5 (1998): 419–35.

———. "'I will wash it out': Holocaust Reconciliation in Agnieszka Holland's 2011 Film, In Darkness." *Holocaust and Genocide Studies* 79, no. 1 (Spring 2015): 57–75.

———. "Katyń Andrzeja Wajdy: melodramatyczny afekt i historia." *Pleograf. Kwartalnik Akademii Polskiego Filmu* 1 (2016). https://akademiapolskiegofilmu.pl/pl/historia-polskiego-filmu/pleograf/andrzej-wajda/1/katyn-andrzeja-wajdy-melo-dramatyczny-afekt-i-historia/536.

Ostrowska, Joanna. "Książę i Dybuk." *Kino*, no. 5 (2018): 70–71.

Paczkowski, Andrzej, and Christina Manetti. *Revolution and Counterrevolution in Poland, 1980-1989: Solidarity, Martial Law, and the End of Communism in Eastern Europe*. Rochester, NY: University of Rochester Press, 2015.

Pajakowski, Philip "Viewing Poland's Cold War through Literature and Film." In *Understanding and Teaching the Cold War*, edited by Matthew Masur, 205–22. Madison: University of Wisconsin Press, 2017.

Pasikowski, Władysław. "Breaking National Taboos: An Interview with Władysław Pasikowski and Dariusz Jabłoński." Interview by Leonard Quart. *Cinéaste* 9, no. 31 (Winter 2013): 22–25, 60.

Patterson, Patrick Hyder. *Bought and Sold: Living and Losing the Good Life in Socialist Yugoslavia*. Ithaca, NY: Cornell University Press, 2012.

Pattison, Mark. "Movie Tells Story of Polish Priest Born a Jew during the Holocaust." *The Forward*, December 6, 2011. https://thedialog.org/featured/movie-tells-story-of-polish-priest-born-a-jew-during-holocaust/.

Patton, Elaina. "In Cold War, Paweł Pawlikowski Tells His Parents' Love Story." *New Yorker*, December 22, 2018. https://www.newyorker.com/culture/culture-desk/in-cold-war-pawel-pawlikowski-tells-his-parents-love-story.

Pawlak, Maciej. "30 Years of the Ronald S. Lauder Foundation in Poland, 1987-2017." *Scripta Judaica Cracoviensia*, 15 (2017): 155–67.

Pawlikowski, Pawel. "'Ida' Director Made Film to 'Recover the Poland of His Childhood." Interview by Terry Gross, February 12, 2015. https://www.npr.org/2015/02/12/385742784/ida-director-made-film-to-recover-the-poland-of-his-childhood.

———. "Ida's Bittersweet Success: An Interview With [sic] Pawel Pawlikowski." Interview by David Sims. *Atlantic*, February 12, 2015. https://www.theatlantic.com/entertainment/archive/2015/02/pawel-pawlikowski-on-the-personal-and-the-historical-in-ida/385568/.

Pawluśkiewicz, Joanna. December 2006. https://culture.pl/pl/dzielo/kochankowie-z -marony.

Pelczar, Jan. "'Pokłosie'—Recenzja filmu," December 3, 2012. https://www.radioram .pl/articles/view/23144/POKLOSIE-Recenzja-filmu.

Picheta, Rob. "Polish Court Rules against Abortion Due to Fetal Defects." CNN, October 22, 2020. https://www.cnn.com/2020/10/22/europe/poland-abortion-fetal -defect-ruling-intl/index.html.

Piepiórka, Michał. "Jestem mordercą." *Kino*, no. 11 (2016): 77. http://kino.org.pl// index.php?option=com_content&task=view&id=2599&Itemid=1746.

Pietrasik, Zdzisław. "'Różyczka,' czyli historia pewnego pisarza." March 12, 2010. https://www.polityka.pl/tygodnikpolityka/kultura/1504012,1,rozyczka-czyli-histo-ria-pewnego-pisarza.read.

———. "Zostaną tylko guziki." September 15, 2007. https://www.polityka.pl/tygod-nikpolityka/kultura/228539,1,zostana-tylko-guziki.read.

Pietrzak, Edyta, and Anna Fligel. "'Black Protest': Abortion Law in Poland in the Context of Division into Private and Public Sphere." In *Mothers in Public and Political Life*, edited by Simone Bohn, Pinar Melisa Yesali Parmaksiz, 287–305. Bradford, Canada: Demeter Press, 2017.

Pietrzyk, Marcin. "Matka-szmatka i inne bajki." January 22, 2018. https://www.film-web.pl/review/Matka-szmatka+i+inne+bajki-20986.

Piotrowska, Anita. "Is Poland a Woman? Feminist and Homosexual Themes in Polish Film from 1989-2009." In *Polish Cinema Now! Focus on Contemporary Polish Cinema*, edited by Mateusz Werner, 104–28. London and Warsaw: John Libbey Publishing-Adam Mickiewicz Institute, 2009.

Pirodsky, Jason. "'Fugue' an Intriguing Polish Mystery." *Prague Reporter*, July 15, 2018. https://www.praguereporter.com/home/2018/7/5/kviff-2018-review-fugue -an-intriguing-polish-mystery.

"Play Poland 2016 Film Festival." http://www.playpoland.org.uk/index.php5?name =newsy&old=737.

Plucinska, Joanna and Anna Wlodarczak-Semczuk, "Poland's Ruling Party Picks LGBT Rights as Election Battlefront." Reuters, March 15, 2019. https://www .reuters.com/article/us-poland-lgbt/polands-ruling-party-picks-lgbt-rights-as-elec-tion-battlefront-idUSKCN1QW0T7.

Płażewski, Jerzy. "Polish Cinema—A Return to Market Economy." In *Polish Cinema Now! Focus on Contemporary Polish Cinema*, edited by Mateusz Werner, 150–69. London and Warsaw: John Libbey Publishing-Adam Mickiewicz Institute, 2009.

"Poland 2019 Crime & Safety Report." March 8, 2019. https://www.osac.gov/ Content/Report/3a89580c-512f-404b-9f9a-15f4aeb14091.

"Poland Corruption Rank." Trading Economics, 2019. https://tradingeconomics.com /poland/corruption-rank.

"Poland Corruption Report." GAN—Business Anti-Corruption Portal, January 2018. https://www.ganintegrity.com/portal/country-profiles/poland/.

"Poland's Leader Slams Church Pathology, Backs Sex Abuse Probe." *CRUX*, May 18, 2019. https://cruxnow.com/church-in-europe/2019/05/18/poland-leader-slams -church-pathology-backs-sex-abuse-probe/.

"Poland's Ruling Chief Speaks Strongly against LGBT Rights." AP, March 16, 2019. https://www.foxnews.com/world/polands-ruling-chief-speaks-strongly-against -lgbt-rights.

"Poland's Ruling Party Confronts the 'LGBT Dictatorship.'" *Economist*, May 4–May 10, 2019.

Polin. https://www.polin.pl/en/support/donor-list.

"Polish Church Turns to Top Court in Pedophile Case." Reuters, October 3, 2018. https://www.reuters.com/article/us-poland-church-paedhophilia/polish-church -turns-to-top-court-in-pedophile-case-idUSKCN1MD1EM.

Połaski, Krzysztof. "Cicha noc: Mocny cios w nasze polskie mordy." November 24, 2017. https://www.telemagazyn.pl/artykuly/cicha-noc-mocny-cios-w-nasze-pol-skie-mordy-recenzja-61616.html.

———. "Dzikie róże: Z rodziną najlepiej wychodzi się na zdjęciu." May 12, 2018. https://www.telemagazyn.pl/artykuly/dzikie-roze-z-rodzina-najlepiej-wychodzi -sie-na-zdjeciu-recenzja-59479.html.

———. "Pomiędzy słowami: krótka opowieść o Polaku, który chciał stać się über Niemcem." February 14, 2018. https://www.telemagazyn.pl/artykuly/pomiedzy -slowami-recenzja-krotka-opowiesc-o-polaku-ktory-chcial-stac-sie-uber-niemcem -63094.html.

"Prominent Nun Says Polish Priests Must Stop Abusing Women Religious." *CRUX/Catholic News Service*, February 15, 2019. https://cruxnow.com/church-in -europe/2019/02/15/prominent-nun-says-polish-priests-must-stop-abusing-women -religious/.

Przeperski, Michał. "'Pokłosie'—reż. Władysława Pasikowskiego, recenzja i ocena filmu." November 15, 2012. https://histmag.org/Poklosie-rez.-Wladyslaw -Pasikowski-7296.

Pulver, Andrew. "Elles—Review." *Guardian*, February 10, 2012. https://www.the-guardian.com/film/2012/feb/10/elles-review.

Pustkowiak, Patrycja. "There the Most Common Method of Contraception Is Prayer." *Aspen Review* 2 (2017). https://www.aspenreview.com/article/2017/where-the -most-common-method-of-contraception-is-prayer/.

Quart, Leonard. "Wajda's Katyń." *Slavic and East European Performance* 29, no. 1 (Winter 2009): 77–82.

Rachwald-Rostkowski. Tomasz. "Polak-koczownik: Recenzja filmu Cicha noc Piotra Domalewskiego." November 18, 2017. https://kulturaliberalna.pl/2017/11/28/ tomasz-rachwald-rostkowski-polak-koczownik-cicha-noc-recenzja/.

Raflesz, Joanna. "Porąbane łóżko. Analiza Domu złego Wojciecha Smarzowskiego." October 4, 2016. https://film.org.pl/a/analiza/porabane-lozko-analiza-domu-zlego -wojciecha-smarzowskiego-32762/.

Ramon, Alex. "Gdynia Film Festival 2015: 'New World' + 'Strange Heaven' + 'The Here After.'" September 24, 2015. https://www.popmatters.com/gdynia-film-festi-val-2015-new-world-strange-heaven-the-here-after-2495486324.html.

Rek, Jan. *Kino Jerzego Kawalerowicza i jego konteksty*. Lodz: Wydawnictwo Universytetu Łódzkiego, 2008.

Reszke, Katka. *Return of the Jew: Identity Narratives of the Third Post-Holocaust Generation of Jews in Poland*. Boston: Academic Studies Press, 2013.

Roache, Madeline. "Poland Is Trying to Make Abortion Dangerous, Illegal, and Impossible." *Foreign Policy*, January 8, 2019. https://foreignpolicy.com/2019/01/08/poland-is-trying-to-make-abortion-dangerous-illegal-and-impossible/.

Roediger, David R. *Working Toward Whiteness: How America's Immigrants Became White, The Strange Journey from Ellis Island to the Suburbs*. New York: Basic Books, 2005.

Rojek, Zofia. "'Ida' pełna antysemickich stereotypów? Krytyka najnowszego filmu Pawlikowskiego." November 5, 2013. https://natemat.pl/80843,ida-pelna-antysemickich-stereotypow.

Rolski, Tomek. "Poland's New Abortion Law Triggers Broader Discontent as Women Lead Protests." October 27, 2020. https://abcnews.go.com/International/polands-abortion-law-triggers-broader-discontent-women-lead/story?id=73853693.

Romańska, Dagmara. "'Rewers': polskie kino w najlepszym amerykańskim stylu." October 13, 2009. https://kultura.onet.pl/film/recenzje/rewers-polskie-kino-w-najlepszym-amerykanskim-stylu/jj7cgxb.

Rostek, Joanna, and Dirk Uffelman, eds. *Contemporary Polish Migrant Culture and Literature in Germany, Ireland, and the UK*. Frankfurt am Main: Peter Lang, 2011.

Rożen-Wojciechowska, Joanna. "The Phenomenon of Polish Independent Cinema in 1989-2009." In *Polish Cinema Now! Focus on Contemporary Polish Cinema*, edited by Mateusz Werner, 130–49. Warsaw-London: Adam Mickiewicz Institute-John Libbey Publishing, 2010.

"Różyczka." http://www.filmpolski.pl/fp/index.php?film=1223331.

Sadowska, Małgorzata. "Małgośka Szumowska wraca z nowym filmem—'W imię.' Pan jest blisko." *Newsweek*, 11 March, 2013. http://www.newsweek.pl/kultura/film/malgoska-szumowska-wraca-z-nowym-filmem---w-imie--pan-jest-blisko,101302,1,1.html.

Sadowska, Maria. "Jestem feministką: Maria Sadowska: Fragment wywiadu z reżyserką." Interview in the booklet accompanying the DVD of *Sztuka Kochania: Historia Michaliny Wisłockiej*. Warsaw: Agora SA, 2017.

Salwa, Ola. "Polish Film: The Art of Loving Tops Local 2017 Box Office." March 21, 2017. https://cineuropa.org/en/newsdetail/325822.

———. "Silent Night: All is (not) calm." November, 23 2017. https://cineuropa.org/en/newsdetail/342933/.

———. "The Polish Film Institute Announces Second Batch of Production Grants for 2020." July 14, 2020. https://cineuropa.org/en/newsdetail/390154/.

Santora, Marc. "Poland's Populists Pick a New Top Enemy: Gay People." *New York Times*, April 7, 2019. https://www.nytimes.com/2019/04/07/world/europe/poland-gay-rights.html.

Santora, Marc, and Joanna Berendt. "Polish Women Protest Proposed Abortion Ban (Again)." *New York Times*, March 23, 2018. https://www.nytimes.com/2018/03/23/world/europe/poland-abortion-women-protest.html.

Saryusz-Wolska, Magdalena. "The Theory of National Memory in Polish Post-War Cinema." *Studia Universitatis Cibiniensis* XI, supp. (2014): 201–14.

Scally, Derek. "Polish Clerical Abuse Film Turns Mirror on Audience." *Irish Times*, October 10, 2018. https://www.irishtimes.com/news/world/europe/polish-clerical-abuse-film-turns-mirror-on-audience-1.3657382.

———. "Robert Biedron Is Latest Political Hope of Poland's Left." *Irish Times*, February 4, 2019. https://www.irishtimes.com/news/world/europe/robert-biedron -is-latest-political-hope-of-poland-s-left-1.3781863.

Schatz, Thomas. *Hollywood Genres: Formulas, Filmmaking, and the Studio System*. Philadelphia: Temple University Press, 1981.

Scheib, Ronnie. "Film Review: 'Aftermath.'" *Variety*, November 1, 2013. https:// variety.com/2013/film/reviews/aftermath-review-1200783281/.

Schrader, Paul. "Notes on Film Noir." *Film Comment*, 8, no. 1 (Spring 1972): 8–13.

Schwarz, Penny. "The Intrepid Couple Who Restored a Gem of a Polish Synagogue." *Times of Israel*, September 30, 2015. https://www.timesofisrael.com/the-intrepid -couple-who-restored-a-gem-of-a-polish-synagogue/.

Scott, A. O. "Unlikely Hero in an Underground Hideout, Away from the Nazis." *New York Times*, December 8, 2011. https://www.nytimes.com/2011/12/09/movies/in -darkness-from-agnieszka-holland-review.html.

Semczuk, Przemysław. *Wampir z Zagłębia*. Warsaw: Znak, 2016.

Shah, Shakhil. "'I Make Films about Things Which Cause Me Pain or Heartache.'" December 1, 2018. https://emerging-europe.com/after-hours/i-make-films-about -things-which-cause-me-pain-or-heartache/.

Shore, Marci. "Conversing with Ghosts: Jedwabne, Żydokomuna, and Totalitarianism." *Kritika: Explorations in Russian and Eurasian History* 6, no. 2 (Spring 2005): 345–74.

Siennica, Adam. "Cicha noc—recenzja filmu." November 24, 2017. https://naekra -nie.pl/recenzje/cicha-noc-recenzja-filmu-festiwal-polskich-filmow-fabularnych -gdyni.

Sifferlin, Alexandra. "It's Almost Impossible to Get An Abortion in Poland. These Women Crossed the Border to Germany for Help." *Time*, January 31, 2018. https:// time.com/poland-abortion-laws-protest/.

Sikorska, Marta. "Rozmowa z Barbarą Sass i Katarzyną Zawadzką." PISF: YouTube, June 8, 2011. https://www.youtube.com/watch?v=kWSjEBjJyLE.

Simon, Alissa. "A Compelling, Strongly Performed Political Thriller Set in Contemporary Poland." *Variety*, June 18, 2013. https://variety.com/2013/film/ reviews/film-review-the-closed-circuit-1200496827/.

———. "In the Name of." *Variety*, February 8, 2013. https://variety.com/2013/film/ markets-festivals/in-the-name-of-1117949193/.

———. "Polish Director Tomasz Wasilewski Delivers a Feel-Bad Coming-out Drama in Artful, Sexually Provocative Fashion." *Variety*, July 3, 2013. https:// variety.com/2013/more/global/film-review-floating-skyscrapers-1200567231/.

———. "Shameless." *Variety*, July 23, 2012. https://variety.com/2012/film/reviews/ shameless-2-1117947933/.

———. "The Dark House." *Variety*, April 5, 2010. https://variety.com/2010/film/ reviews/the-dark-house-1117942542/.

Simon, Julie Hersh. "The Closed Circuit/Układ zamknięty." August 9, 2016. https:// popkult.org/closed-circuit/.

Skilling, Gordon H. *Czechoslovakia's Interrupted Revolution*. Princeton, NJ: Princeton University Press, 1976.

Sklar, Deborah. "Polish Filmmaker Put WWII Massacre on the Map." *Jewish Telegraphic Agency,* July 8, 2001. https://www.jta.org/2001/09/18/lifestyle/polish -filmmaker-put-wwii-massacre-on-the-map.

Smith, Nigel M. "'Little Rose' Wins Big at Tiburion International Film Festival." *IndieWire,* April 18, 2011. https://www.indiewire.com/2011/04/little-rose-wins -big-at-tiburion-international-film-festival-242907/.

Snyder, Timothy. "The Overwhelming Realism of 'In Darkness.'" *New York Times,* Culture Desk, February 22, 2012. https://www.newyorker.com/culture/culture -desk/the-overwhelming-realism-of-in-darkness.

Sobolewski, Tadeusz. *Gazeta Wyborcza,* DVD of *Ida,* opusfilm, 2013.

———. "33 sceny z życia i śmierci." November 7, 2008. http://wyborcza.pl/1,75410 ,5892199,33_sceny_z_zycia_i_smierci.html.

———. "Dzikie róże: Jeden z najlepszych polskich filmów 2017 roku opowiada o dziejach grzechu." December 27, 2017. https://wyborcza.pl/7,101707,22831667 ,dzikie-roze-jeden-z-najlepszych-polskich-filmow-2017-roku.html.

———. "Film 'Czerwony pająk': Morderstwo, czylie dzieło sztuki—rozmowa z reżyserem," November 27, 2015. http://wyborcza.pl/1,75410,19253228,film-czer- wony-pajak-morderstwo-czyli-dzielo-sztuki-rozmowa.html.

———. "Film z tamtego świata." November 8–9, 2008. https://wyborcza.pl/1,75410 ,5896960,Film_z_tamtego_swiata.html.

———. "'Miłość' Fabickiego: Nie wiem, czy jeszcze cię kocham." March 16, 2013. http://wyborcza.pl/1,75410,13570522,_Milosc__Fabickiego__Nie_wiem__czy _jeszcze_cie_kocham.html.

———. "Obce niebo—film podstępny. Zimne piekło Szwecji, gorąco piekło Polski." October 15, 2015. https://wyborcza.pl/1,101707,19024829,obce-niebo-film-pod- stepny-zimne-pieklo-szwecji-gorace.html.

———. "Oscarowa 'Ida' po raz pierwszy w TV. Pawlikowski: nadchodzi czas nacjonalizmu [ROZMOWA]." November 19, 2015. http://wyborcza.pl/1,75410 ,19210750,oscarowa-ida-po-raz-pierwszy-w-tv-pawlikowski-nadchodzi.html.

———. "Sobolewski o filmie 'Ostatnia Rodzina': To nie kryminał, tylko opowieść o miłości i depresij." August 5, 2016. http://wyborcza.pl/7,101707,20501550,sobo- lewski-o-filmie-ostatnia-rodzina-to-nie-kryminal-tylko.html.

———. "Dług." *Gazeta Wyborcza,* no. 2 (1999): 10, Cited in Zuzanna Wiśniewska's translation on culture.pl. https://culture.p./en/work/the-debt-krzysztof-krauze.

Sokolov, Iurii. *Russian Folklore.* Hatboro, PA: Folklore Associates, 1955.

Soltysiak, Grzegorz. *Filmowy przewodnik po Warszawie.* Warszawa: Muzeum Powstania Warszawskiego, 2012.

Sosnowski, Alexandra. "Cinema in Transition: The Polish Film Today." *Popular Film and Television* 24, no.1 (Spring 1996): 10–16.

Staszczyszyn, Bartosz. "'Ach śpij kochanie,' reż. Krzysztof Lang." https://culture.pl/ pl/dzielo/ach-spij-kochanie-rez-krzysztof-lang.

———. "'Cicha noc,' reż. Piotr Domalewski." https://culture.pl/pl/dzielo/cicha-noc -rez-piotr-domalewski.

———. "Closed Circuit—Ryszard Bugajski." March 25, 2013. https://culture.pl/en/ work/closed-circuit-ryszard-bugajski.

———. Staszczyczyn, Bartosz. "Dzikie róże—Anna Jadowska." December 29, 2017. https://culture.pl/pl/dzielo/dzikie-roze-rez-anna-jadowska.

———. "Ida—Paweł Pawlikowski." September 18, 2013. https://culture.pl/en/work /ida-pawel-pawlikowski.

———. "I'm a Killer—Maciej Pieprzyca." October 2016. https://culture.pl/en/work /im-a-killer-maciej-pieprzyca.

———. "In the Name of—Małgorzata Szumowska." October 19, 2013. https://culture.pl/en/work/in-the-name-of-malgorzata-szumowska.

———. "Obce niebo, reż Dariusz Gajewski." https://culture.pl/pl/dzielo/obce-niebo -rez-dariusz-gajewski.

———. "Polish City Placement: A New Kind of Travel Agency." August 31, 2020. https://culture.pl/en/article/polish-city-placement-a-new-kind-of-travel-agency.

———. "Speak of the Devil: Diabolical Plots in Polish Film," July 18, 2017. https:// culture.pl/en/article/speak-of-the-devil-diabolical-plots-in-polish-film.

———. "Tomasz Wasilewski." July, 2016. https://culture.pl/en/artist/tomasz -wasilewski.

Stevenson, Michael. "A Bitter Failure on the Road to Polish Capitalism: Krzysztof Krauze's The Debt (Dług). KinoKultura, 2005. http://www.kinokultura.com/specials/2/dlug.shtml.

Stępniak, Grzegorz. "Majami, padrini i falliczne węże." *Kino*, no. 2 (2019): 28–31.

Stola, Dariusz. "Fighting against the Shadows: The Anti-Zionist Campaign of 1968." In *Antisemitism and Its Opponents in Modern Poland*, edited by Robert Blobaum, 284–300. Ithaca: Cornell University Press, 2005.

———. "Jedwabne: Revisiting the Evidence and Nature of the Crime." *Holocaust and Genocide Studies* 17, no. 1 (Spring 2003): 139–51.

"Sunday Mass Attendance Falls below 40% in Poland." *Catholic World News*, July 24, 2014. https://www.catholicculture.org/news/headlines/index.cfm?storyid=22111.

Szaszewska, Joanna. "'Zimna wojna' to film doskonały. Wywołuje najprawdziwsze ciarki." gazeta.pl, June 7, 2018. https://kultura.gazeta.pl/kultura/7,114628 ,23473033,zimna-wojna-to-film-doskonaly-wywoluje-najprawdziwsze-ciarki .html.

Szczerba, Jacek. "'Ach śpij kochanie': rewelacyjny criminal. Andrzej Chyra jak polski Hannibal Lecter." October 18, 2017. http://wyborcza.pl/7,101707,22529498 ,ach-spij-kochanie-filmowa-rewelacja-made-in-poland-andrzej.html.

———. *Gazeta Wyborcza*, October 23, 1996. Cited by Małgorzata Fiejdasz, "Robert Gliński." August 2007/May 2011, https://culture.pl/en/artist/robert-glinski.

Szpak, Agnieszka. "How to Deal with Migrants and the State's Backlash—Polish Cities' Experience." *European Planning Studies*, 27, no. 6 (2019: 1159–76.

Szporer, Michael. "Woman of Marble: An Interview with Krystyna Janda." *Cineaste* xviii, no. 3 (1991). https://krystynajanda.pl/dorobek/an-interview-with-krystyna -janda/.

"Sztuka kochania." http://www.filmpolski.pl/fp/index.php?film=1239568.

"Sztuka Kochania według Wisłockiej." http://www.filmpolski.pl/fp/index.php?film =4213754.

Szulc, Lukasz. *Transnational Homosexualism in Communist Poland*. Cham, Switzerland: Palgrave Macmillan/Springer International Publishing, 2018.

Szulecki, Kacper. "Nordycka czarna wołga porywa polskie dzieci. Recenzja filmu Obce niebo Dariusza Gajewskiego." October 27, 2015. https://kulturaliberalna.pl /2015/10/27/nordycka-czarna-wolga-porywa-polskie-dzieci-recenzja-filmu-obce -niebo-dariusza-gajewskiego/.

Szumowska, Małgorzata. "Elles: Malgoska Szumowska Interview." Interview by Helen Barlow. SBS, February 29, 2012. https://www.sbs.com.au/movies/article /2012/02/29/elles-malgoska-szumowska-interview.

———. "Interview." Interview by Colette de Castro. *East European Film Bulletin*, 14, February 2012. https://eefb.org/interviews/joanna-kulig-and-malgorzata-szu-mowska-on-elles/.

———. Szumowska, Małgorzata. "Ironia i sarkazm—to klucz do moich filmów." Interview by Kuba Armata. *Kino*, no. 4 (2018): 24–27.

Szwajcowska, Joanna. "The Myth of the Polish Mother." In *Women in Polish Cinema*, edited by Ewa Mazierska and Elżbieta Ostrowska, 15–33. New York/ Oxford: Berghahn Books, 2006.

Szymański, Marek. *Polska na filmowo; Gdzie kręcono znanw filmy i seriale*. Poznan: MJ Media Szymański i Glapiak, 2010, 26.

Śmiałowski, Piotr. *Kino*, no. 9 (2011): 82–83.

———. "A przecież mógł ich wydać." *Kino*, no. 1 (2012): 15–19.

———. "W imię…." *Kino*, no. 9 (2013): 64–65.

Świrek, Krzysztof. "Senność." *Kino*, no. 10 (2008): 80.

———. "Tradition and Diversity: An Outline of Polish Film Education." *In Polish Cinema Now! Focus on Contemporary Polish Cinema*, edited by Mateusz Werner, 220–41. London and Warsaw: John Libbey Publishing-Adam Mickiewicz Institute, 2010.

Tambor, Konrad. "Sponsoring." *Kino*, no. 2 (2012): 85. http://kino.org.pl//index.php ?option=com_content&task=view&id=1328&Itemid=742.

Tatarska, Anna. "'Zimna wojna' Pawła Pawlikowskiego. Dramaturgia przez duże D." June 4, 2018. https://wyborcza.pl/7,101707,23491300,zimna-wojna-recenzja.html.

Tatke, Sukhada. "Meet the 'Abortion Aunts' of Berlin Who Help Polish Women Terminate Unwanted Pregnancies." *GlobalPost*, August 8, 2019. https://www.pri .org/stories/2019-08-08/meet-abortion-aunts-berlin-who-help-polish-women-ter-minate-unwanted-pregnancies.

Tehrani, Bijan. "Ryszard Bugajski, The Closed Circuit, participating at Polish Film Festival." September 24, 2013. https://cinemawithoutborders.com/3491-ryszard -bugajsk-the-closed-circuit-polishfilmla/.

"The Horror Film." In *The Cinema Book*, edited by Pam Cook and Mieke Bernink, 194–208, 2nd edition. London: British Film Institute, 1999.

"The Photography of Zdzisław Beksiński." https://culture.pl/en/video/the-photogra-phy-of-zdzislaw-beksinski-video.

Toro, Gabe. "'Floating Skyscrapers' Never Dodges the Inevitability of the Modern Gay Indie Film Tragedy." *IndieWire*, April 19, 2013. https://www.indiewire.com

/2013/04/tribeca-review-floating-skyscrapers-never-dodges-the-inevitability-of
-the-modern-gay-indie-film-tragedy-99204/.

"Trzęśli Warszawą, dziś znów są na wolności. Co robią teraz dawni bossowie
Pruszkowa?" June 29, 2019. http://warszawa.naszemiasto.pl/artykul/trzesli
-warszawa-dzis-znow-sa-na-wolnosci-co-robia-teraz,3924728,artgal,t,id,tm.html.

Tugend, Tom. "Five Years in the Making: 'The Return' Takes New Look at Polish
Jewish Revival." *Jewish Telegraphic Agency*, January 21, 2015. https://www
.jta.org/2015/01/21/culture/five-years-in-the-making-the-return-takes-new-look-at
-polish-jewish-revival.

Twarze Agnieszki Holland/Faces of Agnieszka Holland. Lodz: Muzeum Kinomatografii
w Łodzi, 2013.

U.S. Holocaust Memorial Museum. https://encyclopedia.ushmm.org/content/en/
article/polish-victims.

U.S. Holocaust Memorial Museum. https://www.ushmm.org/learn/timeline-of-events
/1942-1945/german-poster-announces-death-penalty-for-aiding-jews.

van Heuckelom, Kris. *Polish Migrants in European Film, 1918-2017*. Cham,
Switzerland: Palgrave Macmillan, 2019.

Vasiljuk, Sasha. "We're Here: Polish Jews Today." August 1, 2017. https://culture.pl
/en/article/were-here-polands-jewish-community-today.

Vourlias, Christopher. "Pandemic and Price Wars Put a Dent in the Polish Box
Office." *Variety*, June 23, 2020. https://variety.com/2020/film/spotlight/cannes
-polish-movies-hater-1234645699/.

Wajda, Andrzej. *Kino i reszte świata*. Cracow: Wydawnictwo Znak, 2000.

Wakar, Jacek. "Sławomir Fabicki." Translated by Gabriela Łazarkiewicz. Directors
Guild of Poland. https://polishdirectors.com/en/member_post/fabicki-slawomir/.

Wallace, Marlon. "The M Report." May 22, 2014. http://themreporter.blogspot.com
/2014/05/dvd-review-in-name-of-w-imie.html.

Ward, Sara. "'Beyond Words': Toronto Review." September 8, 2017. https://www
.screendaily.com/reviews/beyond-words-toronto-review/5121719.article.

Warner, Marina. *Alone of All Her Sex: The Myth and the Cult of the Virgin Mary*.
New York: Vintage, 1983.

Weissberg, Jay "33 Scenes from Life." *Variety*, August 19, 2018. https://variety.com
/2008/film/reviews/33-scenes-from-life-1200507656/.

Weitzer, Ronald. "Prostitution: Facts and Fictions." *Contexts* 6, no. 4 (Fall 2007):
28–33. https://journals.sagepub.com/doi/pdf/10.1525/ctx.2007.6.4.28.

Werner, Mateusz, ed. *Polish Cinema Now! Focus on Contemporary Polish Cinema*.
London and Warsaw: John Libbey Publishing-Adam Mickiewicz Institute, 2009.

———. "Whatever Happened to Polish Cinema after 1989?" In *Polish Cinema Now!
Focus on Contemporary Polish Cinema*, edited by Mateusz Werner, 8–21. London
and Warsaw: Adam Mickiewicz Institute-John Libbey Publishing, 2010.

Wheatley, Catherine. "Film of the Week: 'Ida,'" November 28, 2014. https://www2
.bfi.org.uk/news-opinion/sight-sound-magazine/reviews-recommendations/film
-week-ida.

———. "Pawel Pawlikowski Condenses European (and cinematic) History into a 'Sad, Small,' Ineffably Potent Road Movie of the Soul." *Sight and Sound*, November 28, 2014. https://www.bfi.org.uk/news-opinion/sight-sound-magazine/reviews-recommendations/film-week-ida.

White, Anne. *Polish Families and Migration since EU Accession*. Bristol: Bristol University Press, Policy Press, 2011.

Wigura, Karolina. "Dlaczego 'Ida' tak gniewa. Częściowe podsumowanie dyskusji o filmie Pawła Pawlikowskiego." *Kultura liberalna*, no. 255 (48/2013), 26 November 2013. https://kulturaliberalna.pl/2013 /11/26/wigura-dlaczego-ida-tak-gniewa-czesciowe-podsumowanie-dyskusji-o-filmie-pawla-pawlikowskiego/.

Wilkinson, Amber. "Fugue," May 20, 2018. https://www.eyeforfilm.co.uk/review/fugue-2018-film-review-by-amber-wilkinson.

———. "Silent Night (2017) Film Review." April 26, 2018. https://www.eyeforfilm.co.uk/review/silent-night-2017-film-review-by-amber-wilkinson.

"W imieniu diabła, czyli bliskie spotkania z nawiedzeniem." *Kurier poranny*, September 16, 2011. https://poranny.pl/w-imieniu-diabla-czyli-bliskie-spotkania-z-nawiedzeniem/ar/5397336.

Winfield, Nicole. "Pope Francis Issues New Church Law Regarding Clergy Sex Abuse. Victims Say It's Not Enough." *Time*, May 10, 2019. http://time.com /5587051/pope-francis-church-law-clergy-sex-abuse/.

Wisłocka, Michalina. *Sztuka Kochania*. Warsaw: Agora, 2016.

"Władysław Mazurkiewicz—Elegancki morderca." Podcast #5. https://www.kryminatorium.pl/wladyslaw-mazurkiewicz-elegancki-morderca/.

Woch, Agnieszka. "Zaćma." December 28, 2016. https://histmag.org/Zacma-rez.-Ryszard-Bugajski-recenzja-filmu-14512.

Wood, Robin. "An Introduction to the American Horror Film." *Movies and Methods*, edited by Bill Nichols, Volume 2, 195–220. Berkeley: University of California Press, 1985.

World Jewish Congress website. https://www.worldjewishcongress.org/en/about/communities/PL.

Wróblewski, Bartosz. "'Jestem mordercą'—czy Zdzisław Marchwicki naprawdę był 'wampirem z Zagłębia?'" October 27, 2017. http://wyborcza.pl/7,90535,22272389 ,jestem-morderca-czy-zdzislaw-marchwicki-naprawde-byl.html.

Wróblewski, Janusz. "Cicha niemoc. Recenzja filmu Cicha noc." November 21, 2017. https://www.polityka.pl/tygodnikpolityka/kultura/film/1727932,1,recenzja-filmu-cicha-noc-rez-piotr-domalewski.read.

———. "Polish Cinema Success Stories." In *Polish Cinema Now! Focus on Contemporary Polish Cinema*, edited by Mateusz Werner, 170–92. London and Warsaw: John Libbey Publishing-Adam Mickiewicz Institute, 2009.

———. "Recenzja filmu Po-Lin: Okruchy pamięci, reż. Jolanta Dylewska." November 10, 2008. https://www.polityka.pl/tygodnikpolityka/kultura/film /273316,1,recenzja-filmu-po-lin-rez-jolanta-dylewska.read.

————. "Recenzja filmu: 'Pokłosie,' reż. Władysław Pasikowski. Paląca spuścizna." November 6, 2012. https://www.polityka.pl/tygodnikpolityka/kultura/film/1532003 ,1,recenzja-filmu-poklosie-rez-wladyslaw-pasikowski.read.

————. "'Rewers': szydercza gra z narodową pamięcią." November 14, 2009. https://www.polityka.pl/tygodnikpolityka/kultura/1500603,1,rewers-szydercza-gra -z-narodowa-pamiecia.read.

————. "'Zimna wojna,' reż. Paweł Pawlikowski. Polskość dla każdego." June 5, 2018. https://www.polityka.pl/tygodnikpolityka/kultura/film/1750864,1,recenzja -filmu-zimna-wojna-rez-pawel-pawlikowski.read.

Yad Vashem: The World Holocaust Remembrance Center. https://www.yadvashem .org/righteous/statistics.html.

Yoshida, Emily. "*Cold War* is a Stunning Love Story." December 8, 2018. https:// www.vulture.com/2018/12/cold-war-review.html.

Zaborski, Artur. Zaborski, Artur. "Bez wstydu." *Kino*, no. 7–8 (2012): 98.

————. "Cicha noc." *Kino*, no. 11 (2017): 68.

————. "Fuga." *Kino*, no. 12 (2018): 77. http://kino.org.pl//index.php?option=com _content&task=view&id=3124&Itemid=2184.

Zacharczuk, Tomasz. "Chyra jak Lecter, a reszta jest milczeniem. Recenzja filmu 'Ach śpij kochanie.'" October 22, 2017. https://kino.trojmiasto.pl/Chyra-jak-Lecter -a-reszta-jest-milczeniem-Recenzja-filmu-Ach-spij-kochanie-n117694.html.

————. "Mądry, dojrzały i poruszający. Recenzja filmu 'Cicha noc.'" November 24 2017. https://kino.trojmiasto.pl/Zwyciezca-Zlotych-Lwow-juz-w-kinach-Recenzja -filmu-Cicha-noc-n118787.html.

Zarębski, Konrad. "33 ceny z życia." *Kino*, no. 11 (2008): 76. http://kino.org.pl// index.php?option=com_content&task=view&id=266&Itemid=214.

————. "Feature Film Directed by Magdalena Piekorz, 2008." October, 2008. https:// culture.pl/en/work/drowsiness-magdalena-piekorz.

————. "General Nil—Ryszard Bugajski," March 2009. https://culture.pl/en/work/ general-nil-ryszard-bugajski.

————. "Jolanta Dylewska." culture.pl, November 2009. https://culture.pl/pl/tworca /jolanta-dylewska.

————. "Po-Lin: Okruchy pamięci." 2009. https://culture.pl/pl/dzielo/po-lin-okruchy -pamieci.

————. "Wojciech Smarzowski." October 2009. https://culture.pl/pl/tworca/wojciech -smarzowski.

Zarębski, Konrad J. "'W ciemności' -- reż. Agnieszka Holland." December 2011. https://culture.pl/pl/dzielo/w-ciemnosci-rez-agnieszka-holland.

Zawadzka, Anna. "Ida." October 25, 2013. http://lewica.pl/blog/zawadzka/28791/.

"Zdzisław Marchwicki A.K.A.: 'The Silesian Vampire'—'The Zagłębie Vampire.'" https://murderpedia.org/male.M/m/marchwicki-zdzislaw.htm.

Zubrzycki, Geneviève. "The Politics of Jewish Absence in Contemporary Poland." *Journal of Contemporary History* 25, no. 2 (2017): 250–77.

Zucker, Adam. *The Return,* 2014. https://www.thereturndocumentary.com/film/ synopsis.

Źródło, Katarzyna Taras. "Kochankowie z Marony." June 23, 2006. https://kultura
.onet.pl/film/recenzje/kochankowie-z-marony/zncte48.

Żakowska, Magdalena. "Dariusz Gajewski znalazł swoje niebo. 'Ciekawi mnie nasze
życie z Agnieszką.'" Magazyn Viva!, October 21, 2015. https://viva.pl/kultura/film
/dariusz-gajewski-opowiada-o-swoim-nowym-filmie-obce-niebo-i-o-zonie-93408
-r1/.

Żmijewski, Artur. "Katyń, Karole, Świadectwo, czyli praca ideologii." In *Kino polskie, 1989-2009. Historia krytyczna,* edited b. A. Wiśniewska, P. Marecki, 206–10.
Warsaw: Wydawnictwo Krytyki Politycznej, 2010.

Żurawiecki, Bartosz. "Ach śpij kochanie." *Kino* no. 11 (2017). http://kino.org.pl//
index.php?option=com_content&task=view&id=2840&Itemid=1944.

Index

About the Authors

Helena Goscilo is Professor in the Department of Slavic and East European Languages and Culture, and Affiliate Faculty in Comparative Studies, Film Studies, Folklore, Popular Culture, and Women's, Gender & Sexuality Studies at Ohio State University. Earlier she chaired the Slavic Department at the University of Pittsburgh and at her current home institution. Starting as a comparatist in Romantic prose, she gradually shifted focus to gender issues in Slavic culture, and subsequently to visual genres, encompassing art, graphics, and film. She is the coauthor of *Fade from Red: The Cold War Ex-Enemy in Russian and American Film 1990–2005* (2014), coeditor of *Cinepaternity: Fathers and Sons in Soviet and Post-Soviet Film* (2010) and, with Beth Holmgren, *Poles Apart: Women in Modern Polish Culture* (2006), in addition to a dozen authored or (co)edited volumes on women's prose, celebrity culture, aviation, Putin, and St. Petersburg.

Beth Holmgren is Professor in the Department of Slavic and Eurasian Studies; holds secondary appointments in Theater Studies and Gender/Sexuality/Feminist Studies; and is a core faculty member in the Jewish Studies Program at Duke University. Until recently, she chaired her current department and fulfilled the same role in her previous position at the University of North Carolina—Chapel Hill. Holmgren served as President of the Association for Women in Slavic Studies and the Association for Slavic, East European, and Eurasian Studies. Her early work focused on the memoirs and autobiography of Russian women writers and expanded to studies of Russian and Polish popular culture and film. Her recent interest in Polish Jewish culture in the interwar period moved her scholarship entirely into Polish studies. Her publications include *Starring Madame Modjeska: On Tour in Poland and America* (2012), *Warsaw Is My Country: The Story of Krystyna Bierzyńska, 1928–1945* (2018), the coedited volume *Transgressive Women in Russian and East European Cultures: From the Bad to the Blasphemous* (2016), and a wide array of articles on the interwar and wartime Polish literary cabaret.

www.ingramcontent.com/pod-product-compliance
Lightning Source LLC
Chambersburg PA
CBHW050625280326
41932CB00015B/2527